ANIMAL
RIGHTS

ISSN 1546-6736

ANIMAL RIGHTS

Kim Masters Evans

INFORMATION PLUS® REFERENCE SERIES
Formerly published by Information Plus, Wylie, Texas

GALE®

Detroit • New York • San Diego • San Francisco • Cleveland • New Haven, Conn. • Waterville, Maine • London • Munich

THOMSON
━━━━★━━━ ™
GALE

Animal Rights

Kim Masters Evans

Project Editor
Ellice Engdahl

Editorial
Beverly Baer, Andrew Claps, Paula Cutcher-Jackson, Kathleen Edgar, Debra Kirby, Prindle LaBarge, Elizabeth Manar, Sharon McGilvray, Charles B. Montney, Heather Price

Permissions
William Sampson

Imaging and Multimedia
Lezlie Light, Mike Logusz, Denay Wilding

Product Design
Cynthia Baldwin

Composition and Electronic Prepress
Evi Seoud

Manufacturing
Keith Helmling

LIBRARY OF CONGRESS CATALOGING-IN-PUBLICATION DATA

ISBN 0-7876-5103-6 (set)
ISBN 0-7876-7524-5
ISSN 1546-6736

Printed in the United States of America
10 9 8 7 6 5 4 3 2 1

TABLE OF CONTENTS

CHAPTER 1
Humans have interacted with other animals in many ways since the emergence of the human species. This chapter describes hunting and domestication over time, as well as the significance of animals in various cultures and religions, and finally the emergence of laws regulating the use of animals and the animal rights movement.

CHAPTER 2
The concept of "animal rights" means different things to different groups of people, and differences are based on economic, moral, and philosophical grounds. The development and extent of the animal rights movement are discussed, along with the implications of the varied viewpoints and public opinion on animal rights issues.

CHAPTER 3
This chapter discusses the history of human interaction with animals that are not domesticated, from hunting and trapping to the development of legal regulations regarding the use and protection of wildlife. The balance between the needs of humans and those of wildlife and the side effects of their interactions are examined.

CHAPTER 4
The use of domesticated animals for meat and other products has a long history. This chapter describes livestock operations, including factory farms and methods of slaughter of specific animals, and discusses the development of methods and regulations intended to promote more humane treatment of farm animals.

CHAPTER 5
Animals are extensively used for medical, veterinary, drug, and educational research purposes. This chapter discusses the history of animal research and the movement against the use of animals in research, the present-day uses of laboratory animals, the search for alternatives, and genetic engineering.

CHAPTER 6
Animals are featured performers in many sports involving racing, endurance, skill, and fighting. The history, practices, and economics of these sports are discussed, as are the controversies surrounding them, regulations, and the viewpoints of animal rights activists.

CHAPTER 7
From zoos to circuses, theme parks to movies and television, animals are used to provide entertainment and amusement to people. Many animals are trained to do things they otherwise wouldn't do, while others are enjoyed for their natural characteristics. The history, regulation, and viewpoints on entertainment uses are discussed in this chapter.

CHAPTER 8
Humans have long used animals to do work such as manual labor, military roles, and humanitarian services such as guiding the blind. The development of animals for these tasks has moved from domesticated animals to wildlife known for special skills or intelligence, such as dolphins.

CHAPTER 9
Certain animals have been kept for companionship and emotional needs for centuries. Pet ownership is widespread, which has required a system of care, rescue, and disposition of surplus pet animals. Keeping of exotic animals as pets, as well as the health and welfare concerns of both pets and their owners, is discussed in this chapter.

PREFACE

Animal Rights is one of the latest volumes in the Information Plus Reference Series. The purpose of each volume of the series is to present the latest facts on a topic of pressing concern in modern American life. These topics include today's most controversial and most studied social issues: abortion, capital punishment, care for the elderly, crime, health care, the environment, immigration, minorities, social welfare, women, youth, and many more. Although written especially for the high school and undergraduate student, this series is an excellent resource for anyone in need of factual information on current affairs.

By presenting the facts, it is Gale's intention to provide its readers with everything they need to reach an informed opinion on current issues. To that end, there is a particular emphasis in this series on the presentation of scientific studies, surveys, and statistics. These data are generally presented in the form of tables, charts, and other graphics placed within the text of each book. Every graphic is directly referred to and carefully explained in the text. The source of each graphic is presented within the graphic itself. The data used in these graphics are drawn from the most reputable and reliable sources, in particular from the various branches of the U.S. government and from major independent polling organizations. Every effort has been made to secure the most recent information available. The reader should bear in mind that many major studies take years to conduct, and that additional years often pass before the data from these studies are made available to the public. Therefore, in many cases the most recent information available in 2003 dated from 2000 or 2001. Older statistics are sometimes presented as well if they are of particular interest and no more recent information exists.

Although statistics are a major focus of the Information Plus Reference Series, they are by no means its only content. Each book also presents the widely held positions and important ideas that shape how the book's subject is discussed in the United States. These positions are explained in detail and, where possible, in the words of their proponents. Some of the other material to be found in these books includes: historical background; descriptions of major events related to the subject; relevant laws and court cases; and examples of how these issues play out in American life. Some books also feature primary documents or have pro and con debate sections giving the words and opinions of prominent Americans on both sides of a controversial topic. All material is presented in an even-handed and unbiased manner; the reader will never be encouraged to accept one view of an issue over another.

HOW TO USE THIS BOOK

Animals have been important to humans for around 2 million years as sources of food and other natural products, objects of worship and sport, and beasts of burden; but not until the seventeenth century did animal welfare much concern western society. What legal and moral rights do animals currently possess in the United States and how does society balance such rights with animals' enormous economic value? How do "abolitionists" and "welfarists" differ on these and other issues? In what ways should governments protect, regulate, and control wildlife? Under what conditions are farm animals raised and slaughtered? Should research animals be used in medical and veterinary investigations, product testing, and science classes? Do horseracing, greyhound racing, sled dog racing, and rodeos cause unwarranted harm to animal participants? How should entertainment animals, service animals, and pets be treated? These and other basic questions are discussed in this volume.

Animal Rights consists of nine chapters and three appendices. Each of the chapters is devoted to a particular aspect of animal rights in the United States. For a summary of the information covered in each chapter, please see the synopses provided in the Table of Contents at the front of the book. Chapters generally begin with an overview of the basic facts and background information on the chapter's topic, then proceed to examine subtopics of particular interest. For example, Chapter 2, The Animal Rights Debate, begins with a discussion of viewpoints on why, whether, and when humans ought to kill animals. It then gives the history of the modern animal rights movement in the United States, which began during the 1970s, and of related philosophical arguments known as welfarism, utilitarianism, contractarianism, and the "rights view." An exploration of economic, scientific, and personal implications of the rights view rounds out this chapter, along with responses to and analysis of a May, 2003 Gallup poll on animal rights issues. Readers can find their way through a chapter by looking for the section and sub-section headings, which are clearly set off from the text. They can also refer to the book's extensive index if they already know what they are looking for.

Statistical Information

The tables and figures featured throughout *Animal Rights* will be of particular use to the reader in learning about this issue. These tables and figures represent an extensive collection of the most recent and important statistics on animal rights and related issues—for example, graphics in the book cover public opinion on animal rights as of May 2003, resources damaged by injurious wildlife, trends in meat consumption from 1909 to 2001, widely used animal byproducts, pain and distress in regulated research animals, state laws on cockfighting, mounted police programs, and pet ownership survey results. Gale believes that making this information available to the reader is the most important way in which we fulfill the goal of this book: to help readers to understand the issues and controversies surrounding animal rights in the United States and to reach their own conclusions.

Each table or figure has a unique identifier appearing above it for ease of identification and reference. Titles for the tables and figures explain their purpose. At the end of each table or figure, the original source of the data is provided.

In order to help readers understand these often complicated statistics, all tables and figures are explained in the text. References in the text direct the reader to the relevant statistics. Furthermore, the contents of all tables and figures are fully indexed. Please see the opening section of the index at the back of this volume for a description of how to find tables and figures within it.

Appendices

In addition to the main body text and images, *Animal Rights* has three appendices. The first is the Important Names and Addresses directory. Here the reader will find contact information for a number of government and private organizations that can provide further information on animal rights in America. The second appendix is the Resources section, which can also assist the reader in conducting his or her own research. In this section, the author and editors of *Animal Rights* describe some of the sources that were most useful during the compilation of this book. The final appendix is the detailed Index, which facilitates reader access to specific topics in this book.

ADVISORY BOARD CONTRIBUTIONS

The staff of Information Plus would like to extend their heartfelt appreciation to the Information Plus Advisory Board. This dedicated group of media professionals provides feedback on the series on an ongoing basis. Their comments allow the editorial staff who work on the project to make the series better and more user-friendly. Our top priority is to produce the highest-quality and most useful books possible, and the Advisory Board's contributions to this process are invaluable.

The members of the Information Plus Advisory Board are:

- Kathleen R. Bonn, Librarian, Newbury Park High School, Newbury Park, California

- Madelyn Garner, Librarian, San Jacinto College—North Campus, Houston, Texas

- Anne Oxenrider, Media Specialist, Dundee High School, Dundee, Michigan

- Charles R. Rodgers, Director of Libraries, Pasco-Hernando Community College, Dade City, Florida

- James N. Zitzelsberger, Library Media Department Chairman, Oshkosh West High School, Oshkosh, Wisconsin

COMMENTS AND SUGGESTIONS

The editors of the Information Plus Reference Series welcome your feedback on *Animal Rights*. Please direct all correspondence to:

Editors
Information Plus Reference Series
27500 Drake Rd.
Farmington Hills, MI 48331-3535

ACKNOWLEDGMENTS

The editors wish to thank the copyright holders of material included in this volume and the permissions managers of many book and magazine publishing companies for assisting us in securing reproduction rights. We are also grateful to the staffs of the Detroit Public Library, the Library of Congress, the University of Detroit Mercy Library, Wayne State University Purdy/Kresge Library Complex, and the University of Michigan Libraries for making their resources available to us.

Following is a list of the copyright holders who have granted us permission to reproduce material in Animal Rights. *Every effort has been made to trace copyright, but if omissions have been made, please let us know.*

For more detailed source citations, please see the sources listed under each individual table and figure.

American Pet Products Manufacturers Association: Figure 9.1

American Veterinary Medical Association: Figure 9.2, Figure 9.3, Table 9.5

Animal Legal Defense Fund: Table 2.1, Table 2.2

AP/Wide World Photos. Reproduced by permission: Figure 3.1, Figure 4.12, Figure 8.5, Figure 8.6

AP/Wide World Photos/National Park Service. Reproduced by permission: Figure 3.5

AP/Wide World Photos/NBC. Reproduced by permission: Figure 7.3

Association of Veterinarians for Animal Rights: Table 5.7

California Horse Racing Board: Table 6.2

Centers for Disease Control and Prevention: Figure 3.4

Corbis-Bettmann. Reproduced by permission: Figure 2.1

Corbis. Reproduced by permission: Figure 1.1

CORBIS/Kevin Schafer. Reproduced by permission: Figure 1.4

Cory Langley. Reproduced by permission: Figure 8.4

Defenders of Wildlife: Table 3.5

Fur Information Council of America: Figure 4.13

The Gallup Organization: Figure 2.2, Figure 2.3, Figure 2.4

Ganni Dagli Orti/Corbis. Reproduced by permission: Figure 8.9

Greyhound Protection League: Table 6.3

The Humane Society of the United States: Table 1.2, Table 3.8, Table 6.4, Table 6.5, Table 9.1, Table 9.3, Table 9.4

In Defense of Animals: Table 7.2

Jeff Mitchell. Archive Photos, Inc. Reproduced by permission: Figure 5.14

Jim McElhom: Figure 7.4

The Jockey Club: Figure 6.1, Figure 6.2

The Kobal Collection. Reproduced by permission: Figure 7.2

The Library of Congress: Figure 3.2, Figure 3.3, Figure 4.10, Figure 5.4, Figure 5.5, Figure 5.6, Figure 5.7, Figure 5.8, Figure 5.10, Figure 8.7

Michigan Society for Medical Research: Table 5.2, Table 5.6

Minnesota Foundation for Responsible Animal Care: Table 4.3

MountedPolice.com: Table 8.1

National Archives and Records Administration: Figure 4.3, Figure 8.1

National Council on Pet Population Study and Policy: Table 9.2

National Science Foundation, National Science Board: Figure 5.1, Figure 5.2, Figure 5.3

Peter Skinner/Science Source/Photo Researchers, Inc. Reproduced by permission: Figure 8.8

Photo Researchers, Inc. Reproduced by permission: Figure 4.4

RDS: Table 5.3

Robert J. Huffman. Field Mark Publications. Reproduced by permission: Figure 8.2

Society for the Protection of Animal Rights Egypt: Figure 1.3

Temple Grandin's Web Page: Table 4.4

Tim Page/CORBIS. Reproduced by permission: Figure 8.3

U.S. Department of Agriculture, Animal and Plant Health Inspection Service: Figure 4.8, Table 4.5, Table 4.6, Figure 5.11, Figure 5.12, Table 5.4, Table 5.5, Table 5.8, Figure 7.1, Table 7.1

U.S. Department of Agriculture, Economic Research Service: Figure 4.9, Figure 4.11, Table 4.1, Table 4.2

U.S. Department of Agriculture, National Agricultural Statistics Service: Figure 4.2, Figure 4.5, Figure 4.6, Figure 4.7

U.S. Environmental Protection Agency: Figure 4.1

U.S. Fish and Wildlife Service: Table 3.4, Table 3.6, Table 3.7

U.S. General Accounting Office: Table 3.2, Table 3.3

University of Saskatchewan, College of Agriculture: Figure 1.2

Virginia Cooperative Extension: Table 5.9

CHAPTER 1

THE HISTORY OF HUMAN-ANIMAL INTERACTION

At the heart of the animal rights debate is the issue of how humans and animals should interact with each other. Are animals a natural resource for humans to use as they choose? Or are animals free beings with the right to live their lives without human interference? Is there an acceptable compromise somewhere in between? People answer these questions differently depending on their cultural practices, religious and ethical beliefs, and everyday experiences with animals. To understand how the debate has evolved over the centuries, it is necessary to examine history and see how the human-animal relationship developed and changed over time.

PREHISTORIC TIMES

The theory of evolution, adhered to by many scientists, suggests that humans were animals at one time. Biologists classify the human animal as a member of the order Primate, along with chimpanzees and gorillas. Some scientists believe that humans and other primates shared a common ancestor millions of years ago, and that at some point, human animals split off to form their own evolutionary path. Skeletons found throughout parts of Africa show both human and nonhuman characteristics.

Those who believe in the evolution theory think that human primates left the treetops and began walking upright, using their hands to make tools and increase their survivability. Most nonhuman primates ate a mostly vegetarian diet, but human primates began capturing small animals and scavenging for meat from carcasses left behind by predators like lions. About 2 million years ago, human primates began using stone tools and weapons. This was the beginning of the Stone Age. The use of stone-tipped spears allowed humans to hunt large game, such as wooly mammoths.

Hunter-Gatherers

In 1995 archaeologists found three wooden spears in a cave near Helmstedt, Germany. The spears are estimated to be about 400,000 years old. The excavation uncovered the remains of at least 10 horses that appear to have been butchered, suggesting that humans of that time were accomplished hunters. Thousands of bones from elephants, rhinoceros, deer, and horses have also been found in the cave complex. Humans at that time survived by hunting and fishing and by foraging for edible vegetation, nuts, and seeds; hence, they are called hunter-gatherers. Most lived as nomads, traveling in small groups from place to place. Once they had exhausted all the animals and plants in an area, they would move to a new location.

Humans sometimes used their wits along with their weapons to capture prey. Scientists have found the bones of roughly 10,000 horses at the bottom of a cliff in Salutre, France, that date to prehistoric times. Humans may have been unable to catch the very fast horses and somehow tricked them into running off the cliff to their deaths.

Cave Paintings Depict Animals

The earliest known cave drawings date back 30,000 years and are located in France. In October 2001 the British Broadcasting Corporation (BBC) reported that hundreds of prehistoric drawings in the Chauvet Caves of southern France had been analyzed by scientists and found to be between 29,700 and 32,400 years old, making them the oldest known art in the world. Numerous cave drawings depict rhinoceros, lions, buffalo, mammoths, and horses. Figure 1.1 shows a cave painting of a horse.

Other cave drawings indicate that prehistoric peoples interacted with many different kinds of animals, including wooly mammoths, bison, deer, horses, and sea creatures. In fact, scientists believe that most paintings were performed using brushes made of animal hair and paints including animal fat.

The vast majority of prehistoric cave drawings depict animals, not people. Some scientists believe that humans were in awe of the wild and fierce animals that they hunted.

FIGURE 1.1

Cave painting of a horse, circa 13,000 B.C., Lascaux, France © *Corbis.*
Reproduced by permission.

The hunters may have believed that they could exert some kind of magical power over animals by drawing pictures of them. Although little is known for certain about the religious beliefs of the time, it is thought that prehistoric humans believed in a hidden world inhabited by the spirits of their dead ancestors, animals, and birds. Some spirits were good and others were bad. The spirits were offered sacrifices of animals or other food to keep them happy.

A belief called animism has been traced back to the Paleolithic Age (the earliest period of the Stone Age). Animism is the belief that every object, living or not, contains a soul. Thus, animals, trees, and even rocks had spiritual meaning to prehistoric peoples. Anthropologists theorize that humans may have believed that they could capture the spirits (and thus the fierceness, strength, and speed) of wild animals by eating their flesh. Likewise, some wild animals may have been worshipped as gods by early humans.

Changing Climate

Around 15,000–13,000 B.C., the massive glaciers that had covered much of the land during the Great Ice Age began to subside. The habitats and food supplies for both humans and animals began to change. The hunter-gatherers had increasing difficulty finding the big game they had hunted before. Scientists believe that mammoths and many other large animals were driven to extinction around 10,000 B.C. because of climate changes, overhunting by humans, or both. Humans turned to hunting smaller animals and began gathering and cultivating plants in centralized locations. This major shift from nomadic life to settled existence had a tremendous effect on the human-animal relationship.

HUMANS DOMESTICATE ANIMALS

Between 13,000 and 2,500 B.C., humans domesticated dogs, cats, cattle, goats, horses, and sheep from their wild counterparts. Although the terms "taming" and "domestication" are often used interchangeably, they are not the same. Individual wild animals can be tamed to behave in a docile manner around humans. By contrast, domestication is a process that takes place with an entire animal species over many generations.

Characteristics of Domesticated Animals

Domesticated animals are not just tamer than their wild ancestors, they are different genetically. Over the ages, desirable qualities, such as size and disposition, were engrained by breeding only those animals that displayed them. This explains some of the physical differences between wild and domesticated animals. For example, most domesticated species are smaller and fatter and have smaller teeth and brains than their wild ancestors. (See Figure 1.2.)

An article in the journal *Nature* (Jared Diamond, "Evolution, Consequences and Future of Plant and Animal Domestication," August 8, 2002) describes the biological traits and behaviors that wild animals must have to be domesticated. Successful domestication is only possible with species that exhibit these characteristics:

- A diet that can be supplied easily and relatively cheaply by humans

- A relatively fast growth rate with short time intervals between births

- The ability to mate and breed in captivity

- A tendency towards calm predictable behavior rather than panic

- A lack of viciousness towards humans

- A social structure based on hierarchy and cooperative group living without strong territorialism

Lack of any one of the characteristics can mean that domestication is not possible. According to *Nature,* only 14 of the 148 species of large land-based mammals have been domesticated.

Domestication of Dogs and Cats

The dog is thought to be the first animal to be domesticated by humans, sometime around 13,000–10,000 B.C., from its wolflike ancestor *Canis lupus.* Scientists believe that humans either adopted cubs and raised them or just began to accept some of the less fierce wolves that hung around their camps scrounging for leftovers. In either event, humans soon found dogs to be a welcome addition. The arrangement benefited both sides, as domesticated wolves helped humans with hunting and guarding duties and shared the food that was obtained.

Although cat remains have been found in settlements that date back to 8000 B.C., it is not clear if these were domesticated cats or small wild cats that were tolerated or even encouraged by the people living there. Cat bones mixed with human and rat bones found on the island of Cyprus date back to around 5000 B.C. Because wild cats are not native to the island, cats must have been transported there by humans on purpose, probably to control the rat population.

The ancient Egyptians are usually credited with domesticating wild cats (*Felis silvestris libyca*, originating in Africa and southwestern Asia) around 4000 B.C. The Egyptians most likely raised cats from small kittens to protect their grain stores from rats and mice. Cat domestication is strongly associated with the establishment of permanent settlements and the growing and storage of grains. Cats became important to agricultural cultures, just as dogs had been important to hunting cultures.

Domestication of Livestock

The domestication of livestock, chiefly pigs, cows, sheep, horses, and goats, is thought to have occurred between 9000 and 5000 B.C. as agriculture became more of a factor in human societies scattered around Asia and Europe. Scientists can estimate these dates based on evidence from excavated archaeological sites.

The study of historical human-animal interaction is called archaezoology or zooarchaeology. The age, sex, and condition of animal remains found near human settlements provide many clues. Any evidence of sharp knife marks on animal bones indicates that an animal was killed and consumed by humans, not another predator.

Sites associated with hunters feature the bones of mostly large adult male animals. These animals would have been the preferred targets because they provided more meat than younger males or females. By contrast, agricultural sites are more likely to have the bones of younger smaller male animals than those of older larger males. Herd management (then and now) involves keeping mostly female animals. A few large males with desired qualities are kept alive for breeding purposes, but most males are slaughtered at a relatively young age. Likewise when animal bones indicate that a group of animals died at about the same age, this is a strong indication that these animals were domesticated, not wild.

The domestication of pigs, cows, oxen, sheep, goats, and horses all occurred in a relatively short period of time. Although there is disagreement about the order in which these animals were domesticated, many scientists believe that the pig was first, domesticated from wild boars. (See Figure 1.2.) Cows and oxen descend from aurochs, large and fierce wild animals that later became extinct. Sheep and goats were domesticated from their wild counterparts and selectively bred to provide desired coat and meat characteristics. Most historians believe that dogs played

FIGURE 1.2

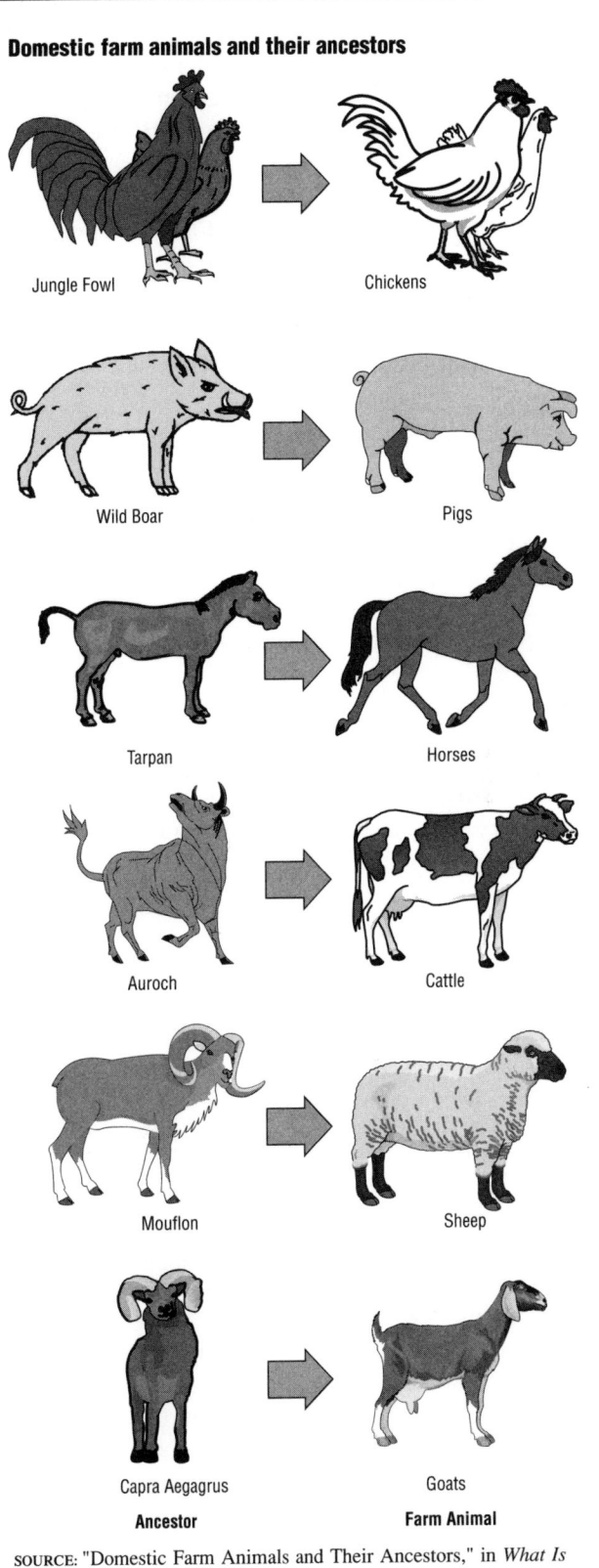

Domestic farm animals and their ancestors

Jungle Fowl → Chickens

Wild Boar → Pigs

Tarpan → Horses

Auroch → Cattle

Mouflon → Sheep

Capra Aegagrus → Goats

Ancestor **Farm Animal**

SOURCE: "Domestic Farm Animals and Their Ancestors," in *What Is Animal Domestication?* University of Saskatchewan, College of Agriculture, Saskatoon, Saskatchewan, Canada, January 29, 1999 [Online] http://www.ag.usask.ca/exhibits/walkway/what/im/animalsdom.jpg [accessed April 22, 2003]

an invaluable role in helping humans to herd and control these animals and protect them from wild predators.

Horses are thought to have been domesticated around 6000 B.C. Archaeological evidence indicates that they were first herded for their meat, hides, and milk. Horse milk was fermented into an alcoholic brew called kummis by ancient peoples living in central Asia. As the growing of crops became more important, horses and oxen became more useful as work animals, pulling carts and wagons, and eventually plows. The Egyptians began using horses to pull plows in the fields sometime after 4000 B.C. Gradually, horses were trained for use in transportation and in warfare.

Donkeys are believed to descend from African wild asses. Domestic donkey remains have been found in Egyptian excavations dating back to around 4000 B.C. Donkeys were probably first used as beasts of burden to supplement the work done by oxen, and later as riding animals. Horses and donkeys allowed people to become much more mobile than they had been, and this led to increased trading between different cultures.

Chickens were domesticated from Asian jungle fowl around 3,500 B.C. as a source of meat and eggs. Camels were domesticated around 2,500 B.C. According to the Agropolis-Museum of France, other early domesticated animals were turkeys and musk ducks in Central America and llamas, guinea pigs, and alpacas in South America.

Domestication Failures

Virtually no other animal species has been domesticated since around 2,500 B.C. Humans tried to domesticate many other types of animals that could be useful for work or provide a good meat source, but were unsuccessful. Zebras are the most notable example. Ancient herdsmen tried for centuries to domesticate zebras. Although they are genetically very similar to horses and can even breed with horses, their behavior is quite different. Zebras are notoriously bad-tempered around humans and have never lost their tendency to bite unexpectedly.

Elephants have historically been used as work animals in some parts of the world, but they grow too slowly to become truly domesticated animals. Grizzly bears and African buffalo have never been domesticated, because of their nasty dispositions. Likewise, deer and antelope are unsuitable because they cannot be herded or penned up (with the exception of reindeer). They flee in panic when they are frightened and do not have the proper social structure for domestication.

History has shown that the most suitable animals for domestication (and use by humans) are those that naturally live in groups and have a hierarchy. This allows humans to assume a dominant role in the hierarchy and exert control over the animals' behavior. Of the animals that have been domesticated, only cats and ferrets are

considered to exhibit solitary lifestyles rather than herd/group behavior. In fact, scientists are not convinced that all species of cats and ferrets are completely domesticated in the classic sense.

Domestication Frees Humans' Time

The domestication of livestock and the dawn of civilization occurred around the same time and are unmistakably linked. The ability to keep and control groups of meat-supplying animals allowed humans to settle down and produce excess food. This freed people to build cities and roads, invent new things, and cultivate the arts.

ANCIENT CULTURES AND RELIGIONS

Scientists believe that the first true settlements sprang up in Mesopotamia (roughly modern-day Iraq) around 8000 B.C., Africa and India (6000 B.C.), China (5000 B.C.), Europe (4000 B.C.), and the Americas (3000 B.C.).

The Mesopotamian region of the Middle East is considered the cradle of civilization because the peoples that settled there were probably the first to form cities and develop writing systems. They produced literature and works of art and began practicing farming and animal husbandry. (Husbandry is the control and management of a resource.) Mesopotamia was home to the Sumerians, Babylonians, Israelites, Assyrians, and Persians, among others. All of these cultures developed from many independent tribes or groups of people that had different religions and cultures.

The peoples of most ancient civilizations were polytheistic (meaning that they believed in more than one god). Many ancient peoples worshipped animals as gods, used animals to represent their gods, or thought that their gods could assume animal form when they wished. The Sumerians believed that they could divine what their gods were thinking by examining the internal organs of animals like goats and sheep. These and other livestock animals were often sacrificed in rituals in attempts to appease the gods and goddesses or obtain favor from them. This practice was common in other major cultures and religions as well.

Many early civilizations also worshipped heavenly bodies, like the sun and moon. These cultures believed that the stars and planets had magical influences over earthly events. They tracked the positions and aspects of the heavenly bodies very closely and believed that such information could be used to foresee the future. Astrology and the zodiac evolved from these beliefs and were adopted by people in many different cultures, including the Babylonians, Egyptians, Hindus, and early Chinese. (See Table 1.1.) Most ancient zodiacs used animals to represent some or all of the constellations. In fact, the word zodiac comes from the Greek words *zodion kuklos*, meaning "circle of little animals."

TABLE 1.1

Chinese zodiac

Rat	Ox	Tiger	Rabbit	Dragon	Snake	Horse	Sheep	Monkey	Rooster	Dog	Boar
1912	1913	1914	1915	1916	1917	1918	1919	1920	1921	1922	1923
1924	1925	1926	1927	1928	1929	1930	1931	1932	1933	1934	1935
1936	1937	1938	1939	1940	1941	1942	1943	1944	1945	1946	1947
1948	1949	1950	1951	1952	1953	1954	1955	1956	1957	1958	1959
1960	1961	1962	1963	1964	1965	1966	1967	1968	1969	1970	1971
1972	1973	1974	1975	1976	1977	1978	1979	1980	1981	1982	1983
1984	1985	1986	1987	1988	1989	1990	1991	1992	1993	1994	1995
1996	1997	1998	1999	2000	2001	2002	2003	2004	2005	2006	2007

SOURCE: Created by Information Plus staff

Egypt

At various times, ancient Egyptians held different animals as sacred and as representations of their gods and goddesses. Some animals may have been worshipped as deities, but others were most likely used to present deities in a recognizable form. Animal worship in Egypt extends back to predynasty times (that is, before 3,100 B.C.). The graves of many ancient Egyptians contain carefully wrapped remains of dogs, sheep, and even cows that were buried along with the humans.

One of the earliest religions was called Apis, or the cult of the bulls. This was one of several bull cults that developed in Egypt. The bull symbolized great strength and courage, and ancient artists sometimes depicted Egyptian kings in bull form. The cults believed that a bull born with very specific markings was sacred—a god to be worshipped. When a sacred bull was born, the people held great celebrations. The bull was housed in a majestic stable and given the best food to eat. Even the mother of the sacred bull was revered and called the Isis cow.

Another animal that the Egyptians are known for worshipping is the cat. Its Egyptian name was "mau" or "myw," which seems very much like the sound that cats make. Many goddesses, including Mafdet and Bast, were represented as cats or cat-human mixes and were thought to be able to switch back and forth from human to cat form. Most representations featured wild cats (like the lion). Bast was usually represented by a domestic cat and called Bastet when she was in cat form. The Sphinx, which dates back to 2,500 B.C., is a massive statue in Egypt with the body of a lion and the head of a pharaoh. As shown in Figure 1.3, some Egyptian gods were depicted with human bodies and animal heads.

A number of cat statues and mummified cats have been found in Egyptian tombs and cemeteries, including hundreds of thousands of mummified cats in the city of Bubastis. All archaeological evidence indicates that cats were treated very well during this time period by the Egyptians, who imposed harsh punishments for killing or harming a cat. The penalty for killing a cat, even if by accident, was execution. Despite their sacred status, cats were also put to work protecting grain stores from rats and other rodents.

India

The first signs of civilization in India date to the fourth millennium B.C., when nomadic people began to form agricultural settlements. The Indus, as they are called, cultivated grains as their main food source, but also ate fish, beef, pork, fowl, and mutton. There is evidence that they used elephants as beasts of burden and kept domesticated dogs and cats.

Although ancient Indians had varied spiritual beliefs, many of these beliefs were blended together into the practice of Hinduism around 3000 B.C. In general, Hindus believe that animals and people experience rebirths after they die. In other words, a human can be reincarnated as an animal, or vice versa. This means that all life forms are to be respected. Because Hindus consider virtually everything to be divine, they worship many animal gods and believe that their gods could take many forms, including human-animal forms. For example, Ganesha has the head of an elephant. Cattle, especially cows and bulls, are particularly sacred.

Buddhism was founded by Siddhartha Gautama (circa 563–483 B.C.), an Indian philosopher who came to be called Buddha. Buddha believed that animals were very important spiritually and were evolving toward a higher consciousness, just as humans were. Therefore, Buddhists consider it wrong to cause any harm to an animal or any other living being.

FIGURE 1.3

Egyptian gods

Anubis   Hathor   Sebek   Seth   Horus

SOURCE: "Egyptian Gods," in *SPARE Pet Name Hieroglyphic Translator,* Society for the Protection of Animal Rights Egypt, Cairo, Egypt, 2001 [Online] http://sparealife.org/images/anigods.JPG [accessed April 22, 2003]

Jainism also originated in India and is similar in many respects to Buddhism, although it is perhaps much older. The Jains are so adamantly opposed to killing any life form that they allow themselves to be bitten by gnats and mosquitoes (rather than swatting them). They often carry brooms so they can brush worms out of their path to avoid stepping on them. The Jains strongly condemn the eating of any meat. They became well-known in later centuries for their animal hospitals.

China

Chinese cities began to appear sometime around 3000 B.C. Archaeological evidence indicates that farming and animal husbandry were practiced at that time and that horse-drawn chariots were in use. The ancient Chinese are also credited with raising silkworms to produce silk. This was important, in part, because it meant that people no longer had to rely on animal skins for their clothing. A Chinese emperor of the first century B.C. established the Garden of Intelligence, one of the largest zoos in the world.

China contained many different cultures, each with its own spiritual and philosophical beliefs and customs. Historians lump these under the heading of Chinese Traditional Religion. This encompasses many local belief systems, as well as Buddhism (which came to China from India), Confucianism, and Taoism.

Confucianism is based on the teachings of Confucius (551–479 B.C.), a Chinese philosopher who became famous for his sayings about how to live a happy and responsible life. In general, Confucius called for respect for animals, but not reverence. In other words, animals were not to be treated as deities. Killing animals for food was allowable, while killing them for sport was not.

Taoism is a spiritual philosophy that developed in China during the fifth and fourth centuries B.C. Although some historians believe that it was founded by Lao-Tse (604–531 B.C.), it may also have developed from the writings of several different philosophers and teachers. Taoism was based around Tao, which is roughly translated in English as "the path" or "the way." Taoists believe that there is a power that envelops and flows through all living and nonliving things and that all life should be respected.

Hebrew Tribes and Judaism

The origins of Judaism lie with Hebrew tribes that populated the Mesopotamian region of the Middle East. Although the Hebrews followed various worship practices, including animism, eventually they developed a central religion known as Judaism. This change was largely brought about by a Hebrew leader named Abraham, who devoted himself to only one god called Yahweh (or Jehovah in Latin). Around 2000 B.C. Abraham led his people to a land that was eventually called Israel. The followers of Judaism came to be called Jews.

Judaism was unique among the many other religions of the time because it is monotheistic. The Jews worship only one god instead of many gods. The Hebrew Bible says that man was created in the image of god. Therefore, the Hebrew god is anthropomorphic, or humanlike.

According to the first book (Genesis) of the Hebrew Bible, God created the Earth and populated it with all kinds of creatures. God granted humans "dominion over the fish of the sea, and over the birds of the air, and over all the wild animals of the earth, and over every creeping thing that creeps upon the earth." This idea of dominion was to have a profound effect on Western civilization for centuries to come.

The book of Genesis also describes a great flood. Noah and his family rescued a male and female of every animal species and took them into an ark. All other life on earth was destroyed. After the floodwaters finally subsided, Noah was instructed to release the animals to repopulate the earth. But first he took some of the animals and offered them as a burnt sacrifice to God. Animal sacrifice was an important and sacred ritual to the Hebrews.

Many domestic and wild animals are mentioned in books of the Hebrew Bible. Domestic animals include asses (donkeys), horses, camels, goats, cattle, sheep, oxen, mules, pigs, and dogs. Most dogs were probably wild, as they are often referred to as scavengers traveling in packs. Small dogs may have been kept as pets.

The Hebrew Bible also includes some very strict dietary rules regarding the eating of meats. Orthodox Jews are only allowed to eat certain animals considered clean by God. These include:

• Animals with parted hooves that are cloven-footed and chew their cud

• Fish with fins and scales

• Most birds, except birds of prey

• Locusts, grasshoppers, and crickets

All other animals, including pigs, are considered unclean by God and are not to be eaten. Animals that are eaten have to have the blood removed because consumption of blood is forbidden.

The Hebrew Bible also contained some directions on how animals were to be treated. For example, animals were supposed to rest and do no work on the Sabbath (Friday evening to Saturday evening), along with the Hebrew people. In another verse, the Bible said that "The righteous person regards the life of his animal."

Arabic Cultures and Islam

The first kingdom appeared in the Arabian Desert around 1000 B.C. Prior to that time, the region was inhabited by scattered families and clans, many of whom were nomadic people, called Bedouins, who raised camels. The Bedouins were animists who believed that spirits lived within all natural things. They also worshipped their ancestors and heavenly bodies.

Over the next few centuries, society became more centralized and the worship of many gods became common in temples and cults throughout the Arabian Peninsula. Islam was founded by the prophet Muhammad (570–632), who believed in only one god, the God of Abraham. This is the same Abraham of Hebrew tradition. However, the followers of Islam called God by the name Allah. Muhammad said that the angel Gabriel had revealed Allah's word to him and named him as his messenger. The Koran contains the sacred writings believed to be the revelations made to Muhammad by Allah.

The Koran includes many references to animals, particularly camels. Falcons, pigeons, cats, and horses were also considered important in Islamic cultures. Legend has it that Muhammad was so fond of cats that he once cut a hole in his robe to keep from disturbing a cat that had fallen asleep on his sleeve. Muhammad also spoke highly of horses and considered the breeding of horses to be an honorable task. The Arabs bred very fine and fast horses that were used in warfare, transportation, and sporting events.

Although the Koran did not specifically mention animal souls, it did teach respect for all living creatures. Muslims, people who practice Islam, sacrificed certain animals to Allah and included meat dishes in their feasts and festivals. However, Muslims were forbidden by the Koran to eat certain animals, mainly swine and those that died of natural causes (such as illness or old age). The Koran also forbade the eating of animal blood or any animal that had not been blessed in the name of Allah.

Classical Greece

The ancient Greeks were polytheistic, but their gods were overwhelmingly anthropomorphic (humanlike). Although Greece was associated with a variety of cultures after its civilization around 2000 B.C., the classical Greek period from 500–336 B.C. was the most influential for future ideas about animals. The classical Greeks did not have one central philosophy but followed the teachings of various schools established by wise men and philosophers. Some of the most famous were Socrates (470–399 B.C.), Plato (circa 427–347 B.C.), and Aristotle (384–322 B.C.).

In general, animals were widely used for food, clothing, and work in Greek society. These uses were not questioned on moral or philosophical grounds because the people believed that everything in nature had a purpose. In other words, plants existed for animals and both plants and animals existed for the welfare and enjoyment of humans.

However, the famous philosopher and mathematician Pythagoras (circa 582–507 B.C.) and his followers did not eat meat because they believed that animals had souls. Many other Greeks, including Plato, recommended a vegetarian diet for ethical or practical reasons. Plato felt that a vegetarian diet made good economic sense because it required less land than animal husbandry to produce food.

Plato's student Aristotle is considered the father of zoology in Western history. He wrote extensively about animal anatomy, behavior, and reproduction in *History of Animals* and *On the Parts of Animals*. Aristotle believed that there was a natural hierarchy in which humans, animals, plants, and inanimate objects were arranged by their level of perfection. This arrangement came to be called the *scala naturae*, or "ladder of nature." Later philosophers called it "The Great Chain of Being."

The top rungs of Aristotle's ladder were occupied by humans, because they alone had rational souls that were capable of belief, reason, and thought. Below the humans were animals. Aristotle believed that animals had limited souls that allowed them to feel, but not to reason. Plants had the lowest forms of souls and ranked the lowest on the ladder. Among humans, Aristotle believed that there was a natural hierarchy, with free men ranked above slaves, women, and children. Aristotle's ideas about the rank of humans and animals in society would influence thinking in Western cultures for centuries.

Christianity

Christianity began as a sect of Judaism during the first century A.D. Its followers believed that God had come among them in the form of a human named Jesus Christ. Jesus preached a message of peace and forgiveness, but his criticism of Jewish rulers and claims of divinity got him into trouble with authorities. He was executed by crucifixion around 33 A.D., but the Christian movement did not end with his death. Jesus' followers believed that he was resurrected. They set down their beliefs in scriptures that came to be known as the New Testament of the Bible.

His followers considered Jesus' death to be a human sacrifice, similar to the animal sacrifices that were common in Jewish religious practice. This symbolism played an important role in the new religion. The New Testament mentions many animals, but mostly in the context of everyday life and as food sources. Jesus ate fish on several occasions and once cast a demon into a herd of pigs, causing them to plunge over a cliff and die. Because the Christian religion had its roots in Judaism, early Christians followed Jewish laws and customs regarding the eating of animals. However, the sect soon split apart from Judaism and abandoned the idea of clean and unclean animals. Christianity had no specific constraints on eating meat or the treatment of animals.

Christians did maintain the belief from the Hebrew Bible that humans had dominion over animals. The importance of the human soul was central to Christian theology. Many Christian philosophers of later centuries, such as Saint Augustine (354–430), argued that only humans (not animals) had rational minds and souls.

Animal symbolism was common in early Christian literature. *Physiologus* is a book that dates back to 200–500 A.D. It describes animals at length in a fanciful manner using Christian symbols and morals. Jesus was often described as a lamb, a lion, or a phoenix in stories.

The Roman Empire

The Roman Empire actually began as a single city, the city of Rome, which became a republic in 510 B.C. The Romans had a warrior mentality and built their empire by conquering other peoples and cultures. They worshipped many different gods and goddesses, most of which were in human form, and often adopted the deities of other cultures, particularly those of Greece. Animal sacrifices were common in Roman religious practices.

The rulers of the Roman Empire delighted in brutal competitions and sports and invented many "games" to entertain their citizens. The Colosseum of Rome was a massive arena that featured events in which wild animals fought to the death with each other or with humans. Ancient texts describe the deaths, very torturous and cruel by today's standards, of thousands of bears, bulls, lions, tigers, elephants, and other animals. Often the animals were chained together or tormented with burning irons and darts to make the fighting fiercer.

Historical evidence shows that the Romans were very fond of horses. Their economy, troops, and postal service were dependent on the work done by horses. A shrine to the horse goddess Epona, who had been adopted from conquered tribes of western Europe, was erected in every Roman stable. Although Epona was usually depicted in human form, she often rode a horse and was followed by dogs and birds. In addition to horses, the Romans practiced animal husbandry with cattle, pigs, sheep, goats, and chickens and kept cats and dogs as either pets or working animals.

Dogs held a special significance in Roman legend. Romans believed that twin babies named Romulus and Remus had been thrown into a river and washed up on shore. Miraculously, they were suckled by a she-wolf and survived. Romulus later killed Remus and founded the city of Rome. Historians believe that Romans were the first to use the dog name Fido, as a shortening of the Latin word *fidus* (meaning trusty) or *fidelis* (meaning faithful and loyal).

Christianity became the official religion of the Roman Empire in the year 325. This put an end to the killing of humans in the Colosseum, because the human soul was sacred to Christianity. There is no evidence that animal games ceased, however, until the Empire became too poor to acquire exotic and wild animals for them.

THE MEDIEVAL PERIOD

In general, historians refer to medieval times (or the Middle Ages) as the time period from the fall of the Roman Empire in the late 5th century lasting through the 16th century. The early centuries of the period are called the Dark Ages because few scientific and cultural achievements were made by Western societies during this time. Once the Roman emperors were gone, the authorities of the Christian church began to hold great power over the peoples of Europe.

Saint Francis of Assisi (1181–1226) is the most famous animal lover of medieval times. The Franciscan friar was said to preach to birds and animals and release captured animals from traps. There are many legends about the saint, the most famous being that he once convinced a wolf to stop terrorizing a town and eating the livestock. Saint Francis was said to have "the gift of sympathy" for animals.

One of the most influential philosophers of the Middle Ages was Saint Thomas Aquinas (1225–1274). In 1264 he published a work called *Of God and His Creatures,* in which he included a section titled "That the Souls of Dumb Animals Are Not Immortal." In this essay, Aquinas argues that animals can neither understand nor reason and that their actions are driven entirely by natural instincts rather than by "art." Because animals could comprehend only the present and not the future, Aquinas believed that their souls were not immortal like human souls.

Animals became the subject of many myths and superstitions during the Middle Ages. Bestiaries were a popular form of literature. They were miniature encyclopedias about animals similar to the *Physiologus* published by early Christian writers. They included descriptions and figures of mostly fanciful, but some real, animals, along with moral teachings. For example, the pelican was described as piercing her own breast to drip blood into the mouths of her young. This was seen as a symbol of the self-sacrifice made by Jesus in shedding his own blood. Symbolism presented in the bestiaries was copied and used throughout medieval art, literature, and architecture.

Aesop's fables had been part of Greek folklore since the Classical period. During the Middle Ages, they were translated into Latin and English and used as textbooks in schools. These fables featured animals or insects learning a moral lesson about life. Some of the more famous include "The Hare and the Tortoise," "The Town Mouse and the Country Mouse," and "The Crow and the Pitcher." Aesop's fables are some of the earliest and most famous examples of talking animals in literature.

During the medieval period, the Christian church worked to stamp out paganism, cults, animal worship, and all other non-Christian beliefs. Numerous Crusades, or holy wars, were launched between 1095 and 1291 to try to conquer the Muslims who had taken over Jerusalem. Many men (and horses) on both sides were killed in these wars.

Domestic crusades were also launched against groups and individuals throughout Europe who were considered dangerous to the church or its teachings. Medieval people became obsessed with the devil and believed that he and his servants assumed human and animal forms. Although different animals were suspected at different times and places, the cat became the most feared.

The Persecution of Cats

Cats came under suspicion for a variety of reasons. Unlike dogs, they did not behave subserviently toward humans. This was considered unnatural, because it violated the biblical view that humans should have dominion over animals. Also, cats were very active at night and engaged in loud raucous mating rituals. Though cats had always behaved in this manner, to the superstitious minds of the Middle Ages, cats were practicing supernatural powers and witchcraft.

Most accused witches were older peasant women who lived alone, often keeping cats as pets for companionship. This guilt by association meant that roughly a million cats were burned at the stake, along with their owners, on suspicion of being witches.

In the early 13th century, Pope Gregory IX (1145–1241) declared that a sect in southern France had been caught worshipping the devil. He said the devil had appeared in the form of a black cat. Cats became the official symbol of heresy (or religious beliefs not advocated by the church). Anyone who showed any compassion or feeling for a cat came under the church's suspicion. By the beginning of the 14th century, Europe's cat population had been severely depleted. Only semi-wild cats survived in many areas.

In 1347 the bubonic plague swept across Europe. Called the Black Death, it killed 25 million people (nearly a third of Europe's population) over only three years. Thousands of farm animals died as well, either from the plague or from lack of care. The death rate peaked in the warm summer months and dropped dramatically in the wintertime because the plague was being spread to humans by fleas on infected rodents. The plague revisited Europe several more times over the next few centuries. In addition, millions of people are thought to have suffered from food poisoning during the Middle Ages because of the presence of rat droppings in the grain supply. Centuries of cat slaughter had allowed the rodent population to surge out of control.

However, cats continued to be exterminated for religious reasons for another 300 years. Queen Elizabeth I (1533–1603) of Britain burned cats alive as part of her coronation celebration. By that time, the Reformation had swept Europe, and many people (including the Queen) were no longer Catholic. Cat hatred had become nondenominational. England's Witchcraft Act of 1563 associated the keeping of cats with "wickedness" and led to the executions of many more cats and owners.

The persecution of cats during the Middle Ages seems to be unique to Europe. In Asia and the Middle East, cats retained their prestige as protectors of grains and other food supplies. Even within Europe, there was a notable exception to the cat persecution. During the 900s the tiny country of Wales was ruled by Hywel the Good. In 945 he established laws for his realm that included protections for cats for their good works in protecting the region's grain supplies. Hywel's laws set the monetary worth of cats (a penny at birth and four pennies after a successful mouse kill) and imposed strict penalties on people for stealing or killing cats. This legal protection lasted for several centuries, until Welsh law was replaced by English law.

The Prosecution of Animals

One of the most bizarre human-animal trends of all recorded history took place during the Middle Ages in Europe. This was the formal prosecution of animals accused of committing crimes against people. Animals charged with such crimes (usually murder) were brought to court, appointed with a lawyer, and tried, just as a person would be. Records show that hundreds of animals were found guilty and then executed by hanging.

Society & Animals: Journal of Human-Animal Studies, published by the organization Psychologists for the Ethical Treatment of Animals, describes the practice in detail in a 1994 article titled "The Law Is an Ass: Reading E. P. Evans' *The Medieval Prosecution and Capital Punishment of Animals*" (Piers Beirne).

The article reviews books by several authors on the subject, focusing on one written by E. P. Evans in 1906. Evans describes 191 animal trials, mostly from the 15th–17th centuries. Most of the trials took place in France, Italy, and Germany. There are a few historical records of trials in other European countries and in the United States, Canada, and Brazil. Animals were tried for a variety of offenses besides murder, mostly fraud and theft. Records show that many were tortured for confessions (just as humans were) prior to the trial. It is not clear how animal confessions were interpreted, considering that animals could not speak human languages.

Criminal proceedings against animals were handled with the utmost seriousness by medieval legal authorities. Animals that harmed humans were considered servants of the devil because they violated God's directive in the Bible that humans should have dominion over animals. A particular Bible verse, Exodus 21:28, was often cited as the grounds for executing an animal convicted of murder: "If an ox gore a man or a woman that they die, then the ox shall be surely stoned, and his flesh shall not be eaten." The penalties for offenses less serious than murder matched those given to humans for the same types of crimes.

Evans lists a variety of domestic and wild animals, as well as rodents, sea creatures, birds, and insects, that were tried at various times by government or church courts. Those that could not be physically brought to court were tried *in absentia*. In general, only the larger domestic animals, such as pigs, bulls, cows, horses, sheep, and dogs, actually appeared in court and were subjected to punishments. A few animals were found innocent or granted pardons or reprieves by authorities. Many wild animals found guilty by church courts were excommunicated (exiled from the church).

The vast majority of criminal defendants were pigs, probably because farmers allowed them to roam free much of the time. In 1386 a pig accused of murdering an infant was tried and convicted by a court in Falaise, France. The pig was hanged at the gallows by the village hangman. Her six piglets were charged with being accessories to the crime but were acquitted "on account of their youth and their mother's bad example."

A lawyer could establish his reputation by performing well in animal trials. In France in the early 1500s, a lawyer named Bartholomé Chassenée was appointed to represent some rats that had eaten and destroyed some barley (a felony). Chassenée used a series of clever legal maneuvers to delay the trial as long as possible. At one point he convinced the judge that it was too dangerous for his clients to come to court on the appointed day because of the many cats in the neighborhood. Chassenée became famous throughout France for his excellent legal skills.

It is not clear why medieval courts went to the trouble to formally try animals before executing them. Some historians believe that these trials were intended to be warnings to animals and people about the consequences of their actions. Others believe the trials represented a philosophical desire to exert some human control over nature.

THE AGE OF ENLIGHTENMENT AND THE USE OF VIVISECTION

The centuries immediately following the Middle Ages are called the Age of Enlightenment because waves of intellectual and scientific advancement swept across Europe. Many superstitions and customs disappeared as societies became more urban and less rural. Church authorities began to lose much of their power over people's lives. Medical researchers gained permission to perform autopsies (mostly on executed prisoners) to learn about human anatomy. Autopsies had been forbidden by the church for centuries, and little medical progress had been made in the field of anatomy since the second century, when the Roman doctor Galen practiced dissection on gladiators and animals. Animal experimentation was to become a major research tool of modern medicine.

In 1543 the Belgian doctor Andreas Vesalius (1514–64) published an article titled "Some Observations on the Dissection of Living Animals" in *De Fabrica Humani Corporis*. Vesalius hoped to convince other doctors that the study of anatomy was key to improving medical care. He advocated cutting open living animals to teach students about blood circulation.

During the 1600s the French philosopher and mathematician René Descartes (1596–1650) published some influential essays in which he argued that animals could not think at all. Descartes said that only humans had eternal souls; thus, only humans could reason. He described the human gift of language as proof that humans were philosophically different from animals. Descartes was fascinated with the field of mechanics and extended its ideas to nonhuman animals. He wrote that animals were mechanical things like clocks and therefore could not feel pain. This helped make it socially acceptable to cut open animals while they were still alive for medical and scientific purposes. The process became known as vivisection and was widespread in Europe in the 17th and 18th centuries.

Literature from this time describes live dogs being nailed to tables in classrooms and dissected to learn about their anatomy. Writers dismissed the cries of the dogs as being similar to the screeching sounds that a piece of machinery makes when it is forcibly taken apart.

BLOOD SPORTS

As the Middle Ages drew to a close, sports in which animals were pitted against each other became very popular in England. These "blood sports" included bull- and bear-baiting with dogs, cockfighting, and dogfighting.

Baiting began as more of a practical matter than a sport. Medieval people believed that an animal that was whipped immediately prior to slaughter would provide more tender meat. Whippings administered by butchers eventually evolved into events where teams of dogs were allowed to set upon bulls and bite and tear at their flesh. Such baitings soon became popular entertainment and were expanded to include other animals, such as bears. Baiting events were generally held in a ring or arena or in a field near the shops.

Baiting was popular with the Tudor family, who ruled England from 1485 to 1603. The monarchs of this time were also fond of hunting and sports and popularized horse and greyhound racing among the upper classes.

King Henry VIII (1491–1547) and Queen Elizabeth I (1533–1603) were legendary for their appreciation of baiting events. In 1585 the British House of Commons tried to ban bear-baiting on Sundays but was overruled by Queen Elizabeth I. Gradually blood sports became associated with the lower classes and were mostly held on holidays and during church festivals.

Most church authorities considered animal blood sports to be harmless pastimes, but this was not true of the Puritans. The Puritans were a Christian group that wanted to change the Church of England. They took power over the British Parliament in the mid-1600s and outlawed baiting and other blood sports for a short time. One Puritan wrote, "What Christian heart can take pleasure to see one poor beast rend, tear, and kill another?" When the Puritans were thrown out of power, blood sports returned and were even more popular than before.

THE MOVE TO AMERICA

During the 17th century, many Puritans fled England for the New World—America. The Puritans brought their unique perspective on animals with them. In 1641 the Massachusetts Bay Colony enacted a Body of Liberties that set out the fundamental rights of the colonists. Included in these rights was Article 92, which stated that "No man shall exercise any Tirranny or Crueltie towards any Bruite creature which are usuallie kept for man's use." This is generally considered the first modern law against animal cruelty; however, it did not have a major effect on American laws or customs regarding animals.

Animals and Indigenous Americans

The Puritans were not the first visitors to America. Anthropologists believe that domesticated dogs traveled from Asia into North America with prehistoric humans before the Ice Age ended. Spanish explorers who visited during the 1500s left behind domesticated horses. By the time the first colonists arrived a century later, they found that dogs and horses were the only two domesticated animals in America.

The Native Americans who had inhabited the land for thousands of years had no domesticated cattle, sheep, goats, pigs, or chickens. Their cultures had not undergone the transition from hunter-gatherer to settled agriculture in the European/Asian way. Native Americans were more nomadic, moving from place to place to find better hunting and fishing grounds. Grain crops, such as wheat and rye, were unknown to them. Corn was their major agricultural crop, along with pumpkins and squash. These crops could be sowed and harvested by hand, so Native Americans had never needed large animals to plow fields and pull hay wagons. They used dogs as beasts of burden or ate them for food. Horses were used by tribes in the Central and Western Plains to hunt large game, like buffalo.

Native Americans also believed in animal spirits. Many tribes thought that some animals, particularly the eagle and the buffalo, had special powers and great spiritual significance. However, these beliefs did not keep Native Americans from eating animals or killing them for other purposes. The European settlers provided new markets for meat, fur, and animal goods, and they introduced guns to hunting tribes. By the 1800s, the wild buffalo of the Plains had been driven to the brink of extinction.

The Colonists Shape the New World

The early colonists were impressed by the wide variety of wild animals that lived along the eastern shores, including elk, deer, beaver, turkey, and quail. However, the Europeans were accustomed to agricultural life based on captive livestock and grain crops. They had difficulty surviving and had to import livestock from Europe. Dogs and cats came along as companions and working animals. Although intended for breeding purposes, the early shipments were eaten by hungry colonists, and more had to be brought.

Livestock became vitally important to the new colonies. Laws were passed making it a capital crime to kill a farm animal without the owner's permission. Livestock herds eventually built up enough to support the expansion of villages and towns. The colonists began exploring and took their animals with them as they migrated south and west.

IN ENGLAND, PHILOSOPHERS ARGUE AGAINST BARBARITY TO ANIMALS

Meanwhile, in Europe, new social and philosophical movements were to have far-reaching effects on the welfare of animals. At the time, domestic animals were frequently treated brutally, either for entertainment or for profit. Blood sports continued to go on, although they were mostly enjoyed by the lower classes. Horses pulling carts and carriages were often beaten in the streets. It was still common practice to whip pigs and bulls prior to slaughter to tenderize the meat. Chickens were often nailed down by their feet to keep them from wandering, and geese were plucked while still alive. Dogs and cats were killed by the thousands as late as 1665, when they were blamed for spreading the plague.

During the 17th and 18th centuries, several notable philosophers and writers spoke out against mistreating animals. John Locke (1632–1704) of England wrote that children should be taught from an early age that torturing and killing any living thing was despicable. In 1713 the poet Alexander Pope (1688–1744) wrote an article titled "Against Barbarity to Animals" for London's *Guardian* newspaper.

David Hume (1711–76) of Scotland advocated "gentle usage" of animals for the sake of humanity. The German philosopher Immanuel Kant (1724–1804) argued that cruelty to animals easily escalated to cruelty to humans and should therefore be stopped. Stopping animal cruelty for the sake of humans became a rather popular idea and was embraced more easily than the idea of preventing cruelty just for animals' sake.

In 1751 the British artist William Hogarth (1697–1764) released a series of etchings and engravings called *The Four Stages of Cruelty*. The graphic images depict the life of a fictional boy named Tom Nero who graduates from harming animals as a child to harming people as an adult. In the first scene, the boy, in a white cap, tortures a dog with an arrow. Although one boy tries to stop him, they are surrounded by other children also torturing animals. In the second scene, Tom Nero is shown as a young man beating a horse on the street, while other acts of animal cruelty take place around him. The third scene shows fully grown Tom Nero immediately after he has murdered his girlfriend. In the fourth scene, Tom Nero has been hanged for his crime, and his body is being dissected at a medical school.

In his notes, Hogarth describes why he created the pictures: "The four stages of cruelty, were done in hopes of preventing in some degree that cruel treatment of poor animals which makes the streets of London more disagreeable to the human mind, than any thing what ever, the very describing of which gives pain." The artist's intention was to illustrate some of the horrors of animal cruelty, but the connection between cruelty to animals and cruelty to humans was what captured people's attention. Even those who did not care about animal issues could see the dangers to civilized society of ignoring animal cruelty.

In 1764 the "mechanical animal" theory advocated by Descartes during the previous century was attacked by French philosopher François-Marie Arouet de Voltaire (1694–1778) in *Dictionnaire Philosophique Portatif*. Voltaire argued that the scientists who dissected live animals found "organs of feeling" within them similar to those of humans, thus proving that animals could indeed feel pain.

In 1776 an Anglican clergyman named Humphry Primatt (circa 1742–90) published *A Dissertation on the Duty of Mercy and the Sin of Cruelty to Brute Animals*. He wrote that "Pain is pain, whether it is inflicted on man or on beast." Primatt equated cruelty to animals with sin and even atheism, and complained that legal authorities were doing little to stop it. Primatt argued that eliminating barbaric practices against animals might cut down on the number of "shocking murders" that were occurring.

One of the most poignant pleas for animals was made by British philosopher and political scientist Jeremy Bentham (1748–1832). In 1780 he wrote a paper ("An Introduction to the Principles of Morals and Legislation," published in 1789) in which he advocated making cruelty to animals punishable by law. He said, "the question is not, Can they reason? Nor, Can they talk? but, Can they suffer?" Toward the end of the century, a few court cases were successfully tried against people who had abused animals, but only because the animals were not their personal property.

BRITISH LAW TAKES HOLD

The modern legal protections for animal welfare date back to 1800s England. A bill was first introduced in 1800 to make bull-baiting illegal, but it was defeated by Parliament members who argued that it would deny poor people an excellent form of entertainment. Over the next 20 years, several politicians sponsored bills that would have protected cattle and/or horses against mistreatment, but all of them failed. The turning point came in 1822 when Parliament member Richard Martin sponsored a bill prohibiting cruelty to cattle, horses, and sheep. Martin had introduced a similar bill the year before and had been greeted with laughter, but the second time, he was able to use his persuasive skills to get the bill passed. It was the first anticruelty law of its kind.

"Humanity Martin," as he came to be called, soon learned that having a law in effect and getting it enforced were two different things. The authorities were not interested in spending time gathering evidence and prosecuting animal abuse cases. Martin conducted his own investigations and managed to get a conviction and fine levied against a man for beating horses. He was helped in his efforts by a group of people led by the Reverend Arthur Broome. In 1824 this group became the Society for the Prevention of Cruelty to Animals (SPCA). Although people had tried to form such societies before, most notably in 1808 in Liverpool, this was the first time that a group fighting against animal abuse had legal backup for its endeavors. The SPCA managed to win 149 convictions against abusers during its first year of operation.

In 1835 Martin's original act was expanded to protect dogs and bulls. In addition, cockfighting and the practice of baiting were outlawed. In 1840 the SPCA was recognized by Queen Victoria (1837–1901) and became the Royal Society for the Prevention of Cruelty to Animals (RSPCA). The RSPCA appointed inspectors to patrol the markets and slaughterhouses of London and other large cities looking for abuses. The group continued to push for new and tougher legislation against animal cruelty, and the Cruelty to Animals Act was passed in 1849 (and amended in 1854). This act made illegal many common abuses against animals, including docking (clipping) a dog's ears. It also spelled out rules for the proper treatment of animals during their impoundment and transport to slaughter. The act was amended again in 1876 to restrict the use of animals in research.

Many people involved in furthering animal welfare in England were also involved in other humanitarian movements of the time, including child welfare and antislavery causes. They believed that these issues were all related by common problems: abuse of power and the domination of the strong over the weak using cruel measures. There was also a growing moral belief that permitting cruelty against animals would lead to violence against humans and weaken society in general. It was also during the mid-1800s that the keeping of pets became popular among the middle classes.

U.S. LAW

Early U.S. law was patterned after British common law, which viewed animals as pieces of property. However, the reform movements that swept England during the 19th century also reached America. In 1828 the state of New York passed the first law against animal cruelty: "Every person who shall maliciously kill, maim or wound any horse, ox or other cattle, or any sheep, belonging to another, or shall maliciously and cruelly beat or torture any such animals, whether belonging to himself or another, shall upon conviction, be adjudged guilty of a misdemeanor."

Within the next decade, similar laws were passed in states throughout the Northeast and Midwest. Some state laws covered only livestock, while others included all domestic animals. Some laws applied only if the animal belonged to someone other than the abuser.

In 1866 Henry Burgh founded the American Society for the Prevention of Cruelty to Animals (ASPCA). Fashioned after the RSPCA, the ASPCA received permission from the New York Legislature to enforce anticruelty laws in the state. This meant that ASPCA officers could arrest and seek convictions of animal abusers. Burgh was elected the first ASPCA president and held that post for 22 years. Similar societies soon formed in other major cities, including Philadelphia and Boston.

Vivisection, practiced at Europe's medical schools for some time, had also been incorporated into U.S. medical training. In 1871 Harvard University established one of the first vivisection laboratories in the country. The Massachusetts SPCA launched an aggressive media campaign to educate the public about the cruelties of vivisection and turn public support against the university. Anti-vivisection societies were also started in Illinois and the New England states; however, their attempts to outlaw the practice failed.

The first federal law in the United States dealing with animal cruelty was the Twenty-Eight Hour Law of 1873. This law required that livestock being transported across state lines be rested and watered at least once every 28 hours during the journey. At the time, livestock were transported mainly by rail from farms and ranches to huge central processing stations equipped with meatpacking plants. Chicago's Union Stock Yard and Transit Company was the largest. By the end of the 19th century, it covered 475 acres, employed 25,000 people, and processed more than 80 percent of the meat consumed in the United States.

THE 20TH CENTURY

As the 20th century dawned, American society was becoming increasingly urban and industrial. Working animals, such as horses, were gradually replaced with machinery on farms, battlefields, and city streets. The growing middle class had more time and money for leisure activities, many of which involved animals—hunting, fishing, keeping pets, and visiting wildlife refuges, circuses, zoos, and animal parks. Horseracing and greyhound racing both became popular sports in the 1930s as many states legalized pari-mutuel gambling.

In 1938 the Pure Food, Drug, and Cosmetics Act was passed. This legislation required animal testing of certain chemicals and drugs to ensure their safety for humans. It was to have a profound effect on the human-animal relationship and later debates on the topic of animal rights. Following World War II (1939–45), the use of animals in medical and scientific research exploded. The demand for dogs and cats in the laboratory led to animal procurement laws in many states, allowing scientists to obtain test subjects from dog pounds and animal shelters.

By this time, the country's animal protection organizations had largely turned their attention from farm animals to pets. Some people within these groups were deeply opposed to the use of animals in research, while others saw it as a regrettable necessity. Differences in opinion led to splintering and the formation of new organizations. The Animal Welfare Institute and the Humane Society of the United States (HSUS) were both founded during the early 1950s. Table 1.2 lists other milestones of the animal movement that occurred between 1951 and 2000.

Animal protection groups began to develop separate identities and missions. Some retained a local focus, while others focused on national issues. They gained an ally in Senator Hubert Humphrey (1911–78) of Minnesota, who championed animal causes along with civil rights and other social movements. Humphrey was instrumental in passage of the Humane Methods of Slaughter Act of 1958. The law required use of humane slaughter methods at slaughterhouses subject to federal inspection. It was the first piece of federal animal protection legislation in 85 years.

The next year, Congress passed the Wild Horses Act to outlaw the use of motorized vehicles and the poisoning of watering holes "for the purpose of trapping, killing, wounding, or maiming" wild horses on federal lands. The passage of this legislation had been driven by grass-roots support, a term used in politics to describe a movement that begins with a handful of people and gains national power from widespread popular support. In 1950 Velma B. Johnston and 146 other residents of Storey County,

Nevada, had signed a petition protesting the use of aircraft to capture wild horses in the county. The practice, known as mustanging, was outlawed.

Johnston then took the fight to the Nevada legislature, where she was mockingly nicknamed "Wild Horse Annie." Johnston kept up the pressure and was successful in getting statewide legislation passed in 1955. She next turned her campaign into a national one and garnered support from millions of schoolchildren. Congress was flooded with letters, and articles appeared in major newspapers. The federal law, passed in 1959, was often referred to as the "Wild Horse Annie Act."

During the 1960s another animal issue, this time dog-related, achieved national prominence because of the efforts of a handful of people. Pepper was a family pet that disappeared from her backyard in Pennsylvania in 1965 and wound up dead in a New York City laboratory. Pepper's family diligently tracked down what had happened to her and helped expose a network of shady animal dealers and pet thieves selling animals by the pound to research laboratories. The public demanded action. In 1966 Congress passed the Laboratory Animal Welfare Act requiring licensing of animal dealers and regulation of laboratory animals.

These laws were joined by several other federal laws during the 1960s and 1970s designed to protect wild animals, including eagles, seals, and endangered species. Some animal protection issues were intertwined with causes devoted to conservation, ecology, and the environment. "Save the Whales" became a popular slogan.

In 1975 a new twist developed in an old movement. Author Peter Singer published a book called *Animal Liberation,* calling for a fundamental change in the human-animal relationship. Singer argued that animals are victimized by humans on a massive scale because of a social evil called "speciesism," a term he envisioned as parallel to such words as racism and sexism to refer to the belief that one species is inherently superior to another. He blamed speciesism for allowing systematic abuse of animals in agriculture, research, and other human activities. The next year Animal Rights International was founded by social reformer Henry Spira (1927–98).

Some people working for animal causes embraced the idea that animals are not resources to be protected by benevolent humans but individual beings with their own interests and rights. This meant that humans could not use animals for any purpose (food, clothing, sport, entertainment, etc.) because it was morally and ethically wrong to do so. This opened a new agenda in the animal movement that went beyond calls for kind treatment and humane methods of slaughter. Adherence to the most radical "animal rights" theory meant that eating meat and killing vermin were wrong. So were zoos and circuses, hunting and fishing, and experimenting on animals to find cures for

TABLE 1.2

Milestones in animal protection, 1951–2000

	Organizations founded	Legislation passed/amended	Other
1951	Animal Welfare Institute		
1954	Humane Society of the U.S.		
1955	Society for Animal Protective Legislation		
1957	Friends of Animals		
1958		Humane Slaughter Act (HSA)	
1959	Catholic Society for Animal Welfare (now ISAR)	Wild Horses Act	*The Principles of Humane Experimental Technique* published
	Beauty Without Cruelty		
1962		Bald and Golden Eagle Act	
1966		Endangered Species Act (ESA) Laboratory Animal Welfare Act (LAWA)	
1967	Fund for Animals United Action for Animals		
1968	Animal Protection Institute Canadian Council on Animal Care		
1969	International Fund for Animal Welfare		
1970		Animal Welfare Act (AWA) amendments	
1971	Greenpeace	Wild Free-Roaming Horse and Burro Act	*Diet for a Small Planet* published
1972		Decompression chamber banned for euthanasia in California Marine Mammal Protection Act (MMPA)	
1973	International Primate Protection League (IPPL)	ESA amendments	Convention on International Trade in Endangered Species (CITES) Air Force beagles campaign *Mankind?* published
1974	North American Vegetarian Society (NAVS)		
1975			*Animal Liberation* published
1976	Animal Rights International (ARI) Committee to Abolish Sport Hunting (CASH)	AWA amendments Horse Protection Act Fur Seal Act	American Museum of Natural History protests *The Question of Animal Awareness* published
1977	Sea Shepherd Conservation Society Scientists Center for Animal Welfare American Fund for Alternatives to Animal Research		"Undersea Railroad" releases porpoises in Hawaii
1978	Animal Legal Defense Fund (ALDF) Medical Research Modernization Committee	HSA amendments	Indian government bans rhesus monkey exports
1979	Committee to End Animal Suffering in Experiments (CEASE)	Metcalf-Hatch Act (authorizing pound seizure) repealed in New York State Packwood-Magnuson Amendment to the International Fishery Conservation Act	Coalition to Abolish the Draize Test launched *The Animals' Agenda* launched Research Modernization Act introduced in Congress Animal Liberation Front (ALF) raid, first in the United States, at New York Univ. Medical Center *Vegetarianism: A Way of Life* published
1980	People for the Ethical Treatment of Animals (PETA) Psychologists for the Ethical Treatment of Animals (PsyETA) Student Action Corps for Animals (SACA)		Action for Life conference launched *Animal Factories* published
1981	Farm Animal Reform Movement (FARM) Trans-Species Unlimited (TSU) Mobilization for Animals (MfA) Association of Veterinarians for Animal Rights (AVAR)		Silver Spring Monkeys confiscated from Institute for Behavioral Research

human diseases, no matter how humanely any of these activities were carried out.

This philosophical leap was too much for most people, and the idea that animals had rights like humans was not generally embraced. The public supported anticruelty laws and animal protection measures (within reason) but did not go so far as to say that animals have a moral standing in society that makes it evil to eat or use them. To do so would go against centuries of tradition and beliefs, disrupt many

TABLE 1.2

Milestones in animal protection, 1951–2000 [CONTINUED]

Organizations founded	Legislation passed/amended	Other
1981 Johns Hopkins Center for Alternatives to Animal Testing (CAAT) Primarily Primates sanctuary		
1982 Food Animal Concerns Trust (FACT) Vegetarian Resource Group (VRG) National Alliance for Animal Legislation (NAA) Feminists for Animal Rights (FAR)	MMPA reauthorized	Veal ban campaign launched
1983 In Defense of Animals (IDA)		*The Case for Animal Rights* published *A Vegetarian Sourcebook* published
1984 Humane Farming Association (HFA) Performing Animal Welfare Society (PAWS)	Pound seizure in Massachusetts repealed	ALF raid at Head Injury Clinical Research Center, Univ. of Pennsylvania *Modern Meat*, focusing on antibiotics in meat production, published
1985 Physicians Committee for Responsible Medicine (PCRM) Last Chance for Animals (LCA) Culture and Animals Foundation (CAF) Tufts Center for Animals and Public Policy	AWA amended to include focus on alternatives and control of pain and distress	ProPets Coalition launched Hegins pigeon shoot campaign launched Campaign for a Fur Free America and Fur Free Friday launched Great American MeatOut launched Federal funding for Head Injury Clinical Research Center suspended
1986 Farm Sanctuary Animal Welfare Information Center (AWIC)		Cambridge Committee for Responsible Research (CCRR) initiative
1987		*The Animals' Voice* launched *Diet for a New America* published Jenifer Graham case filed
1988 Doris Day Animal League (DDAL)		
1989		Avon Corporation ends its animal testing Veal Calf Protection Bill hearings, U.S. Congress
1990 United Poultry Concerns	AWA amended California referendum bans mountain-lion hunting San Mateo County spay/neuter ordinance passed	March for the Animals
1991 Ark Trust	Cambridge, Mass., bans LD50 and Draize tests	Stockyard "downer" campaign launched
1992	Wild Bird Conservation Act International Dolphin Conservation Act Driftnet Fishery Conservation Act Colorado referendum bans spring, bait, and hound bear hunting	Student Right Not to Dissect approved in Pennsylvania
1993	NIH Revitalization [Reauthorization] Act mandates development of research methods using no animals	Marie Moore Chair in Humane Studies and Veterinary Ethics endowed at Univ. of Pennsylvania First World Congress on Alternatives and Animals in the Life Sciences
1994	Arizona bans trapping on public lands (public initiative) Oregon referendum bans bear baiting, bear and cougar hounding	
1995		USDA ends face branding under pressure Spay Day USA launched

accepted systems for feeding and entertaining people, have crippling economic consequences, hurt millions of people who earned their living through animals, and impede scientific progress. Because of such arguments, most Americans of the 1970s rejected the idea of animal rights. So did most of the traditional animal protection organizations, though they continued their work to educate and reform.

But the idea did not go away. More books examining this issue were published, and new organizations formed, including People for the Ethical Treatment of Animals (PETA) in 1980. Many others followed. These animal rights groups were much bolder and "in your face" than traditional animal welfare organizations. They held protest marches and publicly condemned companies and research

TABLE 1.2

Milestones in animal protection, 1951–2000 [CONTINUED]

Organizations founded	Legislation passed/amended	Other
1996	Colorado referendum bans body-gripping traps Massachusetts referendum bans bear baiting, hound hunting, body-gripping traps, and reforms Fisheries and Wildlife Commission Washington referendum bans bear baiting and hound hunting bears, cougars, and bobcats	
1998	Arizona referendum bans cockfighting Missouri referendum bans cockfighting California referendum bans body-gripping traps	
1999		Harvard Univ. announces launch of animal rights law course
2000		Hegins pigeon shoot terminated

SOURCE: Deborah J. Salem and Andrew N. Rowan, "Milestones in Postwar Animal Protection," in *The State of the Animals 2001*, The Humane Society of the United States, Washington, DC, 2001

institutions using animals for various purposes. Radical believers, calling themselves the Animal Liberation Front (ALF), raided laboratories and farms to "free" animals and destroy property. The first such raid happened in 1979 at the New York University Medical Center.

Some animal rights groups worked through the legal system to achieve change. They filed lawsuits and worked with prosecutors to strengthen animal laws. In many of these efforts, they were supported by more traditional animal protection groups. Legal reform was one area in which the entire animal movement found some common ground. The traditional groups increased their political power during the 1980s through swelling membership rolls. Animal issues gained momentum in society, particularly among pet owners.

Animal causes were also championed by movie and television personalities. In 1988 entertainer Doris Day founded the Doris Day Animal League. Since the 1980s, at the end of each of his shows, game-show host Bob Barker has urged television viewers to spay and neuter their pets. He founded his own animal organization in 1995.

It is understandable that movie and television celebrities wanted to become involved in animal activism, as animals had been popular characters in movies and television shows from the time the media were invented. Rin Tin Tin was a famous war dog that starred in silent movies during the 1920s. The story of another dog, Lassie, appeared in book form in 1940, in a movie in 1943, and on television in 1954. The original TV show ran for 17 years. Benji the dog gained movie fame in 1974. Popular animal movies of the 1980s included *White Fang* and *Turner and Hooch*.

Keiko the whale became famous because of the 1993 movie *Free Willy*. In the movie, Keiko portrayed a whale liberated from captivity with the help of a boy. *Life* maga-

zine did a story on Keiko, describing the irony of the poor conditions in which he lived in a Mexican amusement park. In response, the Free Willy Foundation raised millions of dollars to have Keiko moved in 1996 to an aquarium in Oregon. (See Figure 1.4.) There he gained weight and recuperated from various health ailments. In 1998 Keiko was flown to Iceland to live in a baypen in his native waters. Although his handlers hoped that Keiko would leave the pen and join a pod of ocean whales, he had not done so as of 2003. He is still semi-dependent on humans for food and seems reluctant to leave.

Some Recent Events

During the 1990s animal stories became so popular that an entire cable television network was devoted to them. Animal Planet is a project of Discovery Communications. It broadcasts such popular shows as *The Crocodile Hunter, Animal Precinct, The Planet's Funniest Animals,* and *The Jeff Corwin Experience*. In 2001 company executives reported that Animal Planet had nearly 75 million subscribers.

Animal Precinct is a reality show that goes on patrol with New York City's Humane Law Enforcement (HLE) agents. These agents are empowered to respond to cruelty complaints, perform investigations, and arrest people for crimes against animals. They were granted this power in 1866 when the ASPCA established its original charter with the state of New York. In 2001 the HLE department received 44,000 complaints of suspected animal cruelty and investigated 2,922 cases, resulting in the arrest of 40 people. Agents of the Michigan Humane Society (MHS) perform a similar role in Detroit. MHS agents respond to more than 4,000 animal cruelty incidents each year. They are featured in an Animal Planet television show called *Animal Cops*. The state of Arkansas also grants limited police powers to agents of local

FIGURE 1.4

Keiko in 1997 at the Oregon Coast Aquarium in Newport, Oregon. *CORBIS/Kevin Schafer. Reproduced by permission.*

humane societies. Animal welfare organizations are pleased that animal cruelty cases receive so much media attention. Many groups publicize cases on their Web sites and ask members to lobby prosecutors for stiff sentences.

In July 2001 a California man was sentenced to three years in prison after killing a woman's pet dog. The man became angry after he and the woman were involved in a minor traffic accident in February 2000. He grabbed the small fluffy white dog from the woman's car and threw him into oncoming traffic. The dog was killed, and the man fled the scene. The incident received widespread media attention, and people around the country donated $115,000 in reward money. Tips from several people led police to the man responsible. The three-year sentence was

unusually long for an animal case, and animal groups hope that it will encourage other jurisdictions to vigorously prosecute people who abuse and maliciously kill animals.

In February 2003 the SPCA of Suffolk County, New York, reported that two men in Long Island had been arrested for abusing rabbits during a family party. A videotape of the incident was turned in anonymously to a local television station. The videotape is alleged to show the men beating and punching the rabbits and skinning one while still alive and conscious and squealing in pain. Each man was charged with one misdemeanor count of animal cruelty. The alleged offenses are not felonies, because the rabbits were being raised for food. New York's felony animal abuse law only applies to companion animals.

CHAPTER 2
THE ANIMAL RIGHTS DEBATE

According to Webster's dictionary, a right is "a power or privilege to which one is justly entitled." Sociologists James Jasper and Dorothy Nelkin define a right as "a moral trump card that cannot be disputed." The phrase "human rights" came into usage during the late 1700s to refer to generally recognized privileges (or freedoms) that every person should enjoy.

The United Nations (UN) has a Universal Declaration of Human Rights (UDHR) that reads as follows: "Everyone has the right to life, liberty, and security of person." The UDHR specifies dozens of particular human rights, including the right to be free from slavery, torture, and cruel or degrading treatment. Other rights involve equal protection under the law, fair and public trials, freedom of movement, marriage and raising families, ownership of property, worship and religion, peaceful assembly, expression of opinions, access to public services, social security, working conditions, rest and leisure, education, culture, and standard of living.

The U.S. Declaration of Independence was written in 1776. It says, "We hold these truths to be self-evident, that all men are created equal, that they are endowed by their Creator with certain unalienable Rights, that among these are Life, Liberty and the pursuit of Happiness." Although America's founding fathers considered these rights to be God-given, they did note that people form governments to "secure these rights." Thus, rights have a moral basis, but they are upheld through the law.

Since the 1970s, a debate has arisen about whether animals also have moral rights that should be recognized and protected by human society. This is largely a philosophical question, but the answer has many practical consequences. For example, if animals have a right to life, then it is wrong to kill them. If animals have a right to liberty, then it is wrong to hold them in captivity. If animals have a right to pursue happiness and enjoy security, then it is wrong to interfere in their natural lives.

Societies and governments make decisions about who should be granted rights and how those rights should be secured. In general, an individual's legal right to life and liberty ends if that person infringes on someone else's right to life and liberty. In the United States, a person who kills another person can be executed by the government. At the very least, the government can restrict the killer's liberty. People debate the moral issues involved in such affairs, but the legal issues are generally spelled out clearly in U.S. law.

Sometimes it is not considered morally or legally wrong for one person to kill another—for example, in the case of self-defense or in defense of others. The same holds true for a person killing an animal. There is general moral and legal agreement that killing an attacking tiger or rabid dog is reasonable and right behavior. In human society, the moral and legal arguments that protect a person acting in self-defense begin to melt away as the threat level descends. Killing an unarmed burglar or trespasser puts a person on shaky ground. Killing a loud, annoying neighbor crosses over the line.

This line is set much lower when it comes to killing animals. People can sometimes kill animals that burgle or trespass, make too much noise, or become a nuisance without moral or legal condemnation. The same holds true for animals that are tasty, have attractive skin or pelts, or are useful laboratory subjects. Why is it acceptable to kill an animal for these reasons, but not a human?

People answer this question in different ways depending on their belief systems and moral and social influences, including religion, philosophy, and education. Here are some of the most common answers:

- Animals do not have souls.
- God gave humans dominion over the animals.
- Humans are intellectually superior to animals.
- Animals do not reason, think, or feel pain like humans do.

- Animals are a natural resource to be used as humans see fit.

- Animals kill each other.

Some people say that it is not acceptable for humans to kill animals. In fact, some believe it is not acceptable to use animals for any human purpose at all. They believe that animals have moral rights to life, liberty, and other privileges that should be upheld by society and the rule of law. These are hard-core believers in animal rights, the fundamentalists of the animal rights movement. When they speak out, write, march, or otherwise publicize their beliefs, they are called animal rights activists. An activist is someone who takes direct and vigorous action to further a cause (especially a controversial cause).

Other people believe that some animals have (or should have) some moral and/or legal rights under certain circumstances. They may rescue abandoned pets, lobby for legislation against animal abuse, feed pigeons in the park, or do any number of other things on behalf of animals. These people are broadly categorized as animal welfarists. Their adherence to the idea of animal rights generally depends on the circumstances. For example, a welfarist might defend the rights of pet dogs and cats but eat chicken for dinner.

This is unacceptable to animal rights fundamentalists. They argue that all animals (not just the lovable ones) have rights that apply all the time (not just when it is convenient). Such fundamentalists face opposition from a variety of sources. Some of this opposition is driven by moral and philosophical differences of opinion. Some is also driven by economics.

Many animals (alive or dead) have financial value to humans. Livestock farmers, ranchers, zookeepers, circus trainers, jockeys, and breeders are among the many people who have a financial interest in the animal trade. If humans were to quit using animals, these people would be out of work. Many others would be deprived of their favorite sport and leisure activities. Given such economic arguments and the moral and philosophical arguments noted above, those opposed to the idea of animal rights feel as strongly about the topic as those who support it.

HISTORY

Most historians note that the modern animal rights movement began during the 1970s. However, the roots of the movement date back much farther, to a handful of philosophers and thinkers. Celsus was a second-century Greek writer who argued against the Jewish/Christian belief that humans are morally superior to animals. Celsus pointed out that animals might actually be more favored by God because they do not have to sow seeds or plow fields to live, while people do. He did not believe that humans must be superior to animals because they are able to capture and eat animals. He noted that humans have to use weapons, traps, and hunting dogs to capture animals, while animals are naturally equipped with the tools they need to capture humans.

Over time, other writers and thinkers questioned society's attitudes toward animals. Their arguments were usually based on philosophical or ethical ideals. The Italian artist Leonardo da Vinci (1452–1519) refused to eat meat. He once wrote in his notebook: "the time will come when men such as I will look upon the murder of animals as they now look upon the murder of men."

Legal protection was extended to some animals during the 1800s in the form of antiabuse laws. These laws were often passed based on the theory that animal abuse was bad for society in general—they did not protect animals for the animals' sake but for humanity's sake. In 1892 the humanitarian Henry Salt (1851–1939) wrote a book titled *Animal Rights: Considered in Relation to Social Progress,* in which he asks, "Why should the law refuse its protection to any sensitive being? The time will come when humanity will extend its mantle over everything which breathes. . . ."

Society became preoccupied with two world wars during the first half of the 20th century, and it was not until the 1970s that the rights of animals became a major social issue. In 1975 Australian professor Peter Singer published a book called *Animal Liberation,* which described in vivid detail the ways in which Singer felt animals were subjected to pain and suffering on farms, in slaughterhouses, and in laboratory experiments. Singer called for an end to what he called speciesism—prejudice and discrimination against animals by humans. He argued that speciesism is similar to racism and sexism, in that they all deny moral and legal rights to one group in favor of another.

Henry Spira (1927–98) formed Animal Rights International after attending one of Singer's lectures. Spira was a social reformer who had worked in the civil rights and women's liberation movements. He turned his attention to the animal rights movement after he "began to wonder why we cuddle some animals and put a fork in others" (*Animal People,* October 1998). Spira was instrumental in bringing various animal groups together to work for common causes. Many people credit him with pressuring cosmetics companies to seek alternatives to animal testing for their products during the late 1980s.

Philosopher R. G. Frey of Bowling Green State University argued that animals do not have moral rights in a 1980 book titled *Interests and Rights: The Case Against Animals.* Frey insisted that animal lives do not have the same moral value as human lives because animals can not and do not undergo the same emotional and intellectual experiences as humans.

In 1979 the organization Attorneys for Animal Rights was begun by lawyer Joyce Tischler. The group held the first national conference on animal rights law in 1980. The next year, it successfully sued the U.S. Navy and prevented the killing of 5,000 burros at a weapons-testing center in California. Also in 1981, the group adopted a new name, the Animal Legal Defense Fund (ALDF). One of ALDF's goals is to end the view that animals are not more than property. The group's anticruelty division also works with state prosecutors and law enforcement agencies to draft felony anticruelty laws and stiffen penalties for violations. As shown in Table 2.1, as of June 2003, 41 states had felony animal abuse provisions, as did the District of Columbia.

It was during the 1970s and 1980s that some animal advocates began using high-profile tactics, such as sit-ins at buildings and protest marches on the streets, to attract public attention to their cause. (See Figure 2.1.) These are examples of civil disobedience, or refusing in a nonviolent way to obey government regulations. A radical element of the movement went even farther, breaking into laboratories and fur farms to release animals and damaging buildings and equipment. Some people who used these methods referred to themselves as part of the Animal Liberation Front (ALF). ALF followers became known as the "domestic terrorists" of the animal movement.

Many in the scientific community were disturbed by this new wave of moral and social opposition to the use of animals in research. In 1981 the Foundation for Biomedical Research (FBR) was founded to defend such usage and promote greater understanding of its medical and scientific benefits among the general public. The FBR began tracking and reporting on the activities of criminal animal activists who broke into laboratories to release animals and/or destroy property.

The organization People for the Ethical Treatment of Animals (PETA) was begun in 1980 and quickly came to prominence. One of the group's cofounders infiltrated a research laboratory and obtained photographs of the primates being held there. The incident attracted national media attention and greatly helped Henry Spira's efforts to reduce animal use in cosmetic testing. Animal issues also became important to a larger number of Americans. During the 1980s membership in the Humane Society of the United States (HSUS) increased by 500 percent.

In 1981 the Association of Veterinarians for Animal Rights (AVAR) was founded by two veterinarians concerned that animals "were routinely being used and abused by society, sometimes for the most trivial of reasons" (AVAR [Online] http://www.avar.org/avar_history.html [accessed August 13, 2003]). AVAR's goal is to educate the public and people within the veterinary profession about these practices and to change social policy toward animals. The group's philosophy, as cited on its Web site in 2003, echoes that of many other animal rights

TABLE 2.1

Jurisdictions with and without felony animal abuse provisions, 2003

Jurisdictions with felony animal abuse provisions

1. Alabama[2]	25. New Mexico
2. Arizona	26. New York[1]
3. California	27. North Carolina
4. Colorado[4]	28. Ohio[5]
5. Connecticut	29. Oklahoma
6. Delaware	30. Oregon
7. Florida	31. Pennsylvania
8. Georgia[2]	32. Rhode Island
9. Illinois[1]	33. South Carolina[2]
10. Indiana	34. Tennessee[4]
11. Iowa[2]	35. Texas
12. Kentucky[5]	36. Vermont
13. Louisiana	37. Virginia[1]
14. Maine[1]	38. Washington
15. Maryland[3]	39. West Virginia[5]
16. Massachusetts	40. Wisconsin
17. Michigan	41. Wyoming[5]
18. Minnesota[3]	
19. Missouri	
20. Montana	**Territories, districts, & possessions:**
21. Nebraska[4]	District of Columbia[3]
22. Nevada[1]	
23. New Hampshire	
24. New Jersey[3]	

Jurisdictions without felony animal abuse provisions

1. Alaska	**Territories, districts, & possessions:**
2. Arkansas	American Samoa
3. Hawaii	Northern Marianas
4. Idaho	Guam
5. Kansas	Puerto Rico
6. Mississippi	Virgin Islands
7. North Dakota	
8. South Dakota	
9. Utah	

[1]Enacted 1999
[2]Enacted 2000
[3]Enacted 2001
[4]Enacted 2002
[5]Enacted 2003

SOURCE: "Jurisdictions with Felony Animal Abuse Provisions," and "Jurisdictions Without Felony Animal Abuse Provisions," in "Felony Status List," in *ALDF, Animal Legal Defense Fund: Resources: Laws and Legislation,* Animal Legal Defense Fund, Petaluma, CA, 2003 [Online] http://www.aldf.org/content.asp?sect=action&sectionid=3 [accessed July 21, 2003]

groups in that it feels "all nonhuman animals have value and interests independent of the values and interests of other animals, including human beings."

In 1983 philosophy professor Tom Regan published the book *The Case for Animal Rights*. Regan argued that animal pain and suffering are consequences of a bigger problem—the idea that animals are a resource for people. He presents detailed philosophical arguments outlining why he believes animals have moral rights as "subjects-of-a-life." Regan says that acknowledging the rights of animals requires people to cease using them for any purpose, not just those associated with pain and suffering.

R. G. Frey responded with his own 1983 book, *Rights, Killing and Suffering: Moral Vegetarianism and Applied*

FIGURE 2.1

Animal activists dressed in prison outfits and monkey masks stage a public protest. *Corbis-Bettmann. Reproduced by permission.*

Ethics. The idea of moral vegetarianism (adhering to a vegetarian diet for moral reasons, rather than for physical reasons) dates back centuries. It had been advocated by Indian leader Mahatma Gandhi (1869–1948) in the early 1930s as a moral duty of humans toward animals, and gained new life during the animal movement of the 1970s. In his book, Frey points out what he believes would be the practical and economic consequences to society of this philosophy—mainly the collapse of animal agriculture and other animal-based industries and widespread social disruption.

In 1984 philosopher Ernest Partridge attacked Singer's speciesism idea and Regan's animal rights view in an article for the journal *Ethics and Animals.* In "Three Wrong Leads in a Search for an Environmental Ethic: Tom Regan on Animal Rights, Inherent Values and Deep Ecology," Partridge maintained that both authors missed a crucial point about the nature of rights—that rights have no biological basis, only a moral basis. In other words, it does not matter how humans and animals are alike or dissimilar in biology. What really matters is that no animals exhibit the capacities of "personhood," such as rationality and self-consciousness. Partridge believes that lack of personhood effectively disqualifies animals from being rights holders.

Carl Cohen, professor of philosophy at the University of Michigan, also attacked the views of Singer and Regan

with his 1986 article "The Case for the Use of Animals in Biomedical Research" in the *New England Journal of Medicine.* Cohen acknowledged that speciesism exists, but denied that it is similar to racism or sexism. He argued that racism and sexism are unacceptable because there is no moral difference between races or between sexes. However, he believes that there is a moral difference between humans and animals that denies rights to animals and allows animals to be used by humans. Cohen went on to become one of the most well-known and widely published of the critics of the animal rights movement.

In 1988 researchers at Harvard University obtained a patent for the OncoMouse—a mouse that had been genetically engineered to be susceptible to cancer. This was the first patent ever issued for an animal. Animal rights groups led by the ALDF challenged the issuance of the patent in court, but the case was dismissed because the court found that the ALDF had no legal standing in the matter. Since that time, several other animals have been patented, including pigs, sheep, goats, and cattle. According to Tom Regan's *The Case for Animal Rights*, patents can be issued for "nonnaturally occurring nonhuman multicellular living organisms, including animals" as long as they are given "a new form, quality, properties or combination not present in the original article existing in nature."

In 1995 Professor Gary Francione published his book *Animals, Property, and the Law*. Francione argues that there is an enormous contradiction between public sentiment and legal treatment when it comes to animals. He says that the majority of the public agrees that animals should be treated humanely and not subjected to unnecessary suffering. However, he claims that the legal system does not uphold these moral principles because it regards animals as property.

Francione compares the situation to that which existed in slave states prior to the Civil War (1861–65). Although there were laws that supposedly protected slaves from abuse, they were seldom enforced against slave owners. Slaves, like animals, were considered property, and the law protects the right of people to own and use property as they see fit. Property rights date back to English common law. Francione says that the law has always relied on the assumption that property owners will treat their property appropriately to protect its economic value. Under this reasoning, the courts of the 19th century refused to recognize that a badly beaten slave was "abused," as defined by the law.

Francione believes that this same logic gives legal support to common practices in which animals are mistreated—for example, in the farming industry or in laboratory testing. He explains that humans are granted "respect-based" rights by the law while animals are only considered in terms of their utility and economic value. Francione complains that animals are treated by the legal system as "means to ends and never as ends in themselves." In other words, existing animal laws protect animals because animals have value to people, not because animals have inherent value as living beings.

The ideas of Singer, Regan, Francione, and other activists within the animal rights movement became a viable force in American society and politics during the 1990s and 2000s. Industries dealing with negative publicity, protest marches, and acts of domestic terrorism from movement supporters took aggressive steps to defend themselves. In 1991 Americans for Medical Progress (AMP) formed, its mission to educate the public about the beneficial uses of animals in scientific and medical research and to warn about the negative consequences of animal extremism. AMP receives funding from universities and private research facilities, pharmaceutical companies, and science and professional societies.

Companies and individuals from a variety of animal-based industries banded together in 1993 to form the National Animal Interest Alliance (NAIA). The NAIA is determined to fight the animal rights movement on political and philosophical grounds. On its Web site in 2003 the NAIA claimed that the animal rights movement "manipulates the political process to spin concern for animals into laws and regulations that deprive private citizens of the right to make ethical determinations about their relationships with animals."

In 2001 the Animal Agriculture Alliance (AAA) was formed to replace an older trade group and defend the agricultural industry against criticism from animal rights groups. The AAA's Web site in 2003 recorded its fears that continued growth of the animal rights movement could mean that "the very future of America's animal agriculture and those whose livelihood depends on it is in jeopardy." A similar fear is voiced by the Center for Consumer Freedom (CCF), a coalition of restaurant operators and food and beverage companies. The CCF's Web site noted in 2003 that there were more than 100 organizations dedicated to the animal rights movement that together received more than $200 million annually in funding from supporters around the country.

PHILOSOPHICAL ARGUMENTS

At the base of the animal rights debate is philosophy. Philosophical discussions involve abstract ideas and theories about questions of ethics and morality. These can be difficult subjects to comprehend and apply to real-life situations, but philosophy is important because it explains people's motivations and why people believe the way they do about a particular issue. Philosophical arguments are commonly used to either justify or condemn certain actions toward animals.

Not all people involved in "the animal movement" believe in animal rights. Many are motivated to work for animal causes for other reasons. Historically the most common motivator has been concern for animal welfare, or welfarism.

Welfarism

Welfarism is defined as the belief system associated with the social system known as the welfare state. "Welfare state" is a term first used during the 1940s to refer to a society in which the government has the primary responsibility for the individual and social welfare of its citizens. When applied to animals, welfarism assumes that humans have the primary responsibility for the welfare of animals. Welfarists acknowledge that society uses animals for various purposes. Their goal is to reduce the amount of pain and suffering that animals endure. Welfarism centers around compassionate and humane care and treatment.

The best example of a welfarist organization in the United States is the American Society for the Prevention of Cruelty to Animals (ASPCA). The ASPCA has existed since 1866 and as of 2003 had about 750,000 members. It defines its mission as follows: "To promote humane principles, prevent cruelty, and alleviate pain, fear and suffering in animals." The ASPCA defines itself not as an animal rights organization but as an animal welfare or animal protection organization.

The Humane Society of the United States (HSUS) had nearly 7 million members as of 2003. Although it defines itself as an animal-protection organization (the largest in the world), critics charge that the HSUS quietly supports an animal rights agenda. In 2003 the Web site of the CCF claimed that the HSUS is "masquerading as an animal-welfare charity" while it has "deep connections to many other radical animal-rights and environmental groups." The HSUS Web site, on the other hand, does not specifically mention animal rights, but does speak out against the use of animals in research, farming practices, and the fur industry.

Animal welfarists believe that humans have a responsibility to assure the well-being of animals and reduce their suffering. This responsibility is upheld by society in the form of anticruelty laws. However, anticruelty laws do not prevent farm animals from being slaughtered for food or laboratory animals from being injected with chemicals. In these situations, welfarists work for humane slaughtering methods and prevention of "unnecessary" suffering during experimentation.

Throughout history, some people acting on behalf of animals were motivated by their concern for society in general. People have long recognized that animal abuse is a form of violence that can easily escalate to violence against people. Acknowledgement of this potential link has helped animal welfarists gain support for antiabuse laws. Animal welfarism as a philosophy and a social movement has considerable support in modern society.

Utilitarianism

Utilitarianism is a philosophy popularized by Jeremy Bentham during the late 1700s. The basic premise of the philosophy is that right actions are those that maximize utility. Bentham defined utility as either the presence of positive consequences—"benefit, advantage, pleasure, good, or happiness"—or the absence of negative consequences—"mischief, pain, evil, or unhappiness" (*Introduction to the Principles of Morals and Legislation,* 1789). In other words, right actions are those that maximize the best consequences or minimize the worst consequences. An important aspect of utilitarianism is that the interests of all parties involved in a particular situation must be considered. Likewise, the consequences to all parties involved must be considered. This is a difficult enough task when only humans are involved, and becomes much more complicated if one also considers animals.

Peter Singer used a form of utilitarian logic in his 1975 book *Animal Liberation.* Singer argued that the suffering endured by animals on farms and during slaughtering far outweighs the pleasure and nutrition that the meat gives to humans. Likewise, he believes that laboratory animals suffer so much that this outweighs their usefulness to humans as test subjects. Singer concludes that the moral consequences of these practices (and other practices in which animals suffer) are too severe, so that they must be abolished and the animals liberated. As a result, advocates of Singer's theory are often called liberationists or abolitionists. Although his book is frequently called the Bible of the animal rights movement, Singer does not specifically call for animal rights in the book. He has stated that he believes that the term is politically useful for drawing attention to animal suffering.

Many philosophers reject the notion that utilitarianism can be applied to human-animal situations. This is because historically animals have not been considered to have interests at all, or their interests have not been considered equal to human interests. In 1992 philosopher Peter Carruthers wrote *The Animals Issue: Moral Theory in Practice.* In that book, he argued that utilitarianism is not an acceptable moral theory for examining animal issues because it equates animal lives and suffering with human lives and suffering, an idea Carruthers calls "intuitively abhorrent" and a violation of "common-sense beliefs." R. G. Frey also discounts the utilitarian theory as a model of morality for dealing with animals, saying that animals do not have interests because animals do not experience wants, desires, expectations, or remembrances.

Contractarianism

Another philosophy used to examine morality is called contractarianism. According to this theory, society establishes right actions (or moral norms) through an arrangement in which individuals (called agents) voluntarily agree to abide by certain rules of morality. Following these rules is beneficial to both individuals and society in general. Although there are many different models of contractarianism, the most common are based on the writings of Immanuel Kant (1724–1804) and the contemporary philosopher John Rawls (1921–2002). Kant believed that the moral code arising out of contractarianism reflects what rational agents would choose under ideal circumstances. Rawls expanded this view by saying that the right actions are those that rational agents would choose if they were unaware of their own personal ambitions or prejudices.

When contractarianism is used to talk about human society, the rational agents are assumed to have direct duties. In other words, the rational agents know they are bound by a moral contract and are responsible for acting accordingly. The rational agents also have direct rights under the contract and have duties to those that lack the rationality to enter into the contract, such as babies, small children, and the mentally challenged.

Some philosophers have used the contractarian model to explain the moral relationship between humans and animals. In *The Animals Issue: Moral Theory in Practice,* Peter Carruthers argued that contractarianism is the best moral model for describing the human-animal relationship.

However, he concludes that animals do not have moral standing under the contract because they do not qualify as rational agents. Carruthers believes that humans have only indirect duties toward animals, one of which is to treat animals humanely out of respect for the feelings of the rational agents that care about them. He does extend direct rights to human beings who are not rational agents, noting that this is necessary to maintain social stability.

Under the contractarianism philosophy, humans are moral agents, meaning that they make decisions and take actions based on morality. Many philosophers believe that animals are amoral—neither moral or immoral. For example, a lion that kills a baby zebra to feed her cubs is taking an action out of instinct. The action is neither morally good or morally bad. Some opponents of animal rights argue that because animals do not make decisions based on morality, animals are not part of the moral contract and do not have moral rights. Tibor Machan is a philosophy professor at Auburn University and an outspoken critic of the notion of animal rights. In a July 2000 article ("The Myth of Animal Rights"), Machan argued that animals cannot have rights because they are "instinctually driven beasts instead of moral agents."

In practice, the moral code of contractarianism seems to provide some protections for selected species of animals. For example, in American society there is widespread moral repugnance to the idea of eating dogs and cats or killing animals with sentimental or patriotic significance (such as bald eagles). These views might be argued to be rooted in their moral and philosophical impact on humans and could therefore be extensions of the contractarianism model.

Rights View

The rights view was defined and defended by philosopher Tom Regan in *The Case for Animal Rights* and many subsequent books. Regan says that all beings who are "subjects-of-a-life with an experiential welfare" have inherent value that qualifies them to be treated with respect and gives them a right to that treatment. In other words, living beings that have conscious awareness and self-identity deserve moral rights. Regan does not define exactly which animals fall into this category, but it includes higher species, such as vertebrates (animals with a spinal cord).

This philosophy is fundamentally different from welfarism and utilitarianism. The rights view holds that animals have moral rights to certain privileges and freedoms, just as humans have such rights. It does not mean that animals have exactly the same rights as humans. Most animal rights advocates believe that animals at least have the right to life and the right to freedom from bodily interference. Table 2.2 shows an animal bill of rights developed as part of a petition drive by the ALDF.

TABLE 2.2

Animal Bill of Rights

A Petition to the United States Congress

I, the undersigned American citizen, believe that animals, like all sentient beings, are entitled to basic legal rights in our society. Deprived of legal protection, animals are defenseless against exploitation and abuse by humans. As no such rights now exist, I urge you to pass legislation in support of the following basic rights for animals:

- The right of animals to be free from exploitation, cruelty, neglect and abuse.
- The right of laboratory animals not to be used in cruel or unnecessary experiments.
- The right of farm animals to an environment that satisfies their basic physical and psychological needs.
- The right of companion animals to a healthy diet, protective shelter, and adequate medical care.
- The right of wildlife to a natural habitat, ecologically sufficient to a normal existence and self-sustaining species population.
- The right of animals to have their interests represented in court and safeguarded by the law of the land.

SOURCE: "Animal Bill of Rights," in *Take Action*, Animal Legal Defense Fund, Petaluma, CA, 2003 [Online] http://www.aldf.org/windows/bill.html [accessed July 10, 2003]

The philosopher most well known for criticizing the animal rights view is Carl Cohen. In 2001 Cohen and Regan coauthored a book titled *The Animal Rights Debate*, which presents a point/counterpoint examination of the issue. Cohen's argument against animal rights is summed up as follows: "Animals cannot be the bearers of rights, because the concept of rights is essentially human; it is rooted in the human moral world and has force and applicability only within that world." In other words, Cohen defends speciesism as a valid reason for denying that animals have moral rights. He admits that animals are sentient (conscious of sensory impressions), feel pain, and can experience suffering, but insists that sharing these traits with humans does not make animals morally equal to humans.

Cohen says that some people confuse rights and obligations and assume that because humans have obligations toward animals, it means that animals have rights. This assumption is called symmetrical reciprocity, and Cohen believes that it is based on false logic. He points out that an obligation is what "we ought to do" while a right is "what others can justly demand that we do."

Cohen states that humans are moral agents who are restrained by moral principles from treating animals inhumanely. This means that humans should not inflict "gratuitous" pain and suffering on animals. However, it does not mean that humans must stop every activity that could or does harm animals in some way. Medical research on animals is an example. Cohen believes that scientists have moral obligations to humanity to use animals in their experiments if that is the best way for them to achieve their goals. According to Cohen, "our duties to human subjects are of a different moral order from our duties to the rodents we use."

Cohen's overall conclusion—that rights do not apply to animals, because rights are essentially human—is a point commonly made by those who oppose the animal rights movement. Many of them find it ludicrous to even debate the issue. Adrian Morrison is a scientist engaged in animal research and a very vocal critic of the animal rights movement. In a speech he presented to the Association for Research in Otolaryngology on January 27, 2002, Morrison noted that few philosophers besides Cohen and almost no scientists bother to dispute in detail the philosophy behind the animal rights view. Morrison suggested that most scientists and philosophers "think the subject to be too far from reality to be worth the trouble."

PRACTICAL APPLICATIONS

Assuming that animals have rights would have massive consequences to society. If animals have moral rights to life and freedom from bodily interference, then they cannot be purposely killed, harmed, or kept in captivity by humans. Billions of domesticated animals would be spared slaughter and would have to be released from cages and pens.

PETA, which claims to be the largest animal rights organization in the world with more than 750,000 members as of 2003, operates under the motto: "Animals are not ours to eat, wear, experiment on, or use for entertainment—period." Implementation of this motto would mean the elimination of all commercial animal operations—livestock and fur farms, animal research facilities, circuses, zoos, animal parks and aquariums, game ranches, hunting lodges, animal breeding facilities, pet stores, dog and horse racetracks, and so on. All of the people working in these businesses would be put out of work. The economic consequences would be enormous. Animal rights advocates point out that dismantling the slave trade after the Civil War was costly too, but it was done anyway because it was the right thing to do.

Besides an economic cost, there would be a scientific cost. Medical and scientific research has relied on animal test subjects for centuries. Some research and development would come to a halt, especially for new drugs and vaccines. Alternatives to animal testing would have to be found immediately or society would have to make a choice between testing on humans or doing without.

Development of some new household cleaners, cosmetics, and other consumer products would be stopped or delayed. Students in schools and universities would have to learn anatomy and biology without dissecting animals. Doctors, surgeons, and veterinarians in training would have to practice on something besides animals. Cloning, twinning, and other genetic manipulation of animals would have to stop. Eliminating the use of animals would disrupt the entire scientific community. Animal rights

activists believe the move is overdue because it would force scientists to think about their research in new ways.

There are also implications to private individuals in terms of dining, fashion, sport, recreation, and leisure. None of these activities could include personal use of animals. Hunting, fishing, eating meat, wearing leather, and keeping pets would come to a stop. The activity that would affect the most Americans would be the elimination of meat and animal products (milk, eggs, cheese, etc.) from their diet. A *Time*/CNN poll published in July 2002 found that only 4 percent of the respondents considered themselves vegetarians ("Should We All Be Vegetarians?," *Time*, July 15, 2002). Only 5 percent of these vegetarians considered themselves vegans (people who eat no animal products). In other words, less than 1 percent of Americans avoided all animal products in their diets. The other 99 percent consumed some type of animal products. Most animal rights advocates and liberationists are vegetarians or vegans. They believe that a vegetarian diet would not only help animals but would be healthier for humans and better for the environment.

Animal rights opponents are always eager to point out that keeping pets would be forbidden if animals had rights. PETA cofounder Ingrid Newkirk has been quoted as saying that pets are a symbol of the human manipulation of animals, and the notion of pets should be phased out. This idea is seldom mentioned by animal rights advocates because it is so radical. Many involved in the movement refer to pets as "companion animals" and to owners as "animal guardians" or "animal caretakers." These terms are intended to downplay the ownership element between humans and animals.

Legally, most animals are considered property—livestock and pets are owned by someone. In fact, the word "cattle" was derived from a Latin word meaning property. However, pets are slowly gaining status under the law. According to a 2003 article by Rebecca J. Huss in the *University of Colorado Law Review*, between 12 and 27 percent of American pet owners have provisions in their wills relating to their pets ("Separation, Custody, and Estate Planning Issues Relating to Companion Animals"). As of 2003, 17 states (Alaska, Arkansas, California, Colorado, Florida, Michigan, Missouri, Montana, Nevada, New Jersey, New Mexico, New York, North Carolina, Oregon, Tennessee, Utah, and Washington) recognized specific bequests to pets.

In 2000 Tennessee became the first state in the country to allow owners to sue for loss of love and affection if a pet is wrongfully killed. The ALDF helped the legislature draft the bill that was passed. Illinois and Maryland allow recovery of emotional distress damages for loss or injury of a companion animal, and similar cases are becoming more common in courts across the country. Most are thrown out because of the legal precedent that animals are property.

Still, lawyers report many more cases involving animal law today than in the past. Some state bar associations have formed animal law sections to deal with the increase. The Washington State Bar Association has such an organization. The summer 2003 issue of its newsletter describes the spectrum of animal law cases as follows: "Legal disputes over pets arise in actions involving dissolution of property or custody agreements, nuisance actions, assistance animal privileges, cruelty allegations, landlord-tenant contracts, police or dog warden brutality, airline negligence, veterinary malpractice and in the area of wills, trusts and estates." In the same publication, legal scholar Carolyn Matlack suggests that companion animals receive a new property classification under the law—sentient property (feeling property). She argues that courts could determine the best interests of sentient property based on the testimony of experts, as is done for young children and the mentally disabled.

Even wild animals are categorized by ownership. Private landowners assume power of ownership over wild animals on their land. As long as the animals are not protected by specific legislation, property owners may kill them as they please. Wild animals inhabiting government lands are considered public property and are treated as such. Consider the mission statement of the U.S. Fish and Wildlife Service (USFWS): "to conserve, protect, and enhance fish, wildlife, and plants and their habitats for the continuing benefit of the American people."

Public and private landowners exhibit implied animal ownership when they grant hunters permission to hunt on lands under their control. If these animals are assumed to have moral rights, then they can no longer be considered property.

Many animal welfarists are uneasy with the animal rights movement. They worry that it draws attention away from goals that are more easily obtainable for animals in the near future. They also worry that the radical statements and actions of some animal rights activists will turn the public against the entire animal movement. Animal rights activists have been known to demonstrate in the nude, splash paint on people wearing fur coats, and even throw pies in the faces of executives working for companies that test their cosmetic products on animals.

Although welfarists and abolitionists sometimes work together to achieve change, there is a philosophical gulf between them. Abolitionists ask welfarists to give up meat and leather; close down all the circuses, zoos, animal parks, aquariums, and racetracks; and stop laboratories from using animals to find cures for deadly diseases. Most welfarists are not willing to go so far. They might agree with some of these arguments some of the time under certain circumstances, but not all of them all the time.

At the other end of the spectrum is the radical element of the animal movement. This element does not debate

FIGURE 2.2

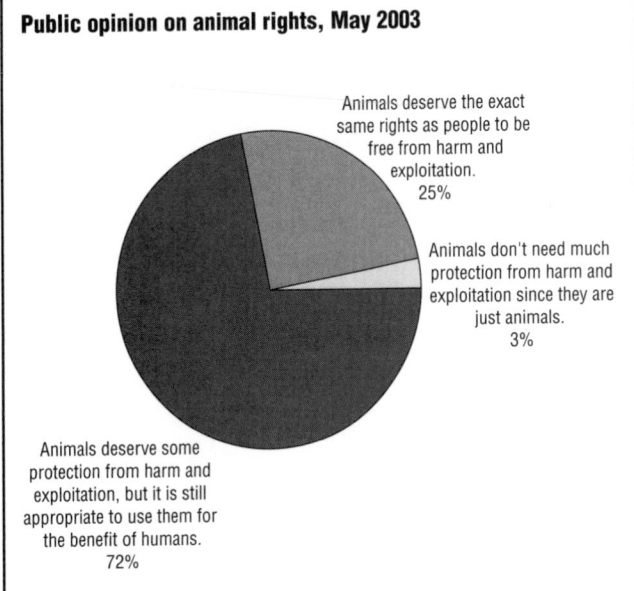

Public opinion on animal rights, May 2003

Animals deserve the exact same rights as people to be free from harm and exploitation.
25%

Animals don't need much protection from harm and exploitation since they are just animals.
3%

Animals deserve some protection from harm and exploitation, but it is still appropriate to use them for the benefit of humans.
72%

SOURCE: Adapted from David Moore, "Opinion of Treatment of Animals," in *Public Lukewarm on Animal Rights,* The Gallup Organization, Princeton, NJ, May 21, 2003 [Online] http://www.gallup.com/ [accessed July 10, 2003] © The Gallup Organization. All rights reserved. Reprinted with permission.

philosophy but takes direct criminal actions to free animals from farms and laboratories. The Animal Liberation Front (ALF) is not really a group, as it has no leadership structure, but is instead a set of guidelines. On its Web site in 2003, ALF's mission was listed as follows: "The . . . short-term aim is to save as many animals as possible and directly disrupt the practice of animal abuse. [The] long term aim is to end all animal suffering by forcing animal abuse companies out of business."

The Web site states that any vegan or vegetarian who carries out actions according to ALF guidelines can regard themselves as part of the ALF. These actions include liberating animals from "places of abuse" and inflicting "economic damage" on the people involved. ALF followers are urged to take precautions to prevent harming humans and animals. ALF receives funding from the ALF Supporters Group, made up of people who believe in the ALF guidelines but do not want to be involved in criminal activities.

PUBLIC OPINION

In May 2003 the Gallup Organization conducted a poll to determine Americans' opinions regarding animal rights issues. The results are based on telephone interviews with 1,005 adults aged 18 and up.

As shown in Figure 2.2, one-quarter (25 percent) of those asked believed that animals deserve the same rights as people. A large majority (72 percent) believed that animals deserve some protection, but can still be used to benefit people. Only a tiny percentage (3 percent) felt that animals do

FIGURE 2.3

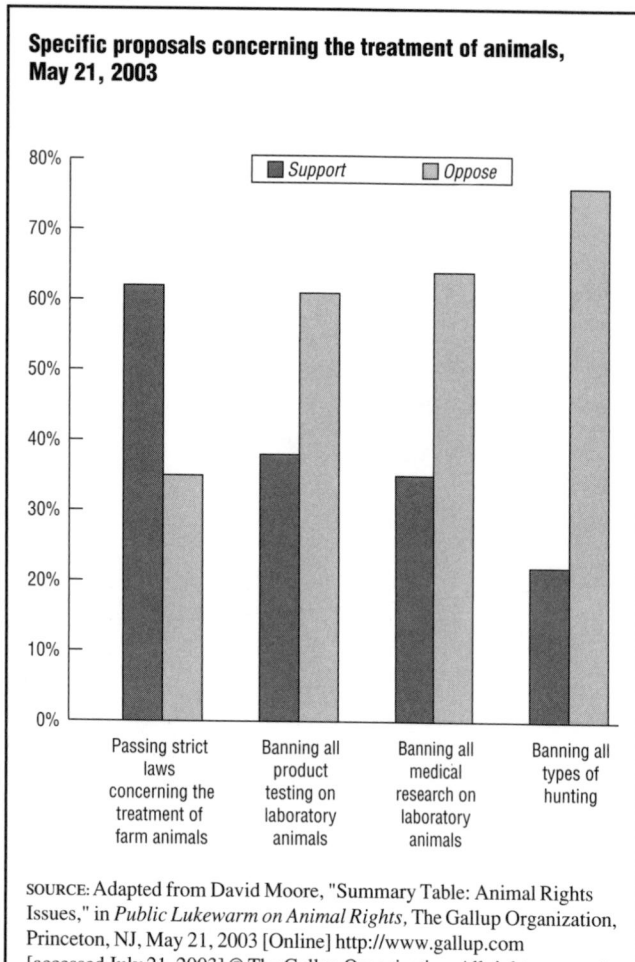

Specific proposals concerning the treatment of animals, May 21, 2003

FIGURE 2.4

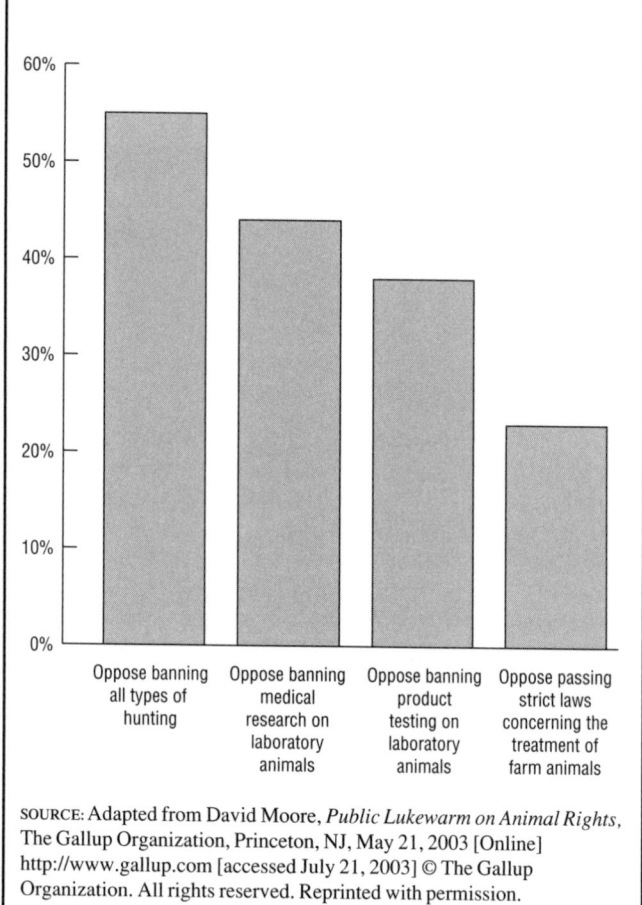

Opinion of those who said they support animal rights, May 21, 2003

not need much protection from harm and exploitation. Support for animal rights was much higher among women (33 percent) than it was among men (17 percent).

The respondents were also asked whether they supported or opposed four specific proposals concerning the treatment of animals. (See Figure 2.3.) More than 60 percent favored passing strict laws regarding the treatment of farm animals. Nearly 40 percent favored a ban on all product testing performed on laboratory animals. Around one-third favored a similar ban on medical research testing. Support was far lower (22 percent) for a total ban on hunting.

Examination of these results by gender, age, and political affiliation reveals far more support for these proposals from women than from men. Support was also significantly higher from Democrats and Independents than it was from Republicans. No significant differences were found between age groups.

Degrees of adherence to the animal rights philosophy varied. Some of the people who said they supported animal rights did not want to eliminate some of the practices in which animals are killed or harmed. (See Figure 2.4.) More than half of those who supported animal rights were opposed to banning hunting. Nearly 45 percent of them did not want to ban medical research on laboratory animals. About 40 percent of them did not want to ban product testing on animals, and more than 20 percent of them opposed passing strict laws concerning the treatment of farm animals.

These answers are somewhat puzzling. Gallup reporter David Moore suggested that the people indicating support for animal rights had pets in mind when they answered that question. Later, when asked about the specific proposals (hunting, research, product testing, and farm animals), these same people may have envisioned different animals. It is also possible that people do not have a clear idea of the concept of animal rights or what they mean in practice.

CHAPTER 3

WILDLIFE

Wildlife are animals that have not been domesticated by humans. This does not mean that wild animals live without human interference. Humans control, manage, manipulate, use, and kill wildlife for various reasons. There are thousands of different wildlife species living all over the world. Humans tend to categorize wild animals based on two factors: threat and value.

Some wildlife threaten human safety, health, property, and/or quality of life. This is true of large carnivores (lions, tigers, alligators, etc.), poisonous snakes and spiders, disease-carrying animals, and animals that endanger moving vehicles. In addition, there are carnivores (like coyotes and bobcats) that prey on livestock and pets, herbivores that eat crops and lawns, beavers that dam up streams, and wild animals that invade or damage human spaces. Many rodents, skunks, rabbits, deer, and birds are considered "nuisance" animals.

However, many wild animals, even dangerous ones, have value to humans. This value might be economic, educational, or emotional in nature. It can help to determine which wild animals live or die and which live in captivity or freedom.

Valuable wildlife fall into these categories:

- Wild animals that produce products people want to eat, wear, or use. This category includes deer, buffalo, elk, wildfowl, fur-bearing creatures, many fish and marine mammals, and animals such as tigers with bones and organs that are used in traditional medicines.

- Wild animals that humans kill for sport through hunting or fishing. In the United States, people primarily hunt native game, such as deer, bears, rabbits, squirrels, and waterfowl. Exotic (foreign) animals are imported and killed at some hunting ranches. African lions and giraffes, antelopes, gazelles, Cape buffalos, Corsican sheep, and Angora goats are some of the most popular. Sport fish include a variety of freshwater and saltwater species.

- Wild animals that can be manipulated to do labor or entertain people. For example, elephants are used as beasts of burden in many Asian countries. They also perform in circuses and shows, along with bears, primates, birds, lions, tigers, dolphins, seals, whales, and other trainable animals. Some wild animals even have military uses, particularly dolphins, whales, and sea lions.

- Wild animals that humans enjoy watching, hearing, feeding, or photographing. This category is very diverse and ranges from songbirds in the backyard to whales in the open sea. (See Figure 3.1.) It includes a variety of animals that humans can encounter in the wild and at refuges, sanctuaries, zoos, parks, and entertainment venues.

- Wild animals that are useful in scientific and medical research. These include primates and some strains of rats, mice, and rabbits.

- Wild animals kept as pets. This includes a wide variety of species, some of which are dangerous to humans.

Some animal rights advocates believe that wild animals should not be used at all—not for food, clothing, entertainment, companionship, or any other purpose. They consider wild animals not commodities but free beings with the right to live undisturbed in their natural habitats. Animal welfarists are concerned that wild animals are exploited and mistreated because of human greed and ignorance. They work to publicize the fate of animals in captivity and to save them from mistreatment.

Most people consider wildlife a valuable natural resource, like water or coal. They may disagree about how wild animals should be used, but they generally agree that humans have the right to use them, especially if the supply is plentiful. Wild species threatened by extinction are a different matter, however, as many people rally to conserve them. Successful conservation ensures that there will be more of the animals around in the future.

FIGURE 3.1

Boaters observe a humpback whale off the coast of Massachusetts. *AP/Wide World Photos*

Every aspect of wild animal–human interaction raises questions in the animal rights debate. For example:

- The American buffalo was nearly extinct in the 19th century. Thanks to conservationists, the species was saved and is even thriving. In the early 2000s, buffalo burgers are sold at trendy restaurants. Is it acceptable to save an endangered species and then eat it?

- The government allows people to kill deer to keep the population down. Otherwise lack of food could lead to starvation among the deer population. Is hunting deer more humane than letting them starve?

- Many people enjoy experiencing wildlife up close. It's entertaining and educational. Should wild animals be kept in captivity to satisfy this desire?

These are just some of the major questions in the animal rights debate.

HISTORY

Prehistoric humans constantly struggled with wildlife. Both sides were sometimes predators and some-times prey. However, humans quickly tipped the balance in their favor with two big advantages—superior intellect and weapons. Many of the large mammals of prehistoric times, such as mammoths, became extinct. Some archeologists, such as Dr. Brian Kooyman of the University of Calgary, believe that overhunting, in combination with climate and environmental factors, may have played a role in those extinctions. When societies became agricultural, some wild species were domesticated. These animals, such as sheep, goats, and cattle, had to be protected from wild animals that wanted to eat them.

As humans gained more control over nature, they began using wild animals not just as a food source but as a source of labor and entertainment. Elephants became beasts of burden. Mongooses and birds of prey were trained to be hunting assistants. Some lions, tigers, and bears were kept in cages to entertain or educate humans. Dangerous animals that could not be contained were often eliminated.

Eventually governments declared their authority over wild animal populations. Some ancient rulers enacted game laws to allow species to multiply. The explorer

Marco Polo described a law of Chinese ruler Kublai Khan (1215–94) that prohibited the killing of deer, rabbits, and large waterfowl during certain months to allow the species time to replenish.

Other rulers restricted the hunting of the most desirable animals to the upper social classes. Under English law, wildlife was the property of royalty. Members of the lower classes were permitted to hunt only low-value animals, such as rabbits. Big game were reserved for the upper classes. English royalty had exclusive hunting rights until 1215, when the Magna Carta was signed.

America

Problems with wildlife management plagued the first European colonists of America. Historical records show that the colonists fought animal predators, including wolves, coyotes, cougars, bears, and mountain lions. They also lost domesticated animals to the wild. Livestock, particularly hogs, sometimes wandered away and survived in the wild. Their offspring were feral animals (animals born and living in the wild that are descendants of domesticated animals). The colonists killed wild and feral animals whenever they could because they were a threat to livestock and crops. Wolves were particularly bothersome. Early governing bodies established wolf bounty acts that paid people for killing wolves. Virginia had a wolf bounty act as early as 1632. It paid colonists and Native Americans for every wolf head they presented.

By the early 1700s, official hunting seasons for certain species were established in some colonies. Over the next century, state governments set up fish and game departments and enacted hunting restrictions, requiring licenses and setting limits on the number of some species that could be killed during each hunting season.

SOME ANIMALS DRIVEN TO THE BRINK OF EXTINCTION—OR BEYOND. Colonization of the New World severely depleted the ranks of some native wild species through a combination of overhunting and disease. The introduction of livestock introduced new animal diseases that were devastating to some native species. Passenger pigeons and heath hens were driven to extinction. Buffalo, elk, and beaver stocks were severely diminished, though they did not become extinct.

Passenger pigeons were once extremely abundant in North America. Biologists estimate that there were billions of them in the United States in the early 1800s. The migratory birds traveled in enormous flocks, and an individual hunter could shoot thousands of them in one outing. They were extremely popular for food, and their numbers begin to dwindle dramatically. The last known passenger pigeon died in the Cincinnati Zoo on September 1, 1914.

Heath hens were small wild fowl prized for their tasty flesh. Although once very common in the eastern United States, heath hens were virtually eliminated by the 1870s. The only surviving colony lived on a tiny island called Martha's Vineyard in Massachusetts. This habitat was made a protected sanctuary, and the birds began to multiply. However, during the early 1900s heath hens were decimated by forest fires, harsh winters, diseases contracted from domesticated turkeys, and natural predators. The last known heath hen died in 1932.

Buffalos once roamed the American West in the millions. Many were killed by colonists and Native Americans during the 1800s. Buffalo tongue was a highly prized delicacy, and buffalo hides were valued as well. Many buffalo also died from diseases imported by domestic cattle. By the end of the 19th century, fewer than 1,000 buffalo were left. Conservation areas established by the U.S. government protected the last remaining buffalo herds and allowed them to repopulate. Similar efforts were required for elk and beaver because both species were also nearly hunted to extinction during the 1800s.

THE DEVELOPMENT OF THE CONSERVATION MOVEMENT. Late in the 19th century, people began to become aware of the value of natural resources, such as land, water, and wildlife, and worked to conserve wilderness spaces and protect them from development. According to Professor Daniel Edge of Oregon State University, five people during this time period were especially notable for their conservation work:

- John Muir (1838–1914) established the Sierra Club in 1892 and worked toward the creation of Yosemite National Park. (See Figure 3.2.)

- President Theodore Roosevelt (1858–1919) set aside millions of acres of land under federal government control for national refuges, forests, parks, and the like.

- Gifford Pinchot (1865–1946) was a firm believer in conservation and a key advisor to President Theodore Roosevelt. (See Figure 3.3.)

- Aldo Leopold (1887–1948) wrote *Game Management* in 1933, the first known publication on the science of wildlife management.

- Ding Darling (1876–1962) advocated the restoration of wetlands and waterfowl habitats and was the driving force behind many wildlife protection programs and laws.

These people (and many others) initiated programs that helped wild animals by preserving natural habitats. However, they were not always motivated by the same concerns that drove people involved in the animal welfare movement. Many prominent conservationists were avid hunters. For example, President Theodore Roosevelt enjoyed hunting big game. Aldo Leopold also hunted and said that it gave him a deep appreciation and respect for

FIGURE 3.2

![John Muir photograph]

John Muir. *The Library of Congress*

FIGURE 3.3

Gifford Pinchot. *The Library of Congress*

wild animals. Many welfarists were (and are) opposed to hunting for sport. The ethical battle over hunting that began between conservationists and welfarists in the 19th century continues today.

THE GOVERNMENT ENACTS LAWS. During the 20th century, dozens of federal laws were enacted that regulated wildlife. Table 3.1 lists the most notable ones. The first federal wildlife law was the Lacey Act of 1900. This law made it illegal to transport illegally taken wildlife across state lines. It also established regulations regarding the importing of wildlife into the country. Many laws were designed to fund conservation efforts through hunting fees. For example, the Duck Stamp Act of 1934 required people to purchase a stamp before they could hunt waterfowl. The Pittman-Robertson Act of 1937 added a special tax to guns and ammunition.

Today the human impact on wildlife is extensively regulated. As of 2003, more than 100 federal laws had been passed dealing with the control, preservation, eradication, and management of wildlife. Many of these laws are described by Ruth Musgrave et al. in *Federal Wildlife Laws Handbook with Related Laws* (Government Institutes, Rockville, Maryland, 1998). Musgrave is the direc-

tor of the Center for Wildlife Law at the University of New Mexico School of Law. She says that at least 40 applicable laws were enacted between 1990 and 1998. Some laws pertain directly to particular species, while others address preservation of habitat and use of federal lands.

THE GOVERNMENT AGENCIES THAT CONTROL WILDLIFE

In the United States, wildlife issues are overseen by various federal and state agencies. At the federal level, the U.S. Fish and Wildlife Service (USFWS) is the primary agency. The USFWS began in 1871 as the U.S. Fish Commission. It was formed to examine problems with declining food-fish stocks and recommend remedies. In 1903 the agency was given oversight of the first national wildlife refuge, Pelican Island, a three-acre bird sanctuary in Florida.

As of 2003, the USFWS managed 94 million acres in nearly 540 refuges in the National Wildlife Refuge System. It also manages migratory bird conservation, oversees thousands of wetlands and other management areas, and operates dozens of national fish hatcheries. The USFWS administers and enforces the following federal wildlife laws:

- The Lacey Act prohibits interstate and international shipment of illegally taken wildlife.

- The Migratory Bird Treaty Act bans the taking, possession, purchase, sale, or barter of any migratory birds and their feathers, eggs, nests, or parts.

- The Migratory Bird Hunting and Conservation Stamp Act requires all waterfowl hunters aged 16 and up to possess a Federal Duck Stamp.

- The Federal Aid in Wildlife Restoration Act distributes to state fish and wildlife agencies money obtained from federal excise taxes on hunting equipment. The states use these funds to acquire, develop, and manage wildlife habitats; educate hunters; develop and manage shooting ranges; and restore wild birds and animals.

- The Eagle Protection Act prohibits the import, export, taking, sale, purchase, or barter of bald and golden eagles.

- The Federal Aid in Sport Fish Restoration Act distributes to state fish and wildlife agencies money obtained from federal excise taxes on fishing and boating equipment. The states use these funds to manage sport fishing, boating access, and aquatic education programs.

- The Endangered Species Act lists, protects, and recovers endangered and threatened fish, wildlife, and plants.

- The Marine Mammal Protection Act prohibits taking and importing of marine mammals, including sea otters, walruses, polar bears, dugongs, and manatees.

- The Wild Bird Conservation Act addresses international trade in wild-caught birds.

- The National Wildlife Refuge System Improvement Act establishes wildlife conservation as the primary goal of the refuge system, but recognizes recreational uses, such as hunting, fishing, wildlife watching and photography, and environmental education as priority public uses of the system.

The USFWS works with U.S. Customs & Border Protection and the U.S. Department of Agriculture to monitor wildlife trade and stop illegal shipments of protected plants and animals. It enforces the country's participation in the Convention on International Trade in Endangered Species of Wild Fauna and Flora (CITES). This international agreement regulates the importing and exporting of thousands of species of concern.

Wildlife control efforts in the United States have historically focused on protecting human interests and preserving endangered species. Human interests include health and safety and also property and resources—livestock, crops, trees, lawns, structures, water, food supplies, vehicles, pets, and so forth. Wild animals that threaten any of these are subject to removal or elimina-

TABLE 3.1

Major federal laws impacting wildlife, 1900–92

Major Federal Laws Impacting Wildlife	Year Enacted
Lacey Act	1900
Game and Bird Preserves Act	1905
Weeks-McLean Act	1912
National Park Service Act	1916
Migratory Bird Treaty Act	1918
Migratory Bird Conservation Act	1920s
Tariff Act (Enhanced Lacey Act)	1930
Animal Damage Control Act	1931
Fish and Wildlife Coordination Act	1934
Migratory Bird Hunting and Conservation Stamp Act (Duck Stamp Act)	1934
Taylor Grazing Act	1934
Federal Aid in Wildlife Restoration Act (Pittman-Robertson Act)	1937
Bald Eagle Protection Act	1940
Federal Aid in Sport Fish Restoration Act (Dingell-Johnson Act)	1950
Whaling Convention Act	1950
Tuna Conventions Act	1950
Fisherman's Protective Act	1954
Fish and Wildlife Act	1956
Great Lakes Fishery Act	1956
Multiple Use Act	1960
Surplus Grain for Wildlife Act	1961
Refuge Recreation Act	1962
Wilderness Act	1964
Refuge Revenue Sharing Act	1964
Land and Water Conservation Fund Act	1965
Anadromous Fish Conservation Act	1965
National Wildlife Refuge System Administration Act	1966
Endangered Species Preservation Act	1966
Fur Seal Act	1966
National Environmental Policy Act	1969
Endangered Species Conservation Act	1969
Federal Wild and Free Roaming Horses and Burros Act	1971
Marine Mammal Protection Act	1972
Endangered Species Act	1973
Alaska National Interest Lands Conservation Act	1980
Fish and Wildlife Conservation Act	1980
National Aquaculture Act	1980
Salmon and Steelhead Conservation and Enhancement Act	1980
Atlantic Salmon Convention Act	1982
Northern Pacific Halibut Act	1982
Atlantic Striped Bass Conservation Act	1984
Pacific Salmon Treaty Act	1985
The North American Wetlands Conservation Act	1986
South Pacific Tuna Act	1988
The African Elephant Conservation Act	1988
Dolphin Protection Consumer Information Act	1990
Non-Indigenous Aquatic Nuisance Prevention and Control Act	1990
Wild Bird Conservation Act	1992
Alien Species Prevention and Enforcement Act	1992
Rhinoceros and Tiger Conservation Act	1994
National Wildlife Refuge System Improvement Act	1997

SOURCE: Compiled by Information Plus staff from various sources

tion. In the past, control was left up to private citizens, who could kill any wild animals that they considered a threat. Today, most control efforts are led or managed by government agencies. For example, hunting requires a license and payment of fees. However, private citizens may legally kill some wildlife "pests" (such as rodents) in and around their homes or businesses.

The U.S. Department of Agriculture (USDA) Wildlife Services (WS) is the agency in charge of controlling wildlife that can damage agriculture, property, and natural resources and threaten public health and safety. The WS operates the National Wildlife Research Center (NWRC) in Fort Collins, Colorado. The agency uses a variety of

TABLE 3.2

Estimates of annual human injuries and fatalities from wildlife bites or attacks, 1995

Species	Injuries	Fatalities
Rodents	27,000	Unknown
Venomous snakes	8,000	15
Skunks	750	0
Foxes	500	0
Bears	30	1
Sharks	28	2
Alligators	18	.5[a]
Coyotes	2	0
Cougars	2	.4[a]

Note: These data are extrapolated from various studies done in various geographic regions over various time periods. They are probably understated because they exclude non-reported bites, which could be quite high in number.

[a]Fewer than one human fatality a year. Alligators, for example, cause an average of one fatality every 2 years.

SOURCE: "Table 2: Estimates of Annual Human Injuries and Fatalities in the United States from Wildlife Bites or Attacks," in *Wildlife Services Program: Information on Activities to Manage Wildlife Damage*, GAO-02-138, U.S. General Accounting Office, Washington, DC, November 2001

FIGURE 3.4

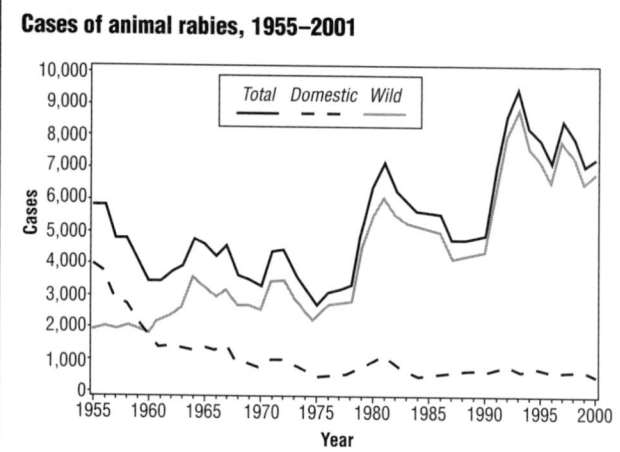

Cases of animal rabies, 1955–2001

SOURCE: Adapted from "Cases of Animal Rabies, 1955–2001," in *Rabies Epidemiology*, U.S. Department of Health and Human Services, Centers for Disease Control, Atlanta, GA, February 12, 2003 [Online] http://www.cdc.gov/ncidod/dvrd/rabies/Epidemiology/Epidemiology.htm [accessed June 16, 2003]

control methods to deal with nuisance wildlife, including relocation, poisons, sharpshooters, contraceptives, and repellents. Lethal control methods are described as "depopulating" or "harvesting" surplus animals.

Controversies over Government Regulation of Wildlife

Animal rights and welfare groups complain that the WS relies far too much on killing as a control method. The WS denies this and claims that 75 percent of the NWRC's 2001 budget was spent on developing or improving non-lethal controls. One example is called the Electronic Guard. This device uses sirens and strobe lights to frighten coyotes away from sheep and lamb herds. The WS says that it successfully dispersed nearly 4 million birds during fiscal year 2000 using nonlethal methods. According to a fiscal year 2002 fact sheet, "USDA Wildlife Services Protects Wildlife," the agency claims that it only uses lethal methods when nonlethal methods have proved ineffective and "strives to select the method that will kill the predator in the quickest and most humane way possible."

Critics say that overuse of lethal methods actually aggravates problems because predators naturally respond by producing more offspring. The WS denies that this is the case. An agency press release reports that a study performed in Yellowstone National Park found that the average number of pups per coyote litter did not increase after some coyotes were eradicated.

THE GOALS OF GOVERNMENT WILDLIFE REGULATION

Protecting Health and Safety

Table 3.2 lists estimated annual numbers of fatalities and injuries to humans from wildlife bites and attacks as provided in a U.S. General Accounting Office (GAO) report titled *Wildlife Services Program: Information on Activities to Manage Wildlife Damage*. The GAO is the investigative division of the U.S. Congress. The report shows that violent confrontations between wild animals and people are relatively rare these days. Of greater concern is the danger from zoonotic diseases. These are diseases that can be passed from animals to people. Zoonotic diseases associated with wild animals include rabies, West Nile virus, Lyme disease, bovine tuberculosis, chlamydiosis, histoplasmosis, salmonellosis, and granulocytic ehrlichiosis.

One of the most feared diseases is rabies. Rabies killed an average of 100 people annually in the early 1900s, but a combination of control methods greatly reduced its threat. By the end of the 20th century, only one or two people died each year from the disease. According to the Centers for Disease Control and Prevention (CDC), there were 7,437 confirmed cases of animal rabies in the United States in 2001. Wild animals accounted for 93 percent of these cases. (See Figure 3.4.) Raccoons, skunks, and bats were the most common wild animals reported with rabies. There were 36 confirmed cases of human rabies in the United States between 1990 and 2002. The vast majority were linked to bat bites.

As shown in Figure 3.4, the number of rabies cases reported in wild animals greatly increased between the mid-1970s and 2001. This was because of an epidemic of rabies in raccoons in the mid-Atlantic states. The scientific name for this type of epidemic that affects many animals of the same type is an epizootic. According to the CDC, the raccoon rabies epizootic began in 1977 along the border between Virginia and West Virginia. It spread

TABLE 3.3

Examples of resources damaged by injurious wildlife, and related emerging concerns, by state, 2001

State	Injurious wildlife	Resource damaged (annual damage estimate, if available)	Emerging concerns
Alabama	Fish-eating birds (e.g., cormorants, pelicans, herons, egrets)	Catfish ($4 million)	Wildlife diseases pose greater threats to humans, livestock, and pets; populations of fish-eating birds continue to increase; and diminished sport trapping is adding to the increase in beaver populations.
	Beavers	Timber ($19 million), transportation infrastructure	
Alaska	Arctic foxes	Aleutian Canada goose (threatened), nesting seabirds	Increased air travel throughout the state, coupled with immense populations of migratory birds and other wildlife, has created an urgent need for state and federal management of wildlife threats. Also, farmers and ranchers need assistance with damage from birds and predators.
Arizona	Coyotes, black bears, mountain lions	Livestock	Increased human populations and increased recreational use of public lands emphasize the need to deal with risks of wildlife disease transmission.
	Blackbirds	Dairy cattle, feedlot cattle (disease risk from contaminated feed and water)	
Arkansas	Blackbirds	Rice crops ($3.5 million)	The growing rice and aquaculture industries require additional protection from the increasing populations of fish-eating birds.
	Fish-eating birds	Catfish ($2.3 million)	
California	Coyotes, black bears, mountain lions	Livestock (nearly $2 million)	Increased airline traffic and population growth of many bird species has created a greater need for wildlife control at airports; the recent surge in the number of direct attacks on humans creates an increased need to protect humans from large predators such as coyotes, black bears, and mountain lions.
	Birds, rodents	Row crops, fruit and nut crops, vineyards	
	Feral cats, red foxes, raccoons, coyotes, striped skunks, raptors	Threatened or endangered species (e.g., California red-legged frog, salt marsh harvest mouse, Sierra Nevada big horn sheep, Monterey Bay western snowy plover)	
Colorado	Coyotes	Sheep and lambs ($1.5 million), black-footed ferrets (endangered)	Human population growth, especially in rural and semi-rural areas, creates an increased potential for human-wildlife conflicts.
Connecticut	Starlings, blackbirds	Dairy cattle (salmonella risk from contaminated feed and water)	Preventing wildlife-borne diseases from affecting humans and livestock has become a growing concern with the recent outbreaks of rabies, West Nile virus, salmonella, and E. coli; increased air travel and growing bird populations also call for increased wildlife control at airports.
	Canada geese, blackbirds, mute swans	Vegetable crops, cranberries	
	Birds, bats, squirrels, monk parakeets, ospreys	Buildings, landscaping, utilities	
Delaware	Snow geese	Coastal salt marsh habitat	West Nile virus is a major health concern. In fiscal year 2000, Delaware reported that four horses tested positive for the virus. Growth in air travel, coupled with growth in deer and bird populations, has created a greater need for wildlife control at airports.
	Canada geese	Grain crops, golf courses ($75,000)	
Florida	Raccoons, red foxes, coyotes, feral hogs, ghost crabs, armadillos	Threatened or endangered sea turtles (e.g., leatherback, hawksbill, loggerhead turtles)	Wildlife continue to threaten the safety of air travelers at many airports, but resource constraints have prevented Wildlife Services from resolving the hazards; livestock producers suffer losses from coyote and vulture predation, and direct assistance from Wildlife Services, rather than advice, would help reduce these losses.
	Foxes, coyotes, black rats, skunks, raccoons, snakes, armadillos, dogs	Endangered beach mice (e.g., Perdido Key, Anastasia Island, Choctawhatchee beach mice)	
	Red foxes, rats, coyotes, raccoons, feral cats	Threatened or endangered birds (e.g., roseate tern, least tern, Puerto Rican parrot)	
	Beavers	Flooded timber lands, croplands, roadways ($620,000)	
Georgia	Armadillos, raccoons, coyotes	Ground-nesting birds (e.g., bobwhite quail)	Increased habitat loss, human population growth, and the adaptability of many wildlife species to human environments increase the need for professional resolution of wildlife problems. Of concern are deer, geese, beavers, vultures, cormorants, pigeons, feral hogs, and raccoons.
	Beavers	Landscapes, pastures, timber, sanitation lines, culverts, highways, wells ($152,000)	
	Resident Canada geese, white-tailed deer	Crops, property, neighborhood landscapes and gardens	

quickly to neighboring states and reached Canada in 1999. State and federal wildlife officials began using baits laden with oral rabies vaccine (ORV) in the early 1990s. Between 1997 and 2002, more than 9 million doses of ORV were placed in Maryland, New York, Ohio, Pennsylvania, Vermont, and West Virginia. In the summer of 2002, the states of Tennessee and Virginia announced plans to join the ORV program. Wildlife

TABLE 3.3

Examples of resources damaged by injurious wildlife, and related emerging concerns, by state, 2001 [CONTINUED]

State	Injurious wildlife	Resource damaged (annual damage estimate, if available)	Emerging concerns
Hawaii	Feral goats, sheep, pigs, deer	Endangered waterbirds, plants	The state is concerned about the time and expense involved in complying with the National Environmental Policy Act (conducting environmental analyses of Wildlife Services' actions performed for nonfederal cooperators), and the associated administrative requirements.
	Tree frogs	Horticulture, parrots, Axis deer	
	Rats	Agricultural products, native plants, seabirds, turtles	
Idaho	Coyotes, black bears, mountain lions, wolves, red foxes	Sheep, lambs ($1.5 million)	Efforts to control crop damage by the sandhill crane have been limited by the lack of resources. Populations of ravens and red foxes have increased, to the detriment of the sage grouse.
	Ravens, coyotes, badgers, red foxes	Sage grouse, endangered northern Idaho ground squirrels	
Illinois	Canada geese, white-tailed deer	Private and municipal property	Bird predation at fish production facilities—an emerging agricultural industry in Illinois—is a concern, as is the transmission of wildlife-borne diseases such as West Nile virus.
	European starlings	Private and industrial property, risk of disease (histoplasmosis)	
Indiana	Canada geese	Private and industrial property ($169,000 in property damage reported in fiscal year 2000)	Over 12,000 people used Indiana's toll-free wildlife conflicts hotline during its first 2 years of service, preventing an estimated $100,000 in wildlife damage; now an additional person is needed to respond to calls.
	Starlings	Property damage (e.g., buildings and equipment), risk of disease (histoplasmosis)	
Iowa	Coyotes	Sheep, cattle, hogs ($20,000 in confirmed losses to coyotes)	Requests for assistance continue to increase, especially in regard to livestock predators (especially coyotes) and beavers.
	Beavers	Roads, crops, bridges	
Kansas	Blackbirds (grackles, starlings, cowbirds)	Livestock feed (more than $660,000 in damage at three feedlots during a recent winter)	Wildlife Services' success in addressing blackbird problems at feedlots has fueled demand for similar services statewide.
Kentucky	Starlings, Canada geese	Agriculture, residential and industrial property, aquaculture, golf courses, parks, utility structures	Increased urbanization and expansion into formerly rural areas, coupled with escalating wildlife populations, have led to a rise in wildlife-human conflicts.
Louisiana	Blackbirds, cowbirds, egrets, cormorants, white pelicans, herons	Sprouting rice ($5 million to $10 million a year in damage), strawberries, pecans, crawfish, catfish	Increased damage by birds is becoming more difficult to control, despite the more than $17 million spent annually by aquaculture facilities throughout the state. Beavers are another source of increasing wildlife damage in the state.
	Beavers	Threatened Louisiana pearlshell (a mussel), timber, roadways, bridges, public utilities. Nearly $5 million in beaver-caused losses was reported between 1998 and 2000.	
Maine	Birds, deer, moose, raccoons, skunks, black bears	Blueberries, strawberries, vegetable crops, beehives, campsites, summer homes, fences	Increasing predation from a rising cormorant population is harming the commercial, pen-raised Atlantic salmon industry and is thought to be the primary cause of the dwindling wild Atlantic salmon population.
	Beavers	Commercial timberlands, municipal roads, highways	
Maryland	Canada geese, vultures	Crops, waterfront properties	The state has an increased need to protect humans, their pets, and livestock from wildlife-borne diseases. Rabies and West Nile virus are two major health concerns on the East Coast.
Massachusetts	Canada geese, blackbirds	Cranberries, vegetables, dairy feed	Preventing the spread of wildlife-borne diseases to humans and livestock is a growing concern, given the recent outbreaks of rabies, West Nile virus, salmonella, Giardia, and E. coli.
	Eider ducks, swans, cormorants, gulls	Trout hatcheries, shellfish	
Michigan	Starlings	Dairies, feedlots	Wolf populations will likely increase and expand from the Upper to the Lower Peninsula, causing increased demand for prompt and professional response in wolf management services. Also, demand for help in reducing damage by congregating starlings has grown significantly.
	Gray wolves (endangered)	Livestock	
	Deer	Bovine tuberculosis in cattle (projected impact to the state's producers is $121 million over 10 years)	
Minnesota	Gray wolves	Cattle, horses, sheep, poultry, dogs	As the wolf population continues to expand, the need for Wildlife Services' professional assistance is expected to increase. Nuisance bear complaints are also increasing.
	Beavers	Private property, roads, timber, fish habitat	

authorities hope to create a barrier to prevent the epizootic from spreading westward.

Increasingly, scientists are worried about emerging and resurging zoonotic diseases in the United States. In May 2003, for example, doctors in Wisconsin, Indiana,

TABLE 3.3

Examples of resources damaged by injurious wildlife, and related emerging concerns, by state, 2001 [CONTINUED]

State	Injurious wildlife	Resource damaged (annual damage estimate, if available)	Emerging concerns
Mississippi	Double-crested cormorants, American white pelicans	Aquaculture (about $5 million)	Feral hogs are causing more crop damage and posing a disease threat (pseudorabies) for the domestic hog industry. Canada geese and black bears are becoming a growing concern for property owners.
	Beavers	Roads, bridges, drainage structures, agricultural fields, private property, timber (several million dollars a year in damage)	
	Black bears	Beehives, crops, private property	
Missouri	Beavers, muskrats	Crops, roads, levees	The state's resident Canada goose population has quadrupled since 1993, causing increased damage; the feral hog population is also increasing, and the state needs Wildlife Services' help with this problem.
	Blackbirds, herons	Rice crops, aquaculture	
	Canada geese	Crops, lawns, golf courses (more than $122,000 in turf and crop damage in fiscal year 2000)	
Montana	Grizzly bears, Rocky Mountain gray wolves (threatened or endangered)	Livestock (predators caused a $1.1 million loss to state's sheep industry in 2000)	With the successful reintroduction and recovery of Rocky Mountain gray wolves in nearby states, Montana Wildlife Services expects a growing demand for its expertise in handling wolf-related livestock predation issues.
Nebraska	Coyotes, foxes, mountain lions, bobcats	Livestock	Areas requiring increased attention include wildlife management at airports, livestock predation, and public protection from wildlife-borne diseases. Increased public awareness of Wildlife Services' professional role in these issues has increased the demand for its services.
	Prairie dogs	Rangeland	
	Blackbirds	Feedlots	
Nevada	Rodents	Public health risk of sylvatic plague (wild form of bubonic plague)	Aviation safety is a growing concern. Population growth and city development around Nevada's major airports has created an ideal habitat for migratory birds such as Canada geese, mallard ducks, and American coots.
	Coyotes, mountain lions	Livestock; humans and pets in urban areas	
New Hampshire	Black bears	Apiaries, row crops, livestock	Controlling the spread of West Nile virus is an emerging concern, along with rabies, Lyme disease, salmonella, and chronic wasting disease. Also, the 10-year trend of increasing conflicts associated with bears and bird feeding activities needs to be addressed.
	Deer	Apples, fruit crops, ornamental shrubbery	
	Woodchucks	Earthen dams and levees, wild lupine (essential to the endangered Karner blue butterfly)	
	Gulls	Roseate and common tern recolonization efforts	
New Jersey	Canada geese	Human health effects of goose feces, human safety threats from aggressive geese, crops, turf	The state's large population of resident Canada geese will pose increasing challenges for the protection of human health and safety, as well as property, at schools, hospitals, airports, and urban and suburban areas. The spread of West Nile virus is another concern.
	Deer, blackbirds	Crops, fruit trees, vegetables	
	Red foxes, raccoons, opossums	Threatened and endangered shorebirds (e.g., piping plovers, least terns, black skimmers)	
New Mexico	Coyotes, cougars, bobcats, black bears	Livestock (losses in excess of $1.6 million in 1999)	Coyotes are becoming an increasing problem in urban and suburban areas, killing pets and other domestic animals and posing safety risks to humans. Wildlife Services' assistance will be needed to resolve conflicts between humans and the black-tailed prairie dog, a candidate threatened species.
	Prairie dogs, pocket gophers, ground squirrels	Agricultural crops, pasture land, turf, human health and safety (nearly $500,000 in rodent damage in fiscal year 2000)	
	Sandhill cranes, snow geese	Crops (e.g., alfalfa, chile, wheat)	
New York	Cormorants, gulls	Catfish, bait fish, crawfish, sport fish	Bat and raccoon rabies remain a health concern, and urban winter crow roosts are emerging as a unique problem to city residents, resulting in conflicts over droppings, noise, odor, and fear associated with zoonotic disease.
	Canada geese	Property, crops	
North Carolina	Beavers	Timber, crops, roads, drainage systems, landscapes. In fiscal year 2000, Wildlife Services prevented about $8.5 million in damage to such resources: nearly $9 saved for every $1 spent.	Threats to public safety, not only by wildlife at airports, but also by the rapidly growing beaver population, must be addressed. A rabid beaver's recent attack on a human has increased public awareness of this issue.

and Illinois reported that several patients had contracted monkeypox from infected prairie dogs purchased as pets. Monkeypox is a disease similar to smallpox, though it is far less lethal to humans. Scientists believe that the prairie dogs caught the disease after being exposed to Gambian rats from Africa in an exotic pet store. Monkeypox is

TABLE 3.3

Examples of resources damaged by injurious wildlife, and related emerging concerns, by state, 2001 [CONTINUED]

State	Injurious wildlife	Resource damaged (annual damage estimate, if available)	Emerging concerns
North Dakota/ South Dakota	Coyotes, foxes	Cattle, sheep, poultry	More work at airports is needed, and concerns over the threat of rabies transferring from skunks to humans or domestic animals continues to be a concern.
	Blackbirds	Sunflowers and other grain crops (over $5 million in losses annually in the upper Great Plains), feedlots	
	Canada geese and other waterfowl	Grain crops (damage increased by 80 percent in 2000, resulting in $162,000 in losses)	
Ohio	Coyotes, vultures	Cattle, sheep, poultry	Increasing populations of gulls, vultures, and starlings are causing significant human health and safety issues and crop and property damage.
	Raccoons	Human health and safety	
	Rooftop nesting gulls	Property	
	Blackbirds, Canada geese	Crops, property	
Oklahoma	Beavers	Dams, timber, crops, roads, private property	Feral hogs cause many problems (livestock predation, crop destruction); Canada geese are growing in number and are damaging crops.
	Coyotes	Cattle, sheep, goats, poultry	
	Canada geese	Crops (especially winter wheat)	
Oregon	Canada geese	Turf grass seed, other crops	Successful wolf reintroduction in Idaho means future wolf conflicts with livestock in Oregon. Wolves will hamper present predator control efforts because control tools and methods will be restricted around wolves.
	Cougars	Human safety (Wildlife Services addressed 386 cougar complaints in 2000; 118 involved threats to humans)	
	Black bears, beavers	Timber	
Pennsylvania	Deer	Human safety (automobile collisions)	The state's large population of resident Canada geese will pose increasing challenges over time, as will increasing populations of deer, vultures, and gulls. Emerging public health issues (e.g., West Nile virus) will also be a challenge.
	Canada geese	Landscape, crops (program annually assists over 300 residents with goose-related problems)	
	Starlings	Livestock facilities	
Rhode Island	Canada geese, gulls, crows, turkey vultures	Property, turf, vegetable crops	The needs of some citizens are currently unmet. Increasingly, the program is able to respond to requests for assistance only from entities that can fully fund it. Preventing wildlife-borne diseases is a growing concern.
	Mute swans	Pond water quality	
	Monk parakeets, ospreys	Landscaping, utilities	
South Carolina	Beavers	Timber, crops, roads, levees, dams	The demand for beaver management has overwhelmed the program, yet some counties cannot afford to share the costs. At the same time, the vulture population and related complaints have increased.
	White-tailed deer	Landscaping, human safety (automobile collisions), human health (tick-borne diseases)	
Tennessee	Canada geese	Turf (at golf courses, parks, etc.)	The growing number and variety of wildlife-human conflicts pose a challenge to the program, especially in terms of wildlife control at airports and urban damage by large birds.
	Beavers	Roads, bridges, timber, wildlife management areas	
	Vultures	Municipal utility structures, residential property	
Texas	Coyotes, foxes	Human health (rabies)	The feral hog population in the state exceeds 1 million. Hogs damage many crops (e.g., corn, rice, peanuts, hay), and they prey on lambs, kids, fawns, and ground nesting birds. Also, damage by migratory birds (e.g., cattle egrets, vultures, cormorants) has increased, taxing the program's response abilities.
	Coyotes	Sheep and goats	
	Beavers	Dams, dikes, railroad track beds, timber, roads, pastures, crops	
	Blackbirds	Citrus crops, rice, feedlot operations	
	Feral hogs	Agricultural crops, livestock	

found in Africa but was previously not found in the Western Hemisphere.

Another emerging disease possibly associated with animals is severe acute respiratory syndrome (SARS).

SARS is a deadly flu-like virus believed to have originated in China. In April 2003 researchers reported that the virus had been found in six palm civet cats purchased at a live animal market in southern China. Palm civets are not really cats but are related to mongooses. They are

TABLE 3.3

Examples of resources damaged by injurious wildlife, and related emerging concerns, by state, 2001 [CONTINUED]

State	Injurious wildlife	Resource damaged (annual damage estimate, if available)	Emerging concerns
Utah	Coyotes, mountain lions, black bears	Sheep and lambs (nearly $2 million in losses in 1999, even with controls in place), endangered black-footed ferrets, sage grouse, mule deer fawns	Demands for wildlife damage management are increasing, yet the program already has more requests than it can address. Protection of native wildlife continues to be of importance.
	Skunks, raccoons, feral and urban waterfowl, pigeons	Human health and safety (threat of rabies, raccoon roundworm, salmonella, plague)	
Vermont	Raccoons	Human health (rabies), threatened Eastern spiney softshell turtle	Wildlife diseases like West Nile virus, Lyme disease, salmonella, and chronic wasting syndrome continue to emerge and need to be addressed.
	Starlings	Cattle feed at dairies	
Virginia	Coyotes, black vultures	Livestock	Challenges include finding a way to provide damage management services to low- and middle-income people and protecting Virginia's rare natural resources (e.g., the threatened piping plover and Wilson's plover).
	Beavers	Roads, railroads	
	Canada geese, crows, vultures, starlings, muskrats	Urban and suburban property, water quality, human health and safety. (Canada geese are involved in 26 percent of all requests for program assistance in Virginia.)	
Washington	Northern pikeminnows, gulls	Threatened and endangered salmon and steelhead	Increasing problems are caused by urban Canada geese and by predators (damage to livestock, agriculture, and forestry resources), but program resources are already strained.
	Starlings, feral pigeons, Canada geese, gulls	Bridges, buildings (bird feces are corrosive to paint and metal), fruit crops, public and private property, human health (over $6 million a year in damage to the fruit industry)	
	Coyotes	Livestock, endangered Columbian white-tailed deer, pygmy rabbits	
West Virginia	Coyotes, vultures	Sheep, cattle, goats	With its limited resources, the program concentrates on the highest priorities (human health and safety). As a result, though, program staff cannot make much-needed on-site evaluations of wildlife damage to property; rather, they make recommendations based on telephone interviews. Also, problems caused by starlings and roosting birds need attention.
	Raccoons	Human health (rabies)	
	Muskrats, beavers	Levees and dams	
Wisconsin	Deer	Crops (over $1 million a year in damage)	The endangered gray wolf population has grown from 34 wolves in 1990 to about 250 in 2000, and the wolf's recovery is considered a success. But problems, such as depredation on livestock and pets, have come with the wolf's recovery. Also problematic is the damage done by the burgeoning population of resident Canada geese, which now numbers over 70,000.
	Black bears	Crops, property, human safety	
	Beavers	Trout streams	
	Gray wolves	Livestock, pets	
	Canada geese	Municipal and private property	
Wyoming	Coyotes, black bears, red foxes, mountain lions, grizzly bears, wolves	Livestock (losses of over $5.6 million to predators in 2000)	As wolf and grizzly bear populations expand, new or different control methods will be needed to prevent unnecessary conflicts with them. Also, skunk rabies seems to be spreading westward across the state, and a program is needed to contain it.
	Skunks	Human health (rabies risk)	
	Coyotes	Black-footed ferrets	
Guam	Brown tree snakes	Power transmission lines, poultry and small animals, endangered species (e.g., Vanikoro swiftlets, Mariana crows, Guam fruit bats, Guam rails, Micronesian kingfishers), human health and safety	The magnitude and complexity of the work to control the brown tree snake pose significant challenges, and the administrative burden is increasing.
U.S. Virgin Islands	Black rats	Endangered sea turtles, migratory birds, native vegetation	Invasive species' impacts on native plants and animals is a major and growing problem.
	Roosting birds	Human health concerns	

SOURCE: "Table 6: Examples of Resources Damaged by Injurious Wildlife, and Related Emerging Concerns, by State," in *Wildlife Services Program: Information on Activities to Manage Wildlife Damage*, GAO-02-138, U.S. General Accounting Office, Washington, DC, November 2001 considered a delicacy in Chinese cuisine. Scientists fear that SARS may have originated in these or other wild animals and then jumped to humans. As of June 2003, SARS had infected thousands of people and killed more than 800, mostly in Asia and Canada.

Besides diseases, humans face dangers posed by collisions between moving vehicles and wild animals and birds. The WS reported in 2001 that more than 1 million collisions between deer and automobiles occur each year, injuring approximately 29,000 people and killing 200 people. Collisions between wildlife (mainly birds) and aircraft caused 140 human deaths between 1990 and 2000.

Protecting Property and Pleasure

According to the WS in 2001, wildlife cause $600 million to $1.6 billion worth of damage annually to agriculture. Each year, farmers and ranchers lose thousands of calves and lambs, worth more than $71 million, to wild predators such as coyotes, wolves, and mountain lions. The National Agricultural Statistics Service estimates that 273,000 sheep and lambs, 147,000 cattle and calves, and 61,000 goats and kids were lost to wild predators in 1999. Coyotes are blamed for the majority of the losses. Wild predators are primarily a problem in western states where ranchers graze their livestock on open rangelands. According to a 2002 report from the USDA Animal and Plant Health Inspection Service (APHIS) (*Wildlife Services: The Facts About Wildlife Damage Management*), wildlife also eat and damage more than $110 million worth of commercially grown berries and flowers annually.

The same APHIS report notes that deer–vehicle collisions cause over $1 billion worth of damage to vehicles each year. Collisions between aircraft and wildlife cause millions of dollars in damage.

In 2001 the GAO did an extensive investigation into wildlife damage across the country. Table 3.3 lists wildlife problems reported by each state. Birds, especially Canadian geese, are a problem in 39 states. Coyotes are mentioned for 20 states. Beavers are a problem in 17 states.

PROBLEM BIRDS. Animal welfare groups are growing increasingly concerned about the eradication efforts being waged against wild birds. They criticized Governor Robert Ehrlich of Maryland for authorizing a plan by the state's Department of Natural Resources to hire a sharpshooter to kill thousands of wild mute swans. The swans are blamed for eating aquatic vegetation essential to natural habitats in Chesapeake Bay. Mute swans are not native to the United States but were introduced during the 19th century from Europe and Asia. As of July 2003, approximately 3,600 of the swans were living in Chesapeake Bay. Officials believed that relocation and repellents were not good options in this case. They hoped to donate the swan meat to food programs for the poor.

In May 2003 the animal activism group Fund for Animals filed a lawsuit in federal court to stop the planned swan killings. The suit alleged that the federal permit issued to the Department of Natural Resources violates the Migratory Bird Treaty Act and the International Convention for the Protection of Migratory Birds. The suit also complains that the department obtained the permit without allowing the public to review and comment on the plan. In response, the department suspended its plan pending further review. In July 2003 the *Baltimore Sun* reported that the department was seeking approval from the USFWS to kill 1,500 of the mute swans and establish a hunting season for them to control the population (Dennis O'Brien, "Maryland Seeks Mute Sawn Hunting Season," July 19, 2003).

In May 2003 the USFWS announced plans to allow fish farmers to kill up to 200,000 cormorants each year to protect their fish stocks. Cormorants are long-necked waterfowl known for their large appetites. The Humane Society of the United States (HSUS) has criticized the plan, which it says will allow the farmers to kill the birds by shooting or gassing them, breaking their necks, or destroying their nests and eggs. The HSUS claims that scientific evidence shows that cormorants have little effect on farmed fish populations. The group has also criticized the WS for its plan to kill 2,500 black vultures and 1,500 turkey vultures in Virginia during 2003. The HSUS insists that preventative measures, such as habitat alteration, should be tried first. In early 2003, the HSUS said that the WS poisoned hundreds of crows in Alexandria, Virginia, after residents complained about droppings and noise.

Some municipalities are using creative methods to deal with nuisance birds. According to the Animal News Center, Inc., park officials in New York City plan to use hawks instead of poison during summer 2003 to rid a Manhattan park of nuisance pigeons. In Plymouth, Massachusetts, local officials called in the HSUS to deal with an aggressive swan chasing canoeists on the Eel River. The bird, nicknamed "Genghis Swan," capsized a canoe in the summer of 2002, spilling several children into the water. Local residents were threatening to kill the swan unless something was done. A team of HSUS volunteers began canoeing the river and squirting the swan with repellent sprays and water pistols when it attacked them. The volunteers used a naturally occurring chemical called methyl anthanilate to deter the swan. This chemical, which is found in Concord grapes, is an effective and approved bird repellent. It can be sprayed at nuisance birds or on grasses where they feed. The birds find its odor and taste repulsive. In May 2003 the *Milford Daily News* reported that the swan had not threatened canoes or kayaks the last two times he was tested ("Ill-Tempered Swan Tamed," May 31, 2003). HSUS officials are hopeful that the swan has been completely rehabilitated.

In May 2003 the HSUS called for animal cruelty charges against a game warden with the Texas Parks and Wildlife Department (TPWD) for dragging an alligator behind his truck through a subdivision. The man then shot the alligator to death in full view of several children. The incident was videotaped by a resident and shown on local television. The HSUS called the warden's actions "outrageous." A group spokesman said that the alligator should have been humanely restrained using a head cover and removed on a trailer instead of being dragged. The HSUS also believes that the incident posed a danger to the people gathered to watch the removal. The TPWD announced that it stands by the warden's actions but will develop new recommendations for dealing with nuisance alligators.

Protecting Endangered and Threatened Species

The federal Endangered Species Act (ESA) was passed in 1973. Its purpose is to conserve the ecosystems upon which endangered and threatened species depend and to conserve and recover listed species. An endangered species is in danger of extinction throughout all or a significant portion of its range. A threatened species is considered likely to become endangered in the foreseeable future. Some species have dual listings. As of June 1, 2003, there were 517 native species on the federal list of endangered and threatened animals—388 endangered species and 129 threatened species. (See Table 3.4.) Another 555 foreign animal species were listed as endangered or threatened. Animals are placed on the list based on their biological status and the threats to their existence. Some species are put on the list because they closely resemble endangered or threatened species.

The USFWS and the National Marine Fisheries Service share responsibility for administering the Endangered Species Act. They work in partnership with state agencies to enforce the act and develop and maintain conservation programs. The federal act prohibits any person from "taking" a listed species. Taking includes actions that "harass, harm, pursue, hunt, shoot, wound, kill, trap, capture, or collect" listed species or attempt to do so. Harm is defined as an action that kills or injures the animal and includes actions that significantly modify or degrade habitats or significantly impair essential behavior patterns such as breeding, feeding, and sheltering.

THE AMERICAN BUFFALO, OR BISON. The measures described above are designed to allow endangered and threatened species to repopulate. However, once a species does repopulate, it can be removed from the list of endangered species and the "taking" prohibition no longer applies. An interesting case illustrating this point is the American buffalo (or bison). In the early 1800s, there were more than 50 million buffalo in the United States. By the end of the century, fewer than 1,000 remained. The animals had been hunted to the verge of extinction. In

TABLE 3.4

Summary of listed species, as of July 1, 2003

Group	Endangered		Threatened		Total Species
	U.S.	Foreign	U.S.	Foreign	
Mammals	65	251	9	17	342
Birds	78	175	14	6	273
Reptiles	14	64	22	15	115
Amphibians	12	8	9	1	30
Fishes	71	11	44	0	126
Clams	62	2	8	0	72
Snails	21	1	11	0	33
Insects	35	4	9	0	48
Arachnids	12	0	0	0	12
Crustaceans	18	0	3	0	21
Total	388	516	129	39	1072

SOURCE: Adapted from "Summary of Listed Species: Species and Recovery Plans as of 07/01/2003," in *Threatened and Endangered Species System (TESS),* U.S. Department of Interior, U.S. Fish and Wildlife Service, Washington, DC, June 1, 2003 [Online] http://ecos.fws.gov/tess_public/html/boxscore.html [accessed June 16, 2003]

1894 President Grover Cleveland outlawed the killing of buffalo. The remaining herds were moved to protected habitats and slowly repopulated.

According to the National Bison Association, in 2003 approximately 244,000 buffalo were on private lands and approximately 10,000 head were on public lands. Dozens of buffalo ranches have sprung up across the West, where the animals are raised for meat. Ranchers and conservationists are excited about the potentials of this market, in large part because buffalo graze much differently than cattle. Cattle tend to eat all the good grass in an area and then move on to another area. Buffalo graze lightly and move around more. This is less harmful to natural vegetation and naturally reseeds grazed areas. The Wild Idea Buffalo Company highlighted these factors in an advertisement for buffalo meat designed to appeal to environmentalists and conservationists: "There are a hundred ways that Americans can support the restoration of the Great Plains, and the revival of the buffalo herds, but the most simple and honest way is to do it one bite at a time."

The decline in buffalo herds is mostly blamed on overhunting, but disease may also have played a factor. Buffalo are believed to have been sickened by brucellosis, a disease imported to the colonies with European cattle. Brucellosis is still a major concern to western ranchers, who fear that buffalo grazing in Yellowstone National Park may have the disease and could spread it to their cattle. Animal welfare groups and conservationists complain that federal authorities are too quick to kill bison that wander from the park and graze near domesticated herds.

BEAVERS. Beavers are another mammal that approached extinction because of overhunting but were saved by conservation efforts. Today most beavers are considered nuisance animals. They cut down trees and build dams that cause creeks to flood and damage property. Many states now allow trapping as a control method, including underwater trapping that drowns the animals.

WOLVES. Dwindling numbers of one species can have adverse affects on others. Some historians believe that the decline in buffalos and other large game during the 16th

TABLE 3.5

Gray wolf populations, 1999–2000

State	Population estimate
Alaska	5,227-8,060
Arizona	22
Central Idaho	141
Greater Yellowstone	118
Isle Royale	29
Michigan	216
Minnesota	2,445
Northwest Montana	63
Wisconsin	250
Total	11,287

Note: The Red Wolf *(Canis rufus)* is not included because it is a separate species from *Canis lupus*. As of 1999, there were up to 100 red wolves roaming North Carolina.

SOURCE: Don Hinrichsen, "Table 2: Gray Wolf Populations in the United States," in *Wolves Around the World,* Defenders of Wildlife, Washington, DC, October 2000

to 18th centuries put wolf populations in grave danger. Wolves that began preying on livestock instead of wild animals were subjected to massive kill-offs. These campaigns were encouraged by the federal government well into the 20th century. The last known wild gray wolf in Yellowstone National Park was killed during the 1920s. Today two wolf species are on the federal list of endangered and threatened species: the gray wolf and the red wolf. Authorities are attempting to reintroduce the species to their historical habitats, including Yellowstone. Gray wolf population estimates for various states are shown in Table 3.5. Figure 3.5 is a photograph of a gray wolf.

MANATEES. An aquatic species of special concern is the West Indian manatee. These large gray mammals inhabit shallow calm waters along the southeastern coast, mainly in Florida. Manatees are gentle creatures that swim slowly just beneath the water surface and eat mostly aquatic vegetation. They can grow to nearly 10 feet long and weigh up to 1,000 pounds. Although their natural life span is about 60 years, manatees are endangered by their close proximity to humans. Many are killed by collisions with speedboats, by ingesting fish hooks and trash, and by crushing or drowning in flood-control structures. As of January 2001

FIGURE 3.5

A gray wolf. *AP/Wide World Photos/National Park Service. Reproduced by permission.*

only about 3,000 West Indian manatees were left in the United States. They are protected under the Marine Mammal Protection Act and the Endangered Species Act. In May 2003 the USFWS announced plans for new manatee refuges to be located throughout the state of Florida.

THE INTERESTS OF HUMANS VERSUS THOSE OF ENDANGERED SPECIES. Protecting endangered and threatened species becomes extremely controversial when it threatens human economic interests. One example is the northern spotted owl. Its primary habitat is among old-growth trees (100–200 years old) in the coniferous forests of the Pacific Northwest. These forests were heavily logged during the 1960s. In 1972 researchers at Oregon State University estimated that 85–90 percent of the owl's suitable habitat had already been eliminated (John Weier, *Spotting the Spotted Owl,* NASA Earth Observatory, June 15, 1999). They assessed the future harvest plans of major logging companies and learned that most of the remaining old-growth trees in these forests were also to be cut down. The resulting publicity caused a major showdown between environmental/conservation groups and the logging industry.

Environmental activists chained themselves to trees and damaged logging equipment to protest removal of the old-growth forests. Protest marches captured national headlines. There was tremendous political pressure to protect the owl's remaining habitat, particularly since approximately half of it was on federal lands. During the mid-1980s the USDA Forest Service (USFS) tried to develop plans for managing federal forests in the Pacific Northwest that balanced timber harvesting with habitat protection. Neither side was happy with the proposals. The timber industry complained that protecting owls would put loggers out of work. Environmentalists insisted that all old-growth forest be saved. In 1990 the USFWS added the northern spotted owl to the federal list of threatened species. The decision followed years of study and lawsuits filed by environmental groups.

The legal battles continued into the 1990s. In 1994 the Clinton administration formulated the Northwest Forest Plan as an attempt to satisfy both sides. The plan requires completion of biological surveys on dozens of plants and animals before logging is allowed on federal timberlands in the Northwest. It also includes other measures designed to protect owl habitat. Critics complain that this protection has a high human cost. According to the *Oregonian,* more than 10,000 jobs in the forest products industry were lost in Oregon and Washington between 1991 and 1998, as mills dependent on federal timber closed down (Hal Bernton, "Forest Service Halts Timber Sales in Northwest Spotted Owl Regions," August 12, 1999).

Similar conflicts between conservation and economic interests have raged in the United States over the protection of other animal species. These include the snail darter (a fish inhabiting the Tennessee River valley), Florida's gopher tortoises, and Coho salmon and sucker fish in Oregon's Klamath River Basin.

A tragedy that killed four young firefighters in 2001 has also raised controversy over the protection of endangered species. The four died in a forest fire raging near the Chewuch River in the state of Washington. The Chewuch River is home to populations of endangered salmon and trout. According to news reports, government officials delayed firefighting helicopters from scooping up water from the river to fight the fire because of concerns over violating the Endangered Species Act (Robin Wallace, "Investigation Into Fire-Fighting Deaths Yields Disturbing Results," August 4, 2001). Although the USFS has downplayed the delay as a major cause of the deaths, the incident is often cited by critics who believe the Endangered Species Act places animal interests above human interests.

INTERNATIONAL EFFORTS. On the international front, endangered wild animals are protected by the Convention on International Trade in Endangered Species of Wild Fauna and Flora (CITES). Under the Endangered Species Act, the United States participates in CITES to prohibit trade in listed species. As of April 2003, 161 nations adhered to CITES. (See Table 3.6.)

The convention includes three lists:

• Appendix I—Species for which no commercial trade is allowed. Noncommercial trade is permitted if it does not jeopardize species survival in the wild. Importers and exporters of Appendix I species must obtain permits.

• Appendix II—Species for which commercial trade is tightly regulated and managed with permits.

• Appendix III—Species that may be negatively impacted by commercial trade. Permits are used to monitor trade in these species.

Listing of any species in Appendix I or Appendix II requires approval by a two-thirds majority of CITES nations. The CITES appendices list thousands of animals from all over the world. They are published on the CITES Web site (http://www.cites.org/eng/append/latest_appendices.shtml).

Animals of major concern internationally include Asian and African elephants and primates. In April 2003 the journal *Nature* reported that gorillas and chimpanzees in western Africa were on the verge of extinction because of poaching (illegal hunting) and the Ebola virus. Researchers estimated that approximately 80 percent of all wild gorillas and the majority of wild chimpanzees lived in the area. Their populations had dropped by more than half since the 1980s and are expected to continue to decrease rapidly unless drastic action is taken.

TABLE 3.6

CITES list of party countries as of April 28, 2003

Afghanistan (1/28/86)	Dominica (11/2/95)	Libyan Arab Jamahiriya (4/28/03)	Saint Vincent and the Grenadines (2/28/89)
Algeria (2/21/84)	Dominican Republic (3/17/87)	Liechtenstein (2/28/80)	Sao Tome and Principe (11/7/01)
Antigua and Barbuda (10/6/97)	Ecuador (7/1/75)	Lithuania (3/9/02)	Saudi Arabia (6/10/96)
Argentina (4/8/81)	Egypt (4/4/78)	Luxembourg (3/12/84)	Senegal (11/3/77)
Australia (10/27/76)	El Salvador (7/29/87)	Macedonia (4/19/00)	Serbia and Montenegro (5/28/02)
Austria (4/27/82)	Equatorial Guinea (6/8/92)	Madagascar (11/18/75)	Seychelles (5/9/77)
Azerbaijan(2/21/99)	Eritrea (1/22/95)	Malawi (5/6/82)	Sierra Leone (1/26/95)
Bahamas (9/18/79)	Estonia (10/20/92)	Malaysia (1/18/78)	Singapore (2/28/87)
Bangladesh (2/18/82)	Ethiopia (7/4/89)	Mali (10/16/94)	Slovakia (1/1/93)
Barbados (3/9/93)	Fiji (12/29/97)	Malta (7/16/89)	Slovenia (4/23/00)
Belarus (11/8/95)	Finland (8/8/76)	Mauritania (6/11/98)	Somalia (3/2/86)
Belgium (1/1/84)	France (8/9/78)	Mauritius (7/27/75)	South Africa (10/13/75)
Belize (9/21/81)	Gabon (5/15/89)	Mexico (9/30/91)	Spain (8/28/86)
Benin (5/28/84)	Gambia (11/24/77)	Moldova (6/27/01)	Sri Lanka (8/2/79)
Bhutan (11/13/02)	Georgia (12/12/96)	Monaco (7/18/78)	Sudan (1/24/83)
Bolivia (10/4/79)	Germany (6/20/76)	Mongolia (4/4/96)	Suriname (2/15/81)
Botswana (2/12/78)	Ghana (2/12/76)	Morocco (1/14/76)	Swaziland (5/27/97)
Brazil (11/14/75)	Greece (1/6/93)	Mozambique (6/23/81)	Sweden (7/1/75)
Brunei Darussalem (8/2/90)	Grenada (11/28/99)	Myanmar (9/11/97)	Switzerland (7/1/75)
Bulgaria (4/16/91)	Guatemala (2/5/80)	Namibia (3/18/91)	Tanzania (2/27/80)
Burkina Faso (1/11/90)	Guinea (12/20/81)	Nepal (9/16/75)	Thailand (4/21/83)
Burundi (11/6/88)	Guinea-Bissau (8/14/90)	Netherlands (7/18/84)	Togo (1/21/79)
Cambodia (10/2/97)	Guyana (8/25/77)	New Zealand (8/8/89)	Trinidad and Tobago (4/19/84)
Cameroon (9/3/81)	Honduras (6/13/85)	Nicaragua (11/4/77)	Tunisia (7/1/75)
Canada (7/9/75)	Hungary (8/27/85)	Niger (12/7/75)	Turkey (12/22/96)
Central African Republic (11/25/80)	Iceland (4/2/00)	Nigeria (7/1/75)	Uganda (10/16/91)
Chad (5/3/89)	India (10/18/76)	Norway (10/25/76)	Ukraine (3/29/00)
Chile (7/1/75)	Indonesia (3/28/79)	Pakistan (7/19/76)	United Arab Emirates (5/9/90)
China, People's Republic of (4/8/81)	Iran (11/1/76)	Panama (11/15/78)	United Kingdom (10/31/76)
Colombia (11/29/81)	Ireland (4/8/02)	Papua New Guinea (3/11/76)	United States (7/1/75)
Comoros (2/21/95)	Israel (3/17/80)	Paraguay (2/13/77)	Uruguay (7/1/75)
Congo (5/1/83)	Italy (12/31/79)	Peru (9/25/75)	Uzbekistan (10/8/97)
Congo, Democratic Republic of (10/18/76)	Jamaica (6/22/97)	Philippines (11/16/81)	Vanuatu (10/15/89)
Costa Rica (9/28/75)	Japan (11/4/80)	Poland (3/12/90)	Venezuela (1/22/78)
Cote d'Ivoire (2/19/95)	Jordan (3/14/79)	Portugal (3/11/81)	Viet Nam (4/20/94)
Croatia (6/12/00)	Kazakhstan (4/19/00)	Qatar (8/6/01)	Yemen (8/3/97)
Cuba (7/19/90)	Kenya (3/13/79)	Romania (11/16/94)	Yugoslavia (5/28/02)
Cyprus (7/1/75)	Korea, Republic of (10/7/93)	Russian Federation (12/8/76)	Zambia (2/22/81)
Czech Republic (1/1/93)	Kuwait (11/10/02)	Rwandese Republic (1/18/81)	Zimbabwe (8/17/81)
Denmark (10/24/77)	Latvia (5/12/97)	Saint Kitts and Nevis (5/15/94)	
Djibouti (5/7/92)	Liberia (6/9/81)	Saint Lucia (3/15/83)	

CITES: Convention on International Trade in Endangered Species of Wild Fauna and Flora

SOURCE: "CITES List of Party Countries," in *U.S. Fish and Wildlife Service, International Affairs,* U.S. Department of Interior, U.S. Fish and Wildlife Service, Washington, DC, April 28, 2003 [Online] http://international.fws.gov/cites/citeslop.html [accessed June 16, 2003]

Logging roads associated with deforestation are allowing poachers easy access to areas that were previously inaccessible. They supply the growing trade in bushmeat (meat from wild animals such as elephants, primates, antelopes, and crocodiles). Although ape meat makes up only a tiny percentage of bushmeat, wild chimpanzees are in great danger from the trade. Scientists say that consumption of contaminated bushmeat passed the Ebola virus from animals to people.

KILLING WILDLIFE

Wildlife all over the world are killed for various reasons, including being threats to human interests, for sport, and for commerce.

Recreational Hunting

Hunting was originally a means of survival for humans. As societies became more dependent on agriculture and livestock, hunting gradually became more an activity of leisure, recreation, and sport than survival (though many hunters do still use the meat they procure to make up varying degrees of their diets). According to the USFWS, 13 million Americans age 16 and over hunted wildlife in 2001. This represents around 13 percent of the population, but the number of hunters was down 7 percent from 1991 levels. The vast majority of the hunters (11 million) pursued big game, such as deer, elk, bear, and wild turkey. (See Table 3.7.) Other popular game includes rabbits, squirrels, pheasants, quail, grouse, doves, ducks, geese, groundhogs, raccoons, foxes, and coyotes.

Hunters use a variety of implements to kill animals, including rifles, shotguns, handguns, and bows and arrows. Animal welfarists argue about which methods they consider the least cruel and which are associated with the smallest number of nonfatal injuries. In general, they consider firearms more humane than arrows.

TABLE 3.7

Hunters and days of hunting, by type of game, 2001

(Population 16 years old and older. Numbers in thousands)

Type of game	Hunters		Days of hunting		Average days per hunter
	Number	Percent	Number	Percent	
Total, all big game	**10,911**	**100**	**153,191**	**100**	**14**
Deer	10,272	94	133,457	87	13
Elk	910	8	6,402	4	7
Bear	360	3	3,334	2	9
Wild turkey	2,504	23	23,165	15	9
Other big game	527	5	5,010	3	10
Total, all small game	**5,434**	**100**	**60,142**	**100**	**11**
Rabbit, hare	2,099	39	22,768	38	11
Quail	991	18	7,926	13	8
Grouse/prairie chicken	1,010	19	9,169	15	9
Squirrel	2,119	39	22,333	37	11
Pheasant	1,723	32	12,769	21	7
Other small game	505	9	5,200	9	10
Total, all migratory birds	**2,956**	**100**	**29,310**	**100**	**10**
Geese	1,000	34	10,508	36	11
Ducks	1,589	54	18,290	62	12
Doves	1,450	49	9,041	31	6
Other migratory bird	210	7	1,523	5	7
Total, all other animals (fox, raccoon, groundhog, etc.)	**1,047**	**100**	**19,207**	**100**	**18**

Note: Detail does not add to total because of multiple responses.

SOURCE: "Table 7: Hunters and Days of Hunting by Type of Game: 2001," in *2001 National Survey of Fishing, Hunting, and Wildlife-Associated Recreation, FHW/01-NAT*, U.S. Department of Interior, U.S. Fish and Wildlife Service, Washington, DC, October 2002.

According to the Web site of the animal welfare group In Defense of Animals (IDA) in 2003, more than 200 million animals are killed by hunters in the United States each year, as follows:

- 42 million mourning doves

- 30 million squirrels

- 28 million quail

- 25 million rabbits

- 20 million pheasants

- 14 million ducks

- 6 million deer

- Thousands of geese, bears, moose, elk, antelope, swans, cougars, turkeys, wolves, foxes, coyotes, bobcats, wild boars, and other game

The IDA claims that hunters injure millions of other animals, damage habitats, and disrupt the eating, migration, hibernation, and mating habits of protected animals. For example, the group estimates that for every animal killed instantly by hunters, at least two wounded animals die slow painful deaths from hunting injuries. Careless hunters also kill and wound domestic animals and people each year. According to the International Hunter Education Association, there were 75 human fatalities and 716 injuries related to hunting in the United States in 2001.

CANNED HUNTS. One type of hunting conducted for commercial purposes is called canned hunting. This is a type of hunting in which animals are fenced in or otherwise enclosed in a space for the enjoyment of trophy hunters. Canned hunting dates back to at least the seventh century B.C., when the Assyrians captured lions and then released them to be hunted to death.

As of 2003 there were approximately 2,000 canned hunt operators in the United States, with 500 in Texas alone. Many offer a "no kill, no pay" policy. Canned hunting of exotic mammals has been banned in 10 states: California, Indiana, Maryland, Nevada, New Jersey, North Carolina, Oregon, Rhode Island, Wisconsin, and Wyoming. The federal Animal Welfare Act does not apply to game and hunting preserves, so canned hunting is not covered by any federal legislation.

The most common animals involved are exotic (foreign) species of antelope, deer, goats, sheep, cattle, swine, bears, zebra, and big cats. Hunters generally pay a set price for each exotic animal killed. Table 3.8 shows a price list compiled by the HSUS that give the price range for various animals involved in canned hunts.

The HSUS and most other animal welfare groups are opposed to canned hunting. They consider it unsportsmanlike and cruel. The HSUS calls it "abuse for the sake of entertainment." Animal welfare groups believe that many relatively tame animals dumped by zoos, circuses, and exhibitors wind up victims of canned hunts. These

TABLE 3.8

Sample prices for canned hunts

Antelope
Addax $1,200–$4,000
Antelope, Sable $3,000–$8,000
Blackbuck $750–$2,500
Blesbok $1,500–$3,000
Eland $1,200–$2,500
Gazelle, Grants $800–$2,000
Gazelle, Dama $800–$3,500
Gazelle, Thompsons $800–$2,400
Gemsbok $800–$3,500
Gnu $1,500–$4,000
Impala $1,000–$2,400
Kudu $3,500–$6,000
Nilgai $1,500
Oryx, horned Scimitar $1,500–$3,500
Oryx, Beisa $1,500–$3,500
Sitatunga $1,000–$2,500
Springbuck $800–$1,600
Waterbuck $1,500–$3,500

Cattle
Buffalo, Cape $4,000–$6,000
Buffalo, Water $3,500

Deer
Barsingha (E) $3,500
Deer, Axis $500–$1,500
Deer, Fallow $500–$1,500
Deer, Red $1,500–$6,000
Deer, Sika $700–$1,500

Goats
Goat, Angora $250–$325
Goat, Catalina $250–$325
Goat, Pygmy $350
Ibex $2,000
Tahr $2,500

Sheep
Aoudad $750–$2,000
Mouflon $400–$1,500
Sheep, Barbados $250–$350
Sheep, Corsican $250–$500
Sheep, Four-Horn $850

Swine
Wild Boar $200–$1,000

Miscellaneous
Rhinoceros (E—all except Southern white subspecies) $10,000–$20,000
Zebra, Grants $800–$2,000

Note: List is a composite based upon actual brochures/price lists from canned hunt operators.
E = Federally listed endangered species.

SOURCE: "Sample Prices for Canned Hunts," in *Canned Hunts*, The Humane Society of the United States, Washington, DC, 2003 [Online] http://www.hsus.org/ace/12066 [accessed June 16, 2003]

animals are not afraid of humans and make easy targets for trophy hunters.

There are many surplus exotic animals in the United States because of overbreeding. The HSUS believes that canned hunts provide a financial incentive that aggravates the problem. Unwanted and purposely overbred exotic animals are passed on by breeders and dealers to game and hunting preserves specializing in canned hunts.

Wildlife Control

HUNTING AS A WILDLIFE CONTROL METHOD. Killing is often the control method of choice on federal lands,

including national parks, forests, wildlife refuges, and other areas overseen by the USFWS, USFS, Bureau of Land Management (BLM), and National Park Service (NPS). According to the USFWS, 40 percent of hunters hunted on public lands in 2001. Federal law allows the government to permit secondary uses, such as hunting, on wildlife refuges if a review of the potential effects indicates that protected wildlife will not be adversely affected. Other allowed secondary uses include fishing, wildlife watching, and environmental education programs.

Hunting is permitted on more than half of the nation's 540 national wildlife refuges. The USFWS insists that hunting is necessary to manage wildlife populations. An agency Web site in 2003 described the role of hunting as follows: "Carefully managed hunts maintain wildlife populations at a level compatible with the environment, provide recreational opportunities, and permit the use of a valuable renewable resource."

Animal rights advocates are often opposed to all hunting and bitterly criticize the federal government for allowing hunting in national refuges. On its Web site in 2003, the HSUS claimed that "the sport is fundamentally at odds with the values of a humane, just, and caring society." Welfare groups are openly skeptical that hunting is an effective solution to overpopulation. For example, the IDA points out that hunters seek out not starving animals but large and healthy ones. The group argues that hunting is not about conserving species but about power, status, and collecting wild animal heads and antlers as trophies.

Deer are the animals most often associated with hunts designed to prevent overpopulation. The deer population has exploded in recent years for a variety of reasons, including lack of natural predators. The USFWS and state wildlife agencies commonly justify hunting as a humane method of killing deer that would otherwise starve because of overpopulation. They argue that death by hunting is more humane than allowing deer to slowly starve to death. Animal welfare groups believe that hunting actually aggravates population problems, claiming it upsets the natural ratio between bucks (male deer) and does (female deer) and results in higher reproduction rates. IDA says that deer make up only a small percentage of the animals killed by hunters and claims that the vast majority of hunted wild species are not considered overpopulated. The group believes that sport hunting should be banned and that natural predators, such as wolves and mountain lions, should be reintroduced wherever possible to control deer populations.

Hunters just as vigorously defend their sport and their role in conserving wildlife. The U.S. Sportsmen's Alliance (USSA) and Safari Club International (SCI) are major groups representing the interests of hunters. The USSA operates the Sportsmen's Legal Defense Fund

(SLDF). The SLDF and the SCI intervene in lawsuits filed by antihunting groups against government wildlife management and natural resources agencies. SCI also operates Sportsmen Against Hunger, a program that donates wild game meat to hunger-relief agencies. The group says that it has fed more than 230 million people in 2002; the program has been operating since 1984.

Hunting proponents note that hunting fees support government conservation programs. According to the USFWS, the duck stamp raised $622 million between its inception in 1934 and 2001, and that money purchased more than 5 million acres of land for the wildlife refuge system. Federal excise taxes on hunting equipment have contributed hundreds of millions of dollars to conservation programs around the country. Nearly $200 million in hunters' federal excise taxes collected annually are distributed to state agencies to support wildlife management programs, the purchase of lands open to hunters, and hunter education and safety classes.

Critics claim that hunting fees account for only a small portion of the money required to operate the country's conservation programs and that the government uses money obtained from hunting fees to set aside more areas for hunting. They want greater focus on activities such as wildlife watching and environmental education at wildlife refuges.

The USFWS says that 66.1 million American adults observed, fed, or photographed wildlife in 2001. This is five times the number that hunted wildlife that year. These wildlife recreationists spent $38.4 billion on travel, equipment, and other items. This represents 35 percent of the total dollars spent on wildlife-related activities in 2001.

In March 2003 the Fund for Animals (FFA) filed suit against the USFWS after the agency decided to begin or expand hunting in 39 National Wildlife Refuges. The FFA claims that hunting will have a negative effect on the endangered species that live in the refuges, particularly migratory birds. The group says that the USFWS did not consider all possible environmental impacts as required by law. Between 1998 and 2002 the federal government opened 42 refuges to hunting. In March 2003 a spokesman for the USFWS commented on the lawsuit (Dean Schabner, "No Refuge," ABC News, March 18, 2003 [Online] http://abcnews.go.com/Sections/US/SciTech/refuge03031 8.html [accessed August 1, 2003]): "The refuges were never created to be sanctuaries where no hunting would be allowed. Ever since the inception of the refuge system, hunting has been allowed, largely because hunting is good for conservation—hunters contribute enormously to conservation. Without hunting, we couldn't do what we do."

OTHER WILDLIFE CONTROL METHODS. Some animal groups choose to fight against particular kinds of wildlife killing. The HSUS, for example, supports passage of the "Don't Feed the Bears Act." This act would prohibit bear-baiting on lands overseen by the USFS and BLM. Bearbaiting is a hunting technique in which food (such as rotting meat, doughnuts, or grease) is used to lure bears to an open location where they can be easily shot. The technique is popular with hunting guides and outfitters (companies that cater to trophy hunters). Bearbaiting is already prohibited on lands overseen by the NPS and USFWS.

According to the HSUS, in 2002 bearbaiting was still allowed on federal lands in nine of the states that permit bear hunting: Alaska, Idaho, Maine, Michigan, Minnesota, New Hampshire, Utah, Wisconsin, and Wyoming. The HSUS believes that the practice is unsportsmanlike and encourages bears to seek out table scraps and garbage around human encampments. The HSUS accuses the BLM and USFS of being hypocritical, because the agencies warn campers not to feed the bears but allow hunters to do so.

Another killing method that receives a lot of criticism is the trapping of fur-bearing animals. Welfarists consider traps to be especially cruel because the panicked animals are often trapped for a lengthy period of time before being discovered and killed. Welfare groups describe gruesome instances in which trapped animals have chewed off their own paws to escape. Trapping is used as a control method on federal lands, including refuges. It is done by refuge staff, by trappers under contract to the refuges, and by members of the public who obtain special permits.

The Animal Protection Institute (API) examined USFWS data collected in 1997 as part of an investigative study of trapping at wildlife refuges around the country. The API claims that many nontarget species were captured in body-gripping traps at refuges, including river otters, feral and domestic cats and dogs, rabbits, geese, alligators, ducks, hawks, owls, eagles, and bears. Some of these animals were killed immediately by the trapping devices or died from injuries sustained during trapping. Others were released unharmed upon their discovery by the trappers.

Fur and Other Products

Many wild animals are killed purely for their fur or parts. The most common wildlife commodities are:

• Fur from mink, beaver, foxes, rabbits, bears, and seals.

• Hides from tigers, leopards, and other big cats.

• Rhinoceros horns, reindeer antlers, snake blood, shark fins, and the penises from seals, tigers, and rhinoceros are popular aphrodisiacs (supplements designed to enhance sexual performance).

• Bones, claws, paws, fangs, brains, eyeballs, tails, and internal organs from tigers are used in traditional Asian medicines.

• Bile from wild boars, bears, and snakes is used in aphrodisiacs and traditional Asian medicines.

- Elephant tusks are a source of ivory.

- Bear paws are considered a delicacy in some Asian countries.

SEALS. Most animals used in the fur trade are bred and raised in cages on farms. Some animals, however, are still trapped or killed in the wild, particularly seals. The killing of seals for fur was a high-profile issue of the animal rights movement during the 1970s. Greenpeace activists traveled to hunting areas to splash dye on seals and draw media attention to their slaughter. As a result the seal fur industry was virtually eliminated. As of 1999 there were more than 5 million harp seals in Canada.

The killing of seals particularly caught public attention because seals on ice floes are usually clubbed in the head, then dragged with hooks across the ice. Animal welfarists who have witnessed seal hunts claim to have seen seals skinned while still alive and conscious. Seal hunters argue that clubbing is humane and kills the seals quickly. Seals swimming in the water are shot instead of clubbed. Critics claim that many of these seals are injured and drown after they sink below the surface.

In May 2002 *U.S. News and World Report* published a story on the comeback of the sealing industry in recent years (Stacey Schultz and Julian Barnes, "Red Tide Rising," May 6, 2002). According to the report, the Canadian government has been quietly paying subsidies to seal hunters to boost the economy in Newfoundland. As a result more seals were killed annually in the early 2000s than were killed three decades earlier.

Government and industry officials insist that increasing demand has driven rising harvests. They also point out that seals are eating large numbers of northern codfish. The codfishing industry collapsed in Canada in the early 1990s after the government imposed strict catch limits in response to declining fish counts. Thousands of fishermen were put out of work. *U.S. News and World Report* suggests that the Canadian government ignored scientific warnings for years that cod populations were too low and then blamed seals when the industry collapsed. Seal quotas were raised substantially, and seal subsidies were begun. The number of seals killed increased from 65,400 in 1995 to 275,000 in 1997. At the same time pelt prices more than doubled to $20 per pelt.

According to the May 6, 2002, issue of *U.S. News and World Report,* the fisheries minister of Newfoundland insists that sealers no longer receive government subsidies. However, *U.S. News and World Report* claims that government agencies had provided nearly $1 million in grants and loans since 2000 to businesses involved in the seal industry. Some biologists believe that the industry would collapse without these funds.

In March 2003 the Canadian Ministry of Fisheries and Oceans announced a new harp seal quota of 975,000 seals over the next three years. The International Fund for Animal Welfare plans to protest at seal hunts during 2003 and bring renewed media attention to the controversial practice.

BIG CATS. There is a huge market for wild animal parts throughout Asia, particularly in China. Many parts are used in traditional remedies for various illnesses and diseases. In addition, animal penises are sold as aphrodisiacs (supplements believed to enhance sexual performance). The animal most sought after is the tiger. Tiger hides sell for as much $20,000 each, and tiger bones are ground up and used in medicines for rheumatism and arthritis. Tiger penises are used in aphrodisiacs, soups, and various medicines.

Tigers are listed as endangered under the federal Endangered Species Act. Leopards are classified as either endangered or threatened, depending on the location of the wild population. According to the USFWS, many tigers are worth more dead than alive. The animals breed easily in captivity and have been extremely overbred in the United States. Baby tigers are popular at zoos and animal parks, but they grow up quickly and are expensive to care for as adults. Unwanted and overbred tigers from zoos, refuges, and game parks can wind up in the hands of unscrupulous dealers who kill the animals for their valuable parts. Federal law allows the possession of captive-bred tigers, but only if their use enhances the propagation or survival of the species. It is illegal to kill the animals for profit or sell their parts, meat, or hide in interstate commerce. It is not illegal to donate the animals.

During the late 1990s, federal and state wildlife officials conducted a massive undercover investigation into the trade of endangered tigers and leopards in the Midwest. In 2001 charges were brought against 17 people. Several dealers, owners, and employees of exotic animal ranches in Missouri, Oklahoma, and Arkansas were charged with illegally purchasing, transporting, and selling four tigers. The animals were allegedly purchased from the Wild Wilderness Drive Through Safari in Gentry, Arkansas, and taken to the 5H Ranch in Cape Girardeau, Missouri, where they were killed. The suit alleges that the conspirators prepared false federal forms stating that the animals were donated from one ranch to another, when in fact they were purchased with the knowledge that the animals would be killed for their parts. In February 2002 three of the people involved pleaded guilty. Additional suits were filed against several people from the Chicago area (including the owner of an exotic meat market) for killing leopards and tigers and selling their parts. Three men from Detroit were charged with buying the hides of protected tigers.

A LARGE PROBLEM. International trade in exotic animals and their parts is a multibillion-dollar industry. Donald J. Barry, the acting assistant secretary of the USFWS, noted in 1997 that such trade ranks right below drug and gun trafficking in terms of the money involved. TRAFFIC is an organization that monitors worldwide wildlife trade. According to an organization spokesperson in 2002, U.S. consumers account for approximately 30 percent of global trade in illegal wildlife.

Whaling and Commercial Fishing

WHALING. Whaling has been an industry in northern seas for hundreds of years. The oil and blubber from whales were popular commodities in many markets. During the mid-1800s, nearly 70,000 people were employed in the industry, but the number of whales declined dramatically through the 19th and early 20th centuries. The United States banned commercial whaling in 1928. In 1946 the International Whaling Commission (IWC) was founded by 24 member countries (including the United States) as a means to self-regulate the industry and limit the number and type of whales that could be killed. In 1986 all IWC countries agreed to ban commercial whaling after virtually all whale populations were placed under Appendix I of the CITES agreement. Whaling was still allowed for "scientific purposes."

Conservation and animal rights groups have complained for years that some IWC countries, particularly Japan, kill a large number of whales under this loophole. Japan has admitted killing 440 minke whales during an Antarctic expedition conducted in late 2002 and early 2003. The worldwide minke population is estimated to be more than 1 million. Whalers and some scientists say that minkes and a few other species (mainly pilot, gray, and sperm whales) are not endangered and should be subjected to controlled hunts. In 2002 Japan proposed downlisting many populations of minke and Bryde's whales from CITES Appendix I to Appendix II, making them available for commercial whaling. The proposal was voted down by CITES member nations.

In 2002 Norway asked to rejoin the IWC after dropping out 10 years earlier. Norway rejoined, but with the reservation that it will not support a ban on commercial whaling. This started an internal battle within the IWC about what its role should be. Some countries believe that the IWC's focus should be entirely on conservation. Other countries believe that the IWC should be more industry-friendly. In May 2003 Iceland announced that it would restart commercial whaling in 2006 and allow the taking of 250 whales annually—100 northern minke whales, 100 fin whales, and 50 sei whales. In response, the U.S. State Department issued an official objection to the IWC.

As of July 2003, 51 countries were members of the IWC. At the IWC's 2003 meeting, 18 of those countries (including the United States) sponsored a resolution called the Berlin Initiative, which clarified the primary goal of the IWC to be whale conservation. The resolution passed, and the IWC plans to establish a committee to set up a conservation agenda for the organization. Many conservation and animal organizations supported the resolution. An HSUS spokesperson notes that the IWC should not "conserve whale populations so that certain countries can then turn around and kill them."

COMMERCIAL FISHING. Commercial fishing of many species is blamed for a host of environmental and conservation problems in the world's oceans. Overfishing and poor management have caused severe declines in some populations. In May 2003 researchers from Dalhousie University in Halifax, Nova Scotia, Canada, reported in the journal *Nature* that commercial fishing has decreased the world's population of large predatory ocean fishes by 90 percent (Ransom Myers and Boris Worm, "Rapid Worldwide Depletion of Predatory Fish Communities," May 15, 2003). These fish include blue marlin, cod, tuna, and swordfish. Scientists found that the most sought-after species were quickly diminished by overfishing and then replaced by less desirable species. These replacement species were also depleted quickly. Technological advances such as global positioning systems and sonar have allowed commercial fisherman to better find and follow great schools of fish in previously uncharted waters.

The Monterey Bay Aquarium issues a seafood guide for consumers, *Seafood Watch,* that lists which fish and shellfish are being harvested in a sustainable and responsible manner and which are being depleted because of overfishing and poor management. The guide is updated twice per year. The spring/summer 2003 edition of the list included items such as sardines, farmed oysters, and trap-caught squid/prawns as "best choices"; mahi-mahi, Alaskan king crab, and bay/sea scallops under "caution"; and monkfish, imported shrimp, and bluefin tuna under "avoid."

Another criticism of commercial fishing is that it endangers marine mammals and other fish besides those the fisherman want to catch. Even nontarget fish and mammals are endangered by commercial fishing. Experts estimate that thousands of nontarget specimens are killed each year after becoming entangled in fishing nets and devices. According to Earthtrust, a nonprofit wildlife conservation organization headquartered in Honolulu, Hawaii, approximately 7 million dolphins were killed between 1959 and 1991 due to purse-seining in the eastern tropical Pacific. Purse-seining is a fishing technique in which giant nets are encircled around schools of fish. It is a popular way to capture tuna. However, tuna schools are frequently accompanied by pods of dolphins. In fact some fishermen chase and set their nets around dolphins to capture the nearby tuna. Since dolphins are mammals, they require air to breathe. The dolphins can get caught and drown in the nets. Negative publicity about the problem during the 1980s led consumers to demand changes in tuna fishing and labeling.

In 1991 the Dolphin Protection Consumer Information Act was passed, establishing an official definition of "dolphin-safe" tuna. Canners must meet certain criteria before they can label their tuna dolphin-safe, and U.S. fishermen modified their fishing techniques to meet the criteria. Purse-seine fishing is still widely practiced by foreign fishing industries, particularly in Mexico and South America.

On December 31, 2002, the National Marine Fisheries Service (NMFS) announced its finding that the tuna purse-seine industry has "no significant adverse impact" on dolphin populations in the eastern tropical Pacific. This finding allows foreign fishermen using the technique to import their fish into the United States as dolphin-safe if an onboard observer certifies that no dolphins were killed or seriously injured during the catch.

Critics claim that purse-seine fishing is stressful to dolphins even if they are released from the nets alive because it can separate baby dolphins from their mothers. In January 2003 Earth Island Institute and eight other environmental, conservation, and animal welfare groups (including the HSUS) filed suit against the NMFS in federal court to halt implementation of the ruling. Late in that month, the court issued a stay, meaning that the existing labeling standards continue in effect until the lawsuit is settled.

RESCUE AND REHABILITATION OF WILDLIFE

A variety of individuals, groups, and agencies are involved in rescue or rehabilitation of wildlife. Most state wildlife and fish and game agencies operate rehabilitation programs and require private individuals and groups rehabilitating and releasing native wildlife to be licensed. In addition, the USFWS requires federal permits for those rehabilitating migratory bird species.

The HSUS operates the five-acre Cape Wildlife Center in West Barnstable, Massachusetts. The center includes a wildlife rehabilitation facility and a veterinary clinic for injured, sick, and orphaned wild animals. Nearly 1,400 animals received care there during 2002. Although the center is not open to the public, it operates a hotline to answer questions and offer suggestions about ways in which wildlife and humans can coexist.

The Association of Sanctuaries (AOS) is a nonprofit organization founded in 1992 to accredit sanctuaries that rescue and care for all kinds of animals, including wild animals. The rescued animals are not used for commercial purposes or allowed to breed in captivity. Seven AOS-accredited facilities in the United States rehabilitate and release wild animals. Dozens more provide sanctuary for wild animals that cannot be returned to their natural habitat for some reason. These include unwanted exotic pets and circus and zoo animals. One example is The Elephant Sanctuary near Hohenwald, Tennessee. It was founded in 1995 as the country's first natural habitat refuge specifically for endangered Asian and African elephants. The 800-acre sanctuary is surrounded by a 3,000-acre natural buffer. As of July 2003 the sanctuary housed six female elephants. Four more elephants were expected to arrive there during mid- to late 2003.

There are hundreds of other rescue and rehabilitation facilities around the country. Many are nonprofit tax-exempt operations run by individuals or animal groups. The quality of care offered by these facilities depends on the expertise of the staff and the funds available. The HSUS is critical of some of these facilities. In April 2003 the HSUS vice president said, "We call them pseudo-sanctuaries. They're primarily engaged in commercial activities while passing themselves off as a nonprofit."

These comments followed a raid on the home of a California couple operating Tiger Rescue, a nonprofit sanctuary for big cats. State and county wildlife authorities found the corpses of 30 adult tigers and 61 cubs when they raided the couple's property on April 22, 2003. Thirteen cubs found alive were turned over to the Fund for Animals Wildlife Rehabilitation Center near San Diego. The California Department of Fish and Game had removed 10 tiger cubs from Tiger Rescue in November 2002, citing concerns about the animals' welfare. At a preliminary hearing held in July 2003, a veterinarian testified that some of the dead cubs had starved to death. Authorities said the property was littered with decaying animal corpses. As of mid-2003, the owners had been bound over for trial and will face 63 charges, including 17 felony counts related to allegations of animal cruelty and child endangerment. (The couple's eight-year-old son lived in the house with them.) The two operate a popular roadside zoo in Colton, California, that features dozens of exotic animals, a petting zoo, and a big cat exhibit.

CHAPTER 4
FARM ANIMALS

Farm animals are animals that are kept for agricultural purposes. This includes domesticated animals, such as cows and chickens, and wild animals that are raised in confinement, such as mink and fish. Animals are farmed for a variety of reasons. Most are raised to be killed. Meat from cattle, hogs, and chickens provides the bulk of protein in the American diet, while animals with beautiful fur are killed for their pelts. However, some farm animals are more useful and profitable alive. These animals produce something of value to humans, such as milk, eggs, wool, or honey, or are farmed for their skills, like horses, mules, and burros. Whatever the reason, the cultivation of farm animals is an enormous business.

Table 4.1 lists the top 25 moneymaking agricultural products in the United States during 2001. Six are animals or animal products. In fact, farm animals and their by-products accounted for about half (49.9 percent) of all agricultural income in the United States.

The number of animals involved is staggering. As of 2002 U.S. farms included:

• 8.3 billion chickens

• 275 million turkeys

• 105 million cattle

• 59 million hogs

• 6.5 million sheep

• 3.6 million ducks

• 3 million mink, rabbits, etc.

• 2 million goats

In addition, there were millions of horses, quail, pheasants, and honeybees and several hundred thousand geese, mules, burros, donkeys, fish, and other farmed animals.

In 2002 more farm animals were living in the United States than there were humans on earth. The use and well-being of these animals is of major importance to people concerned with animal rights and welfare. Animal rights activists abhor the idea that animals are commodities at all. Many believe that animals should not be used for any purpose, especially to feed humans. Welfarists focus their attention on the treatment of farmed animals—how they are housed, fed, transported, and slaughtered.

People in the American livestock business argue that farm animals are well treated. They point to the high productivity of the industry as proof. In other words, farm animals must be thriving because there are so many of them. The American Meat Institute (AMI) is a trade organization that represents the meat and poultry industry. On its Web site in 2003, the AMI summed up its viewpoint: "Healthy animals whose welfare is carefully respected result in safe, wholesome, high quality meat and poultry products." In January 2001 the AMI published a brochure titled "Animal Welfare in the Meat Industry: A Commitment to Consumers and Livestock," in which it noted that livestock farmers practice humane animal care because it is ethical and results in calmer animals. In turn, calmer animals help make farms and meat plants safer working environments, resulting in higher quality meat. The link between humane animal treatment and high production of good-quality products is commonly cited by the livestock industry.

Critics argue that high productivity is an indicator of the efficiency of the overall system, not the welfare of individual animals. They have a long list of complaints about how farm animals are raised and slaughtered in this country.

Farming animals is a very old and respected business. It feeds hungry people and supplies products that people want. Forcing farmers to radically change the way they treat animals might jeopardize the relatively cheap and plentiful supply of animal products that Americans enjoy. Would society tolerate this just for the sake of the animals? This is the ultimate question at the center of the farm animal debate.

TABLE 4.1

Leading commodities for cash receipts, 2001

(dollar amounts in thousands)

Rank	Item	Value of receipts	Percent of total receipts	Cumulative percent[1]	Percent of U.S. value[2]	Value of U.S. receipts
	All commodities	202,849,408	100.0	—	100.0	202,849,408
	Livestock and products	106,431,172	52.5	—	100.0	106,431,172
	Crops	96,418,236	47.5	—	100.0	96,418,236
1	Cattle and calves	40,439,877	19.9	19.9	100.0	40,439,877
2	Dairy products	24,694,531	12.2	32.1	100.0	24,694,531
3	Corn	17,108,878	8.4	40.5	100.0	17,108,878
4	Broilers	16,688,339	8.2	48.8	100.0	16,688,339
5	Greenhouse/nursery	13,794,634	6.8	55.6	100.0	13,794,634
6	Soybeans	12,777,099	6.3	61.9	100.0	12,777,099
7	Hogs	12,455,792	6.1	68.0	100.0	12,455,792
8	Wheat	5,719,222	2.8	70.8	100.0	5,719,222
9	Cotton	4,954,043	2.4	73.3	100.0	4,954,043
10	Hay	4,556,955	2.2	75.5	100.0	4,556,955
11	Chicken eggs	4,444,864	2.2	77.7	100.0	4,444,864
12	Grapes	2,924,049	1.4	79.2	100.0	2,924,049
13	Turkeys	2,729,457	1.3	80.5	100.0	2,729,457
14	Potatoes	2,464,275	1.2	81.7	100.0	2,464,275
15	Lettuce	1,907,083	0.9	82.7	100.0	1,907,083
16	Tobacco	1,880,300	0.9	83.6	100.0	1,880,300
17	Tomatoes	1,664,890	0.8	84.4	100.0	1,664,890
18	Apples	1,369,980	0.7	85.1	100.0	1,369,980
19	Oranges	1,369,014	0.7	85.7	100.0	1,369,014
20	Strawberries	1,086,082	0.5	86.3	100.0	1,086,082
21	Peanuts	1,001,845	0.5	86.8	100.0	1,001,845
22	Horses/mules	984,700	0.5	87.3	100.0	984,700
23	Cane for sugar	917,991	0.5	87.7	100.0	917,991
24	Sorghum grain	905,052	0.4	88.2	100.0	905,052
25	Sugar beets	885,172	0.4	88.6	100.0	885,172
	Government payments[3]	12,380,016	—	—	100.0	12,380,016
	Net farm income[4]	45,582,427	—	—	100.0	45,582,427

— = Not applicable

[1]The cumulative percentage is the sum of the percent of total receipts for each commodity and all preceding commodities.
[2]Percent state receipts are of U.S. receipts for same line item.
[3]Government payments made directly to farmers in cash or Payment-in-Kind.
[4]Net farm income, a value of production measure, is the farm operator's share of the sector's net value added to the National economy from production activities within a calendar year.

SOURCE: "United States: Leading Commodities for Cash Receipts, 2001," in *United States Fact Sheet,* U.S. Department of Agriculture, Economic Research Service, Washington, DC, 2001 [Online] http://www.ers.usda.gov/StateFacts/TopAgCommodities/TOP25US.txt [accessed May 20, 2003]

HISTORY

Humans have been farming animals for thousands of years, dating back to when animals were first domesticated. The ability to keep and control animals allowed people to turn their focus away from hunting and toward building civilizations. It also changed the fundamental attitudes that humans had about animals. Domesticated animals lost the status that their ancestors had as independent free-roaming creatures, and became pieces of property.

Humans devoted a great deal of energy to maximizing the value of their new property. Control over breeding was particularly important. Certain animals were mated with each other to produce offspring that were even more valuable, while animals with undesirable properties were eliminated from the gene pool. Because farm animals were viewed as property, many decisions were based on logic and economics. Society at large benefited from the ready availability of meat and other products from this system.

Livestock Protection Laws

During the 1800s a number of laws were enacted in England and the United States to protect animals from abuse, neglect, and mistreatment by their owners. Some of these laws specifically included livestock, while others did not. Many state anticruelty laws excluded what they called "customary agricultural practices." These laws were often interpreted not to apply to animals raised for food.

The Twenty-Eight Hour Law of 1873 was the first federal law dealing with livestock welfare. It required that livestock being transported across state lines be rested and watered at least once every 28 hours during the journey. At the time, livestock transport was done by rail, and as of 2003, the law had never been changed to reflect new methods of transport and was only enforced on railroad transport. The federal Animal Welfare Act was enacted in 1966 to provide protection for animals used for certain purposes, but the regulations enforcing the law specifically excluded livestock.

The major legislation of the 20th century to affect livestock was the Humane Methods of Slaughter Act of 1958. The law required slaughter by humane methods at slaughterhouses subject to federal inspection. This meant that livestock had to be rendered insensitive to pain before being slaughtered. The act excluded chickens and all animals slaughtered using techniques associated with religious rituals. Enforcement of the act was turned over to the U.S. Department of Agriculture (USDA).

Concern Grows

Farm animals received little more attention until a 1964 book by Ruth Harrison was published. *Animal Machines* described the brutality inflicted on livestock in Britain by the modern farming industry. In 1975 Peter Singer published *Animal Liberation,* which detailed similar problems on America's "factory farms." It was also during the 1960s and 1970s that the vegetarian movement picked up steam.

The plight of farm animals became a major issue with animal rights activists and welfarists. During the 1980s and early 1990s, several groups dedicated to livestock concerns formed, among them the Farm Animal Reform Movement (FARM), Humane Farming Association, Farm Sanctuary, and United Poultry Concerns. Today these and other groups work to publicize abuses that occur in the agricultural industry and achieve new legislation to protect farm animals.

Some of the major farm animal campaigns being pursued by these groups in 2003 included:

• Banning the slaughter of horses for food

• Protecting animals at the slaughterhouse that are unable to walk (so-called "down animals")

• Outlawing the keeping of veal calves and pregnant and nursing hogs in small crates

• Publicizing the abuse and mishandling of animals at slaughterhouses

ANIMAL PRODUCTS

Animal products are used in many ways by modern society. People consume them and wear them and buy items every day that contain animal-derived components. According to the USDA, Americans consumed 193.8 pounds of meat per capita during 2001. (See Table 4.2.) Since the early 1970s, demand for red meat (such as beef, pork, lamb, veal, and mutton) has declined, while demand for chicken and turkey has skyrocketed. Fish and shellfish consumption has increased only slightly. Overall meat consumption has increased dramatically since the early 1900s.

Animals killed for meat must be processed immediately. This means that meat animals must arrive alive at the

TABLE 4.2

Total meat consumption, 1909–2001

BONELESS, TRIMMED (EDIBLE) WEIGHT, POUNDS PER CAPITA PER YEAR

Year	Red meats (beef, pork, lamb, veal & mutton)	Poultry (chicken & turkey)	Fish and shellfish	Total meats
1909	101.7	11.2	11	123.9
1910	96	11.8	11.2	118.9
1911	99.3	12	11.3	122.5
1912	95.2	11.5	11.3	118
1913	93.7	11.2	11.5	116.4
1914	91.3	11.1	11.7	114.2
1915	87.7	11.2	11.2	110.1
1916	91.2	10.6	11	112.8
1917	88.6	10.3	10.9	109.8
1918	92.8	10.3	10.9	114.1
1919	90.7	11.2	11.6	113.5
1920	88.8	10.8	11.8	111.4
1921	87.2	10.5	10.5	108.2
1922	89.8	11.1	11.3	112.2
1923	95.7	11.4	10.7	117.8
1924	95.7	10.7	11	117.5
1925	91.3	11.2	11.1	113.6
1926	90.1	11.1	11.4	112.5
1927	87.6	11.9	12.2	111.7
1928	85.2	11.5	12.1	108.7
1929	85	11.3	11.8	108.1
1930	83.6	12.3	10.2	106.2
1931	84.6	11.1	8.8	104.6
1932	84.7	11.6	8.4	104.7
1933	88.2	12	8.6	108.8
1934	94	11	9.2	114.2
1935	76.9	10.7	10.5	98.1
1936	85.5	11.4	11.6	108.5
1937	82.4	11.5	11.7	105.7
1938	82.9	10.8	10.8	104.5
1939	86.9	11.9	10.8	109.6
1940	92.4	12.3	11	115.6
1941	94.7	13.4	11.1	119.1
1942	98.9	15.3	8.8	122.9
1943	105	18.5	8	131.5
1944	113.2	18.4	8.7	140.3
1945	104.3	18.7	9.8	132.7
1946	102.5	17.1	10.8	130.4
1947	103.6	15.5	10.3	129.4
1948	96.1	15.1	11.2	122.4
1949	95.5	16.1	10.9	122.6
1950	95.8	17.6	11.9	125.3
1951	93.3	18.7	11.3	123.3
1952	96.7	19.1	11.1	126.9
1953	103.5	19.1	11.3	133.9
1954	103.1	20	11.1	134.2
1955	117.1	18.8	10.4	146.3
1956	120	21	10.4	151.4
1957	114	22.3	10.2	146.5
1958	108.7	24.1	10.6	143.4
1959	114.7	24.8	10.9	150.5
1960	115.1	24.1	10.3	149.5
1961	115	26.5	10.7	152.3
1962	116.3	26.2	10.6	153.1
1963	120.5	26.6	10.5	157.6
1964	125.7	27.2	10.5	163.4
1965	120.1	28.9	10.9	159.9
1966	122.3	30.7	10.9	163.9
1967	127.6	31.9	10.6	170.2
1968	130.6	31.6	11	173.2
1969	129.4	32.9	11.2	173.4
1970	131.9	33.8	11.7	177.5
1971	135.5	34	11.5	181
1972	131.8	35.4	12.5	179.7
1973	121.8	33.7	12.7	168.2
1974	130.4	33.8	12.1	176.3

TABLE 4.2

Total meat consumption, 1909–2001 [CONTINUED]

BONELESS, TRIMMED (EDIBLE) WEIGHT, POUNDS PER CAPITA PER YEAR

Year	Red meats (beef, pork, lamb, veal & mutton)	Poultry (chicken & turkey)	Fish and shellfish	Total meats
1975	125.4	32.9	12.1	170.5
1976	133.4	35.5	12.9	181.7
1977	132.3	35.9	12.6	180.9
1978	127.5	37.3	13.4	178.2
1979	124.4	40.1	13	177.6
1980	126.4	40.8	12.4	179.6
1981	125.1	42.1	12.6	179.7
1982	119.8	42.2	12.4	174.4
1983	123.9	42.7	13.3	180
1984	123.6	44	14.1	181.7
1985	124.9	45.5	15	185.4
1986	122.2	47.4	15.4	184.9
1987	117.4	51	16.1	184.5
1988	119.5	51.9	15.1	186.6
1989	115.6	53.9	15.6	185.1
1990	112.3	56.3	15	183.5
1991	111.6	58.2	14.8	184.5
1992	113.5	60.5	14.6	188.6
1993	111.3	62	14.8	188.1
1994	113.6	62.7	15	191.3
1995	113.6	62.1	14.8	190.5
1996	111.1	63.1	14.5	188.7
1997	109.1	63.1	14.3	186.4
1998	113.3	63.7	14.5	191.5
1999	115.1	66.7	14.9	196.7
2000	113.6	66.8	15.2	195.7
2001	111	67.6	15.2	193.8

Note: Includes processed red meat, poultry, and fish on a fresh (raw) basis. Excludes game, game fish consumption, and edible offals.
Calculated from unrounded data.

SOURCE: Adapted from *Food Consumption (per capita) Data System,* U.S. Department of Agriculture, Economic Research Service, Washington, DC, 2003 [Online] http://www.ers.usda.gov/Data/FoodConsumption/DataSystem.asp?ERSTab=3 [accessed May 20, 2003]

slaughterhouse. They cannot be humanely euthanized with drugs as pets put to sleep are, because humans will be consuming them. Those parts that are not readily edible by humans are "rendered" into other marketable products.

According to the National Renderers Association, 9.4 million tons of animal by-products were produced by the rendering industry in 2002. Only about 50 percent of a cow, 60 percent of a pig, 72 percent of a chicken, and 78 percent of a turkey become edible products. The bones, hooves, beaks, feet, feathers, fat, and inedible organs and tissues are recycled at a couple of hundred rendering plants in the United States. The fat is processed for industrial use, and the other by-products are ground into a powder or boiled to make gelatin.

Rendered by-products are sold to a variety of industries and become ingredients in lubricants, paints, varnishes, waxes, soaps, candles, cement, pharmaceuticals, pet food, toothpaste, and cosmetics (such as lipstick and shampoo). Gelatin is an ingredient in many food products including some ice cream, yogurt, candy, and marshmallows. However, the main use of rendered by-products is as a protein supplement (or food source) for livestock. (In 1997 the FDA outlawed the use of most mammal-based protein in feed intended for cattle. This is to prevent the spread of mad cow disease, should it appear in the United States.) Rendering plants also process whole carcasses of farm animals that die of illness or injury and other dead animals, including euthanized pets.

Table 4.3 lists some of the many products that contain animal-derived ingredients. In addition, animal products are increasingly used for human medical and health purposes. An undated American Meat Institute (AMI) fact sheet titled *Products from Animals* and available on the AMI Web site in mid-2003 reports that the adrenal glands of cattle are a source of epinephrine, a drug administered to people suffering from allergies, asthma, and hay fever. Epinephrine is also used as a heart stimulant and to enhance the effect of some anesthetics. Thrombin is a substance derived from cattle blood that is used to help promote blood clotting in humans and for skin grafting. Other cattle-derived products with medical benefits include insulin, rennet, heparin, TSH (thyroid stimulating hormone), ACTH (adrenocorticotrophic hormone), cholesterol, and estrogen. Similar products derived from hogs include cortisone, norepinephrine, estrogen, insulin, pepsin, plasmin, blood fibrin, and oxytocin. Pig organs and skin are also increasingly used in human medicine. According to the AMI, hog heart implants saved 250,000 lives over a period of 12 years preceding the publication of the fact sheet.

After meat, one of the most popular animal products is leather. Produced from the skins of calves, cows, pigs, sheep, lambs, and other animals used in food production, leather is utilized for everything from clothing and shoes to luggage and office supplies to car seats. Industry organizations, such as the Leather Apparel Association, argue that no animal is killed for leather only; however, animal rights organizations argue that the value of the leather makes up a significant portion of the value of the animal. In 2003 information available on the Web site of People for the Ethical Treatment of Animals (PETA) suggested that leather accounts for 55–60 percent of the by-product value of cattle.

ROUTINE FARMING PRACTICES

Farm animals have historically not been covered by animal welfare legislation. As a result, some practices relating to the treatment of farm animals are considered standard by farmers but may be thought of as cruel or inhumane by animal activists. Such practices include culling, castration, dehorning, branding, and various forms of physical alteration. Culling means the rejection of inferior or undesirable animals. Because it costs money to feed and care for livestock, unwanted farm animals are often killed. This is particularly true in the hen-breeding business. Male chicks of laying breeds will never lay eggs and are not suitable meat chickens. Millions of them are routinely killed each year when they are only one day old.

TABLE 4.3

Animal byproducts in our daily lives

Intestines	Fats and fatty acids	Bones, horns and hooves	From hide & wool
Sausage casings	Explosives	Syringes	Lanolin
Instrument strings	Solvents	Piano keys	Clothing
Surgical sutures	Chewing gum	Marshmallow	Drum heads
Tennis racket strings	Paints	Pet food ingredients	Luggage
	Industrial lubricants	Bandage strips	Yarns
	Cosmetics, shampoo	Bone charcoal products	Artist's brushes
	Dog food	Gelatin	Sports equipment
	Mink oil	Adhesive tape	Fabrics
	Oleo margarine	Phonograph records	Pelt products
	Ceramics	Combs & toothbrushes	Insulation
	Medicines	Buttons	Textiles
	Soaps	Jewelry	Tennis balls
	Creams & lotions	Bone meal	Carpet
	Tires, rubber products	Emery boards & cloth	Footwear
	Paraffin	Ice cream	Woolen goods
	Biodegradable detergents	Horn & bone handles	Baseballs
	Antifreeze	Wallpaper and wallpaper paste	Upholstery
	Crayons	Dog biscuits	Hide glue
	Floor wax	Steel ball bearings	
	Chemicals	Fertilizer	
	Insecticides	Neatsfoot oil	
	Candles	Adhesives	
	Herbicides	Plywood & paneling	
	Shaving cream	Shampoo & conditioner	
		Dice	
		Collagen cold cream	
		Crochet needles	
		Cellophane products	
		Glycerine	
		Photographic film	
		Laminated wood products	

SOURCE: Adapted from "Animal Byproducts in Our Daily Lives," Minnesota Foundation for Responsible Animal Care, Minneapolis, MN, 2000 [Online] http://www.mnbeef.org/MnFRAC/byproducts.htm [accessed May 20, 2003]; http://www.mnfrac.org

Another ancient farming practice is animal castration (removal of the male sex organs). Humans have used castration to control the reproduction of farm animals for centuries. This is particularly true in cattle and hog farming. Only the males with the most desirable characteristics are allowed to remain intact for breeding purposes. This is believed to be beneficial for herd management, because castration reduces aggressive behavior and physical confrontations between males that might damage their meat. In addition, farmers believe that castrated males gain weight better and do not release male hormones that could taint the taste of the meat.

Dehorning

The vast majority of cattle are dehorned to make them easier to handle and to prevent them from accidentally or intentionally injuring each other. In grown cattle, the fully developed horns are cut off, but a more common practice is to treat the emerging horn buds of baby calves with a caustic salve to prevent horns from developing.

Branding

Branding and other forms of identification, such as ear-notching, are used to distinguish ownership. In the American Old West, most cattle were not fenced in but roamed free across ranches. At roundup time, the distinctive brand burned into each hide allowed cowboys to sort the cattle by owner. Cattle branding is still practiced today as a precaution against theft and to establish ownership. Also, the ears of cattle and hogs are often given distinctive notches using sharp knives to permit easier identification from a distance.

Other Physical Alterations

Other forms of physical alteration widely accepted in animal husbandry include beak trimming of poultry and tail clipping of cattle and swine. Chicken beaks are trimmed to reduce injuries that might result from the animals pecking at each other. Cattle and swine have their tails clipped to prevent them from chewing on each other's tails and to improve cleanliness and reduce disease.

Ongoing Controversy

All of these procedures are considered practical and necessary by farm animal producers and considered inhumane by many animal welfarists. Castration, dehorning, branding, beak trimming, tail clipping, and ear notching are widely conducted in the United States without the use of anesthetics or pain medicine. Use of a local anesthetic is recommended (but not required) in Canada and required by law in most cases in the United Kingdom.

FIGURE 4.1

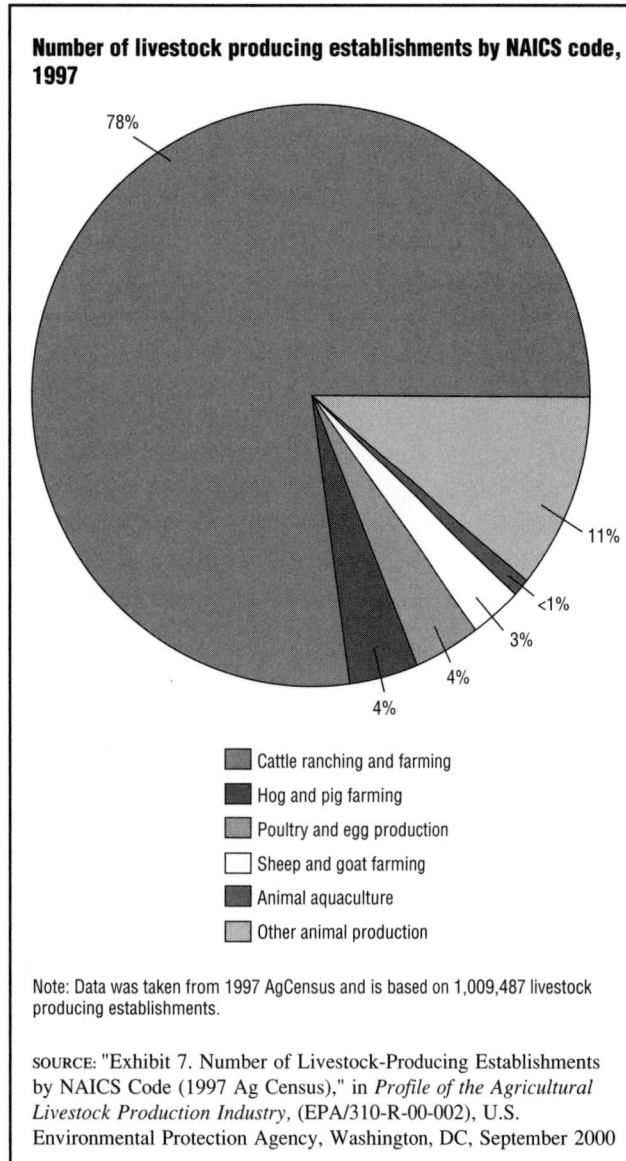

Number of livestock producing establishments by NAICS code, 1997

- Cattle ranching and farming
- Hog and pig farming
- Poultry and egg production
- Sheep and goat farming
- Animal aquaculture
- Other animal production

Note: Data was taken from 1997 AgCensus and is based on 1,009,487 livestock producing establishments.

SOURCE: "Exhibit 7. Number of Livestock-Producing Establishments by NAICS Code (1997 Ag Census)," in *Profile of the Agricultural Livestock Production Industry,* (EPA/310-R-00-002), U.S. Environmental Protection Agency, Washington, DC, September 2000

FACTORY FARMING

What Is a Farm?

The farming of livestock has changed dramatically over the past century. Many people think of a farm as a rural collection of barns and fields run by one farming family. In reality, some farms are massive industrial-type facilities owned and operated by large corporations. These are called factory farms. Although they make up a small percentage of American farms, they handle a large percentage of the animals killed for food in this country.

In its most recent Census of Agriculture (1997), the USDA defined a farm as an establishment that produces or sells $1,000 or more of agricultural products during a year. According to the 1997 census, there were more than 1.9 million farms in the United States, more than half of which produced livestock. The breakdown by animal type is shown in Figure 4.1. Cattle were raised at 78 percent of

farms, while equines, swine, poultry, sheep, and goats were raised at far fewer farms. The "other" category includes specialty animals, such as fur-bearing animals, honeybees, buffalo, llamas, snakes, and worms.

Consolidation of Agricultural Businesses

In 1997 approximately 86 percent of all farms were owned and operated by individuals and families. Partnerships accounted for 8.8 percent of farm ownership, and only 4.4 percent of establishments were owned by corporations. However, many small farms operate under contract to corporations. The farmers may sign away ownership of their animals and be paid to raise them to a contracted age or weight. Then, the animals are turned over to the companies for finishing or slaughtering.

Agribusiness underwent much consolidation between the 1950s and 1990s. For example, according to researchers at the University of Missouri, only four companies controlled 81 percent of the U.S. cattle slaughter/packing market in 2000: IBP Fresh Meats (a subsidiary of Tyson Foods, Inc.), Monfort Meats (part of ConAgra Foods), Excel Corporation (a subsidiary of Cargill, Inc.), and Farmland National Beef. Many corporations have vertically integrated their operations. In other words, they not only own facilities that raise animals, but they also own the facilities that produce feed for them and the facilities that slaughter and process them. Economies of scale—that is, larger volumes—allow corporations to spend less on each of these steps than small farmers do.

How Factory Farms Work

The most visible symbol of factory farming is the animal feeding operation (AFO) or concentrated animal feeding operation (CAFO). By federal definition, an AFO is a facility that "congregates animals, feed, manure and urine, dead animals, and production operations on a small area of land." The difference between an AFO and a CAFO is based in part on how many animals are involved. Both feature highly concentrated confinement areas with no pasture or grazing land.

In this way, the animals can be housed, fed, medicated, and processed with utmost efficiency. Every aspect of animal life and behavior is controlled to ensure that productivity and profits are maximized. The animals are kept in the smallest space possible and fed the cheapest food that will quickly and effectively fatten them up. Breeding facilities ensure a constant supply of replacements.

Modern technology is employed whenever it is economically feasible. Females are artificially inseminated rather than mated. Pregnancies are spaced close together to increase production. Mothers and offspring are separated quickly to keep the process moving. Antibiotics, hormones, and growth-enhancing drugs are administered to ensure rapid growth and to prevent deadly diseases.

FIGURE 4.2

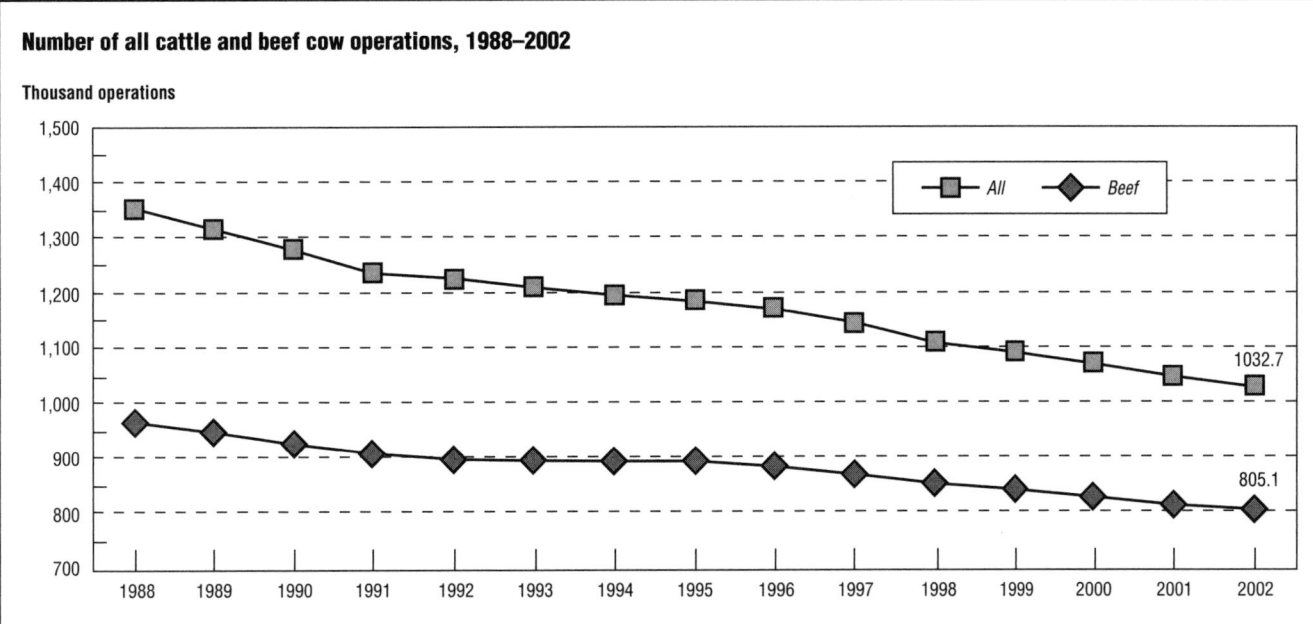

Number of all cattle and beef cow operations, 1988–2002

SOURCE: "Number of All Cattle and Beef Cow Operations, United States, 1988–2002," in *Cattle,* United States Department of Agriculture, National Agricultural Statistics Service, Washington, DC, January 31, 2003 [Online] http://www.usda.gov/nass/aggraphs/acbc_ops.htm [accessed May 20, 2003]

Slaughterhouses are run like assembly lines with an emphasis on speed and meat quality.

The Pros and Cons

The overwhelming advantage of the factory farming system to society is economics—satisfaction of supply and demand. Factory farming provides the United States with a continuous and relatively inexpensive meat supply. On the other hand, animal rights activists blame the factory farming system for many animal abuses. They believe that the industry's emphasis on profits, efficiency, and productivity has contributed greatly to inhumane treatment and sloppy slaughtering of farm animals.

There is no doubt that industrial methods have changed the way in which farmers and animals interact. Traditionally, farmers had a lot of personal interaction with their animals during feeding and handling. However, this did not change the ultimate usage of the animals. Some theorize it built a bond that led farmers to care more about the welfare of individual animals. Certainly sick or injured animals were more likely to be noticed and cared for in this system. Many small farms, particularly in communities that use traditional methods (such as Amish farms) still achieve this level of human-animal contact.

By contrast, factory farms are almost entirely automated. For example, in most chicken farms the food is dispensed by machines and the eggs are collected on conveyor belts. The chickens rarely see people until they are gathered by human handlers into crates for their journey to the slaughterhouse. Such automation in modern animal

husbandry saves money by reducing labor costs and increasing efficiency.

Factory farming is increasingly being criticized for adverse effects on the environment. AFOs and CAFOs produce incredibly huge amounts of manure and droppings. According to information available on its Web site in 2003, the Sierra Club says that factory farms produce 2.7 trillion pounds of waste each year. Traditionally, small farms have recycled manure by spreading it on their crops for fertilizer. This is not practical for large industrial operations. Most of them collect and store the waste in open lagoons or concrete cisterns. Runoff into streams, rivers, and lakes can kill fish and contaminate human drinking water supplies.

On its Web site in 2003, the Sierra Club claimed that 35,000 miles of rivers in 22 states and groundwater in 17 states has been polluted by hog, chicken, and cattle waste products. The Web site of the Humane Society of the United States (HSUS) in 2003 blamed Iowa's massive hog farms for contributing 25 percent of the pollutants found in the Mississippi River watershed. Factory farms, particularly those raising hogs, are also considered a hazard to air quality and are notorious for their odor problems.

CATTLE

Cattle are bovines that descend from ancient animals called aurochs. They have complex four-compartment stomachs called rumens and eat vegetation. In nature, cattle swallow their food whole. Later the partially digested food, or cud, is regurgitated into their mouths for them to chew. "Chewing the cud" is a well-known cattle trait. The natural lifespan for cattle is 20–25 years.

FIGURE 4.3

The Chicago stockyards, circa 1947. *National Archives and Records Administration*

There are many different breeds of cattle. Some are specially bred for meat (such as Angus and Hereford), while others are bred to produce milk (such as Jerseys). Adult female cattle are called cows. They produce milk for their newborn calves for months. People learned long ago to take calves away from their mothers and collect the milk for human consumption. Young female cows that have not yet given birth are called heifers. Uncastrated adult male cattle are called bulls. They are used only for breeding purposes. Male cattle castrated before they reach sexual maturity are called steers. They are a major source of beef in this country.

The 2002 USDA cattle inventory reveals that there were around 105 million cattle in this country in that year. Roughly one-third were beef cattle. Dairy cows were far less common—only about 9 million. As shown in Figure 4.2, there were more than 1 million cattle farms (including just over 800,000 beef cow farms) in the United States in 2002. In addition, the USDA reports that approximately 90,000 dairy farms operated in 2002.

Beef Cattle

HISTORY. At the beginning of the 20th century, America's cattle industry was concentrated in the western states. Cattle were herded by cowboys to markets in large cities with railroad hubs. Cattle were shipped by rail to massive stockyards and slaughter/processing centers in places like Chicago and Kansas City. (See Figure 4.3.) As refrigeration and electricity spread throughout the country, slaughterhouses were able to move away from the big cities and into rural areas.

During the 1950s, large meat companies began setting up feedlots for cattle, first in the Great Plains and later further west. (See Figure 4.4.) Before that time, cattle mostly ate grass, with some corn and other grains added to fatten them. They were slaughtered when they reached marketable size, around three to four years of age. America's farmers produced a surplus of corn in the mid-1950s, and it became a primary feed for beef cattle. Cattle fed a diet rich in corn got fatter much faster and could be slaughtered much earlier than grass-fed cattle. Corn-fed beef had a rich fatty taste with a marbled texture and was more tender than grass-fed beef. It was also much cheaper. Heavy marketing by grocery stores led to huge demand for corn-fed beef.

CURRENT CONDITIONS. Today most beef cattle are slaughtered around the age of 14–16 months. Calves

FIGURE 4.4

A cattle feedlot. *Photo Researchers, Inc.*

spend the first 6–8 months of their lives with their mothers, drinking milk and grazing on grass at farms and ranches around the country. This is called the "cow-calf" stage of the business. Following weaning, most calves are moved to large crowded feedlots—outdoor grassless enclosures—to be "finished" for slaughter. During finishing the cattle receive virtually no exercise to prevent muscle buildup and fat loss. The animals are given various drugs to help them digest the rich corn diet and fend off disease from the crowded and often dirty conditions.

In March 2002 reporter Michael Pollen purchased an eight-month-old calf from a South Dakota ranch and chronicled the calf's life for a newspaper article ("Power Steer," *New York Times,* March 31, 2002). Following weaning, Pollen's calf spent several months in a backgrounding pen becoming accustomed to a corn diet before being shipped to a feedlot. At the feedlot, crowded with 37,000 cattle, the calf was fed a diet of corn, fat, protein supplements, and some alfalfa hay and corn silage for roughage. The calf was given antibiotics to help it digest this new diet.

Pollen noted that feedlot cattle must be fed antibiotics and antacids to overcome digestive problems from eating corn rather than grass. Corn-fed cattle are prone to severe bloat, indigestion, and other conditions that can weaken

their immune systems and make them susceptible to serious diseases. Thus, many are fed continuous low-level doses of antibiotics to keep them reasonably healthy. The corn diet damages their livers, but this is a trade-off acceptable to the beef industry because cow liver is not in high demand. Pollen's steer also received a hormone injection of synthetic estrogen to help him gain weight, a common and legal practice.

According to Pollen, the cattle on the feedlot lived amidst a thick layer of manure during their entire stay, another reason that antibiotics are required for feedlot cattle. Generally manure is not a concern until slaughtering time, when it is washed off the carcasses during processing. Pollen suggests that this practice is not healthy for the people who will eat the beef or for the cattle living in this environment.

Ranchers use the feedlot system because it is much cheaper for them than finishing the cattle at the ranch. The price of beef is so low that profit margins on cattle are very slim. Ranchers and farmers must cut costs wherever they can. Many ranchers sell their calves to corporations and companies running feedlots. Others retain ownership and pay rent to the feedlot during the finishing process.

FIGURE 4.5

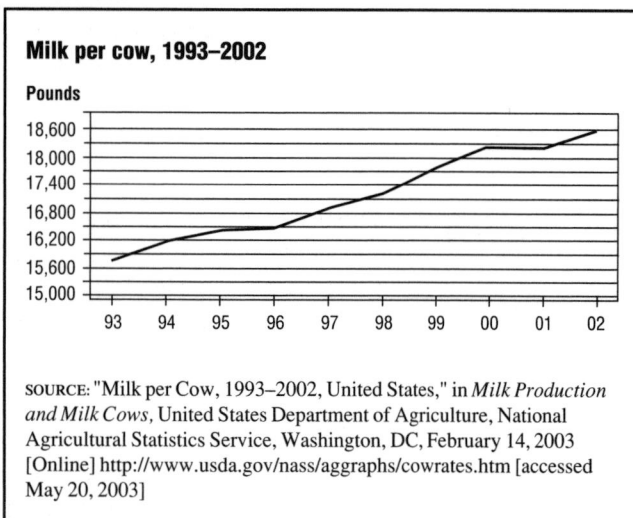

Milk per cow, 1993–2002

Pounds

SOURCE: "Milk per Cow, 1993–2002, United States," in *Milk Production and Milk Cows,* United States Department of Agriculture, National Agricultural Statistics Service, Washington, DC, February 14, 2003 [Online] http://www.usda.gov/nass/aggraphs/cowrates.htm [accessed May 20, 2003]

In April 2002 the PBS television program *Frontline* examined factory farming in a documentary titled *Modern Meat.* PBS interviewed various people involved in the beef industry, including Bill Haw, the chief executive officer of National Farms, a Kansas City beef company. Haw defended the feedlot system as humane, arguing that feedlot cattle are better fed, nourished, sheltered, and cared for than range cattle. He believes that if cattle had a choice "the vast majority of them would vote to be in the feedlot" because "all of their wants and needs are really taken care of in a very pampered sort of a way."

Dairy Cattle

Dairy cattle are a valuable commodity because they produce milk that can be consumed as a drink or used to make other dairy products. Average per capita consumption in the United States during 2000 was 25 gallons of milk, 30 pounds of cheese, and 4 pounds of butter. The combination of factory farming, high-tech breeding, and modern medicine means that the average dairy cow produced three times as much milk in 2002 as did a cow in 1955. Milk production per cow increased by 18 percent just between 1993 and 2002. (See Figure 4.5.)

While some people assume that dairy cattle spend leisurely days in rolling fields of grass and are only occasionally milked by machines, the reality is that dairy cows have become milk-producing machines. Most dairy cows live in small indoor stalls or are confined to large dirt pens called dry lots.

In order to produce milk, the cows must have calves. Modern farmers keep dairy cows pregnant almost continuously, often through artificial insemination. They take the calves away from their mothers as soon as possible after birth to prevent the calves from drinking the valuable milk. Male calves and any cows that cease to produce milk are slaughtered for beef. Common health problems in dairy cows include mastitis (an udder infection) and lameness due to back and leg problems.

Many dairy cattle are given antibiotics and other drugs on a routine basis. One of the most controversial drugs is called bovine growth hormone (BGH). BGH can increase by 25 percent the amount of milk that a cow can produce. Animal welfarists complain that BGH enlarges cows' udders to such a degree that the cows suffer from spine and back problems and have difficulty keeping their udders from dragging in dirt and manure. In a 1999 fact sheet, the Animal Protection Institute estimated that BGH was given to 7–25 percent of U.S. cattle. The use of BGH, which is also called bovine somatotropin or BST, is banned in Europe.

Another criticism of the factory farming of dairy cattle is that the cows spend long periods standing on hard surfaces. This includes concrete floors, metal gratings, and dirt-packed dry lots. Welfarists complain that this contributes to lameness problems in dairy cattle. Lameness is a major reason for cows to be culled (killed) during the raising process. Experts studying downed animals (those that cannot stand and walk because of injury or illness) arriving at slaughterhouses report that a large percentage of downers are dairy cows.

Veal

Veal is meat from very young calves that are raised in a way that produces tender, light-colored flesh. This meat is highly prized for its pale color and delicate flavor. Per information available on the Cattlemen's Beef Board and National Cattlemen's Beef Association Web site (www.veal.org) in 2003, U.S. veal production is 300–400 million pounds per year.

There are 3 main types of veal. Special-fed veal is the premier category and accounts for 85 percent of the veal consumed in this country. It is sold in upscale grocery stores and finer restaurants. It comes from calves that are fed a totally liquid diet consisting of reconstituted or liquid whey. The calves live for 16–20 weeks and may grow to 500 pounds. They are kept in very narrow stalls or boxes that prevent them from turning around and receive no exercise, because that would build muscle. Bob veal comes from calves that are fed a milk diet and slaughtered at around 150 pounds, typically 3 weeks of age. Grain-fed veal comes from calves started on milk and finished on grains and hay. They are slaughtered at age 5–6 months and weigh 450–600 pounds.

WHO PRODUCES VEAL? According to the book *Animal Liberation* by Peter Singer, the modern U.S. veal industry was started in 1962 by a company called Provimi, Inc. Provimi pioneered the use of a special mixture of proteins, vitamins, and minerals to bring veal calves to slaughter weight as quickly as possible with the most desirable flesh. According to the 2002 edition of *Animal Liberation,* Provimi controls as much as three-fourths of the U.S. veal market. According to the company's Web site in 2003, Provimi veal comes from calves that are "raised in environmentally controlled barns."

The American Veal Association (AVA) says that the seven major veal-producing states are Indiana, Maryland, Michigan, New York, Ohio, Pennsylvania, and Wisconsin. Most veal producers do not raise their own calves but purchase them at auction. Veal farmers typically use unwanted male calves from the dairy industry. Some dairy beef ranchers switch to raising veal when market conditions are favorable. According to information available on the AVA's Web site in 2003, the average veal farm is raising 250 calves at any given time.

THE CONTROVERSY. Veal production is harshly criticized by animal welfarists. They view the early separation of calves from their mothers and the extremely confined conditions under which the calves live as inhumane. Also, they accuse producers of feeding the calves diets that are extremely low in iron in order to prevent the flesh from darkening. This results in anemic calves that suffer from health problems and stress brought on by their living conditions. The British government has banned the use of veal crates that do not allow a calf to turn around and requires that calves be fed a diet containing sufficient iron and fiber.

American veal producers defend the use of individual stalls to raise their calves. They point out that this method reduces the spread of disease by preventing interaction between the calves. Each calf receives its own feed and does not have to compete with others for food. Also, each calf can receive individual attention to its nutrition and health needs. On its Web site in 2003, the AVA claimed that the stalls "are of adequate size to allow the calves to stand, stretch, lie down and groom themselves."

THE PREVALENCE OF VEAL. In 1986 there were 1.2 million calves raised for veal in the United States. This number has steadily decreased through 2003. However, because of the rising weight of calves at slaughter, the total pounds of veal available have decreased only slightly. Special-fed veal is a $700 million industry, the AVA's Web site reported in 2003.

Cattle Slaughter

Cattle slaughtered at federally-inspected slaughterhouses are required by law to be killed humanely. In most plants, the preferred method is use of a stun gun. Cattle are directed single-file through chutes that lead to the stunner. As each animal passes by, the stunner shoots a stun bolt into the animal's forehead to render it unconscious.

The animal is then hoisted up by one rear leg to hang from a bleed-rail. At that time, its throat is cut so that the blood can all drain out. Federal law requires that no animal fall into the blood of other slaughtered animals. This is why bloodletting is performed while the animal is suspended in the air. Following bloodletting, the animal moves down the line to a number of processing stations where the tail and hocks are cut off, the belly is cut open, and the hide is removed.

SPECIALLY DESIGNED METHODS. Dr. Temple Grandin is a professor at Colorado State University and a renowned expert on cattle handling and slaughter. She designed the systems in use at most U.S. slaughterhouses and has written numerous guidance documents for the American Meat Institute (AMI). The AMI is a large trade organization that represents people engaged in meat production and processing.

Dr. Grandin suffers from autism and says that this allows her to see the world "in pictures," as animals see it. She has published many books and articles on the proper design of livestock chute systems. For example, chutes must be curved to trick the animals into thinking they are going back to where they came. The chutes must have high walls to keep the animals from seeing what is going on around them. Each animal should only see the rear end of the animal in front of it as it walks toward the stunner.

Dr. Grandin's recommendations are designed to keep cattle moving efficiently and peacefully. This has both economic and welfare benefits. Cattle that balk (refuse to move ahead or try to go back down a chute) hold up production. Also, animals that panic are believed to release stress chemicals that taint their meat. Therefore, it is in the best interest of producers that their cattle remain calm in the slaughterhouse. Maintaining quiet and calm also leads to less stress for the animals, which is of importance to animal welfarists.

Dr. Grandin says that she is often asked if animals entering the slaughterhouse know they are about to die. She believes that the animals do not suspect their fate, because if they did, they would all balk and panic. She reports that cattle will calmly walk into restraining devices covered with the blood of other cattle, as long as the previous cattle were also calm. However, cattle will refuse to approach a location in which a stressed animal has been killed. Dr. Grandin believes that animals that become agitated for several minutes release fear pheromones that other animals can smell.

Dr. Grandin has developed an audit procedure with which slaughterhouses can be graded on how well they meet AMI guidelines. (See Table 4.4.) In 1996 Dr. Grandin conducted an audit for the USDA of 10 federally inspected slaughterhouses in various states. Only three of the plants were able to stun at least 95 percent of the cattle with a single shot. Grandin also described problems with poor equipment maintenance, lack of management supervision, excessive use of electric prods, transport of downed animals with forklifts, and other such practices.

TABLE 4.4

Cattle slaughter audit form

Plant_____ Auditor_____ Date_____ Contact Person _____ Line Speed _____

Numerical scoring of handling and stunning in slaughter plants. Score 100 cattle in plants with line speeds over 100 cattle per hour. Fifty cattle in slower plants.

CCP 1. Percentage of cattle stunned correctly on the first shot. Must be 95% or better for a minimum acceptable score. Missed cattle must be restunned immediately. 99% to 100% is excellent.

X = stunned correctly   _____ Percent stunned correctly
G = stunning failed due to lack of gun maintenance _____ Percent poor aim
A = missed stun due to poor aim   _____ Percent poor maintenance

Animal #
1__	2__	3__	4__	5__	6__	7__	8__	9__	10__	11__	12__	13__	14__	15__
16__	17__	18__	19__	20__	21__	22__	23__	24__	25__	26__	27__	28__	29__	30__
31__	32__	33__	34__	35__	36__	37__	38__	39__	40__	41__	42__	43__	44__	45__
46__	47__	48__	49__	50__	51__	52__	53__	54__	55__	56__	57__	58__	59__	60__
61__	62__	63__	64__	65__	66__	67__	68__	69__	70__	71__	72__	73__	74__	75__
76__	77__	78__	79__	80__	81__	82__	83__	84__	85__	86__	87__	88__	89__	90__
91__	92__	93__	94__	95__	96__	97__	98__	99__	100__					

CCP 2. Percentage of cattle that are insensible on the bleed rail. Must be 499/500 or better. The limbs may kick but the head must be limp and floppy. There is a zero tolerance for starting any slaughter procedure on an animal showing any sign of sensibility. On a 50 to 100 head audit must have 100% insensibility to pass the audit.

X = completely insensible
E = eye moves when touched   _____ Percent insensible
BL = blinking
RB = rhythmic breathing
VO = vocalization no matter how small (moo or bellow)
RR = righting reflex - animal attempts to lift head while hanging on the rail

Animal #
1__	2__	3__	4__	5__	6__	7__	8__	9__	10__	11__	12__	13__	14__	15__
16__	17__	18__	19__	20__	21__	22__	23__	24__	25__	26__	27__	28__	29__	30__
31__	32__	33__	34__	35__	36__	37__	38__	39__	40__	41__	42__	43__	44__	45__
46__	47__	48__	49__	50__	51__	52__	53__	54__	55__	56__	57__	58__	59__	60__
61__	62__	63__	64__	65__	66__	67__	68__	69__	70__	71__	72__	73__	74__	75__
76__	77__	78__	79__	80__	81__	82__	83__	84__	85__	86__	87__	88__	89__	90__
91__	92__	93__	94__	95__	96__	97__	98__	99__	100__					

CCP 3. Percentage of cattle prodded with an electric prod. In some plants depending on the layout, three CCP's can be observed simultaneously in the stunning chute area. Must be 25% or less for a minimum passing score. An excellent percentage is 5%.

X = moved quietly without an electric prod   _____ Percent electric prodding
P = electric prod   _____ Percent balking
A = used an abusive method such as hitting hard with a stick
B = electric prodded because the animal backed up and balked.
This indicates a facility problem.

Animal #
1__	2__	3__	4__	5__	6__	7__	8__	9__	10__	11__	12__	13__	14__	15__
16__	17__	18__	19__	20__	21__	22__	23__	24__	25__	26__	27__	28__	29__	30__
31__	32__	33__	34__	35__	36__	37__	38__	39__	40__	41__	42__	43__	44__	45__
46__	47__	48__	49__	50__	51__	52__	53__	54__	55__	56__	57__	58__	59__	60__
61__	62__	63__	64__	65__	66__	67__	68__	69__	70__	71__	72__	73__	74__	75__
76__	77__	78__	79__	80__	81__	82__	83__	84__	85__	86__	87__	88__	89__	90__
91__	92__	93__	94__	95__	96__	97__	98__	99__	100__					

CCP 4. Percentage of cattle that slip and fall during handling in the crowd pen, single file chute, or stunning box. A fall is recorded if the body touches the floor. This CCP should also be recorded in the truck unloading ramp. Must be 99% or better no falls and 97% or better no slipping. Slight slipping often occurs in stunning boxes and it makes the animal agitated and difficult to stun. Slight slipping must be noted.

X = no slipping or falling   _____ Percent falling
F = fell   _____ Percent slipping
S = slip
Where did slipping and falling occur? _____

Animal #
1__	2__	3__	4__	5__	6__	7__	8__	9__	10__	11__	12__	13__	14__	15__
16__	17__	18__	19__	20__	21__	22__	23__	24__	25__	26__	27__	28__	29__	30__
31__	32__	33__	34__	35__	36__	37__	38__	39__	40__	41__	42__	43__	44__	45__
46__	47__	48__	49__	50__	51__	52__	53__	54__	55__	56__	57__	58__	59__	60__
61__	62__	63__	64__	65__	66__	67__	68__	69__	70__	71__	72__	73__	74__	75__
76__	77__	78__	79__	80__	81__	82__	83__	84__	85__	86__	87__	88__	89__	90__
91__	92__	93__	94__	95__	96__	97__	98__	99__	100__					

In 1999 Grandin was hired by McDonald's Corporation to audit the company's beef and pork suppliers for their compliance with the standards. Grandin reports that compliance greatly improved after McDonald's fired a supplier that failed the audit. For example, 90 percent of the plants audited after that firing were able to stun at least 95 percent of the cattle with a single shot. In addition, the use of electric prods was reduced or eliminated, and most abusive behavior by employees stopped. (These data were reported in Temple Grandin, "Corporations Can Be Agents of Great Improvements in Animal Welfare and Food Safety and the Need for Minimum Decent Standards," National Institute of Animal Agriculture Seminar, April 4, 2001.)

PROBLEMS WITH THE PROCESS? Stories in the media in the late 1990s and early 2000s exposed some problems with slaughterhouse procedures. In 2001 the *Washington Post* published an article called "They Die Piece by Piece"

TABLE 4.4

Cattle slaughter audit form [CONTINUED]

CCP 5. Percentage of cattle that vocalize during handling or stunning in the crowd pen, single file chute, and the stunning box or restrainer. Score in these areas only. Score an animal as a vocalizer if it makes any audible vocalization. Must be 3% or less of the cattle moo or bellow. Each animal is scored on a yes/no basis vocalizer or nonvocalizer.

Reasons for Vocalization

X = non-vocalizer   _____ Percent vocalizing
P = prod
S = stun
F = fall or slipping
R = excessive pressure from restraint

Animal #	1__	2__	3__	4__	5__	6__	7__	8__	9__	10__	11__	12__	13__	14__	15__
	16__	17__	18__	19__	20__	21__	22__	23__	24__	25__	26__	27__	28__	29__	30__
	31__	32__	33__	34__	35__	36__	37__	38__	39__	40__	41__	42__	43__	44__	45__
	46__	47__	48__	49__	50__	51__	52__	53__	54__	55__	56__	57__	58__	59__	60__
	61__	62__	63__	64__	65__	66__	67__	68__	69__	70__	71__	72__	73__	74__	75__
	76__	77__	78__	79__	80__	81__	82__	83__	84__	85__	86__	87__	88__	89__	90__
	91__	92__	93__	94__	95__	96__	97__	98__	99__	100__					

Standards for Objective Numerical Percentage Scores

		American Meat Institute Guidelines		
	Actual %	Min. Passing Score	Excellent	Final Score / Excellent / Pass/Fail
1. Percentage stunned correctly with one shot		95%	99%	
2. Percentage rendered completely insensible prior to being hung on the bleed rail		100%	100%	
3. Percentage of cattle prodded with an electric prod		25%	5%	
4a. Percentage of cattle that slip		3%	0%	
4b. Percentage of cattle that fall		1%	0%	
5. Percentage of cattle vocalizing		3%	1%	

Reasons for scores that are not acceptable minimum passing score:
_____
_____
_____
_____

Walk Through Audit of Items that are not Numerically Scored

Pass/Fail

1. **Downers** - Handling of non-ambulatory animals. There is a zero tolerance for dragging sensible animals. To pass the audit, the plant must either stun non-ambulatory cattle on the truck or have a way to move them comfortably without dragging. Stunned cattle may be dragged consistent with the Humane Slaughter Act Regulations. Describe:
_____
_____
_____
_____

2. **Drinking water** - Is clean drinking water available in holding pens. Required by Humane Slaughter Act Regulations.
3. **Non-slip flooring** is required on unloading ramps, pens, alleys, chutes, and stunning areas.
    A. Stun Area _____
    B. Single File Chute_____
    C. Crowd Pen _____
    D. Holding Pen _____
    E. Unloading Ramp _____
4. **Pen condition** - Fencing must be in good repair and free of sharp edges that could cause bruises or injuries. Floors must drain and be free of large puddles. Describe:
_____
_____
_____
_____

5. **Pen stocking** - Are holding pens overcrowded? If cattle are held overnight there must be enough room for cattle to lie down.
6. **Truck unloading** - If possible, observe truck unloading. To pass, 75% of the animals should move at a walk or a trot and none fall down.
7. **Handling** - Cattle in the yards are moved at a walk or trot and none fall down.
8. **Cattle condition** - Note any animals that are in poor body condition (emaciated), advanced cancer eyes, or are obviously lame. Estimate percentage of animals with serious problems.

    A. Emaciated _____
    B. Advanced cancer eye_____
    C. Severe lameness / difficulty walking _____
    D. Non ambulatory Downers _____
    E. Foundered hooves - Double normal length _____

(Joby Warrick, April 10, 2001). The article analyzed USDA records and conducted interviews with current and former slaughterhouse workers and federal inspectors. The workers, who made about $9 an hour, claimed to have seen many conscious cattle moving down the bleed-rail.

A worker responsible for cutting off the cattle's hocks reported that dozens of conscious animals reached his station each day. He says the animals were blinking, moving, looking around, and making noises. Other workers also reported having to cut into living cattle. Workers in charge of stunning complained that the line moved so fast that they did not have time to do their job properly.

The *Post* article noted that the USDA has relaxed its oversight of slaughtering plants since 1998 and does not track the number of humane slaughter violations that occur each year. However, a records review showed that inspectors

TABLE 4.4

Cattle slaughter audit form [CONTINUED]

9. Acts of abuse - Was an obvious act of animal abuse observed such as poking an object into sensitive parts of the animal such as the eyes or anus? If yes, the plant fails the audit. Paralyzing conscious cattle with electricity is an automatic failure. See AMI guide for more information. Describe observations:

_____
_____
_____
_____

10. Stunner maintenance - Stunner maintenance program. Describe the program:

_____
_____
_____
_____

11. Employee training - Does the plant have an employee training program for animal handling and stunning? Describe:

_____
_____
_____
_____

12. Ritual Slaughter - The animal should be held in a comfortable upright position during ritual slaughter. Plants that shackle and hoist fully conscious animals or use devices that clamp the legs and feet of fully conscious animals will fail the audit. Describe the handling system:

_____
_____
_____
_____

13. Mud Score - Feedlot cattle.
    A. Clean animals. Some mud on ankles._____
    B. Mud on the legs and knees. Sides and belly clean._____
    C. Belly is mud caked. Sides are clean._____
    D. Belly and sides of the animal have mud caked on them._____

Final Scoring

To pass the audit the plant must have acceptable scores on the five numerically scored items. On the walk through items, they must comply with the guidelines of non-ambulatory animals, no obvious acts of cruelty and follow the guidelines on restraint and handling for ritual slaughter. Plants which fail on other walk through items would get a conditional pass and they would need to take corrective action.

	Pass or Fail
Numerically scored items	_____
Handling of non ambulatory cattle	_____
No acts of obvious abuse	_____
Ritual slaughter handling	_____

The above 4 items must receive a passing score to pass the audit at the minimum acceptable level. To receive an excellent rating, the numerically scored items must be at the excellent level and all walk through items must receive a passing score.

SOURCE: Temple Grandin, "Standards for Objective Numerical Percentage Scores," in *Cattle Slaughter Audit Form (Updated October 2001) Based on American Meat Institute Guidelines,* Temple Grandin's Web Page, Fort Collins, CO, October 2001 [Online] http://www.grandin.com/cattle.audit.form.html [accessed May 20, 2003]

---

found 527 violations in 1996–97, including incidents in which "live animals were cut, skinned, or scalded."

The *Post* claimed that secretly filmed videotapes from slaughterhouses showed blinking cattle hanging from bleed-rails. Other cattle twisted, turned, and arched their backs as if trying to pull themselves upright. Footage also showed squealing hogs being lowered into the scalding water baths that are designed to soften the hides of dead animals. Industry officials claimed that the videotaped incidents were staged by disgruntled employees and that unconscious animals kick and twitch by reflex.

Live animals on the bleed-rail are a danger to line workers. According to the *Post,* many workers are kicked by the animals and suffer broken bones and teeth. Although the line is supposed to be stopped when a conscious animal is detected, workers complained that this does not happen.

Animal welfare activists say that the allegations made in the *Washington Post* article are not unusual. They blame many of the problems on the extremely fast line speed at slaughterhouses and the use of low-paid workers. According to the *Post* article, most plants process around 400 animals per hour. This figure has more than doubled since the 1970s. Meatpacking is an extremely dangerous job. According to the U.S. Department of Labor, meat packers had the third highest rate of occupational injuries in 2001. In previous years, the industry has had the highest injury rate of all private industries.

Another major concern of welfarists relates to the problem of downed animals. According to the organization Farm Sanctuary, tens of thousands of farm animals become downed each year. These are animals (primarily dairy cattle) that collapse from illness, injury, or other causes. They are often tossed alive onto trash heaps, or dragged by chains or pushed by forklifts around stockyards and slaughterhouses. Animal rights activists consider processing of these animals inhumane and a possible threat to the safety of the U.S. meat supply (if the animals happened to be sick with diseases that could be transmitted to humans through meat consumption, such as mad cow disease).

In February 2001 Senator Daniel Akaka of Hawaii introduced a bill that would amend the Packers and Stockyards Act of 1921 to make illegal the transfer or marketing of nonambulatory livestock. The bill (H.R. 1421/S. 267) is called the Downed Animal Protection Act. The act, if passed, would require critically ill or injured farm animals be humanely euthanized at the stockyards. Although originally part of the 2002 Farm Bill, the act was stripped from the final version of that bill. It was expected to be reintroduced in 2003.

RITUAL SLAUGHTER. The Humane Methods of Slaughter Act does not apply to ritual slaughter—that is, slaughter conducted according to religious dictates. Ritual slaughter is practiced by some orthodox Jews and Muslims. Their teachings require that animals killed for food be moving and healthy when they are killed by having their throats slit. This was likely intended to ensure that sick animals were not eaten. However, strict interpretation of this directive means that cattle are not stunned prior to being bled out. They may be jerked up to the bleed-rail by a hind leg while still fully conscious. The jerking action can break the leg and tear apart joints, causing them severe pain. Their thrashing makes it more difficult for the cutter to cleanly cut their throats, which prolongs the entire process.

There are upright restraining devices that hold animals more humanely while their throats are being cut. The AMI strongly recommends the use of these devices, both for the welfare of the animals and the safety of the plant workers. Dr. Grandin reports that throat cutting must be done precisely with a long razor-sharp knife to induce "near-immediate collapse." Otherwise, the animal can remain conscious for more than a minute. Animals that struggle against their restraints or become agitated stay conscious the longest.

In his book *Animal Liberation,* Peter Singer complained that critics of ritual slaughter are often accused of being racist or anti-Semitic. He points out that portions of ritually killed animals wind up on supermarket shelves and are purchased by people who may not be aware of how the animal was killed. This is because Jewish law requires the removal of the lymph nodes and sciatic nerve from cattle. Singer says that this is difficult to do efficiently on the hindquarters of cattle, so often only the front portion is sold as kosher. The hindquarters are processed and sold in usual commercial markets.

POULTRY

Poultry are domesticated birds cultivated for their eggs or meat. This includes chickens, turkeys, geese, and ducks. Chickens are, by far, the most common type of poultry raised in America. The USDA estimated that there were 8.3 billion chickens living in the United States in 2002.

Chickens

Chickens were originally domesticated from wild Asian jungle fowl. In natural conditions, chickens tend to live in small groups composed of one male chicken (called a rooster or cock) and a dozen or more female chickens (called hens). Chickens are known for their hierarchy, or "pecking order." Each member of the group has a particular rank that determines its place in society. The average natural lifespan of a chicken is six to 10 years, although they can live to be as old as twenty-five.

Chickens are omnivores, meaning that they will feed on both vegetable and animal substances. They spend a good part of their day foraging and pecking at the ground for food. They also like to perch, flap their wings, and take dust baths. Hens prefer to lay eggs in a private nest. Young hens above the age of 5 months produce 200–300 eggs per year. Unless the hen has recently mated with a rooster, however, the egg is infertile and does not develop into a chick. In the wild, the hen would leave infertile eggs to rot or be eaten by predators.

CHICKEN BECOMES BIG BUSINESS. Prior to the 1920s, chicken meat was not common in the American diet. Female chickens were valued on the farm for egg production. Besides being sometimes used for cockfighting, male chickens were considered to have little value at all. They were relatively scrawny and aggressive. This began to change in the 1920s when enterprising farmers started cultivating chickens for meat. Scientific advances led to chicken breeds that were much meatier and grew faster. The use of vitamins, antibiotics, and growth hormones allowed mass production of chickens to become a thriving business. During the 1950s, producers began using large confined animal feeding operations (CAFOs).

Today, the vast majority of U.S. chickens are raised by contract farmers and finished in CAFOs. Nearly half of the chickens sold in the United States during 2001 were produced by only four companies: Tyson Foods, Gold Kist, Pilgrim's Pride, and ConAgra Foods.

Chickens raised in crowded conditions are prone to violent behavior. They peck and claw at each other, which can cause feather loss and even injury. Injured chickens may be pecked to death and even eaten by other chickens. It is common practice in factory farming of chickens to debeak a certain percentage of chickens by removing part of the upper and/or lower beak. Toe clipping involves cutting off parts of the chicken claw. Producers say that these practices are for the good of the chickens, to spare them injury. They claim that the chickens do not experience any pain because beaks are similar to human fingernails.

United Poultry Concerns (UPC) is a nonprofit group based in Maryland that is concerned with the treatment of domestic poultry. UPC claims that scientific studies show that chicken beaks contain nerves and pain receptors.

FIGURE 4.6

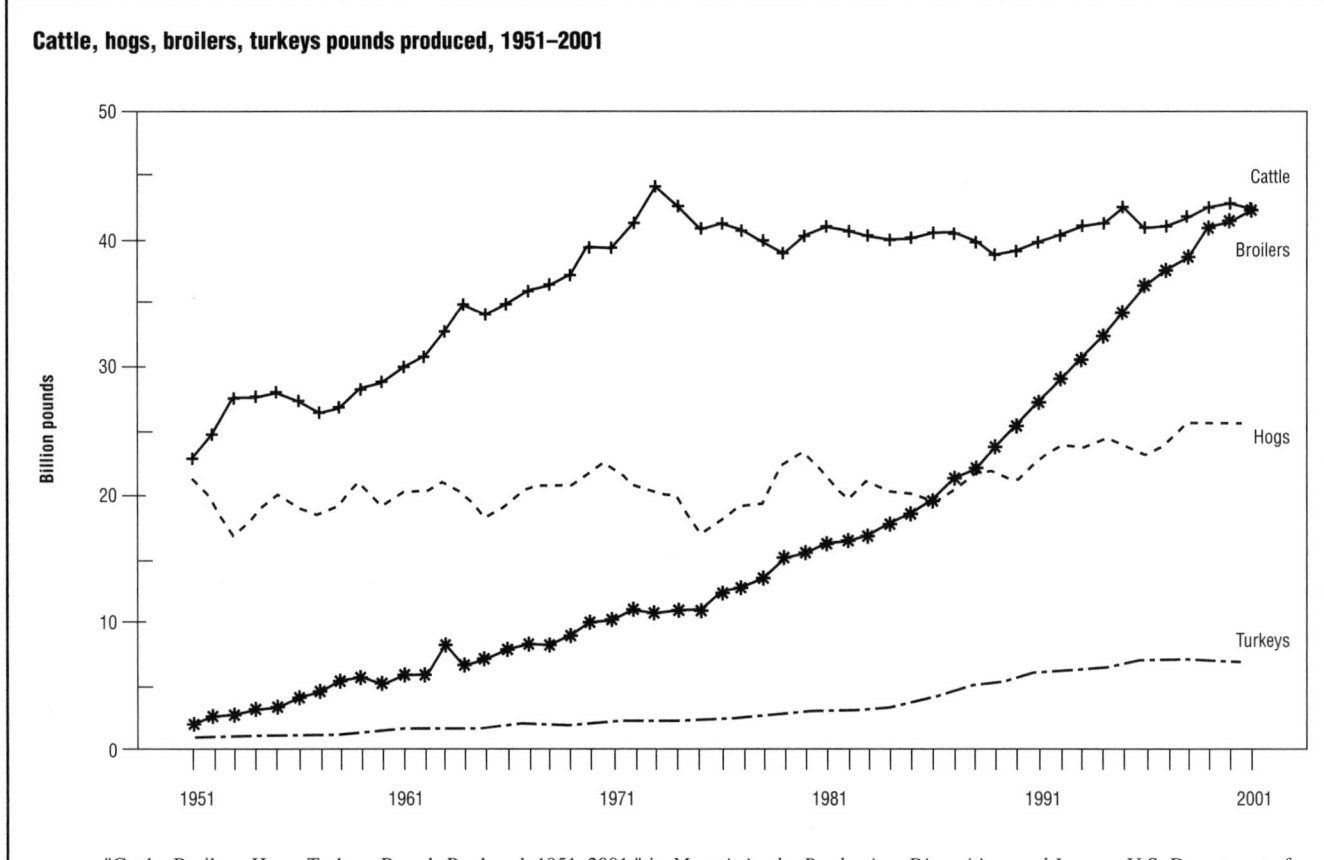

Cattle, hogs, broilers, turkeys pounds produced, 1951–2001

SOURCE: "Cattle, Broilers, Hogs, Turkeys Pounds Produced, 1951–2001," in *Meat Animals: Production, Disposition, and Income,* U.S. Department of Agriculture, National Agricultural Statistics Service, Washington, DC, April 2002 [Online] http://www.usda.gov/nass/aggraphs/lbspr.htm [accessed May 20, 2003]

Thus, UPC suggests, debeaked chickens suffer pain that is evident through their decreased desire to eat for several weeks following debeaking. The group describes debeaking operations as "haphazard and uncontrollable."

Animal welfarists say that debeaking and toe clipping would not be necessary if chickens were raised in more natural environments. They believe that it is the stress of living in cramped cages in buildings housing tens of thousands of other chickens that drives chickens to overly aggressive behavior. Instead of changing the way in which chickens are raised, producers accommodate these brutal systems by mutilating the chickens.

Chicken producers defend these practices as necessary. In March 2003 the National Chicken Council (NCC) made the following statement: "Today's chicken has been purposefully selected to thrive under modern management. We believe current good management practices that avoid destructive behavior, prevent disease, and promote good health and production, are consistent with the generally accepted criteria of humane treatment." On its Web site in 2003, the NCC stated, "Criticism of the industry's practices comes largely from people who are opposed to using animals for food under any circumstances."

Although there are many different breeds of chickens, they fall into two main categories: meat producers and egg producers. According to the USDA's 2002 inventory there were about 8 billion meat-producing chickens (broilers) and 335 million egg-laying chickens in the United States.

BROILERS. Broiler-type chicks are bred to gain weight fast so they can be used for meat. Although commonly called broilers, these chickens have different cooking names, depending on how they are raised and when they are slaughtered:

- Cornish hens are slaughtered at 5 weeks old and weigh around 2 pounds.

- Broilers or fryers are slaughtered at 7–8 weeks old and weigh 4–5 pounds.

- Roasters are slaughtered at 12–13 weeks old and weigh about 8 pounds.

- Capons are castrated at 3–4 weeks, slaughtered at 17–19 weeks, and weigh around 11 pounds.

Chicken meat is extremely popular in the United States. The total number of pounds of chickens produced for meat was the same as the number of pounds of cattle

FIGURE 4.7

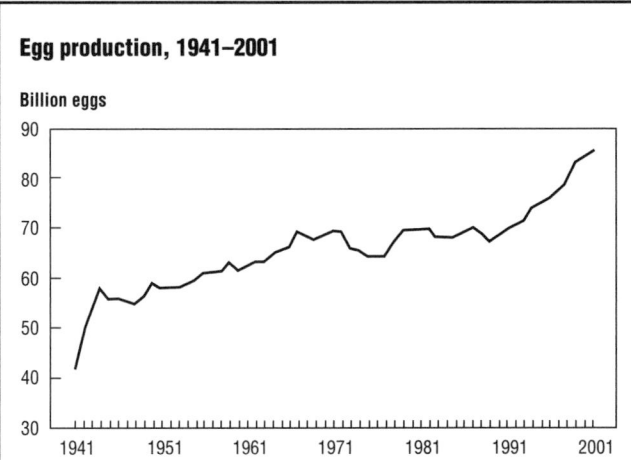

Egg production, 1941–2001

Billion eggs

TABLE 4.5

Percent of farm sites by number of square inches of floor space per hen placed, 1999

Number square inches	Percent farm sites	Standard error
Less than 48.0	16.6	(3.6)
48.0 - 53.9	45.1	(5.3)
54.0 or more	38.3	(6.2)
Total	100.0	

produced for meat in 2001. (See Figure 4.6.) Billions of broilers are raised each year to keep up with the demand for chicken meat.

Broilers start their lives at hatcheries. Day-old chicks are moved into chicken houses that may be hundreds of feet long and contain tens of thousands of chickens. These buildings are windowless and usually have dim lighting, because this is considered more calming. Under the crowded conditions and unused to the presence of humans, the chickens are prone to panic attacks at sudden loud noises. In modern chicken houses nearly everything is automated. Food and water are dispensed by machine. Broilers are routinely given antibiotics and other drugs to overcome disease and speed up growth.

LAYING HENS. Layers, or laying hens, are chickens bred for their egg-laying abilities. The chicks are sorted by sex when they are one day old. Only the females are kept. The males are discarded because they have not been bred for meat production and will not grow up to be plump and tasty, so are of no use for meat. According to animal rights groups, millions of culled male chicks are thrown into garbage bags where they suffocate. The poultry industry does not generally discuss its methods of culling male chicks, but it is widely believed that methods including suffocation and maceration (instantaneous death in a high-speed grinder) are commonly used.

U.S. egg production has more than doubled since the 1940s. As shown in Figure 4.7, around 85 billion eggs were produced in 2001, up from about 40 billion in 1941. These eggs are produced by millions of laying hens. Under natural conditions, hens can lay eggs for more than a decade, but egg-laying production of hens in factory farms ceases dramatically after the first year.

One method used by producers to rejuvenate laying is called forced molting. In forced molting all food is withheld from the hens for either a set number of days (usually 5–14), or until the hens lose a particular amount of weight. This forced fast mimics the conditions that wild chickens experience in the fall or winter when food is not as plentiful. Lower food intake causes a hen to molt (lose her feathers). Also, her reproductive system temporarily ceases producing eggs. When food is fully restored, the hen is much more productive at making eggs than she was before.

Many chicken producers use forced molting to extract more eggs from their chicken flocks. The USDA reports that 83 percent of egg-laying facilities used forced molting on a routine basis in 1999. Animal welfarists are extremely critical of forced molting, saying that because all food is withheld from the hens, it is much more brutal than natural molting. They equate the practice to forced starvation, and note that food deprivation for the purpose of forced molting is banned in Europe.

Once a hen dramatically reduces her egg output, she is considered "spent." Spent hens are slaughtered for lower-grade meat uses such as canned soups or pet food. They are replaced with young hens called pullets.

Welfarists point to data from the USDA to illustrate the point that laying hens are overcrowded and stressed by it. The National Animal Health Monitoring System's (NAHMS) *Layers '99* examined laying hens in 15 states, accounting for more than 75 percent of layers in the United States at the end of 1998. The study showed that the vast majority of the facilities had at least 4 rows (or batteries) of cages. Half of the facilities had cages stacked at least 3 tiers high. On average, each cage contained 5.6 hens. The average space for each bird was 53.4 square inches. About 1 out of 6 farms provided each bird with less than 48 square inches of space. (See Table 4.5.) For comparison purposes, a standard piece of notebook paper is 93.5 square inches.

As shown in Figure 4.8, one of the most widespread problems among laying hens in 1999 was cannibalism

FIGURE 4.8

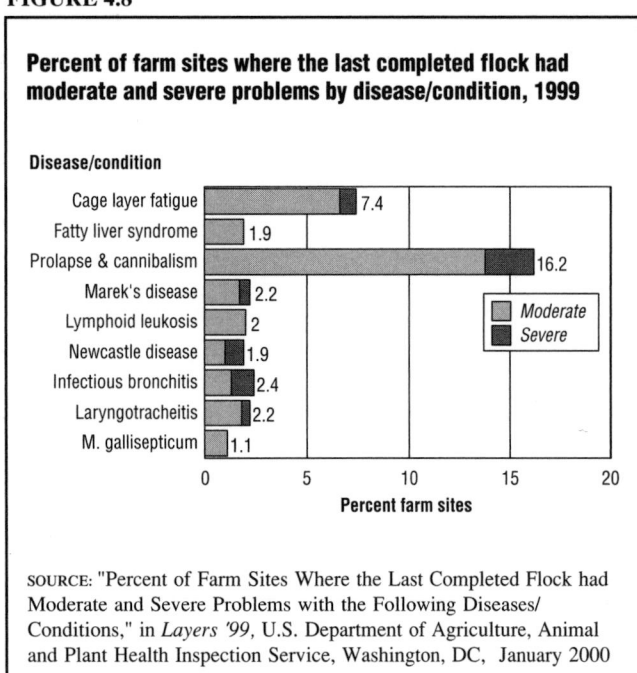

Percent of farm sites where the last completed flock had moderate and severe problems by disease/condition, 1999

Disease/condition

Disease/condition	Value
Cage layer fatigue	7.4
Fatty liver syndrome	1.9
Prolapse & cannibalism	16.2
Marek's disease	2.2
Lymphoid leukosis	2
Newcastle disease	1.9
Infectious bronchitis	2.4
Laryngotracheitis	2.2
M. gallisepticum	1.1

Moderate
Severe

Percent farm sites

SOURCE: "Percent of Farm Sites Where the Last Completed Flock had Moderate and Severe Problems with the Following Diseases/ Conditions," in *Layers '99*, U.S. Department of Agriculture, Animal and Plant Health Inspection Service, Washington, DC, January 2000

associated with prolapse. Prolapse is a condition in which a hen's shell gland does not retract. When a hen lays an egg, a gland from her reproductive tract temporarily protrudes and is turned inside out as the egg leaves her body. If this gland does not retract back into her body as it should, other hens will peck at it. If pecking draws blood, the hens may go into a frenzy, peck the prolapsed hen to death, and eat her.

Egg producers blame prolapse on a variety of physical factors, including weak muscle tone. Beak trimming is commonly seen as the best method to prevent injuries and deaths associated with prolapse. Animal welfarists, on the other hand, believe that cannibalism is aggravated by the stressed and overcrowded conditions in which the hens are forced to live.

In early 2002 egg producer Cypress Foods went out of business. The company had about 1.7 million layers in facilities in Georgia and Florida at the time. Animal rights groups say that 20,000–30,000 of the hens starved to death after the company declared bankruptcy. Another half a million hens had to be euthanized by authorities because they were half-starved and not salvageable. State authorities refused to prosecute the company for animal cruelty, saying that the deaths were due to economic factors rather than criminal intent. A spokesman for the animal welfare group Farm Sanctuary criticized the decision, saying "running out of money is no defense for animal cruelty."

The U.S. poultry industry had to destroy millions of birds in California, Nevada, and Arizona beginning in 2002 because of exotic Newcastle disease (END). END is a highly contagious and deadly viral disease that affects

birds' nervous, respiratory, and digestive systems. Industry and government officials feared that millions of birds would have to be killed as a preventative measure to halt the spread of the disease.

In early 2003 a mass chicken kill at the Ward Egg Ranch near San Diego, California, received widespread media attention. Employees reportedly tossed more than 30,000 live chickens into wood chippers to dispose of them. The chickens were spent hens that were no longer wanted. Ordinarily, they would have been shipped to a slaughterhouse in northern California. However, the county had enacted a chicken quarantine because of fears about the spread of END in the state.

Local authorities were harshly criticized by animal welfare groups, including the HSUS, for not filing animal cruelty charges in the case. The county district attorney defended the decision, saying that the ranch owners did not act with criminal intent. Also, the owners insisted that they had consulted with a veterinarian before destroying the animals and were told that use of a wood chipper was acceptable.

CHICKEN SLAUGHTER. When they are ready to go to the slaughterhouse, chickens are gathered by their feet by handlers, who carry them upside down to put into crates. At the slaughterhouse the chickens are shackled upside down by their feet to a conveyor belt. The Humane Methods of Slaughter Act does not apply to poultry, which means that chickens do not have to be stunned unconscious before having their throats slit. However, some plants do use a stunning method based on electricity.

Each live chicken strapped to the conveyor belt has its head dunked into a water bath containing salt. An electric current is passed through the shackles to knock the chicken unconscious. Immediately the birds pass by an automated cutting blade that slits their throats. After the blood is drained (about 90 seconds) the birds are dipped into scalding water baths to loosen their feathers before moving on to cutting stations.

In January 2003 PETA and UPC obtained a signed affidavit from a former worker at a chicken slaughterhouse in Arkansas. The man, who worked at the plant from 1997 to 2002, claims to have witnessed many acts of brutality toward the birds. He says that other workers regularly ran over chickens with forklifts, stomped them to death, and threw snowballs made of dry ice at them for fun. He also claims that chickens were often not stunned or killed prior to entering the scalding baths. He describes working one night when equipment breakdowns delayed the conveyer belt and allowed stunned chickens to wake up before their throats were slit. The workers did not have time to do the slitting so they sent the chickens straight to the scalding baths. The animal welfare groups turned the affidavit over to local authorities in hopes that cruelty charges will be brought against the workers named.

Turkeys

Turkeys are one of the few domesticated animals native to North America. Today's turkeys have little resemblance to their wild ancestors, however. They have been bred to gain weight quickly, particularly in the breast. Around 275 million turkeys were being raised in the United States in 2002. According to National Turkey Federation statistics from the same year, 46 million turkeys are eaten at Thanksgiving, 22 million at Christmas, and 19 million at Easter. Annual per capita turkey consumption increased from 8.7 pounds in 1974 to 17.9 pounds in 2002. Americans ate 5 billion pounds of turkey in 2002.

Turkeys are raised much the same way that broiler chickens are raised. At around six weeks of age, the baby birds are moved into growing houses in which they spend the remainder of their lives. Conditions there are crowded, as they are for chickens, and can lead to feather pecking and cannibalism. Turkeys are slaughtered similarly to chickens at around three to six months of age.

Ducks and Geese

Domestic ducks and geese are raised for their meat, eggs, and feathers. The most controversial product associated with these poultry is *foie gras,* which is pronounced "fwah grah" and means "fat liver" in French. The birds are force-fed a very rich corn diet over a short amount of time to make their livers fatty and hugely swollen, six to ten times their normal size.

The feeding process, called *gavage,* is usually started 2–4 weeks before slaughter. It is accomplished using an electronic pump that forces food through a 12- to 16-inch tube that is placed down the bird's throat. The birds are force-fed several times a day and held in cramped cages or pens so that they cannot move. This prevents them from losing weight during the fattening process.

Animal welfarists are highly critical of *gavage.* The HSUS says that the birds suffer pain from swollen abdomens and lesions in their throats. The organization also says that autopsies conducted on dead birds subjected to *gavage* show severe liver, heart, and esophagus disorders.

Foie gras is a gourmet delicacy that is very expensive, around $40 per pound. It is available at upscale restaurants and specialty stores. Most foie gras comes from France. As of 2003, there were only two commercial producers in the United States, both of which used ducks, located in the Hudson Valley of New York and the Sonoma Valley of California. The producers defend the use of the gavage process, saying that it does not gag the birds because they do not chew their food anyway.

HOGS AND PIGS

Hogs and pigs are domestic swine. A pig is a young swine that is not yet sexually mature. A young female hog

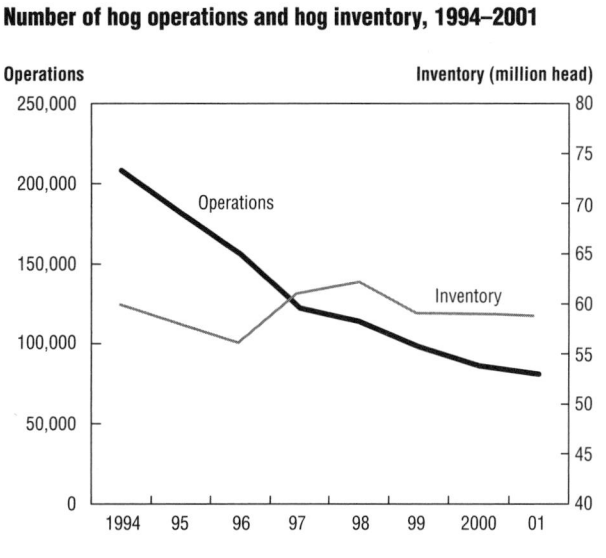

FIGURE 4.9

Number of hog operations and hog inventory, 1994–2001

Note: An operation is any place having one or more hogs on hand at any time during the year.

SOURCE: William D. McBride and Nigel Key, "Figure 3: Number of U.S. Hog Operations and Hog Inventory," in *Economic and Structural Relationships in U.S. Hog Production* (AER-818), United States Department of Agriculture, Economic Research Service, Washington, DC, February 2003

is called a gilt. A female adult hog is called a sow. Hogs are curious and intelligent animals, supposedly smarter than dogs. They have very sensitive noses, which they use to root around the ground for their food and explore their surroundings. Pregnant sows like to build nests of grass. Under natural conditions, sows give birth to (farrow) a litter of piglets twice a year. Each litter includes 8 piglets, on average, that suckle for about 3 months. The normal life expectancy of a hog is 12–15 years.

The Modern Hog Industry

Hogs have been popular farm animals for centuries. According to the USDA, the 1850 agricultural census showed an inventory of around 30 million swine. This number doubled to 60 million by 1900. At that time, 76 percent of American farms produced hogs. Hogs were favored because hog meat and fat were so versatile. Pork could be canned, smoked, or cured to provide food for long periods of time. Lard, or fat produced from hogs, was widely used as cooking oil and in making candles.

Today the U.S. inventory of hogs is around 59 million, only slightly less than a century ago. (See Figure 4.9.) However, hogs are now produced on only 4 percent of the country's farms. The hog industry has undergone tremendous consolidation, and 5 companies control two-thirds of the market: Tyson Industries, Smithfield, ConAgra Foods, Excel, and Farmland. According to the USDA, nearly 75 percent of all hog farms in 2001 had at least 2,000 hogs. This percentage was double the 1994 level.

Hog production takes place mostly in the Midwest and South. Iowa was, by far, the top-producing state as of March 2003 in terms of number of hogs. North Carolina, Minnesota, Illinois, and Indiana completed the top five states.

The vast majority of hogs raised in the United States are concentrated on a few massive CAFOs. These facilities not only finish the hogs, as is done in the cattle industry, but actually raise them. Major pork producers operate farrowing complexes, nurseries, and growing-feeding units.

Hog-Raising Practices

Confinement buildings for hogs can be hundreds of feet long and contain up to 12,000 hogs. They typically feature concrete or slatted floors—concrete floors can be easily cleaned and slatted floors allow manure and urine to fall into pits below. Hogs are kept on short tethers or confined in cages and pens to prevent them from getting exercise, which might build muscle instead of fat and toughen the meat. Crowded conditions can lead to aggressive behavior among the hogs, including tail chewing, biting, and fighting. Tail docking and teeth clipping are commonly practiced to help prevent injuries from these behaviors. Antibiotics, hormones, and other drugs are routinely administered to speed growth and prevent deadly diseases.

GESTATION CRATES. Breeding sows are often kept in individual stalls or confined with tethers until they are ready to farrow. Gestation crates, as they are called, are typically around seven feet long and just wide enough for the sow to lie down but not turn around (about two feet). The sow eats, urinates, and defecates where she stands. When she is ready to give birth, the sow may be moved to a farrowing pen in which she and her piglets will be kept tightly confined.

The use of gestation crates has been banned in the United Kingdom and Sweden. The European Union plans to phase out use of the crates over the next 10 years. In November 2002 Florida voters passed an amendment to the state constitution that will outlaw the use of gestation crates. The move is largely symbolic, as the state is not a major hog producer. Following the vote, the Florida Farm Bureau reported that only two small hog farms in the state used gestation crates, and that one of them had already shut down and the other was phasing out of business. According to the USDA's *Swine 2000* report, 83.4 percent of sows are farrowed in total confinement facilities and 81.8 percent of pigs are raised in total confinement nurseries.

Industry officials defend the use of gestation crates, saying that the crates are necessary to keep aggressive sows from fighting with each other over food. Fighting can cause injuries that lead to aborted fetuses. Pork producers believe that caged sows receive beneficial individual attention to their health and nutrition needs. The National Pork Producers Council says that hogs are better off raised indoors because they are protected from "extreme changes in temperature, snow, rain, mud and parasites."

SEGREGATED EARLY WEANING (SEW). Pork producers increasingly use artificial insemination and early separation of piglets from their mothers to produce more piglets each year. Early separation is possible because piglets can be bottle-fed by machines. Pork producers call it segregated early weaning (SEW). An undated publication of the National Pork Board in reaction to a December 1996 meeting called SEW an "exciting breakthrough" for improving profits in the industry (Steve Meyer and Bill Lazarus, *How Can We Price Early-Weaned Pigs?*, National Pork Producers Council).

The document recommends SEW be done before the piglets reach 19 days old. The primary advantage of SEW is that young nursing piglets receive high levels of natural antibodies from the sow's milk. This protection only lasts for about three weeks. After that, the piglets are more susceptible to diseases and can catch them from their mothers. SEW gives the piglets a better chance of remaining disease-free later, in the growing-feeding units where they are often susceptible to respiratory problems.

OTHER PRACTICES. Generally, week-old pigs are subjected to teeth clipping, tail docking, and ear notching. The males are castrated at this time. These procedures are done without anesthesia. Once the piglets reach around 55 pounds, they are moved to indoor finishing pens. Piglets are raised to slaughter weight, typically 250 pounds, at around 4–6 months of age. Spent breeding sows are usually slaughtered around 2–3 years of age.

According to the USDA's *Swine 2000* report, nearly 18 percent of sows and gilts were culled during the first 5 months of 2000. The primary reasons were age (42 percent), reproductive failure (21 percent), and lameness (16 percent). Respiratory disease was also a cause of mortality, accounting for 28.9 percent of nursery deaths and 39.1 percent of deaths in grower/finisher pigs.

Animal welfarists are critical of hog-raising practices in the United States. They consider the intense confinement too stressful for intelligent and social animals like hogs. They also condemn early weaning as cruel to sows and piglets. Factory-farmed hogs not only suffer from excessive crowding, stress, and boredom but also experience serious breathing disorders because of high concentrations of ammonia from their waste materials. Critics also say that hogs experience feet and leg deformities from standing on floors made of improper materials.

Hog Slaughter

Hogs are generally killed via electrocution or by stunning followed by bleeding out. Electrocution is accomplished by stunning the hog with a wand with sufficient

FIGURE 4.10

Dead hogs being processed at a meat-packing plant. *The Library of Congress*

shock to stop its heart. This is called cardiac arrest stunning and is the technique most large hog slaughter plants use. Hogs can also be given an electrical shock to the head to render them unconscious. Next, the animals are hoisted up by their back feet and bled via a small incision in the chest. Fully electrocuted hogs are also bled out in this manner. The dead hogs are then lowered into vats of scalding water to remove hair. The meat can then be processed. (See Figure 4.10.)

According to Dr. Temple Grandin's instructions for electrical stunning, a hog stunned with sufficient amperage in the correct location will feel no pain. Insufficient amperage and an improper current path will cause the animal pain. Dr. Grandin recommends that head-stunned hogs be bled out within 30 seconds of being stunned to prevent them from regaining consciousness.

HORSES

In 1900 approximately 20 million horses lived on U.S. farms. In 1999 that number was 2–3 million. The country's total horse inventory is somewhere around 5 million; however, this figure includes horses kept for racing, breeding, showing, and pleasure purposes.

Although horses are not specifically cultivated in this country for meat for human consumption, there is a growing overseas market for this meat, primarily in Europe and Asia. Horse meat is increasingly popular among Europeans because of the scares concerning mad cow disease. According to the USDA, 42,312 horses were slaughtered in the United States for human consumption in foreign countries in 2002.

Controversy over Premarin

One issue of concern to animal rights activists is the use of urine from pregnant mares (pregnant mare urine, or PMU) to provide an estrogen drug called Premarin. Premarin is widely used by menopausal women as an estrogen replacement therapy. It is also prescribed for people suffering from heart disease and osteoporosis. On its Web site in 2003, the HSUS estimated that there were approximately

500 PMU farms in North America, mostly in western Canada, and that more than 100,000 horses were involved in the PMU industry.

PMU-producing mares are tethered in tight stalls for 6–7 months of their 11-month pregnancies. A collection system including a rubber cup is placed beneath each mare's vulva to collect her urine. Welfarists complain that the horses are prevented from moving around and usually cannot lie down in a comfortable position. The mares are released from the system to give birth and then are reimpregnated as soon as possible. The HSUS claims that spent mares often wind up at slaughterhouses. They have little commercial value because they receive no training in riding and are difficult to handle.

FISH

According to the United Nations, fish farming, or aquaculture, accounted for 42 million tons of fish production worldwide and 29 percent of the world's fish supply in 2001. Fish farming has been around for at least a millennium. Historians believe that the Chinese practiced aquaculture around 900 A.D. to raise fish for their emperor's dinner table. China is still a leading producer of farmed fish. Commercial aquaculture is also a big business in the United States. Nearly all of the rainbow trout and catfish raised in this country come from farm operations. Besides freshwater fish, saltwater fish are also raised in farm environments.

Fish farming is accomplished in one of two ways. Producers use netted enclosures in near offshore ocean waters or they build separate enclosures inland. The second method is considered more environmentally friendly because the farmed fish and their waste are separated from fish living in natural waters. In-ocean farms occasionally lose fish to the surrounding waters, and environmentalists fear that these fish could spread diseases to their wild counterparts. In-ocean farms can also only be used for saltwater species, not freshwater. Fish farms typically keep as many fish as possible in the smallest amount of space possible. These confined operations can cause health problems, particularly sea lice infestation, in the farmed fish.

OTHER FARM ANIMALS

Several other animal species are farmed for meat and other products in the United States, mainly sheep, goats, honeybees, rabbits, and bison (buffalo).

Sheep and Goats

SHEEP. According to the USDA, there were around 6.5 million sheep on U.S. farms in 2002. Just over 3.3 million of them were slaughtered for food, producing 222 million pounds of meat. Lambs accounted for 95 percent of the slaughtered sheep. Most meat sold as lamb comes from animals that are less than 14 months old. Major lamb markets are metropolitan areas of the Northeast and West Coast with large populations of people from the Middle East, Greece, the Caribbean, and African countries. Demand for lamb meat in these markets is higher than the domestic supply. The USDA estimates that lamb imported from Australia and New Zealand satisfies one-third of U.S. demand. Lamb legs and loins are the preferred cuts of meat in the United States. Less desirable cuts are widely used in the pet food industry. Texas accounted for nearly one-sixth of the total sheep inventory during 2002, the largest of any one state.

Sheep herds have diminished significantly in the United States since 1942, when there were more than 50 million of the animals. USDA statistics from June 2003 show that per capita consumption of lamb and mutton (meat from adult sheep) in the United States decreased from nearly five pounds per year in the 1960s to just over one pound. The USDA blames competition from poultry, pork, and beef, and "declining acceptance of lamb" as the reasons for decreased consumption in the United States.

Nearly 5.5 million sheep and lambs were shorn in 2002, resulting in 41 million pounds of wool. Wool production was down 60 percent from the late 1970s. Farmers raising sheep balance production of meat and wool animals depending on market demand. When demand for wool increases, fewer animals are sent to slaughter and vice versa. The 2002 Farm Bill implemented financial incentives for sheep farmers to produce more wool over the time period 2002–2007. This is expected to increase domestic wool production.

GOATS. The USDA estimates that around 2 million goats were raised on U.S. farms in 2002. Nearly 600,000 were slaughtered for food in federally-inspected slaughterhouses. Most goat meat consumption in the United States is associated with ethnic populations (particularly Hispanics and people from the Middle East and Africa). Demand is seasonal and peaks around religious holidays, such as Christmas, Easter, and the Muslim festival Ramadan. In 1997 the USDA estimated that approximately 11,000 goats were kept on U.S. farms for milk and cheese production.

During 2002 there were around 280,000 goats of the Angora breed raised for their mohair (long silky hair used to make fabrics). The vast majority of these goats (99 percent) were farmed in Arizona, New Mexico, and Texas. Just over 2 million pounds of mohair were produced in 2002. Mohair goats are generally shorn twice a year, in the spring and the fall.

CONTROVERSY OVER WOOL AND HAIR COLLECTION. Animal rights activists are opposed to the harvesting of wool and hair from sheep and goats. On its Web site in 2003, PETA claimed that animals suffer from brutal treatment and bloody wounds during shearing. PETA says that sheep, goats, and other animals raised for their wool or hair are bred to produce overheavy coats that cause the animals to suffer from the heat during warm weather. Likewise, the shorn animals can suffer from cold exposure.

Bees

The USDA reports that 2.5 million honeybee colonies were kept in the United States in 2002, producing 171 million pounds of honey. Honey production was down 8 percent from 2001. California was home to 440,000 of the colonies, the most for any one state. Animal rights groups are critical of beekeeping because the bees are kept in captivity. PETA claims that commercial beekeepers often cut the wings off of queen bees to keep them from moving the hive.

Sericulture and Down Production

Other farming methods not widely practiced in the United States draw criticism from animal rights groups. These include sericulture (silkworm cultivation) and the plucking of downy feathers from geese and ducks. Sericulture is widely practiced in China to harvest silk fibers. The fibers are produced by silkworm larvae when they weave elaborate cocoons around themselves. The live larvae are boiled or baked to death in order to detach the silk fibers from the cocoons. Approximately 3,000 cocooned larvae are needed to produce a single pound of silk. Down production involves the plucking of soft underbelly feathers from geese and ducks. Plucking down from live birds is practiced in some eastern European countries and is considered cruel by animal rights activists and welfarists.

Rabbits

MEAT. Although the USDA does not consider rabbits livestock animals, there is a meat rabbit industry in the United States. The Professional Rabbit Meat Association (PRMA) is a nonprofit organization devoted to growing and processing rabbits for meat, either commercially or in backyard operations. Rabbit meat is classified similarly to poultry. Young, tender rabbits are sold as fryers, while older rabbits are sold as stewers. The New Zealand white rabbit is the most popular meat breed.

According to an article in the November/December 2001 issue of the PRMA newsletter, approximately 1 million fryer rabbits are sold in the United States annually. Meat rabbit farming is far more prevalent in Italy and France, where up to 300 million of the animals are slaughtered for food each year (Max Raivio, "Modern Rabbit Production").

FUR. Rabbits are also farmed for fur and hair. The USDA's 1997 Census of Agriculture found that approximately 13,000 American farms were raising 530,000 rabbits for their pelts or hair. The most popular fur rabbits are hybrid Rex rabbits featuring thick, plush fur. Angora rab-

bits are prized for their long silky hair. The hair is generally collected by plucking or combing the rabbits.

Bison

The USDA reports that 25,340 bison (buffalo) were slaughtered at federally-inspected plants in 2002. Buffalo meat is being heavily marketed by entrepreneur Ted Turner of Atlanta, Georgia. In June 2003 the *Boston Globe* reported that Turner owns 35,000 bison at his ranches in Montana, New Mexico, and Nebraska. The entire U.S. buffalo population is estimated to be around 300,000. In 2001 Turner opened a chain of restaurants called Ted's Montana Grills that feature buffalo meat. He also formed a company called U.S. Bison to market buffalo meat to upscale restaurants and consumers.

WELFARE-FRIENDLY FARMING?

The most strict animal rights activists are opposed to the farming of animals to produce products for human consumption and use. They often embrace a vegan lifestyle, in which such products are not consumed or used. Still others are vegetarians. Vegetarians do not eat meat, but may consume secondary products, such as milk or eggs. For example, lacto-vegetarians eat dairy products, while ovo-vegetarians eat eggs. Lacto-ovo vegetarians eat both.

Vegans and vegetarians make up a small but increasing minority of the U.S. population. National polling conducted in 2000 by Zogby for the Vegetarian Resource Group suggests that 2.5 percent of U.S. adults consider themselves strict vegetarians. This equates to roughly 5 million people. Many more people are part-time vegetarians or occasionally eat vegetarian meals. Not all vegetarians embrace their chosen diet for animal rights reasons—many have health, environmental, and/or religious reasons instead of or in addition to ethical ones.

There is also growing demand in the United States for meat and other products from animals that are raised or slaughtered using more humane methods. Food suppliers are beginning to make changes that represent significant reforms in animal welfare and slaughter. Some of these changes have no doubt been driven by pressure from vocal animal rights groups. For example, PETA has been conducting aggressive publicity and picketing campaigns against major fast-food chains in the United States, and many fast-food chains are implementing more welfare-friendly policies. Some of these include:

- In 1999 the McDonald's Corporation established new animal welfare principles for its meat suppliers. The company began auditing the handling and slaughtering practices used by its beef suppliers and fired one supplier after it failed the audits. In 2001 the company added guidelines for laying hen suppliers that require more cage space per hen and forbid the practice of forced molting.

- The Wendy's Corporation adopted the AMI animal welfare guidelines for beef and pork in 1998 and established an animal welfare council to oversee company animal policies. In 2002 Wendy's reported that it had forbidden its suppliers to use forced molting to increase egg production.

- Burger King Corporation announced in 2002 that it was working with animal industry groups to create uniform standards for the humane handling of food animals. The company also created an auditing program and planned to initiate audits for its suppliers in late 2003. Burger King introduced the BK veggie burger (a vegetarian burger) to its menu in 2002, drawing praise from vegetarians and animal rights groups.

- In May 2003 the Kentucky Fried Chicken (KFC) Corporation announced plans to adopt new guidelines and auditing procedures for its poultry suppliers. These include increasing the cage space for chickens and installing video cameras in slaughterhouses to ensure that proper procedures are followed. As of 2003, the company also is investigating the use of gas to kill chickens at slaughter plants.

Animal rights groups claim that all of the welfare incentives implemented by these companies were driven by pressure from animal rights activists. Although the companies deny it, there is no doubt that some animal rights groups (particularly PETA) have conducted aggressive public relations campaigns against them. In 2003 PETA launched a publicity blitz against KFC, calling the company "Kentucky Fried Cruelty" and criticizing it harshly for the treatment of chickens by its suppliers.

In June 2002 the National Council of Chain Restaurants and the Food Marketing Institute published new welfare recommendations for suppliers providing meat products to their members. According to information on their Web site in 2003, the two organizations represent nearly 150,000 stores and restaurants across the country. They made a number of recommendations that would improve the housing and care of the animals involved. Although compliance with the guidelines is voluntary, many people believe that it is a hopeful start to true reform in farm animal welfare.

Some farmers have initiated reforms on their own. For example, some smaller hog farms are allowing their sows to farrow in straw-filled huts or barns instead of in gestation crates. Welfare-friendly farming is considered part of a larger movement called organic farming. Organic farming of crops involves no use of pesticides and herbicides. This produces a more natural product that many consumers consider healthier and more environmentally

FIGURE 4.11

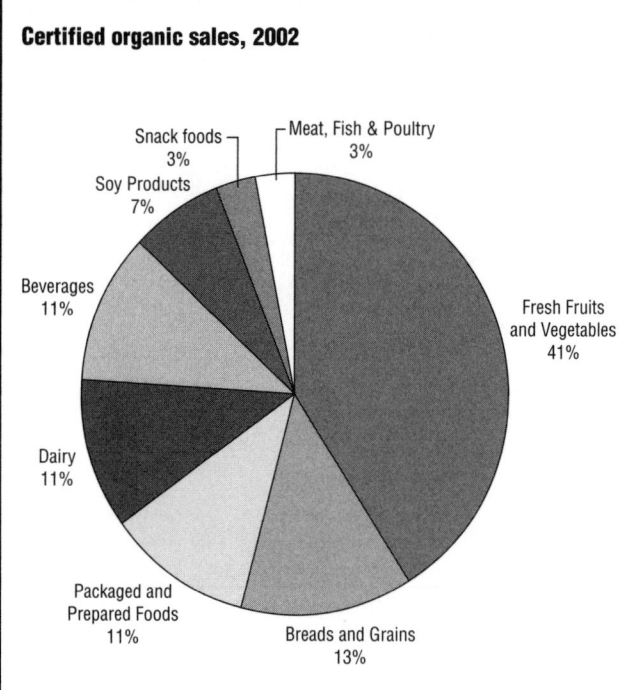

Certified organic sales, 2002

SOURCE: Adapted from "What Is The Size Of The U.S. Market For Organic Foods?," in *Organic Farming And Marketing: Questions And Answers,* U.S. Department of Agriculture, Economic Research Service, Washington, DC, June 24, 2003 [Online] http://www.ers.usda.gov/Briefing/Organic/Questions/orgqa5.htm [accessed July 21, 2003]

friendly. According to the USDA, organic farming was one of the fastest-growing segments of U.S. agriculture during the 1990s. Retail sales grew from $3.3 billion in 1996 to $7.1 billion in 2001.

Some livestock farmers offer meat and other products from animals cultivated using organic methods. The animals are not given antibiotics or other drugs (except some necessary vaccines) and are housed in more natural conditions than those used in factory farms. The farmers accommodate the animals' natural nutritional and behavior requirements. For example, ruminating animals are given access to pasture.

Farmers are not allowed to label their products as organic unless they meet specific requirements established by the U.S. government in the National Organic Program. The organic standards govern living conditions, access to the outdoors, feed rations, and health-care practices. No growth hormones or genetic engineering are allowed, and the animals are not fed animal by-products. There are also restrictions on manure management and slaughter procedures. The farmers must provide documentation to the USDA demonstrating that they are following these standards in order to use the organic label.

During the 1990s, organic dairy experienced tremendous growth with sales up over 500 percent between 1994 and 1999. The market for organic meats has not grown as

TABLE 4.6

Percent of sites that gave antibiotics or other feed additives to grower/finisher pigs by primary reason and route of administration, 2000

Primary reason	Route of administration (percent)			
	Feed	Water	Injection	Any route
Growth promotion	63.7	0.0	0.0	63.7
Treat respiratory disease	27.4	25.2	57.2	61.9
Disease prevention	37.9	4.0	6.4	42.8
Treat enteric disease	15.2	7.5	15.4	27.5
Treat other disease	0.2	1.0	14.1	14.7
Any reason	88.5	31.2	64.5	92.6

SOURCE: "Table 2: Percent Sites that Gave Antibiotics or Other Feed Additives to Grower/Finisher Pigs, by Primary Reason and Route of Administration," in *Preventive Practices in Swine: Administration of Iron and Antibiotics,* U.S. Department of Agriculture, Animal and Plant Health Inspection Service, Washington, DC, March 2002

quickly, but this may be because organic meat labels were not approved until 1999. Organic meat sales accounted for only 3 percent of total organic sales in 2002. (See Figure 4.11.) The number of certified livestock and poultry increased from 73,010 in 1992 to just over 5 million in 2001. The 2001 numbers were as follows:

- Beef cows—15,197

- Milk cows—48,677

- Hogs and pigs—3,135

- Sheep and lambs—4,207

- Laying hens—1,611,662

- Broilers—3,286,456

- Turkeys—98,653

Some livestock farmers are marketing products from grass-fed, pasture-raised, or free-range animals. These products may or may not also be organic. The USDA allows producers to label a product as "all natural" as long as it is "minimally processed and contains no artificial ingredients." However, the label can be applied to meat from animals that received antibiotics and other drugs to promote growth.

HUMAN HEALTH ISSUES

Because humans consume so many animal products, there is a correlation between the health of farm animals and human health. Even people who do not have moral or philosophical problems with the treatment or consumption of livestock are concerned about some factory farming methods.

Use of Antibiotics

One of the biggest concerns is the routine administration of low doses of antibiotics to farm animals to prevent them from developing diseases and to cure any that might already have diseases. This is called nontherapeutic, subtherapeutic, or preventative antibiotic use. Many people fear that it could lead to development of antibiotic-resistant diseases in animals and humans. Scientists already know that some bacteria are able to adjust to and tolerate low dosages of weaker antibiotics. Once they achieve this resistance it is much more difficult to kill them and requires increasingly stronger types of antibiotics.

According to data on its Web site in 2003, the Union of Concerned Scientists estimates that more than 70 percent of the antibiotics used in this country are administered to farm animals. A 2000 report from the USDA showed that 92.6 percent of hog-producing sites administered preventative antibiotics or other feed additives to their hogs. (See Table 4.6.) The American Medical Association and the World Health Organization have called for a ban on nontherapeutic use of antibiotics in farm animals. They have already been banned by the European Union.

In February 2002 McDonald's, Wendy's, and Popeye's announced that they will no longer buy chickens from suppliers that administer fluoroquinolone antibiotics to their poultry. Fluoroquinolone is similar to a powerful human antibiotic called Cipro. The HSUS claims that fluoroquinolone is often administered via drinking water to entire chicken flocks because it is too difficult or costly for the producers to individually treat sick birds.

Animal-to-Human Disease Transmission

Another concern related to animal welfare is the fear that U.S. farm animals could transmit diseases to humans. Such diseases are called zoonoses. They include anthrax, scrapie, brucellosis, leptospirosis, bovine tuberculosis, streptococcus suis, orf, and ringworm. Of major concern is a group of diseases called transmissible spongiform encephalopathies (TSEs).

One TSE is called bovine spongiform encephalopathy (BSE), commonly known as mad cow disease. This disease devastated farm animal populations in England during the 1980s and 1990s. Millions of animals were killed because they either had the disease or as a precaution against the disease. Scientists suspect that BSE is a fairly new disease that emerged in cattle that had been fed animal by-products from sheep contaminated with scrapie. By-products from slaughtered infected cattle were inadvertently fed to healthy cattle, leading to widespread infection. To prevent the spread of the disease, "cattle passports" are now supposed to be presented whenever an animal is moved to show where it has been. (See Figure 4.12.)

There have been no documented cases of BSE in the United States. The variant Creutzfeldt-Jakob disease (vCJD) is a TSE disease that humans can catch. Medical authorities suspect that humans can contract vCJD from

FIGURE 4.12

Cattle passports. *AP/Wide World Photos*

eating meat from BSE-infected animals. The Centers for Disease Control and Prevention (CDC) reports that 125 people worldwide were confirmed to have vCJD as of April 2002. Nearly all had consumed beef in the United Kingdom during the BSE epidemic. According to the CDC's Web site in 2003, the risk of acquiring vCJD from British beef and beef products is approximately 1 case per 10 billion servings.

Foodborne Illnesses

Food poisoning from meat products has received a lot of attention in recent years. Humans can become very sick from ingesting bacteria that are found in the intestinal tracts and manure of some farm animals. These pathogens include *Salmonella, Listeria, Escherichia coli,* and *Campylobacter.*

In December 2002 the CDC estimated that as many as 76 million illnesses, 325,000 hospitalizations, and 5,000 deaths annually are caused by foodborne hazards. However, the CDC notes that some foodborne illnesses declined dramatically between 1996 and 2001, thanks to increased public awareness, pathogen reduction measures implemented by the USDA at meat and poultry slaughterhouses and processing plants, and product recalls. When USDA or internal inspections reveal potential problems at processing plants, producers issue market recalls. In October 2002 Pilgrim's Pride had to recall 27 million pounds of deli meat processed at a plant that tested positive for *Listeria*. This is considered the largest meat recall in U.S. history.

The USDA is advocating the use of irradiation to safeguard the U.S. meat supply. Irradiation is a process in which meat is treated with low levels of radiation to kill bacteria. In October 2002 the USDA announced that meat supplied to public schools can undergo irradiation. Some people are concerned that irradiation could cause unforeseen problems in meat that might be harmful to humans. Animal rights activists and welfarists claim that irradiation of meat would not be required if farming and slaughtering processes were reformed to reduce animal-waste contact.

FUR FARMING

Fur farming is a unique agricultural enterprise for two reasons. First of all, most of the animals involved are wild instead of domesticated. Second, the animals are raised and killed for their pelts only. The most popular fur animal is the mink. It takes about 40 mink pelts to produce one fur coat.

FIGURE 4.13

Fur sales, 1991–2001

SOURCE: Adapted from "How Have Fur Sales Fared in Recent Years?", in *FAQS Facts,* Fur Information Council of America, West Hollywood, CA, 2003 [Online] http://www.fur.org/fica2003/faqs/facts.asp [accessed July 21, 2003]

Mink are wild animals that are kept in cages on fur farms. They typically breed in the early spring and give birth to litters in late spring. An average litter contains four or five babies, or kits, that are weaned after six to eight weeks. The kits are vaccinated against common diseases. During the late summer and early fall, the mink naturally molt (lose their summer fur) and regrow a thick winter coat. The mink are killed in late autumn or early winter. Some are retained for breeding purposes.

According to the USDA, there were about 300 mink farms in the United States in 2001, down from more than 1,000 in the 1970s. Approximately 2.5 million pelts were produced in 2001, each worth about $33. The industry produced nearly $86 million worth of mink pelts that year.

According to the U.S. Fur Commission, the top 5 mink-pelt producing states in 2001 were Wisconsin, Utah, Minnesota, Oregon, and Idaho.

The fur industry is harshly criticized by animal rights activists and welfarists. They claim that the animals are kept in miserable conditions and in small cages. The HSUS says that overbreeding by farmers to produce desirable coat colors leads to serious and painful deformities in the animals. Farming and slaughter of fur animals are not regulated by the USDA. The most common killing techniques are gassing, electrocution, and breaking of the animals' necks. Fur farming has been banned in many western European countries.

Animal welfarists and rights activists have conducted antifur campaigns since the 1960s. PETA's "I'd rather go naked than wear fur" campaign was begun in the 1990s and has featured celebrities like Pamela Anderson and Kim Basinger posing nude. PETA activists also regularly disrupt fashion shows featuring fur-clad models and protest outside stores selling fur. However, fur sales have continued to rise in the United States. According to the Fur Information Council of America, fur sales increased from $1 billion in 1991 to $1.53 billion in 2001. (See Figure 4.13.) Industry analysts say that fur demand is driven by weather and economy rather than animal issues.

Mink farmers defend their animal husbandry and slaughtering procedures as humane. They argue that mink in the wild rarely live longer than one year and insist that the mink are handled carefully, both for their welfare and to protect their valuable coats from damage. Producers also insist that the mink are killed quickly and humanely using veterinary-approved methods. In a 2001 media interview a veteran mink farmer claimed that "animals raised for their fur are inherently the best cared for farm animals" (Delia Montgomery, "Fur Ethics," U.S. Fur Commission, http://www.furcommission.com/resource/perspect999as.htm).

CHAPTER 5
RESEARCH ANIMALS

Research animals are animals that humans use solely for scientific purposes. They are used in medical and veterinary investigations and training; in the testing of drugs, cosmetics, and other consumer products; and in educational programs. Though no official statistics exist, estimates collected in 2003 from various animal protection and biomedical research groups suggest that 20–25 million animals are used in research, testing, and training programs in the United States each year, and more than 100 million are used worldwide. Millions more research animals are kept as classroom pets or teaching aids to educate children in schools.

Living animals used as specimens to test drugs and products, practice medical and surgical procedures, and investigate diseases and bodily systems are called laboratory animals. Laboratory animals often die from these procedures or are euthanized by researchers after they are no longer needed. The plight of laboratory animals has been a major issue for animal rights advocates since the 1970s.

Increasingly, the use of dead animals to teach dissection skills to children is coming under fire. Dissection is a procedure in which an organism is cut apart for scientific examination. If the organism is alive at the time, the procedure is called vivisection. The term vivisection has come to be used to refer to all invasive research and testing performed on live animals for scientific purposes.

Live animals are used in modern medical research because some of their bodily systems mimic those of humans. This makes them useful test subjects for drugs, vaccines, and other products that could be dangerous to humans. They are also useful training tools for doctors, surgeons, and veterinarians who need to practice medical procedures, such as inserting a catheter, administering anesthesia, or performing operations.

People who support the use of animals in research are passionate in their belief that the benefits to people far outweigh the consequences to animals. They point out the important medical and veterinary advances that have resulted. Animal rights activists, on the other hand, uniformly condemn this use. Some of the most radical have broken into laboratories, released animals, and physically harassed the researchers involved. Animal welfarists work to minimize the pain these animals experience during testing and to improve their living conditions.

The Gallup Organization includes a question about laboratory animals in the morality poll it conducts each year. The poll conducted in May 2003 showed that 63 percent of Americans find "medical testing on animals" to be morally acceptable, while 33 percent find it morally wrong. Another 3 percent said the morality depends on the situation, and 1 percent had no opinion. These numbers were virtually unchanged from those obtained in 2001 and 2002.

Science and Engineering Indicators is a report published by the National Science Board every two years. The latest available report included the results of public opinion polls conducted in 2001 on various topics related to science and engineering. Figure 5.1 and Figure 5.2 compare public opinion on the use of mice versus the use of dogs and chimpanzees in medical research that causes pain and injury to the animals but produces new information on human health problems. The results show that 67 percent of respondents approve of the use of mice in such a manner, while only 44 percent approve of the use of dogs and chimpanzees. This finding is not surprising, as people typically have more charitable feelings toward dogs and chimpanzees than they do toward mice. Figure 5.3 shows that approval for painful tests on dogs and chimpanzees has generally decreased since 1988.

This decrease may be the result in part of the fact that many people react emotionally to the thought of animals in distress. Scientists and researchers, those who work with the animals directly, use clinical terms to describe

FIGURE 5.1

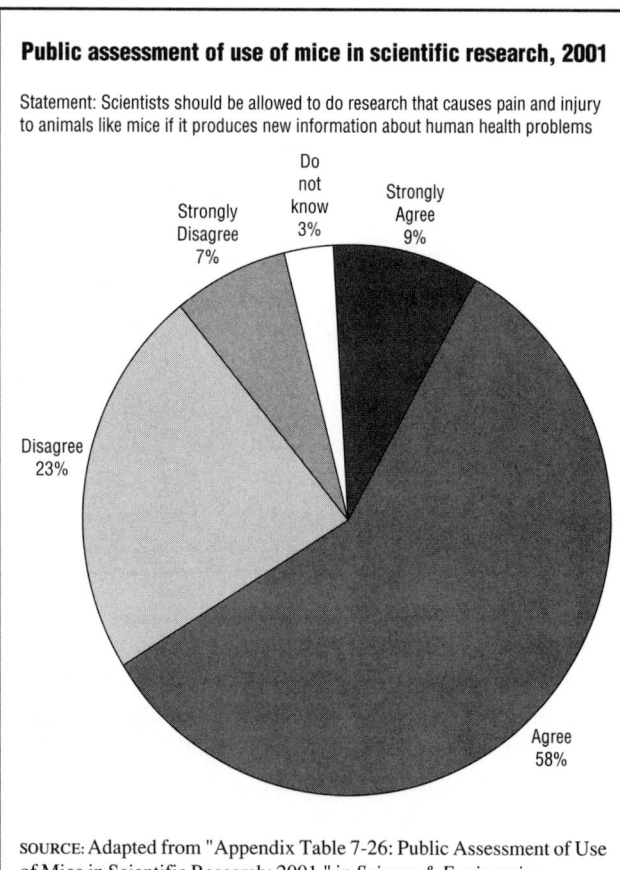

Public assessment of use of mice in scientific research, 2001

Statement: Scientists should be allowed to do research that causes pain and injury to animals like mice if it produces new information about human health problems

- Do not know 3%
- Strongly Agree 9%
- Strongly Disagree 7%
- Disagree 23%
- Agree 58%

SOURCE: Adapted from "Appendix Table 7-26: Public Assessment of Use of Mice in Scientific Research: 2001," in *Science & Engineering Indicators—2002*, (NSB-02-1), National Science Foundation, National Science Board, Arlington, VA, 2002

FIGURE 5.2

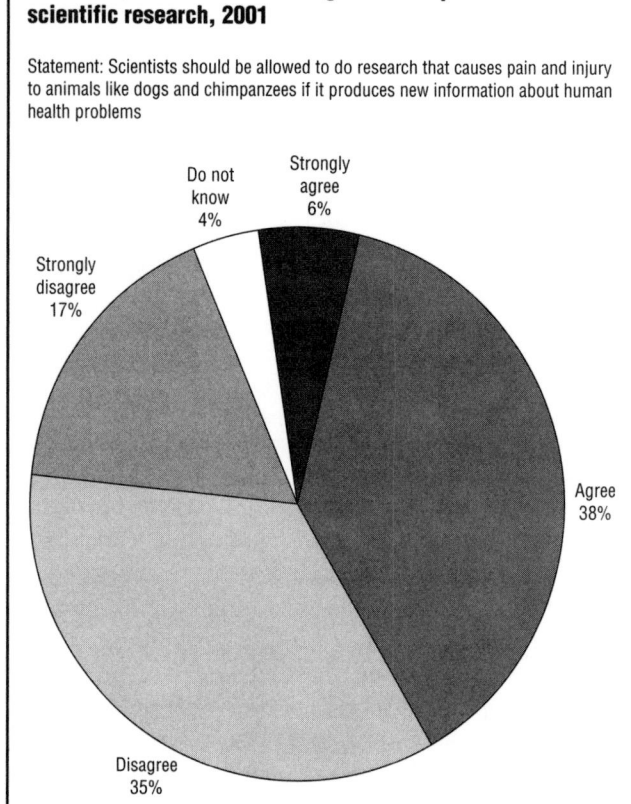

Public assessment of use of dogs and chimpanzees in scientific research, 2001

Statement: Scientists should be allowed to do research that causes pain and injury to animals like dogs and chimpanzees if it produces new information about human health problems

- Do not know 4%
- Strongly agree 6%
- Strongly disagree 17%
- Agree 38%
- Disagree 35%

SOURCE: Adapted from "Appendix Table 7-27: Public Assessment of Use of Dogs and Chimpanzees in Scientific Research: 1988–2001," in *Science & Engineering Indicators—2002*, (NSB-02-1), National Science Foundation, National Science Board, Arlington, VA, 2002

their work. They refer to laboratory animals as animal models and speak of them as specimens. Antivivisection groups gain support for their views by publicizing the gruesome details of experiments. Photographs of restrained animals with bolts through their brains or sores on their bodies can disturb the public, no matter how scientifically justified the experiments may be.

The modern antivivisection movement began during the 19th century. In 1892 humanitarian Henry Salt wrote, "the practice of vivisection is revolting to the human conscience, even among the ordinary members of a not over-sensitive society." This was only 75 years after the publication of Mary Shelley's *Frankenstein,* a story about a scientist who creates a mutant human from spare parts. Anthropologist Susan Sperling believes that the antivivisectionists of the 19th century and the 21st century have shared a common fear—scientific manipulation of living beings.

HISTORY

Early Times

Vivisection on animals and humans dates back to at least the ancient Greeks and Romans. During the third and second centuries B.C., human bodies were vivisected and dissected at the medical school in Alexandria, Egypt, by Herophilus and Erasistratus. Historians believe that more than 600 living criminals were subjected to vivisection. Human dissection and vivisection were generally forbidden throughout the rest of Egypt and in the Roman Empire because of moral concerns.

Galen (circa 130–200) was a Greek physician who moved to Rome and administered to gladiators and emperors. (See Figure 5.4.) He frequently practiced vivisection on animals, particularly goats, pigs, monkeys, oxen, and dogs. Although Galen made some important anatomical discoveries, such as the importance of the brain and the presence of blood inside arteries, he did not grasp the role of the heart in blood circulation. Modern historians believe that Galen relied too much on animal models. One of his most famous misconceptions involved the *rete mirabile*. This is a network of blood vessels found in some hoofed animals, but not in humans. Galen mistakenly assumed that humans also had this network.

Galen wrote extensively, and his teachings formed the basis of Western medical science well into the Middle Ages. The Christian church frowned upon human

FIGURE 5.3

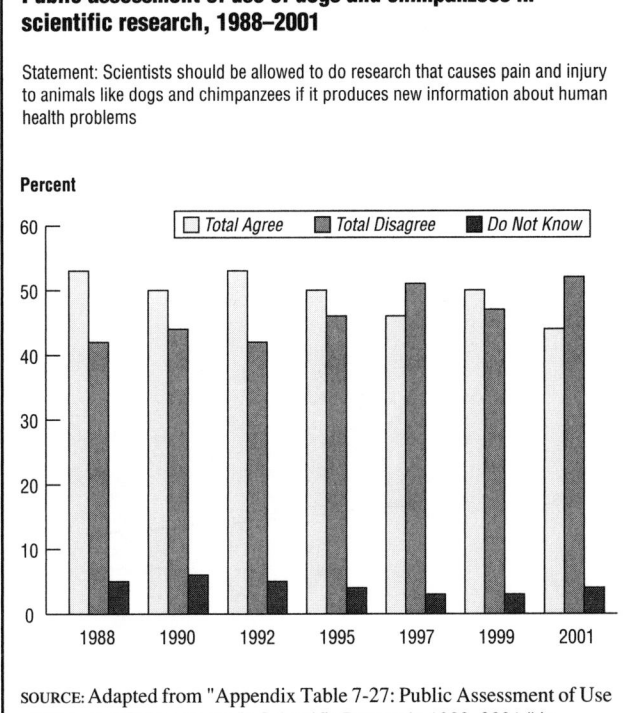

Public assessment of use of dogs and chimpanzees in scientific research, 1988–2001

Statement: Scientists should be allowed to do research that causes pain and injury to animals like dogs and chimpanzees if it produces new information about human health problems

SOURCE: Adapted from "Appendix Table 7-27: Public Assessment of Use of Dogs and Chimpanzees in Scientific Research: 1988–2001," in *Science & Engineering Indicators—2002*, (NSB-02-1), National Science Foundation, National Science Board, Arlington, VA, 2002

FIGURE 5.4

Galen. *The Library of Congress*

dissection/vivisection during this period, meaning that only animals were generally available for anatomical study, though some adventurous souls still used humans in their research. (See Figure 5.5.) Few advances in medical science were made until the 1500s, when the Belgian doctor Andreas Vesalius (1514–64) challenged many of Galen's ideas. (See Figure 5.6.) Vesalius began to uncover the mysteries of blood circulation after performing autopsies on human corpses. He also practiced vivisection on animals and wrote about its importance in the study of anatomy. Vesalius was followed by British physician and anatomist William Harvey (1578–1657). (See Figure 5.7.) By performing animal vivisection and dissecting the corpses of executed criminals, Harvey discovered the true role of the heart in pumping blood throughout the body.

The 17th, 18th, and 19th Centuries

During the 17th century, a new philosophy was introduced by French philosopher René Descartes (1596–1650). (See Figure 5.8.) Descartes' Cartesian philosophy taught that animals were unthinking, unfeeling machines. This allowed researchers to perform all manner of experiments on live animals without any moral concerns. In 1764 the philosophy was criticized by French philosopher François-Marie Arouet de Voltaire (1694–1778). (See Figure 5.9.) Voltaire noted that vivisection uncovered organs of feeling in animals, proving

that animals were not machines, but feeling beings. Later in the century British philosopher Jeremy Bentham (1748–1832) wrote his famous line: "the question is not, Can they reason? Nor, Can they talk? but, Can they suffer?" (See Figure 5.10.)

Throughout the 18th and 19th centuries, philosophers debated the moral issues involved in animal vivisection. According to historians, the poor and working-class people of the time opposed animal vivisection because they associated it with the dissection of human corpses. The unclaimed bodies of poor people and criminals were often turned over to medical colleges for dissection. There were also well-publicized cases of grave robbing and body snatching to supply researchers with human corpses. These events horrified the common people and made them suspicious of scientists and doctors engaged in medical research.

The 19th century also witnessed organized efforts from animal welfare organizations to achieve legislation against animal cruelty in the United Kingdom and United States. The Cruelty to Animals Act was passed in Britain in 1849 and amended in 1876 to restrict the use of animals in research. In December 1875 the Society for the Protection of Animals Liable to Vivisection was founded by Frances Power Cobbe (1822–1904). It was later called the Victorian Street Society. In 1898 Cobbe founded the

FIGURE 5.5

Italian anatomist Mondino de' Luzzi (circa 1265–1326) presides over a human dissection in the early 14th century. *The Library of Congress*

British Union for the Abolition of Vivisection, an organization still active as of 2003.

Vivisection was also fought by welfarists in the United States. In 1871 Harvard University founded one of the first vivisection laboratories in the country, despite opposition from the Massachusetts Society for the Prevention of Cruelty to Animals (SPCA). Various antivivisection groups were founded, including the American Anti-Vivisection Society (AAVS) in 1883 and the New England Anti-Vivisection Society (NEAVS) in 1896. (Table 5.1 provides a list of some of the major U.S. organizations involved in advocating or opposing the use of animals in scientific research over the years.) The new antivivisection groups tried, but were unsuccessful at outlawing the practice of vivisection. Legislation was passed during the 1890s that outlawed repetition of painful animal experiments for the purpose of teaching or demonstrating well-known and accepted facts.

FIGURE 5.6

Andreas Vesalius. *The Library of Congress*

The First Half of the 20th Century

In December 1903 writer Mark Twain (1835–1910) published a short story called "A Dog's Tale" in *Harper's Magazine*. The story was written to protest cruelty to animals and their use in research. It is told from the viewpoint of a dog that lives with the family of a scientist. The dog saves the family's baby from a nursery fire but later sees her own puppy blinded and killed during an experiment performed by the scientist to impress his friends. Although some critics condemned the work as overly sentimental, animal welfarists of the time were pleased that it brought public attention to the issue of animal experimentation.

In 1906 the U.S. Congress passed the Pure Food and Drug Act (PFDA). The original act did not require any type of testing to ensure that a product was safe or effective. This would change after some tragic events occurred. According to Professor Susan Wilson-Sanders of the University of Arizona, many Americans were injured, sickened, or even killed by unsafe potions, snake oils, and patent medicines sold by entrepreneurs during the early decades of the 20th century ("Mrs. Brown's Sad Story: A History of the Food, Drug, and Cosmetic Act" [Online] http://www.ahsc.arizona.edu/uac/notes/classes/Altern-method/mrsBrownstoryFDA.htm [accessed August 11, 2003]). Some of these products contained incredibly toxic

FIGURE 5.7

FIGURE 5.8

William Harvey. *The Library of Congress*

René Descartes. *The Library of Congress*

substances, such as dinitrophenol, a compound used to make explosives.

During the 1920s and 1930s, hair dyes containing an aniline compound called paraphenylenediamine became popular. It was well known that aniline compounds were harmful to the eyes, but a cosmetics company introduced a brand of mascara called Lash-Lure containing these chemicals. Doctors reported thousands of eye injuries caused by the product, and even a few deaths after patients suffered serious infections. Many states banned the use of aniline dyes in personal-care products. Professor Wilson-Sanders reports that Lash-Lure contained 25–30 times more aniline than the amount commonly used in hair dyes.

Other popular cosmetic products of the time that caused injury were called Anti-Mole, Berry's Freckle Ointment, Bleachodent (a teeth whitener), Dr. Dennis's Compound, Koremlu cream, and Dewsberry Hair Tonic. These products contained high concentrations of acids or other toxic chemicals. Whisker dyes marketed to men contained dangerous levels of silver or lead acetate. A popular depilatory (hair removal cream) contained rat poison.

Doctors lobbied Congress throughout the 1930s to crack down on dangerous drugs and personal products sold to Americans, but they were opposed by powerful marketing groups. In 1937 nearly 100 people (mostly children) died after drinking a product called Elixir of Sulfanilamide containing sulfa drugs dissolved in diethylene glycol (antifreeze). The public was outraged and pressured Congress to strengthen the original PFDA and include cosmetics. The Pure Food, Drug, and Cosmetic Act (PFDCA) was passed in 1938. It contained a requirement for animal testing.

Professor Wilson-Sanders notes that the first tests were conducted on rats and could last less than one month. The testing requirements were gradually amended to include different species and to last for longer time periods. By 1957 drug testing had to be performed on rats or dogs for up to six months. By the 1980s testing required 12–18 months. Testing on pregnant animals was instituted in the 1960s following the thalidomide tragedy. Thalidomide is a drug that was widely prescribed in Canada and Europe during the late 1950s to treat nausea in pregnant women. More than 10,000 deformed babies resulted. Although the drug had been extensively tested on animals, it had not been tested on pregnant animals. New guidelines for testing the effects of drugs on animal reproduction and fetus development were incorporated into the PFDCA.

FIGURE 5.9

Voltaire.

FIGURE 5.10

Jeremy Bentham. *The Library of Congress*

The Latter Half of the 20th Century

Historians note that the antivivisection movement subsided with the advent of World War I (1914–17) and did not resurge until the 1960s. One of the driving forces was the story of Pepper. Pepper was a Dalmatian who disappeared from her family's backyard in Pennsylvania in July 1965. The family tracked the dog to an animal dealer in New York, but he refused to return the dog. The family enlisted the help of the Animal Welfare Institute, the Pennsylvania State Police, and New York Congressman Joseph Resnick, but they were too late. Pepper had been sold to a hospital in New York City that conducted an experiment on her and euthanized her.

The story was widely publicized and led to public outrage. Bills were introduced in the House and Senate calling for animal dealers and laboratories to be licensed and inspected by the U.S. Department of Agriculture (USDA) and required to meet certain humane standards of care. During the debate, which took place during 1965 and 1966, Senator Warren Magnuson (1905–89) of Washington said, "we do not think we can allow the needs of research, great as they may be, to promote either the theft of a child's pet or the growth of unscrupulous animal dealers." The bills were opposed by strong lobbying groups

and were in danger of failing, until a story ran in the February 1966 issue of *Life* magazine.

"Concentration Camps for Dogs" was the story of a police raid on a dog dealer's facility in Maryland. The story included horrific photographs of abused dogs kept in filthy cages until they could be sold to research laboratories. According to the article, the dogs were to be sold at auction for 30 cents per pound. The offices of politicians were flooded with letters. Editorials appeared in major newspapers around the country calling for federal legislation.

A few months later, Congress passed the Laboratory Animal Welfare Act of 1966. It called for the licensing of animal dealers and regulation of laboratory animals. The original act applied to dogs, cats, primates, guinea pigs, hamsters, and rabbits. In 1970 the act was renamed the Animal Welfare Act (AWA) and amended to cover several other warm-blooded animals. A year later, the USDA decided to exclude rats, mice, and birds from coverage under the act, arguing that the department did not have the staff needed to regulate the huge numbers of such animals involved. The USDA has also noted that most of these small animals are used at research institutions that have other oversight protections in place to regulate their use.

TABLE 5.1

Major organizations, founded from 1883 to 1992, that are devoted to issues involving animal research

Founding date	Organization	Stated mission
1883	American Anti-Vivisection Society (AAVS)	Devoted to legally and effectively ending the use of animals in science through education, advocacy, and the development of alternative methods to animal use.
1895	New England Anti-Vivisection Society (NEAVS)	Works to expose and replace animal experiments in laboratories and classrooms with ethically and scientifically responsible modern research methods.
1929	National Anti-Vivisection Society (NAVS)	Goals include ending the use of animals in research, product testing, and education; educating the public about the cruelty and waste of vivisection; and encouraging development of non-animal methodologies.
1950	American Association for Laboratory Animal Science (AALAS)	Advances responsible care and use of laboratory animals to benefit people and animals.
1965	American Association for Accreditation of Laboratory Animal Care (AAALAC)	Voluntary accreditation organization founded by veterinary and scientific groups to promote uniform animal-care standards.
1974	Public Responsibility in Medicine and Research (PRIM&R)	Group dedicated to furthering research and promoting ethical ideals within the research community.
1979	National Association for Biomedical Research (NABR)	Provides the collective voice for the scientific community on national policy involving animal use in research, education and product safety testing.
1981	Johns Hopkins University Center for Alternatives to Animal Testing (CAAT)	Funded by the Cosmetics, Toiletry, and Fragrance Association to research alternatives to animal testing.
1981	Michigan Society for Medical Research	Non-profit science education organization that supports biomedical research and the judicious use of animals in research.
1985	Physicians Committee for Responsible Medicine (PCRM)	Advocates alternatives to harming animals for educational or research purposes.
1986	The Scientists Center for Animal Welfare (SCAW)	A non-profit educational association of individuals and institutions involved in research. The group's goal is to promote the welfare of animals used in research, testing, and educational programs.
1991	Americans for Medical Progress (AMP)	Non-profit organization devoted to protecting society's investment in research by promoting public understanding of and support for the appropriate role of animals in biomedical research so that scientists are able to continue their quest for cures and improved methods of treatment for illness, injury and disease.
1991	Ethical Science & Education Coalition (ESEC)	Educational affiliate of the NEAVS that works to protect the rights of students who decide not to dissect or otherwise use animals in a harmful way.
1992	Center for Laboratory Animal Welfare (CLAW)	Affiliated with the Massachusetts SPCA, this organization advocates alternatives to animal testing.

SOURCE: Created by Information Plus staff

In 1975 Australian philosopher Peter Singer published a book called *Animal Liberation* that was highly critical of the use of animals in scientific research. The book included disturbing photographs and descriptions of animals being subjected to all sorts of painful procedures for questionable purposes. Singer argued that the pain and suffering inflicted on the animals was too high a moral price to pay for scientific research. His book was very influential and is often considered the bible of the modern animal rights movement.

In 1976 animal activist Henry Spira (1927–98) led a campaign protesting research at the American Museum of Natural History on the effects of castration and mutilation on cats' sexual behavior. The campaign was hailed as a success by activists after the museum halted the research a year later. Spira then turned his attention to the testing of cosmetics on animals, particularly the Draize test, in which chemicals are put into the eyes of rabbits.

He formed a coalition of animal welfare and antivivisection groups to educate the public about animal testing of cosmetics. In full-page advertisements in major newspapers, Spira accused major cosmetics companies of being cruel to animals. Public response was immediate. Several companies, including Revlon and Avon, announced their intention to cease animal testing and find new alternatives. In 1981 the Cosmetics, Toiletries, and Fragrance Association funded the founding of the Center for Alternatives to Animal Testing (CAAT) at Johns Hopkins University in Baltimore, Maryland. By the end of the 1980s, Revlon and Avon had ceased animal testing.

In 1985 Congress amended the Animal Welfare Act to require that researchers minimize animal pain and distress whenever possible through use of anesthesia, analgesics (painkillers), and humane euthanasia. New requirements were added regarding the physical and psychological well-being of dogs and primates used in research work. Throughout the 1980s and 1990s, animal welfare groups petitioned and sued the USDA to add mice, rats, and birds to the animals covered under the AWA, but were unsuccessful. In 1990 AWA coverage was extended to horses and other farm animals.

Scientists engaged in animal research watched with concern as animal welfare and antivivisection groups launched aggressive publicity campaigns against them. In 1979 the National Association for Biomedical Research was founded in Washington, D.C., with the mission of "advocating sound public policy that recognizes the vital role of humane animal use in biomedical research, higher

TABLE 5.2

The important role of animals in Nobel Prizes, 1975–2002

Year		
1975	**Monkey, Horse, Chicken, Mouse**	Interaction between tumor viruses and genetic material.
1979	**Pig**	Development of computer assisted tomography (CAT scan).
1981	**Cat, Monkey**	Processing of visual data by the brain.
1988	**Mouse, Chick, Snake**	Nerve and epidermal growth factor.
1990	**Dog**	Organ transplantation techniques.
1995	**Fruitfly**	Genetic control of early embryonic development.
1998	**Rabbit**	Regulating blood pressure with nitric oxide (NO).
1999	**Mice**	Discovery that proteins have intrinsic signals that govern their transport and localization in the cell.
2000	**Sea Slug**	Signal transduction in the nervous system.
2001	**Sea Urchins**	Key regulators of the cell cycle.
2002	**Nematode (worm)**	Genetic regulation of organ development and programmed cell death.

SOURCE: "The Important Role of Animals in Nobel Prizes," in *Educational Materials,* Michigan Society for Medical Research, Ann Arbor, MI, 2003

education, and product safety testing." In 1981 the Foundation for Biomedical Research and the Michigan Society for Medical Research (MISMR) were founded with similar goals.

These organizations work to counter claims by animal rights activists that animal research and testing are cruel practices with little to no scientific value. For example, the MISMR says that animals have played a major role in the work of at least 11 Nobel Prize winners since 1975. (See Table 5.2.) RDS is an organization based in the United Kingdom that represents the interests of British researchers conducting animal research. On its Web site, RDS maintains a timeline of the major medical and veterinary breakthroughs of each decade that were achieved through animal testing. (See Table 5.3.)

PEOPLE FOR THE ETHICAL TREATMENT OF ANIMALS (PETA) AND THE SILVER SPRINGS MONKEY CASE. In 1981 a little-known organization called People for the Ethical Treatment of Animals (PETA) gained national prominence through an exposé on paralysis experiments on monkeys at the Institute of Behavioral Research in Silver Springs, Maryland. The research was funded by the National Institutes of Health (NIH) and led by Dr. Edward Taub. It involved depriving monkeys of sensory input into their spinal cords in order to give them denervated arms, or arms

in which the nerves were not active. The monkeys gnawed and licked their arms, producing wounds. Taub hired a young man named Alex Pacheco to work as a laboratory assistant. Unbeknownst to Taub, Pacheco had cofounded PETA the year before. Pacheco photographed the monkeys, then reported the lab to authorities. A subsequent raid led to the filing of animal cruelty charges against Taub.

The incident came to be known as the Silver Springs Monkey Case. Although the charges against Taub were eventually dropped, the publicity made PETA famous. The monkeys were confiscated, and Congress forced the NIH to cease the research. This was viewed as a major triumph by people involved in antivivisection and the growing animal rights movement.

HUNTINGDON LIFE SCIENCES (HLS) BECOMES A TARGET. PETA continued to use infiltration and secretly obtained photographs (and videotapes) to publicize the realities of animal research. In 1997 the group conducted an eight-month undercover investigation at a Huntingdon Life Sciences (HLS) facility in New Jersey. HLS is a major target of antivivisection groups because it is one of the largest contract companies conducting animal research. PETA turned over to the USDA the documents, photographs, and videotapes its investigators obtained during the undercover operation, and filed a formal complaint against HLS. HLS countersued PETA, claiming that the materials were obtained by illegal means. In 2000 the group In Defense of Animals (IDA) asked the USDA for access to the materials under the Freedom of Information Act. The USDA refused, citing ongoing litigation as its reason. IDA then sued the USDA for failure to comply with the Freedom of Information Act.

Some activists within the animal movement have become more and more radical in their actions and now break into laboratories to free animals or destroy property and harass researchers. This is particularly true in Britain, where activists have targeted HLS facilities and even companies that provide HLS with services, funding, and equipment. The tactics have had a degree of success in that they have convinced some companies to sever their association with HLS (at least publicly). However, they alienate some people who view them as terrorist actions.

THE COULSTON FOUNDATION IS DRIVEN OUT OF BUSINESS. Mainstream antivivisection and welfarist groups have condemned such radical tactics and instead wage public relations and political campaigns against the use of research animals. One of their primary targets has been the Coulston Foundation (TCF), a primate breeding and research facility operated by toxicologist Fred Coulston in Alamogordo, New Mexico. The facility began operations in 1980 and at one time housed as many as 650 chimpanzees, making it the largest captive chimpanzee colony in the world.

TABLE 5.3

Animal research used in human and animal medicine, 1900s–2000s

1900's **Local anesthetics**
Cocaine was the first local anesthetic, but its dangers led to the development of the safer procaine. *Rabbits, dogs*

Corneal transplants
The first successful human transplant was of the cornea, the clear covering of the eye. It is normally out-of-reach of white blood cells, so rejection is not a problem. *Rabbits*

1910's **Blood transfusion**
Many doctors and scientists were involved in the research that led to the safe storage and routine transfusion of sterile, compatible blood. *Dogs, guinea pigs, rabbits*

1920's **Insulin for diabetes**
Before the development of insulin, Type 1 diabetes was a death sentence. Millions of lives, both human and animal, have been saved by insulin. *Dogs, rabbits, mice*

Canine distemper vaccine
Distemper (hard pad) in dogs was rife a century ago. Research on the disease—only possible with very careful isolation and disinfection routines—revealed a virus as the cause and ultimately yielded a vaccine. *Dogs*

1930's **Modern anesthetics**
Intravenous anesthetics were first used successfully for short surgical procedures in human patients in the mid 1930s. Modern inhaled anesthetics began to be developed from the 1950s. *Rats, rabbits, dogs, cats, monkeys*

Diphtheria vaccine
Before the antitoxin and the vaccine, this disease was widespread, serious and fatal for one in ten. They died from suffocation, paralysis and heart failure. *Guinea pigs, rabbits, horses, monkeys*

Anticoagulants
Anticoagulants prevent potentially fatal blood clots. Heparin and warfarin were the first anticoagulants developed for human use. *Rabbits, guinea pigs, mice, dogs*

1940's **Kidney dialysis**
Dialysis saves the lives of hundreds of thousands of patients with kidney failure, and is often used until a kidney is available for transplant. *Guinea pigs, rabbits, dogs, monkeys*

Broad spectrum antibiotics for infections
The development of penicillin and other broad spectrum antibiotics revolutionised the treatment of bacterial infections in both humans and animals. *Mice*

Whooping cough vaccine
Whooping cough, also known as pertussis, is potentially a major cause of child death. Its incidence has dropped steadily wherever the vaccine has been introduced. *Mice, rabbits*

Heart-lung machine for open heart surgery
Open-heart surgery for severe heart conditions would be impossible without the heart–lung machine to take over circulation and oxygenation of the blood. *Dogs*

1950's **Hip replacement surgery**
Rheumatoid and osteoarthritis take their toll on our joints and can cause years of suffering. Failing hips, and other joints, can be replaced using artificial joints made of strong, inert material. *Dogs, sheep, goats*

Kidney transplants
The best and most cost effective treatment for chronic kidney failure is a transplant. Around 2,000 patients in the UK receive a new kidney every year. *Dogs*

Cardiac pacemakers
Pacemakers are like implanted electronic clocks, sending a small current through a lead to stimulate the heart beat. About 10,000 patients benefit every year in the UK. *Dogs*

Polio vaccine
The vaccine has eradicated polio in the western world, and a worldwide vaccination program aims to eliminate this crippling disease completely. Mice, monkeys

Drugs for high blood pressure
Annual deaths in the UK from high blood pressure were about 20,000 before the introduction of effective medicines. These medicines also reduce the risk of stroke, heart and kidney disease. *Rats, mice, cats, dogs*

Replacement heart valves
Artificial heart valves give a new lease on life to patients—some 6,000 a year in the UK—whose own valves are failing due to congenital defects or disease. Valves from pigs have also been used successfully since the 1970s. *Dogs, calves, rabbits, guinea pigs, rats*

1960's **German measles vaccine**
This epidemic disease, also known as rubella, mainly affects children, but can also cause severe defects in the unborn child. *Monkeys*

Coronary bypass operations
Healthy arteries can be transplanted from the leg to replace dangerously blocked heart arteries. This operation is now routine and at least 13,000 UK patients benefit every year. *Dogs*

Drugs to treat mental illness
Lithium was one of the first drugs developed to treat depression, the fourth most common illness worldwide. *Rats, guinea pigs, rabbits*

Heart transplants
The first successful human transplant was in 1967, building on experience gained in transplanting other organs and animal experiments. *Dogs*

Some of the chimps came from the U.S. Air Force, which had been using them in space flight research. Others came from various government and academic institutions. TCF conducted numerous experiments on the chimps during the 1980s and 1990s with funding provided by the NIH. Areas of research included HIV, hepatitis, and herpes-B viruses, as well as spinal cord experiments. The president of the animal protection group In Defense of Animals (IDA) accused Coulston in a September 17, 2002, news release of using primates as "hairy test tubes."

TABLE 5.3

Animal research used in human and animal medicine, 1900s–2000s [CONTINUED]

1970's   **Cat scanning for improved diagnosis**
The use of 3D scanners and injected chemicals to improve contrast means that X-rays can show the organs of the body more clearly. *Pigs*

Chemotherapy for leukemia
Treatments for the commonest form of childhood leukemia mean that eight out of ten with the disease are long-ter m survivors. *Mice*

Drugs to treat ulcers
Drug treatment for ulcers means that surgery to remove ulcers is no longer necessary. *Rats, dogs*

Inhaled asthma medication
Inhaled drugs for asthma prevent or relieve the suffering of asthmatics and save lives. *Guinea pigs, rabbits*

1980's   **Life support systems for premature babies**
Tiny babies depend for their survival on specialized ventilators, incubators and monitoring systems. *Monkeys*

Drugs to control transplant rejection
Without drugs to suppress the immune system, organs could only be transplanted successfully between close relatives, preferably identical twins. *Mice, rabbits, dogs, monkeys*

Hepatitis vaccines
Vaccines are helping the fight against the infectious (A) and serum (B) virus, which cause hepatitis, cirrhosis and liver cancer. *Monkeys*

Drugs to treat viral diseases
Drugs such as amantadine and acyclovir are used to control serious viral infections in both people and animals. *Many species*

Treatment for river blindness
A drug first developed to treat heartworm in dogs has been donated by a pharmaceutical company to save the sight of millions of people in tropical countries threatened by a similar parasitic infection. *Rodents, cattle*

1990's   **Feline leukemia vaccine**
A type of potentially fatal leukemia in cats caused by a retrovirus (FeLV) can now be prevented. *Cats*

Meningitis vaccine
Hib meningitis, once a major cause of meningitis leading to brain damage and death in young children, is now very rare thanks to the vaccine. *Mice*

Better drugs for depression
The new class of antidepressants—selective serotonin re-uptake inhibitors (SSRIs) such as Prozac—act in a very specific way in the brain and thus have fewer side effects. *Rats*

Combined drug therapy for HIV infection
Combinations of antiviral drugs are currently the best therapy for HIV, often keeping full-blown AIDS at bay for many years. *Mice, monkeys*

Drugs for breast and prostate cancer
The survival rates for breast cancer and prostate cancer have improved significantly since the introduction of new drugs. *Mice, rats, dogs*

2000's   **Drugs for adult leukemia and lymphoma**
Effective monoclonal antibody therapy for these cancers has been developed. *Mice, rats, monkeys*

Alzheimer's disease vaccine?
A vaccine has been shown to be effective in mice in reducing the brain damage caused by Alzheimer's disease, and is now being tested in patients. *Mice*

Gene therapy for inherited diseases?
The insertion of healthy genes to correct gene defects, for instance in cystic fibrosis, muscular dystrophy and thalassaemia, is a new idea. It is being guided by studies in animals, which have shown some success. *Mice*

Malaria vaccine?
A huge effort has been mounted to find an effective vaccine against malaria, which kills three million people every year in tropical countries. *Mice, monkeys*

SOURCE: "Timeline," in "Medical Milestones," in *RDS: Understanding Animal Research in Medicine,* RDS, London, England, 2003 [Online] http://www.rds-online.org.uk/pages/page.asp?i_ToolbarID=3&i_PageID=37 [accessed June 30, 2003]

Coulston was quoted in a February 4, 1997, *New York Times* article as saying that he wanted to raise primates "like cattle" to harvest their blood and organs for medical research (David Berreby, "Unneeded Lab Chimps Face Hazy Future").

IDA began investigating TCF in 1993 after claims surfaced that the facility was not providing proper care for its primates. Information on IDA's Web site in 2003 charged that TCF repeatedly violated AWA regulations, but was staunchly defended by NIH bureaucrats. As of 2002, TCF had received more than $40 million in government funding.

The AWA violations stem from the deaths of several primates from heat stress, water deprivation, and improper surgical techniques. TCF was also cited by the USDA numerous times for housing and care violations and lack of qualified veterinarians. It was fined by the Occupational Safety and Health Administration (OSHA) for serious human safety violations and was in trouble with the Food and Drug Administration (FDA) regarding its animal testing procedures. During the late 1990s, TCF's regulatory problems were accompanied by severe economic problems. Government auditors found that TCF was deep in debt and had depleted funds that were intended to provide lifelong care for some of the primates.

In September 2002 the TCF facility closed, on the verge of bankruptcy after it could not acquire additional government funding. The remaining 266 chimpanzees and 61 monkeys at the facility were retired from research (though not necessarily permanently, as the NIH says it may recall them if it needs to). They are now wards of the Center for Captive Chimpanzee Care (CCCC), a well-respected primate sanctuary in Florida featuring Dr. Jane Goodall as one of its founders. The CCCC raised millions of dollars, donated by various animal welfare groups, to buy out TCF. Because the CCCC did not yet have room for the chimps, as of mid-2003 they remained at the TCF New Mexico facility, which the CCCC has modified to be more comfortable for them, where they will stay until the CCCC can expand its Florida facility. The New Mexico attorney general has announced plans to investigate TCF for alleged misspending of government funds, though TCF argues this is not within the attorney general's realm of authority.

FEDERAL LEGISLATION AND OVERSIGHT

Facilities that use certain species of live laboratory animals for research purposes must abide by laws and policies governing their use. Although there are a few state laws that also apply, most of the applicable legislation and oversight is provided by federal agencies.

The Animal Welfare Act (AWA)

AWA regulations are enforced by the Animal Care unit of the USDA Animal and Plant Health Inspection Service (APHIS). The regulations govern the housing and care of the animals and include licensing, registration, veterinary, and recordkeeping requirements. Covered facilities must register with the USDA.

The AWA does not apply to cold-blooded animals, or to rats of the genus *Rattus,* mice of the genus *Mus,* and birds. These animals do not fall under the definition of "animal" written into the law. This condition was made permanent in May 2002 as part of new federal legislation. The AWA does cover dogs and cats, rabbits, primates, guinea pigs, hamsters, marine mammals, and "other warm-blooded animals."

Under the AWA, each research facility must have an attending veterinarian who is required to provide adequate veterinary care to the facility's animals. The law defines adequate veterinary care as "what is currently the accepted professional practice or treatment for that particular circumstance or condition." Each research facility must have an institutional officer who is responsible for legally committing the facility to meet AWA requirements. This officer or the chief executive officer (CEO) of the facility must appoint an institutional animal care and use committee (IACUC) to assess the research facility's animal program, facilities, and procedures. An IACUC must include at least three members—a chairperson, a veterinarian, and a person not affiliated with the institute to represent "general community interests." IACUC members have to be qualified based on their experience and expertise.

An IACUC is responsible for reviewing a research facility's animal use program and inspecting the facilities in which animals are housed and studied. These evaluations must be done at least once every six months. Written reports are required and must be made available to APHIS and any federal agencies that provide funding to the facility. An IACUC is also responsible for investigating any complaints lodged against the facility regarding the care and use of the animals. This includes complaints from the general public. An IACUC has the power to approve or disapprove proposed animal care and use activities and to ask for modifications in these activities. It can also suspend particular animal activities if it believes they are not being conducted in accordance with its wishes.

Under the AWA any proposed activities must meet certain criteria. Some of the major requirements are as follows:

- Procedures must "avoid or minimize discomfort, distress, and pain to the animals."

- Researchers must consider alternative procedures that will not cause more than momentary or slight pain and justify why those cannot be used.

- Researchers must provide written assurance that the activities "do not unnecessarily duplicate previous experiments."

Any procedures that may cause more than momentary or slight pain or distress require that pain-relieving drugs be administered, unless withholding the drugs is "scientifically justified." Animals cannot be administered paralyzing drugs unless they are also given anesthesia. Animals that experience severe or chronic pain or distress that cannot be relieved are required to be painlessly euthanized as soon as possible, unless researchers seek and receive an exemption from the IACUC.

According to APHIS, there were 1,216 registered research facilities in the United States in 2001. (See Table 5.4.) California had the most facilities (179), followed by New York (86) and Massachusetts (83). A list of the research institutions is maintained on the APHIS Web site at http://www.aphis.usda.gov/ac/lists/listr.pdf. The list includes the names and addresses of the facilities, mostly colleges and universities, pharmaceutical companies, and hospitals.

All research facilities are required to comply with AWA regulations. Federal facilities are not required to register with the USDA and are not subject to USDA inspections, though they are required to comply with USDA standards for animal care established under the AWA and must submit annual reports to the USDA regarding their use of regulated laboratory animals. The AWA requires that nonfederal research facilities receive at least one inspection per year to determine compliance with the law.

TABLE 5.4

Active research facilities, fiscal year 2001

	Active research facilities	
	Facilities	Sites
Total United States	**1,216**	**1,868**
Alabama	13	17
Alaska	3	4
Arizona	10	11
Arkansas	8	10
California	179	229
Colorado	25	26
Connecticut	17	30
Delaware	8	13
District of Columbia	5	8
Florida	21	40
Georgia	15	33
Guam	0	0
Hawaii	2	2
Idaho	4	6
Illinois	41	45
Indiana	21	29
Iowa	16	21
Kansas	18	21
Kentucky	7	13
Louisiana	14	28
Maine	10	23
Maryland	41	71
Massachusetts	83	189
Michigan	32	45
Minnesota	26	41
Mississippi	5	5
Missouri	37	38
Montana	9	11
Nebraska	14	16
Nevada	2	10
New Hampshire	4	12
New Jersey	45	86
New Mexico	10	10
New York	86	138
North Carolina	23	35
North Dakota	3	5
Ohio	44	68
Oklahoma	17	26
Oregon	10	10
Pennsylvania	71	114
Puerto Rico	7	14
Rhode Island	6	13
South Carolina	10	18
South Dakota	6	6
Tennessee	16	26
Texas	78	102
Utah	8	8
Vermont	4	4
Virgin Islands	0	0
Virginia	15	36
Washington	31	35
West Virginia	5	6
Wisconsin	28	58
Wyoming	3	3

SOURCE: Adapted from "Table 1: Number of Licensees and Registrants, By Facilities and Number of Sites (FY 2001)," in *Animal Welfare Report, Fiscal Year 2001,* (APHIS 41-35-075), U.S. Department of Agriculture, Animal and Plant Health Inspection Service, Washington, DC, 2002

In fiscal year 2001 the Animal Care unit of USDA/APHIS conducted 1,556 compliance inspections. (See Figure 5.11.) This number was down slightly from 1999 (1,816).

All registered research facilities must submit annual reports to the USDA listing the number and species of animals used in research, testing, and experimentation and

FIGURE 5.11

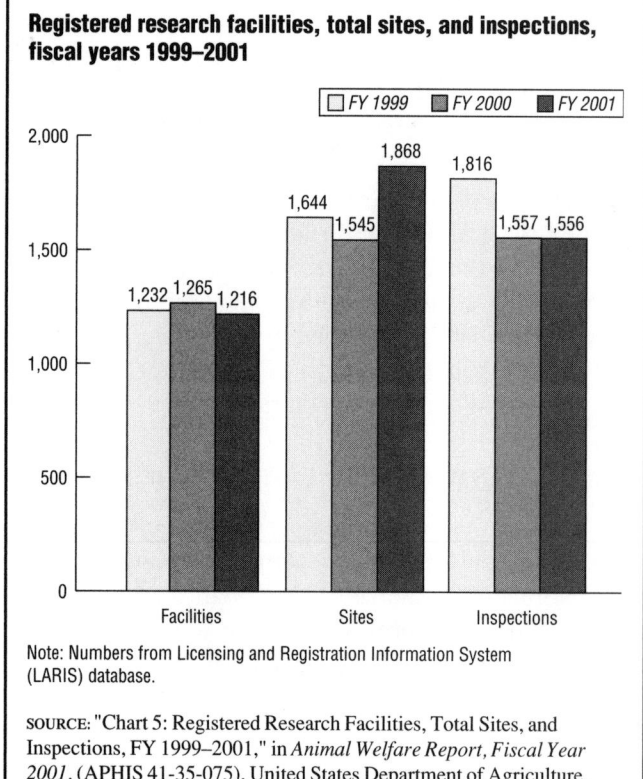

Registered research facilities, total sites, and inspections, fiscal years 1999–2001

Note: Numbers from Licensing and Registration Information System (LARIS) database.

SOURCE: "Chart 5: Registered Research Facilities, Total Sites, and Inspections, FY 1999–2001," in *Animal Welfare Report, Fiscal Year 2001,* (APHIS 41-35-075), United States Department of Agriculture, Animal and Plant Health Inspection Service, Washington, DC, 2002

indicating whether pain-relieving drugs were administered. If the drugs were not administered for procedures that cause pain or distress, the report must explain why their use would have interfered with the research or experiment.

The Health Research Extension Act (HREA)

In 1985 the Health Research Extension Act (HREA) was passed. This legislation requires that facilities conducting animal research, training, and testing activities that receive funding from the Public Health Service (PHS) follow an animal welfare policy called the Public Health Service Policy on the Humane Care and Use of Laboratory Animals (PHSP). The PHS includes government agencies such as the Centers for Disease Control and Prevention (CDC), the FDA, and the NIH. The NIH is the main public source of funding for biomedical research in the United States.

Affected animal research facilities must follow the recommendations given in the PHS's *Guide for the Care and Use of Laboratory Animals* regarding housing, cleanliness, husbandry, veterinary care, and use of measures to alleviate pain and distress. The standards are similar to those found in the Animal Welfare Act (AWA). However, the HREA applies to all vertebrates, including mice, rats, and birds.

The HREA requires facilities to file annual reports that describe their animal care and use programs and how they comply with the AWA and the PHSP. The PHSP is administered by the NIH Office for Protection from Research Risks (OPRR). Research facilities that receive funding from the NIH must have at least five people on their IACUC. The NIH also reviews planned animal studies to ensure that animal models are appropriate and that no more animals than are necessary are used.

The Food, Drug, and Cosmetic Act (FDCA)

Another major piece of federal legislation that affects laboratory animals is the Food, Drug, and Cosmetic Act (FDCA). The FDCA defines drugs as follows:

- Articles intended for use in the diagnosis, cure, mitigation, treatment, or prevention of disease

- Articles (other than food) intended to affect the structure or any function of the body of man or other animals

Drugs must receive FDA approval before they can be sold in the United States. Although the FDA does not specify the tests that must be done, the agency does not allow human testing to occur if animal safety testing is considered inadequate or incomplete.

Cosmetics are defined as articles other than soap that are applied to the human body for "cleansing, beautifying, promoting attractiveness, or altering the appearance." Soaps are specifically excluded from the regulatory definition of cosmetics, and so do not fall under the FDCA.

The FDA divides cosmetics into 13 categories:

- Skin care (creams, lotions, powders, and sprays)
- Fragrances
- Eye makeup
- Manicure products
- Makeup other than eye (lipstick, foundation, and blush)
- Hair coloring preparations
- Shampoos, permanent waves, and other hair products
- Deodorants
- Shaving products
- Baby products (shampoos, lotions, and powders)
- Bath oils and bubble baths
- Mouthwashes
- Tanning products

Cosmetic products and their ingredients (except for color additives) are not subject to premarket FDA approval. However, it is illegal to distribute cosmetics that contain substances that could harm consumers under normal use. Although animal testing is not required by the law, it is recommended by the FDA to ensure product safety. On its Web site in 2003, the agency said:

FDA continues to work with other governments and private organizations to develop validated alternatives to animal testing in assessing cosmetic safety and considerable progress has been made in some areas. Nevertheless, until a method has been proven to be reliable and accepted by the scientific community, FDA believes that the use of animals remains necessary to ensure the safety of cosmetic ingredients and products.

Cosmetic products that are not adequately tested for safety must have a warning statement on their front label reading "WARNING—The safety of this product has not been determined."

Some consumer products are considered both a drug and a cosmetic under the law—for example, dandruff shampoos, fluoride-containing toothpastes, combination antiperspirants/deodorants, and makeup products or moisturizers that contain sunscreens. These products are subject to provisions of the laws that apply to both drugs and cosmetics.

Other Federal Legislation

The Federal Hazardous Substances Labeling Act was passed in 1960. The Consumer Product Safety Commission (CPSC) administers the law as it applies to household products. This law affects animals because household products (like cleaners) that contain hazardous chemicals must warn consumers about their potential hazards. A hazardous substance is defined as one that is toxic, corrosive, flammable, or combustible; that is extremely irritating or sensitizing; or that generates pressure through heat, decomposition, or other means. Toxicity tests are required to determine these conditions.

Other laws governing chemicals that must be tested for toxicity include the Toxic Substances Control Act and the Federal Insecticide, Fungicide, and Rodenticide Act. Both of these laws are administered by the Environmental Protection Agency (EPA). Animals are commonly used to test the products regulated by all of this legislation.

In 2000 the Chimpanzee Health Improvement, Maintenance, and Protection (CHIMP) Act was passed, calling for the creation of a national sanctuary system for chimpanzees no longer needed in research programs conducted or supported by federal agencies. As of 2003, there were approximately 900 chimpanzees involved in federal research programs. Most were bred or captured from the wild for the performance of AIDS research. Several hundred of the animals were considered surplus by the government.

In 2002 the NIH awarded a contract to Chimp Haven, Inc. to establish and operate a sanctuary under the CHIMP Act in Shreveport, Louisiana. A groundbreaking ceremony was held at the property in May 2003. The CHIMP Act is extremely controversial because it allows the animals to be recalled for research purposes if there is a "public health need." Because the act does not call for permanent

TABLE 5.5

Animals used in research, fiscal year 2001

	Number of all animals	Dogs	Cats	Primates	Guinea pigs	Hamsters	Rabbits	Sheep	Pigs	Other farm animals	Other animals
Total United States	1,236,903	70,082	22,755	49,382	256,193	167,231	267,351	26,236	60,253	75,169	242,251
Total research	1,122,403	68,945	22,374	43,838	244,482	155,557	259,043	13,595	48,679	39,216	226,674
Federal agencies	114,500	1,137	381	5,544	11,711	11,674	8,308	12,641	11,574	35,953	15,577
Alabama	8,163	1,796	308	941	587	32	2,228	166	519	658	928
Alaska	26	8	0	0	0	0	8	0	0	0	10
Arizona	6,134	302	84	102	109	563	721	107	273	204	3,669
Arkansas	2,833	1,109	31	0	505	0	884	0	215	2	87
California	119,286	2,911	1,588	5,872	29,516	7,497	50,098	3,537	4,378	4,898	8,991
Colorado	8,368	859	291	18	2,794	1,553	784	633	515	62	859
Connecticut	7,103	728	90	485	1,383	1,037	1,783	6	559	8	1,024
Delaware	56,778	2,126	1,227	31	11,348	16,253	19,037	75	2,204	1,113	3,364
District of Columbia	1,867	168	35	22	64	281	460	56	741	0	40
Florida	7,094	360	347	402	1,012	206	1,126	186	1,007	13	2,235
Georgia	19,470	1,507	597	3,310	382	4,765	4,474	15	774	185	3,461
Guam	0	0	0	0	0	0	0	0	0	0	0
Hawaii	113	0	1	5	0	80	16	0	0	0	11
Idaho	889	45	12	0	0	0	88	0	0	3	741
Illinois	39,128	2,532	727	683	10,861	1,778	14,912	560	3,843	592	2,640
Indiana	23,505	2,437	1,130	291	3,560	802	3,109	50	476	27	11,623
Iowa	58,612	1,708	1,468	19	5,712	38,650	3,697	164	332	869	5,993
Kansas	19,423	989	731	178	77	530	424	48	310	12,407	3,729
Kentucky	2,794	184	76	101	215	504	1,023	1	206	10	474
Louisiana	14,289	745	221	2,913	426	30	2,625	10	337	233	6,749
Maine	3,457	9	13	0	3	12	225	0	102	274	2,819
Maryland	26,679	852	358	2,503	8,742	2,195	6,911	332	489	184	4,113
Massachusetts	134,568	1,408	410	3,819	20,847	8,946	9,769	864	3,018	3,426	82,061
Michigan	39,023	5,236	808	1,305	13,293	1,622	5,316	314	558	447	10,124
Minnesota	16,365	1,858	589	311	4,794	853	3,697	632	2,633	605	393
Mississippi	1,502	341	36	134	0	332	224	25	199	14	197
Missouri	34,722	2,551	1,956	111	5,453	6,461	3,681	521	1,823	1,847	10,318
Montana	1,981	12	32	28	397	0	1,273	107	0	63	69
Nebraska	44,269	826	971	67	2,297	31,251	3,488	193	1,416	1,728	2,032
Nevada	1,979	100	0	0	460	0	128	253	0	0	1,038
New Hampshire	817	27	11	10	0	113	91	447	63	0	55
New Jersey	78,736	6,388	516	2,937	33,478	8,690	13,528	17	2,647	300	10,235
New Mexico	1,159	186	0	57	32	70	60	0	40	33	681
New York	50,888	5,636	2,023	1,947	9,665	6,116	8,198	445	1,927	256	14,675
North Carolina	21,289	1,501	587	1,298	7,416	688	5,289	131	2,474	141	1,764
North Dakota	309	19	29	0	0	0	0	221	20	20	0
Ohio	63,387	4,923	1,042	717	30,281	3,126	15,215	283	4,058	405	3,337
Oklahoma	4,586	698	134	63	483	132	793	48	43	134	2,058
Oregon	3,993	130	59	1,200	859	677	384	249	276	59	100
Pennsylvania	85,356	5,431	1,611	2,395	19,100	2,337	44,133	718	2,459	1,006	6,166
Puerto Rico	328	0	0	35	20	112	74	0	18	0	69
Rhode Island	1,491	56	46	1	45	169	192	108	247	47	580
South Carolina	3,146	241	98	200	251	8	742	0	342	8	1,256
South Dakota	5,135	62	31	8	0	6	360	388	1,259	2,850	171
Tennessee	7,103	941	194	298	1,226	501	979	115	1,491	69	1,289
Texas	37,176	2,079	603	2,897	5,745	3,158	13,216	954	1,681	3,186	3,657
Utah	4,686	215	106	35	1,292	247	1,258	176	86	60	1,211
Vermont	1,213	39	13	0	473	263	172	60	0	2	191
Virgin Islands	0	0	0	0	0	0	0	0	0	0	0
Virginia	15,129	1,761	186	1,676	220	854	4,548	32	1,118	158	4,576
Washington	13,380	1,209	320	1,815	3,718	323	2,245	159	477	148	2,966
West Virginia	722	19	50	0	111	53	214	89	22	0	164
Wisconsin	21,584	3,651	565	2,598	5,214	1,679	5,087	100	1,004	246	1,440
Wyoming	370	26	13	0	16	2	56	0	0	16	241

SOURCE: "Table 2: Animals Used in Research (FY 2001)," in *Animal Welfare Report, Fiscal Year 2001*, (APHIS 41-35-075), U.S. Department of Agriculture, Animal and Plant Health Inspection Service, Washington, DC, 2002

retirement of chimpanzees, many animal activist groups have been calling for its repeal.

LABORATORY ANIMALS AND THEIR USES

Table 5.5 notes that there were nearly 1.24 million AWA-registered animals used in live research during fiscal year 2001. (Note that rats, mice, birds, and cold-blooded animals are not regulated by the AWA and are not included.) This number is down from an annual average of 1.75 million for the period between 1974 and 1992. The number of regulated laboratory animals has steadily declined since 1992. During 2001 rabbits comprised the single largest species of regulated animals used, accounting for 21 percent. (See Figure 5.12.)

FIGURE 5.12

Research animals registered with the U.S. Department of Agriculture, fiscal year 2001

Sheep 2%
Cats 2%
Primates 4%
Pigs 5%
Dogs 6%
Other farm animals 6%
Rabbits 21%
Hamsters 14%
Guinea pigs 20%
Other animals 20%

Note: Excludes rats, mice, birds, and cold-blooded animals

SOURCE: Adapted from "Table 2: Animals Used in Research (FY 2001)," in *Animal Welfare Report, Fiscal Year 2001*, (APHIS 41-35-075), U.S. Department of Agriculture, Animal and Plant Health Inspection Service, Washington, DC, 2002

FIGURE 5.13

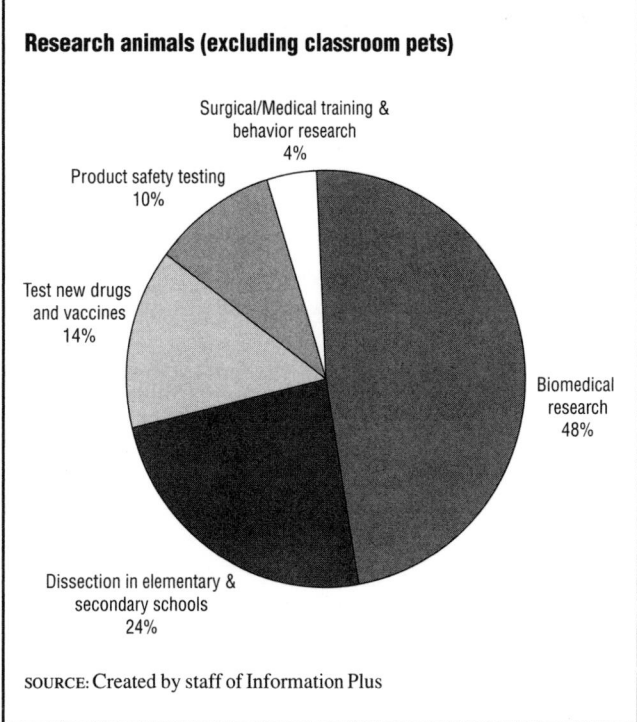

Research animals (excluding classroom pets)

Surgical/Medical training & behavior research 4%
Product safety testing 10%
Test new drugs and vaccines 14%
Biomedical research 48%
Dissection in elementary & secondary schools 24%

SOURCE: Created by staff of Information Plus

Since the USDA does not regulate all lab animals (notably rats and mice), there are no official total numbers of animals used in research. Composite numbers taken from the estimates of a number of animal welfare and biomedical research groups in 2003 indicate that approximately 25 million total animals (regulated and nonregulated) are used in research annually. This would mean that regulated animals comprise only 5 percent of the total number of animals used. This figure seems reasonable, given that groups advocating animal research usually estimate that rats and mice account for 95 percent of all animals used.

If a total of 25 million is assumed, then primates, dogs, and cats together comprised just over one-half of 1 percent of the total animals used during 2001. These species are the ones that arouse the most public concern in the research animal debate. According to the USDA, the usage of dogs and cats declined by 65 percent between 1973—when 195,157 dogs and 66,165 cats were used—and 2001—when 70,082 dogs and 22,755 cats were used. Annual primate usage fluctuated between 35,000 and 60,000 animals over this time period.

Biomedicine and Dissection

According to statistics and estimates gathered from various animal welfare groups in 2003, nearly half of all research animals (excluding classroom pets) are used in biomedicine. (See Figure 5.13.) Biomedicine is a medical

discipline based on principles of the natural sciences, particularly biology and biochemistry. Table 5.6 shows some of the animals associated with particular areas of biomedical research.

Dead animals used for dissection in schools comprise the second largest category of research animals. An HSUS estimate on the organization's Web site in 2003 suggests that approximately 6 million animals are dissected by schoolchildren each year, mostly frogs, pig fetuses, and cats. Dissection has been considered a staple of biology classes since the 1960s, when the National Science Foundation urged schools to implement a more hands-on science curriculum.

According to the NEAVS, the first legal challenge against school dissection lodged by a student occurred in 1987 in California. A high school student sued her school for not allowing her to perform an alternative to dissection. California and Florida became the first states to allow students to opt out of dissection in the mid- to late 1980s. According to information available on the HSUS Web site in mid-2003, six other states have since followed suit with "choice-in-dissection" laws or policies—Maine, Pennsylvania, Louisiana, New York, Rhode Island, and Illinois. Today many students are expressing ethical and moral concerns about the practice of dissection in the classroom. Some school districts now offer students alternatives, such as computer models. The National Science Teachers Association defends dissection as a valuable learning tool for children, but urges teachers to be flexible in offering alternatives.

TABLE 5.6

Roles animals have played in biomedical research

Armadillos
Leprosy

Cats
Cataract Surgery
Deafness
Epilepsy
Feline Leukemia
Glaucoma
Lupus

Chinchillas
Cholera Vaccine
Sleep Research

Dogs
Aging
Artificial Hips & Joints
Behavioral Studies
Organ Transplants

Ferrets
Canine Distemper
Influenza Virus
Reproductive Research
Toxicology Research

Flies
Genetic Research

Frogs
Antibiotics

Guinea pigs
Diptheria Vaccine
Immune Systems

Hamsters
Diabetes
Lyme Disease

Marine sponges
Human Immune System

Mice
Addictive Drugs
Cancer Treatments
Genetic Models
Organ Transplants
Whooping Cough Vaccine

Monkfish
Hormone Research
Insulin for Diabetes

Pigs
Atherosclerosis
Heart Transplants
Motion Sickness Patches
Plastic Surgery
Stress Studies

Primates
AIDS
Alzheimer's Disease
Gum Disease
In Vitro Fertilization
Polio Vaccine
rH Factor

Rabbits
Emphysema
Eye & Ear Infections
Rabies Vaccine
Skin Disorders

Salamanders
Heart Attack Research

Sheep
Anthrax Vaccine
Fetal Alcohol Syndrome
Joint Reconstruction
Pregnancy Research

Woodchucks
Hepatitis B

SOURCE: "Roles Animals Have Played in Biomedical Research," in *Educational Materials,* Michigan Society for Medical Research, Ann Arbor, MI, 2003

The use of dissection as an educational tool in secondary schools has been banned in Israel, Switzerland, Holland, the Slovak Republic, Poland, Argentina, and the Indian state of Rajasthan.

Drug and Product Testing

Though no official statistics exist, estimates obtained from various animal rights groups in 2003 suggest that nearly one-quarter of all research animals are used in the testing of new drugs, vaccines, and consumer products. These tests are required or recommended by federal law.

According to the FDA, drug companies typically test new drugs on at least two different animal species to see if they are affected differently. Animal testing is performed to determine specific characteristics, such as:

- How much of the drug is absorbed into the bloodstream

- Any toxic side effects

- Appropriate dosage levels

- How the drug is metabolized (broken down)

- How quickly the drug is excreted from the body

The results from animal tests tell researchers if and how new drugs should then be tested on humans. Product safety testing exposes animals to chemicals to determine factors such as eye and skin irritancy. Common product safety tests conducted with animals include the following:

- Acute toxicity tests determine the immediate effects of chemical exposure. The LD-50 test is an example. In this test, animals are exposed to chemicals through ingestion, inhalation, or skin contact to determine the concentration necessary to kill 50 percent of the test group within a specific time period.

- Skin and eye irritancy tests determine the effects on skin and eyes of chemical exposure. One example is the Draize eye test, in which chemicals are placed in the eyes of restrained animals. Rabbits are commonly used because they cannot blink and wash out the chemicals.

- Subchronic and chronic toxicity tests determine the effects of long-term chemical exposure.

- Genetic toxicity tests determine the effects of chemical exposure on reproductive organs.

- Birth defects tests determine the effects of chemical exposure on offspring.

- Cancer potential tests determine the potential of chemical exposures for causing cancer.

Some cosmetics companies advertise that they do not conduct animal testing on their products or that their products are cruelty-free. This can be a confusing issue to consumers. According to the Johns Hopkins Center for Alternatives to Animal Testing (CAAT), such claims can mean various things, including:

- Animal testing has not been performed on the products and/or their ingredients in the previous five years.

- Animal testing was performed on the products and/or ingredients by another company (for example, a supplier).

- Non-animal testing was performed on finished products made from ingredients already known to be safe because of previous animal testing.

The CAAT points out that the vast majority of cosmetic ingredients used by the industry have been tested on animals at some point in time, or are known to be safe based upon decades of use. It notes that smaller cosmetics companies tend to produce final products made from purchased ingredients, rather than from ingredients developed in-house. Larger companies that develop new ingredients for cosmetics must use animal testing or viable alternatives to prove that the ingredients are safe for consumer use.

The National Anti-Vivisection Society publishes a book called *Personal Care for People Who Care.* The book lists hundreds of companies that produce personal care (e.g., bath products, deodorants and antiperspirants), household (e.g., bathroom and kitchen cleaners, furniture polishes), pet care, and cosmetic products and tells whether they do or do not test their products on animals. The companies are distinguished as follows:

- Companies that do not test products or ingredients on animals, nor do any of their outside suppliers

- Individual subsidiaries/divisions that do not test products or ingredients on animals even though their parent companies do test on animals

- Companies that do not test their finished products or ingredients on animals but do not have agreements with suppliers stating that they do not test their ingredients on animals

- Companies that do test products and/or ingredients on animals

In addition, the book identifies companies that do not use any animal-derived ingredients in their products. Other animal rights organizations, such as PETA, maintain similar types of lists. Some provide a seal compliant companies can use to mark their products for easy identification by shoppers.

In February 2003 the Council of the European Union and the European Parliament approved the 7th Amendment of Council Directive 76/768/EEC (the Cosmetics Directive). It will place a ban on the testing of cosmetics on animals in Europe in 2009. In addition, in 2009 the sale and import of new cosmetics tested on animals using 11 specific tests will be banned. Another ban will be implemented in 2013 on the sale and import of cosmetics tested on animals for three toxicity tests (assuming that valid alternative tests have been established by that time).

Surgical/Medical Training and Behavior Research

As shown in Figure 5.13, it is estimated that the use of laboratory animals for surgical/medical training and behavior research comprises only a small part (4 percent) of the number of research animals used. However, this category is one that is particularly criticized by antivivisection groups. In the past, surgeons training to operate on humans and animals almost always practiced on live animals. Many of these surgeries were "terminal surgeries," or those conducted on animals that are not allowed to regain consciousness. The animals are euthanized while they are under the effects of anesthesia.

According to the Physicians Committee for Responsible Medicine (PCRM), as of February 2003, two-thirds of all U.S. medical schools had eliminated live animal labs. Its list of medical schools that continued to use such labs to train students in human physiology, pharmacology, and/or surgery as of that date included 27 schools. PCRM

TABLE 5.7

Animals in veterinary medical schools, 1998–99

School	Students	Animals used	Animals killed	Multiple sessions
Auburn University	360	836	373	0
Colorado State University	537	1,910	582	10
Cornell University	NS	NS	NS	NS
Iowa State University	392	1,402	591	0
Kansas State University	390	817	245	0
Louisiana State University	NS	NS	NS	NS
Michigan State University	398	839	254	7
Mississippi State University	188	1,176	502	9
North Carolina State Universit	290	12,744	1,152	20
Ohio State University, The	530	874	526	48
Oklahoma State University	297	324	220	136
Oregon State University	144	355	122	74
Purdue University	260	746	251	30
Texas A&M University	499	1,443	941	0
Tufts University	320	1,027	52	0
Tuskegee University	NS	NS	NS	NS
University of California	429	2,378	802	24
University of Florida	312	739	173	0
University of Georgia	306	502	387	60
University of Illinois	400	2,242	677	50
University of Minnesota, The	304	1,315	468	20
University of Missouri	NS	NS	NS	NS
University of Pennsylvania	NS	NS	NS	NS
University of Tennessee	261	1,004	425	40
University of Wisconsin	318	1,395	192	7
Virginia Tech and University of Maryland	345	1,068	234	0
Washington State University	277	1,230	484	0
Totals:	**7,557**	**36,366**	**9,653**	**535**

Note: NS = Not supplied

SOURCE: Susan B. Krebsbach, "Summary Data for Number of Animals Used," in *Educational Use of Nonhuman Animals in U.S. Veterinary Medical Schools for the 1998–99 School Year*, Association of Veterinarians for Animal Rights, Davis, CA, September 17, 2000 [Online] http://www.avar.org [accessed July 21, 2003]

notes that many of the medical schools that have dropped the use of live animal labs are well-respected institutions, among them Harvard, Stanford, and Yale.

In 1999 the Association of Veterinarians for Animal Rights (AVAR) conducted a survey of U.S. veterinary medical schools regarding their use of animals in education and training. The summary data are included in Table 5.7. More than 36,000 animals were used during the 1998–99 school year, and 9,653 of these were killed. The vast majority of the animals used were associated with the teaching of anesthesiology and surgery. The data also include the number of animals that were subjected to multiple sessions—that is, multiple surgeries involving invasive procedures. More than 500 animals were involved in multiple sessions at the schools.

Many veterinary schools are limiting the number of terminal surgeries required of their students. In August 2002 the University of Pennsylvania School of Veterinary Medicine eliminated the last small-animal terminal surgery course that it offered. Formerly, each student was required to perform terminal surgery on two dogs and one cat. Each student now performs recovery surgery on one dog and one cat and performs a sterilization of one dog for the Massachusetts SPCA. The Tufts University School of Veterinary Medicine in North Grafton, Massachusetts, and the Western University of Health Sciences College of Veterinary Medicine in Pomona, California, have also eliminated requirements for terminal surgery.

Some veterinary schools conduct dissection labs. According to the NEAVS, many schools now use animal cadavers donated by people whose pets or livestock have died of natural causes or have been humanely euthanized due to illness or injury.

SOURCES OF RESEARCH ANIMALS

Live animals used in research come from one of two sources. Most are purpose-bred for laboratory research, meaning that they are born and raised under controlled conditions. Purpose-breeding of laboratory animals is becoming more and more common as researchers demand animals with particular genetic makeups. For example, researchers investigating narcolepsy use dogs bred to be born with the condition.

Purpose-bred animals are obtained by laboratories from animal breeders licensed by the USDA. As of 2003, the largest breeder and supplier of these animals was Charles River Laboratories, headquartered in Wilmington, Massachusetts. Lab animal suppliers advertise their animals in the *Lab Animal Buyer's Guide*, available on the Internet at http://guide.labanimal.com/guide/. The 2003 edition included frogs, toads, salamanders, newts, cats, dogs, ferrets, chickens, ducks, cattle, goats, sheep, swine, rabbits, nonhuman primates (monkeys, chimpanzees, etc.), birds, fish, opossums, invertebrates, and a wide assortment of rodents.

Live animals for research can also be purchased from random sources. For example, dogs and cats obtained from animal shelters are considered random-source animals. Researchers acquire these animals from licensed dealers or directly from shelters. Random-source dealers are also listed in the *Lab Animal Buyer's Guide*.

Random-source animals are used in experiments where genetic diversity is important. Random-source dogs and cats are far less expensive than purpose-bred ones. According to information available on the MISMR Web site in 2003, the cost of a shelter dog or cat was $60–$200, compared to $400–$600 for a purpose-bred one. The site also claimed that less than 2 percent of the 10 million animals that visit shelters each year are used for medical research. The organization points out that these animals would be euthanized in the shelters anyway because of the pet overpopulation problem.

MISMR says that random-source animals are primarily used in biomedical research on cardiovascular dis-

eases, cancer, diabetes, arthritis, lung disorders, orthopedics, birth defects, hearing loss, and blindness. Dogs are the subject of choice for heart and kidney disease research. Cats are frequently used in research devoted to the central nervous system, strokes, and disorders of the brain, eyes, and ears. MISMR notes that use of these animals in research benefits not only human medicine but also veterinary medicine.

Animal welfare organizations often criticize the NIH for funding research projects that use shelter dogs and cats. The NIH leaves source decisions to individual research institutions. Although some people are pushing for legislation to outlaw the use of shelter animals in medical research, MISMR argues that this would drive up the cost of research and costs to local communities that must house and euthanize unwanted animals.

In April 2002 executives with a company called LABS of Virginia, Inc., were indicted by federal authorities for importing wild-caught monkeys in violation of wildlife protection laws. The firm breeds and sells primates to research institutions. It allegedly planned to establish a breeding colony of the monkeys at its facility in Yemassee, South Carolina, with monkeys that were shipped into the United States from Indonesia in 1997. Witnesses at Chicago's O'Hare International Airport reported the firm to authorities after seeing crying baby monkeys in shipping crates.

Animals used in dissection labs are usually purchased from biological supply companies. One of the largest is the Carolina Biological Supply Company of Burlington, North Carolina. Carolina sells a variety of preserved specimens for dissection, including earthworms, amphibians, sharks, fish, bats, mice, cats, mink, rabbits, cows, sheep, dogs, rats, pigs, and pig fetuses.

The company says that it obtains its animals from many sources, including cultures (breeding facilities), the food industry, animal shelters, and "natural or managed habitats where seasonal collections are made." Carolina notes that many of the organisms that it sells were already dead when the company purchased them, such as euthanized cats from animal shelters and fetal pigs from slaughterhouses.

Animal welfare and conservation organizations are particularly critical of the use of wild-caught animals in dissection labs. The NEAVS said as of 2001 that approximately 3 million wild-caught frogs are sold each year for dissection purposes. This is troublesome because some feel it could threaten natural populations of these species. Welfarists worry that wild-caught animals might not be harvested, housed, and transported in a humane manner.

The World Society for the Protection of Animals (WSPA) claims that American biological supply firms purchase large numbers of cats from Mexico and that many of these cats are stolen pets. The allegations are based on a 1994 investigation that the organization conducted.

REDUCTION, REFINEMENT, AND REPLACEMENT (THE 3R'S)

In 1959 scientists William Russell and Rex Burch published a book titled *Principles of Humane Experimental Technique* that advocated three principles for the animal research industry: reduction, refinement, and replacement. The authors called these principles "the three R's for the removal of inhumanity."

The book was largely ignored until the 1980s, when public protest against the use of animals in laboratory testing became more widespread. Scientists and animal welfare organizations then embraced the 3R's as scientifically reasonable and humane goals for the industry. However, they are guiding principles, not legal requirements.

The 3R's are defined as follows:

- Reduction is a goal to reduce the number of animals used in research overall by reducing the number required for individual experiments or areas of study without sacrificing the statistical validity of the results. In other words, researchers are urged to use statistics to determine the minimum number of animals that can be used in an experiment and still provide valid data. Another goal is to reduce the number of procedures that require whole animals. For example, tissues from an animal used in one experiment could be used in other experiments in place of live whole animals.

- Refinement is a goal to refine experimental and care practices to reduce animal suffering and distress and encourage well-being. Such practices include the use of painkillers during and after experiments, the use of humane euthanasia techniques, and improvements in animals' living environments.

- Replacement is a goal to replace live laboratory animals with suitable alternatives (for example, computer simulations) and to replace higher animal species with lower species.

The Search for Alternatives to Animal Tests

In 1993 the National Institutes of Health Revitalization Act was passed, requiring formation of an agency to oversee validation of alternatives to toxicological animal testing. The result was the Interagency Coordinating Committee for the Validation of Alternative Methods (ICCVAM) and the National Toxicology Program Interagency Center for the Evaluation of Alternative Toxicological Methods (NICEATM).

The ICCVAM is responsible for establishing validation criteria and for encouraging government agencies that regulate toxicity testing to accept validated methods. The NICEATM facilitates information sharing among all the parties involved.

The ICCVAM and NICEATM work with 15 federal agencies:

- Agency for Toxic Substances and Disease Registry

- Consumer Product Safety Commission

- Department of Agriculture

- Department of Defense

- Department of Energy

- Department of the Interior

- Department of Transportation

- Environmental Protection Agency

- Food and Drug Administration

- National Institutes of Health

- National Cancer Institute

- National Institute of Environmental Health Sciences

- National Institute for Occupational Safety and Health

- National Library of Medicine

- Occupational Safety and Health Administration

The ICCVAM also works with the European Centre for the Validation of Alternative Methods (ECVAM) to coordinate international validation efforts.

Between 1999 and 2003 the ICCVAM has recommended two alternative tests to regulatory agencies: the local lymph node assay (LLNA) and Corrositex. LLNA is a mouse-based test for determining if new chemicals cause allergic contact dermatitis (skin reactions). The traditional test for this condition used guinea pigs. The LLNA is reported to use fewer animals and cause much less pain and distress than the traditional test. It is also much faster.

Corrositex is an *in vitro* test in which synthetic skin is used to test chemical irritancy. *In vitro* is a Latin phrase that means "in glass." *In vitro* tests are commonly conducted in test tubes. The traditional test for skin irritancy relied on rabbits and could take several weeks. The new takes between a few minutes and a few hours.

Pain and Distress

One of the goals of refinement is to relieve animal pain and distress. The USDA tracks the occurrence of pain and distress in regulated animals, as shown in Table 5.8. These numbers are based on reports by research institutions to the USDA for fiscal year 2001. During that year, 57 percent of the regulated animals (705,602)

TABLE 5.8

Pain and distress in regulated research animals reported to the U.S. Department of Agriculture, fiscal year 2001

	No pain or distress— no drugs needed for relief	With pain or distress— drugs used for relief	With pain or distress—no drugs used for relief	Total United States
Dogs	34,533	33,878	1,671	70,082
Cats	13,008	9,339	408	22,755
Primates	22,069	26,460	853	49,382
Guinea pigs	150,677	69,371	36,145	256,193
Hamsters	79,056	43,254	44,921	167,231
Rabbits	156,364	105,951	5,036	267,351
Sheep	16,585	9,154	497	26,236
Pigs	22,140	36,883	1,230	60,253
Other farm animals	59,900	13,471	1,798	75,169
Other animals	151,270	78,025	12,956	242,251
TOTAL	**705,602**	**425,786**	**105,515**	**1,236,903**

SOURCE: Adapted from "Table 3: Animals Used in Research, No Pain or Distress—No Drugs Needed for Relief (FY 2001)," and "Table 4: Animals Used in Research, With Pain or Distress—Drugs Used for Relief (FY 2001)," and "Table 5: Animals Used in Research, With Pain or Distress—No Drugs Used for Relief (FY 2001)," in *Animal Welfare Report, Fiscal Year 2001*, (APHIS 41-35-075), U.S. Department of Agriculture, Animal and Plant Health Inspection Service, Washington, DC, 2002

TABLE 5.9

Proteins with therapeutic and industrial value that have been produced (but not commercialized) in the milk of transgenic animals, 2002

Protein	Animal	Use
Antithrombin III	Goat	Reduce the amount of blood needed in some surgeries
Factor VIII, Factor IX	Goat, Pig, Sheep	Treatment of hemophilia
CFTR	Sheep	Treatment of cystic fibrosis
Lactoferrin	Cow	Natural antibiotic and used in coronary surgery
Alpha-1-antitrypsin	Sheep	Treatment of cystic fibrosis and emphysema
Lysostaphin	Cow	An anti-bacterial compound that prevents mastitis in cows
Spider silk protein	Goat	Production of ultra-strong, lightweight medical and industrial materials

SOURCE: Randy Vines, "Table 1: Proteins with Therapeutic and Industrial Value That Have Been Produced (But Not Commercialized) in the Milk of Transgenic Animals," in *Animal Biotechnology*, (443-003), Virginia Cooperative Extension, Blacksburg, VA, 2002

experienced no pain or distress, 34 percent experienced pain or distress but were administered drugs for relief (425,786), and 9 percent suffered pain and distress but were not given drugs for relief (105,515).

Animal welfare groups have expressed doubts about the validity of USDA pain and distress numbers, making accusations that these numbers are greatly underreported by research institutions. In 1998 the HSUS launched a Pain and Distress Initiative to focus attention on issues involved in assessing and relieving pain in laboratory animals. The HSUS publishes a newsletter titled *Pain and Distress Report* to publicize these issues. The goal of the initiative is to eliminate pain and distress in research animals by the year 2020.

The HSUS acknowledges that animal rights advocates want to eliminate animal testing, not reform it. The organization states, "The HSUS would like to see the day when animals are no longer used in harmful research. However, we believe the most urgent public priority is eliminating pain and distress among laboratory animals."

Scientists recognize that eliminating pain and distress in laboratory animals is not only humane but good scientific practice. The animal use policy at Vanderbilt University, for example, acknowledges that experimental results can be compromised by a physical or mental state of distress in the subject and recommends relieving pain and distress in animal subjects.

One concept embraced by the HSUS is the use of humane endpoints. This means that test animals can be humanely euthanized after exhibiting specific symptoms of a disease rather than dying of the disease itself. The October 2002 issue of *Pain and Distress Report* describes a study performed to determine a humane endpoint for the L1210 model of murine leukemia. Researchers injected mice with lymphocytic leukemia cells and recorded their symptoms and appearance every six hours until all of the mice died. They concluded that a humane endpoint was the appearance of hunched posture, decreased activity, or abdominal swelling in two consecutive examinations or the appearance of two specific symptoms during a single examination. According to the HSUS, the researchers concluded that early euthanasia at these humane endpoints would not compromise the research results but would substantially reduce animal pain and distress.

GENETIC ENGINEERING

Genetic engineering is the scientific manipulation of genetic material, like genes and DNA. Animals have been the subject of genetic engineering research and experiments for several decades. Transgenic animals are animals that carry a foreign gene that has been deliberately inserted through genetic engineering. They are widely used in biomedical research. As shown in Table 5.9, scientists have invented transgenic sheep and goats that produce foreign proteins in their milk. Production of these proteins could have enormous medical and industrial benefits for humans.

Research continues on the genetic engineering of pigs so that they can grow organs that will not be rejected by human bodies. Scientists believe that harvesting organs from transgenic pigs could one day solve the human organ shortage that presently exists, saving millions of human lives. The technology is almost to the point to make this possible. Some people consider this to be medical progress, but others see it as another injustice perpetrated against animals for the sake of humans.

A clone is a later-born genetic twin. In July 1996 the first mammal cloned from adult cells was born, a product of research at the Roslin Institute in Edinburgh, Scotland. Dolly was cloned from an udder cell taken from a six-year-old sheep. (See Figure 5.14.) Between 1996 and 2003, several other animals were cloned, including sheep, mice, cows, a guar (an endangered Asian ox), goats, pigs, rabbits, and a cat. Not all of the animals have survived. Cloning is still new technology, and the success rate is low.

A company named Genetic Savings & Clone has invested $2 million in producing the first cloned dog. Entrepreneurs hope to one day clone beloved pets for people willing to pay thousands of dollars for the service. Farmers may be able to vastly increase meat, milk, and egg production by cloning their best-producing animals. The scientific implications of cloning are impressive. It could benefit millions of people. Yet the ethical questions are troubling to some.

A Gallup poll conducted in 2001 found that only 32 percent of those asked believed that cloning of animals should be allowed. This was higher than the percentage approving of human cloning (9 percent). In a 2002 poll, Gallup asked people their opinions about cloning particular categories of animals. In that poll, 38 percent of respondents favored the cloning of endangered species to keep them from becoming extinct. Only 15 percent favored the cloning of pets. Public support therefore does not seem to be fully behind animal cloning, even though it proceeds in the laboratory.

FIGURE 5.14

Dolly. *Photograph by Jeff Mitchell. Archive Photos. Reproduced by permission.*

CHAPTER 6
ANIMALS IN SPORTS

Webster's dictionary defines a sport as a recreation including physical activity. Most people would think of a sport as an athletic competition that demonstrates skills such as physical strength, stamina, agility, and speed. Humans recognized centuries ago that many animals possess such skills naturally and could be used in sporting events.

In the United States today, the major sports in which animals are involved are horseracing, greyhound racing, sled dog racing, rodeos, and organized animal fighting. Besides animal fighting, all of these are considered legitimate sports.

These legitimate sports probably began as friendly competitions between people wanting to show off their animals. However, the most popular evolved into businesses in which large amounts of money are involved. Horseracing and greyhound racing are intertwined with the legalized gambling industry. Rodeos and sled dog races largely depend on sponsors. These are companies that provide financial backing in exchange for being allowed to advertise during the event—for example, by placing advertisements around an arena or in the program. Even animal fighting has become a business of sorts, with profits driven almost entirely by illegal gambling.

In all of these sports, skilled animals can be quite profitable for the people who own, train, and manage them. Therefore, it makes sense that these animals receive the best possible care during their athletic "careers." Sports animals that are less skilled, injured, past their prime, or unwilling or unable to compete anymore have different prospects. Some retire and live comfortably, while others are sold to the slaughterhouse or are killed.

The fate and well-being of animals in sports lie in the hands of humans. To some animal rights activists, this is the root of the problem. They believe that animals should not be used by people for any purpose at all, including sports. Animal welfarists focus their attention on uncovering, publicizing, and outlawing practices in animal sports that they consider harmful to the animals. Animal participation is defended by insiders and fans who feel that their right to enjoy a recreational activity is being threatened by overzealous activists who do not understand the nature of these sports.

THE ROOTS OF ANIMAL SPORTS

All animal sports have their roots in historical customs: religious rituals; contests staged for audience entertainment; and warfare, hunting, and herding practices.

Use of Bulls

Centuries ago the Minoans of Crete practiced religious rituals in which they grabbed running bulls by the horns and flipped or jumped over them. Many ancient religions had rituals that involved bull slaughter. Roman gladiators also fought against bulls in the Colosseum. The Moors, tribes of Arab and African descent that conquered Spain in the eighth century, fought bulls from horseback, a practice that evolved into bullfighting during the Middle Ages.

Blood Sports

Blood sports, such as animal fighting, may have their roots in animal sacrifice, but were really popularized by the Romans as entertainment. Thousands of wild animals died in Rome's Colosseum while doing battle with each other or with gladiators. These events were often more like slaughters than sports. The animals were usually tortured with hot spikes or even dabbed with burning pitch to make them fight more ferociously and violently.

Baiting

Blood sports surged in popularity in Europe during the Middle Ages. These included bears, bulls, and dogs or cocks (roosters) fighting with each other in various forums. Baiting involved a large animal, such as a bull or bear, being set upon by a group of dogs. Originally, baiting did have a practical purpose. Medieval people believed that whipping a bull before it was slaughtered tenderized the meat. Mauling by dogs was considered the same as tenderizing. In fact many customers refused to buy bull meat unless they knew the bull had been baited.

Some baitings were held in small arenas, but many occurred in front of shops and bars. These events were staged by merchants, particularly bar owners, to attract a crowd. Baitings provided so much public entertainment that they were expanded to include other animals. Witnesses at some medieval baitings describe donkeys and other farm animals being tied to bulls and bears and attacked by the dogs. Baitings were imported to the United States with the colonists.

When legislation was passed in England and the United States outlawing bear- and bullbaiting, cockfighting and dogfighting became more popular. These blood sports required less space than baiting and could be conducted without drawing as much public attention.

Horseracing

Sports involving horses originated from warfare, hunting, and herding practices, where fast horses were a great asset. Archaeological records indicate that horseracing occurred in ancient Babylon, Syria, and Egypt. It was an event in the Greek Olympic Games as early as 664 B.C. Selective breeding of horses dates back thousands of years and was practiced by ancient Arabs and Romans.

Organized racing of horses in athletic competitions was an inevitable outcome of human efforts to breed ever-faster horses that performed well in battle. The Romans held chariot races in huge arenas called hippodromes, the most famous of which was Circus Maximus.

Horseracing with riders became widespread during the Middle Ages, particularly in England. Knights returning from the Crusades brought back fast Arabian stallions that were bred with sturdy English mares to produce a new line of horses called Thoroughbreds. Thoroughbred racing was popular with the aristocrats and royalty of British society, earning it the title "Sport of Kings." Human dependence on the horse during hunting and herding led to the creation of many other competitions in which horses excelled, such as jumping over obstacles or chasing lost cows. Rodeo sports thus were born.

Greyhound Racing

Greyhound racing probably began several millennia ago with the Bedouin tribes of Africa and Asia. It was popular with the Egyptian pharaohs and in ancient Greece and Rome. Aristocrats of the Middle Ages used greyhounds to hunt rabbits, deer, and foxes. During the 1500s, Queen Elizabeth I is credited with inventing a hunting sport called

TABLE 6.1

Horse sports

Category	Description	Organizations
Cattle Events	Cutting or Herd Work: Rider on horseback selects a single calf from a herd in the arena, guides it into the center of the arena, and then using fast starts and turns, prevents it from escaping back to the herd.	National Reined Cow Horse Association, National Reining Horse Association, National Cutting Horse Association, United States Team Penning Association
	Reining: Rider maneuvers horse through various moves, including figure-eight patterns, 360 degree spins, and sliding stops.	
	Cow Work: Rider maneuvers horse to control the movements of a running steer, including herding it back and forth along a fence and circling around an arena.	
	Team Penning or Sorting: Team of 2 or 3 riders on horseback must cut specifically marked cattle from a herd and herd them to designated areas.	
Dressage	Rider moves horse through a series of carefully choreographed movements and patterns.	United States Dressage Federation
Endurance	Long-distance trail riding conducted over natural terrain.	American Endurance Ride Conference
Eventing or Combined Training	A three-in-one competition including dressage, cross-country jumping, and show jumping.	Fédération Equestre Internationale
Foxhunting	A sport in which riders and dogs hunt foxes in the countryside.	American Masters of Foxhound Association
Hunter-Jumper	Equestrian event in which horses and riders jump over obstacles.	National Hunter and Jumper Association
Polo	Two teams of players riding thoroughbred horses play a game similar to hockey using a small ball and mallets.	United States Polo Association
Polocrosse	Combination of polo and lacrosse in which riders use racquets instead of mallets.	American Polocrosse Association
Ride and Tie	Long-distance race in which two people and one horse form a racing team. During a race the people alternate riding the horse and running.	Ride and Tie Association
Steeple Chase	Equestrian event in which horses and riders jump over fences.	National Steeplechase Association
Vaulting	Sport in which a rider uses gymnastic moves to vault onto and dismount from moving horse.	American Vaulting Association

SOURCE: Compiled by Information Plus staff from various sources

coursing in which greyhounds were used to pursue hares. Greyhound racing came to be called the "Sport of Queens." It did not become popular in America until the 1800s.

SPORTS ANIMALS TODAY

The only animals used in major sports today are domesticated ones: horses, bovines (calves, bulls, and steers), dogs, and cocks (or roosters).

Horses are the most versatile sporting animal, participating on a large scale in sports besides racing and rodeos. (See Table 6.1.) However, none of these sports are performed by horses alone. All of them include humans, who ride the horses, run alongside them, or are pulled behind in carts.

Although bovines are not nearly as glamorous as horses, they still play a major role in two organized sports: bullfighting and rodeos. Bullfighting has a long and illustrious past, but it has never caught on in North America. It is extremely popular in Spain and Portugal, some Latin American countries (Mexico, Peru, Colombia, Venezuela, and Ecuador), southern France, and the African island of Pemba. In Portugal the bull is not killed in the ring but may be slaughtered afterwards.

Rodeos have a much shorter history. They evolved in North America to show off the work done by ranch hands and cowboys during the 1800s to herd and control cattle. Besides their dependence on bovines, bullfighting and rodeos are unique among sports for another reason. They are the only major animal sports in which humans compete against (or must vanquish) animals.

Dogs participate on a large scale in three sports: sled dog racing, greyhound racing, and organized fighting. These sports differ widely in their legitimacy. Sled dog racing evolved as a sport to show off the skills of hardy dogs that have been pulling sleds in snowbound regions for centuries. Greyhound racing, by contrast, began as a competition between fast and graceful dogs but evolved into a gambling pastime. Organized dogfighting is illegal in every state. Despite its illegitimacy, or maybe because of it, dogfighting continues to be popular. Its roots lie in the blood sports enjoyed by the ancient Romans at the Colosseum.

All three of these dog sports are largely breed-specific. Only sled dog racing pairs humans and dogs during the sporting event. Greyhound racing and dogfighting are dog-only competitions.

There are also a variety of new amateur sporting events that are emerging for dogs. Agility-based competitions, such as catching Frisbees and traversing obstacles, are growing in popularity. One of the newest dog sports is called fly ball. This is a relay event in which teams of dogs compete against each other to jump over hurdles and race to retrieve a ball. In 2000 the International Federation of Cynological Sports (IFCS) was formed in Europe to unite organizations holding dog sports in various countries around the world. (Cynology is the scientific study of canines.) The IFCS is working to bring dog sports, such as agility, to the Olympic Games.

A cock is the adult male of the domestic fowl (*Gallus gallus*), also known as a rooster. Cocks participate in only one organized sport, and that is cockfighting. This sport also has its roots in the blood sports of the past.

MAJOR ANIMAL SPORTS AND THEIR CONTROVERSIES

Animal sports enthusiasts argue that the animals are doing what they do naturally. Horses and greyhounds love to run, cocks naturally fight with each other in the barnyard, wild dogs fight over who will lead the pack, and unbroken livestock naturally try to buck off a rider. People involved in legitimate animal sports argue that the animals are well cared for because their welfare is crucial to the success of the sport and the people involved. In other words, it makes no sense for the owner or manager of a sports animal to mistreat that animal and perhaps lose money as a result. They also insist that safeguards are in place to ensure that animals are not mistreated during a sporting event and receive proper medical care if they are injured.

Critics say that animal sports are not sports at all, but performances forced out of animals that have no choice in the matter. They believe that sports animals are not behaving naturally. They argue that animal sports are not intended to show off animal skills but to make money. General complaints about animal sports revolve around four main issues:

- Overbreeding of the animals
- Mistreatment during training, performances, and the off-season
- Lack of veterinary care
- The ways in which unwanted sports animals are destroyed

Horseracing

Thoroughbred horse racing is the king of animal sports in the United States. It is a multibillion-dollar industry that as of 1996, according to the Animal and Plant Health Inspection Service (APHIS) of the U.S. Department of Agriculture (USDA), employed roughly half a million people. Horseracing is a big business, involving people who breed, manage, train, own, and ride the horses, and the people who own and manage racetracks. Indirectly, the industry provides income to feed and equipment suppliers, veterinarians, and other support personnel. The industry is also a source of income for those state governments that allow gambling at racetracks and/or off-track betting locations.

Thoroughbred horse racing was taking place on Long Island, New York, as far back as 1665. However, the advent of organized Thoroughbred racing is attributed to Governor Samuel Ogle of Maryland, who staged a race "between pedigreed horses in the English style" in Annapolis, Maryland, in 1745. The Annapolis Jockey Club, which sponsored the race, later became the Maryland Jockey Club. Among its initial members were George Washington and Thomas Jefferson.

Horse populations were severely depleted during the Revolutionary War and Civil War because horses were pressed into battle. However, breeding stocks were soon replenished. In 1894 the American Jockey Club was founded to oversee the breeding and racing of Thoroughbreds. Horse racing declined in popularity again around

FIGURE 6.1

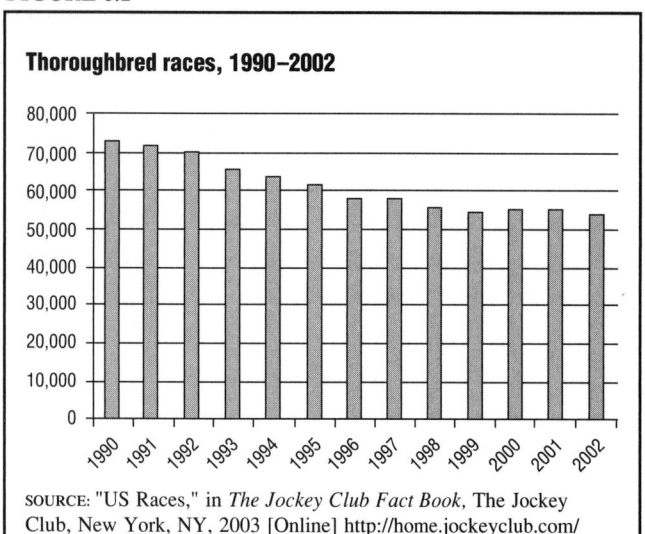

Thoroughbred races, 1990–2002

SOURCE: "US Races," in *The Jockey Club Fact Book,* The Jockey Club, New York, NY, 2003 [Online] http://home.jockeyclub.com/FACTBOOK/index.html [accessed April 23, 2003]

FIGURE 6.2

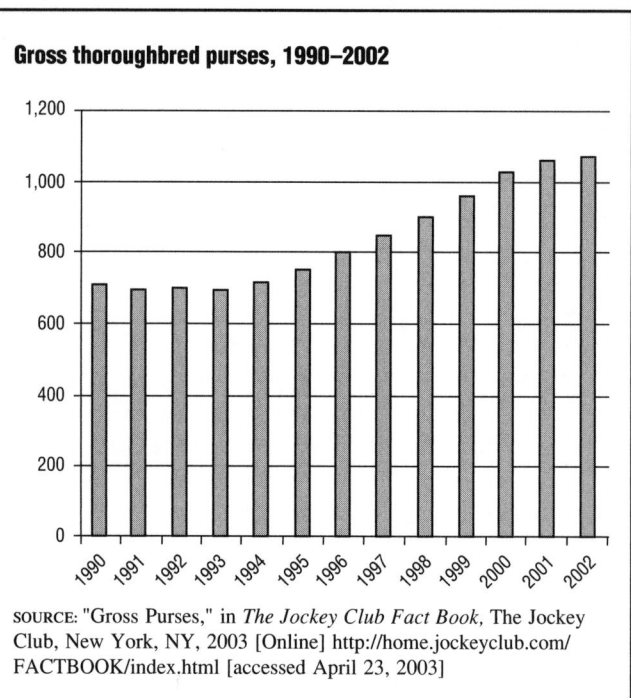

Gross thoroughbred purses, 1990–2002

SOURCE: "Gross Purses," in *The Jockey Club Fact Book,* The Jockey Club, New York, NY, 2003 [Online] http://home.jockeyclub.com/FACTBOOK/index.html [accessed April 23, 2003]

the turn of the century, after gambling was outlawed throughout much of the country.

The industry rebounded in the mid-1930s when several states legalized pari-mutuel gambling on horseracing. Legalization was seen as a means of regulating the industry and gaining some revenue from it. Horseracing and gambling spread to many other states over the following decades.

THE RACES. According to the Jockey Club, there were 54,304 Thoroughbred horseraces in the United States during 2002. California hosted the most events, with 5,111 races, followed by West Virginia, Pennsylvania, New York, and Florida. The total purse, or amount won by the owners of the winning horses, for all races was $1.1 billion. As shown in Figure 6.1, the number of Thoroughbred races held each year has generally declined since 1990. Although the number of races is declining, the purses are going up because people are gambling more money on horseraces than ever before. (See Figure 6.2.)

As of July 2003, there were about 90 Thoroughbred racetracks around the country. Some racetracks are only open seasonally, while those in warm climates are open year-round. Racetracks vary in size and in ownership; some are government-owned and some are owned by private and public companies.

The three most prestigious Thoroughbred races in the United States are the Kentucky Derby at the Churchill Downs track in Kentucky, the Preakness Stakes at Pimlico in Maryland, and the Belmont Stakes at Belmont Park in New York. The races are held over a five-week period during May and June of each year. A horse that wins all three races in one year is said to have won the "Triple Crown." Only 11 horses have ever captured the Triple Crown, most recently, a horse named Affirmed in 1978.

There are two other types of professional horseracing associated with pari-mutuel wagering, harness racing and the racing of quarter horses and Arabian horses.

In harness racing, horses trot or pace rather than gallop. They have to be specially trained to run races in this manner. Typically the horse pulls behind it a two-wheeled cart, known as a sulky, carrying a jockey who controls the reins. Harness racing is performed by a breed of horse called the Standardbred, which is shorter, more muscled, and longer in body than the Thoroughbred. In 1879 the National Association of Trotting Horse Breeders in America established the official registry for Standardbred horses. While Thoroughbred horses were the favorite of high society, Standardbred racing became popular among the common folk. As of July 2003, there were approximately 30 licensed harness racetracks around the country at which pari-mutuel betting takes place. Harness racing is also conducted at county fairs and exhibitions and sometimes with the jockey seated on the horse rather than in a sulky.

A third type of horse known for racing is the quarter horse, so named because of its high speed over distances of less than one-quarter mile. It was originally bred by American colonists to be both hardworking and athletic. As of July 2003, there were nearly 40 quarter horse racetracks around the country.

Arabian horses are considered the only true purebred horses on the race circuit, as they have not been mixed with other breeds. Arabian horseracing was conducted at about 15 tracks in the United States as of July 2003.

THE WELFARE OF RACING HORSES. The racehorse industry prides itself on the enormous investments it has

TABLE 6.2

California racehorse fatalities, November 6, 2001–November 6, 2002

Associations	Breed of horse						Occurred during		
Thoroughbred	**TB**	**QH**	**ST**	**APP**	**AR**	**P**	**Racing**	**Training***	**Other***
Los Angeles Turf Club/SA	29						5	19	5
Churchill Downs Operating Co./HP	29						12	14	3
Del Mar Thoroughbred Club/DM	17						4	9	4
Oak Tree Racing Assn./SA	18						7	8	3
Churchill Downs Fall Operating Co./HP	11						8	2	1
Bay Meadows Operating Co./BM	20						8	7	5
Bay Meadows Operating Co. (Fall)/BM	10						5	4	1
Pacific Racing Assn./GGF	37						16	17	4
Harness									
Capitol Racing LLC/CE			5				1	1	3
Quarter Horse									
Los Alamitos Quarter Horse Racing Assn./LA	18	35		2			33	11	11
Fairs									
Stockton	3			2			2	3	
Pleasanton	2							1	1
Vallejo	4						1	3	
Santa Rosa	2						2		
San Mateo	1						1		
Ferndale									
Cal Expo	3	1					3	1	
Pomona	7						3	4	
Fresno	1								1
Totals	212	36	5	4			111	104	42

Total fatalities 257

TB = thoroughbreds   QH = quarter horses   ST = standardbreds   APP = appaloosas   AR = Arabians   P= paints
* Training and other fatalities include fatalities that occurred at auxiliary training facilities.

SOURCE: "Racehorse Fatalities," in *Thirty-Second Annual Report of the California Horse Racing Board: A Summary of Fiscal Year 2001–2002 Racing in California,* California Horse Racing Board, Sacramento, CA, 2003

made in horse health issues. Millions of dollars have been spent on veterinarian research concerning the injuries and illnesses that affect racehorses. The Grayson-Jockey Club Research Foundation is the leading private source of funding for research into horse health issues. The foundation, which dates back to 1940, is operated by the Jockey Club, though it accepts donations from private individuals, Thoroughbred clubs, racetracks, and other organizations. It allocated more than $700,000 during 2001 to universities conducting equine research projects, and has contributed more than $6.7 million since 1983. The foundation receives financial support from donations and from special racing events staged by horse racetracks.

Two horse health issues of major concern are mare reproductive loss syndrome (MRLS) and exercise-induced pulmonary hemorrhage (EIPH). MRLS is a mysterious illness blamed for an unusually high number of spontaneous abortions and stillborn births in pregnant mares and for births of weak foals (sometimes with respiratory problems) that require intense veterinary treatment. The syndrome killed more than 5,000 Kentucky foals, or horses less than one year old, during 2001. Analysts estimate that the MRLS tragedy had an economic impact of $336 million in the same year. EIPH is a common condition in racehorses, associated with bleeding from the lungs during strenuous exercise. Horses that experience EIPH are called "bleeders" and can be temporarily or permanently barred from racing depending on state regulations and the severity of the problem.

Most animal welfare groups are opposed to horseracing and contend that racehorses are treated as investments rather than as living beings. Specifically, they have the following complaints about horseracing:

- Thoroughbred racehorses have been inbred to the point that their bodies are too heavy for their slender, fragile legs.

- Broodmares are forced to come into season too often and at unnatural times to lengthen the potential training season for their offspring.

- Racehorses are drugged when they have injuries or illnesses (such as hairline fractures) so that they can still compete.

- Track surfaces are too hard.

- The racing season is too long.

- Horses are run too young, risking damage to bones that are not fully mature.

- The industry is regulated by state governments that have a vested interest in making the industry profitable, not safeguarding animal welfare.

- Racehorses suffer injuries and deaths during training and performances.

As shown in Table 6.2, there were 257 racehorse fatalities in California alone between November 2001 and November 2002. In addition, 517 racing-related injuries to horses were reported in the state, most of them to Thoroughbreds.

The slaughter of racehorses is a particularly controversial topic. Demand for horse meat has skyrocketed in parts of Asia and Europe. Horse meat sells for as much as $20 per pound in some markets. However, horses intended for human consumption cannot be injected with drugs, either as painkillers or as a humane method of euthanization. By contrast, horses sold to rendering plants can be given drugs for pain in transit and can be euthanized by lethal injection. Horses sold for horse meat are given no painkillers in transit, and when they reach the slaughterhouse, they are knocked unconscious, then have their throats cut (in the same way that cattle are slaughtered).

The USDA reports that more than 50,000 horses were slaughtered in the United States in 2001 for human consumption overseas. It is unknown how many of these horses came from the racing industry. Animal welfare groups allege that many injured racehorses are not humanely euthanized but are shipped off to slaughter without being giving painkillers. Besides a handful of horse meat slaughterhouses in the United States, there are many in Mexico and Canada.

Welfarists say that racehorses going to meat slaughterhouses travel for many hours in cramped carriers with no food or water. Transport in double-decker cattle trailers is common. These carriers were designed for short-necked livestock, and horses riding in them must remain stooped over or on their knees for the entire trip.

In 1996 the U.S. Congress passed the Commercial Transportation of Equines for Slaughter Act. However, the regulations enforcing the act were not published until December 2001. According to the Humane Society of the United States (HSUS), the new rules permit the use of double-decker trailers until 2006 and allow the horses to be transported for up to 28 hours without water, food, or rest. The transport of horses in double-decker cattle trucks is prohibited in some states, including New York and Pennsylvania.

A bill was introduced in the House of Representatives in February 2003 that would prohibit the slaughter of horses in the United States for human consumption and also prohibit the trade and transport of live horses intended for human consumption. As of April 2003 the bill was still in committee.

RETIRED RACING HORSE ADOPTION. There are several organizations around the country that rescue retired racehorses and either adopt them out or provide lifetime sanctuary and care for them. In August 2003 an article in the *New York Times* reported on a partnership between the Thoroughbred Retirement Foundation (TRF) and a prison facility in upstate New York (Mike Wise, "Partners, Horse and Man, in Prison Pasture," August 10, 2003).

The TRF is a nonprofit organization founded in 1982 by Monique Koehler. Since 1986 it has placed hundreds of horses in adoptive homes, at horse sanctuaries, or in programs for mentally- and physically-challenged people. The TRF also partners with several prison facilities around the country to operate work programs in which inmates feed and care for retired racehorses at stables built at the prisons. The TRF estimates that 3,000–5,000 thoroughbreds are retired from racing each year because of injury or lack of ability. The article describes racehorses rescued by TRF from miserable conditions and suffering due to serious neglect and untreated medical conditions.

The New Vocations Racehorse Adoption Program adopts out retired racehorses (Thoroughbred and Standardbred) at 2 facilities in Ohio. The group placed more than 1,000 horses between 1992 and 2002. Most of the horses had suffered injuries during their racing careers and required rehabilitation prior to placement. In addition, adopted racehorses must undergo training to be acceptable pleasure-riding horses. The program has strict requirements for people considering adoption and charges an adoption fee of $400–$700 per horse, depending on its age and physical condition.

Greyhound Racing

Greyhounds were brought to America during the late 1800s to help control the jackrabbit population on farms in the Midwest. Soon local farmers began holding races. Early races were held using a live rabbit to lure the dogs to race. In the early 1900s, Owen Patrick Smith invented a mechanical lure for this purpose. The first circular greyhound track opened in Emeryville, California, in 1919.

THE SPORT. In 2002 there were 49 greyhound racetracks operating around the country in 15 states: Alabama, Arizona, Arkansas, Colorado, Connecticut, Florida, Iowa, Kansas, Massachusetts, New Hampshire, Oregon, Rhode Island, Texas, West Virginia, and Wisconsin. Greyhound racing is legal in South Dakota, but the state has no operating racetracks. Greyhound racing is most prevalent in Florida, where there are 16 tracks. Florida's greyhound racing industry paid out purses of $34.9 million during 2000-2001.

According to the HSUS, revenue from greyhound racing declined by 45 percent during the 1990s, leading to closure of or cessation of live racing at many tracks around the country. In addition seven states specifically banned live greyhound racing during the 1990s: Idaho, Maine, North Carolina, Nevada, Vermont, Virginia, and Washington.

Three major organizations manage greyhound racing in the United States: the National Greyhound Association

TABLE 6.3

Racing greyhound breeding statistics and analysis of the annual numbers of dogs killed, 1986–2001

Year	Number of litters born (Source: NGA)	Estimated number born	Dogs individually registered to race (Source: NGA)	Farm puppies culled before racing	Estimated greyhounds adopted**	Estimated dogs retained for breeding	Racing dogs killed	Total killed
2001	5,015	32,698	26,797	5,901	13,000	1,800	11,997	17,898
2000	5,234	34,126	26,464	7,662	13,000	2,000	11,464	19,126
1999	5,266	34,334	27,059	7,275	13,000	2,000	12,059	19,334
1998	5,034	32,822	26,036	6,786	13,000	2,000	11,036	17,822
1997	5,192	33,852	28,025	5,827	12,500	2,000	13,525	19,352
1996	5,438	35,456	28,877	6,579	12,000	2,000	13,977	21,456
1995	5,749	37,483	31,688	5,795	10,000	2,100	19,588	25,383
1994	6,232	40,633	34,746	5,887	8,500	2,200	24,046	29,933
1993	6,805	44,369	39,139	5,230	6,000	2,500	30,639	35,869
1992	7,690	50,139	38,023	12,116	3,000	2,500	32,523	44,639
1991	8,049	52,479	38,430	14,049	1,000	3,500	33,930	47,979
1990	9,473	61,764	38,615	23,149	650	3,200	34,765	57,914
1989	7,690	50,139	38,443	11,696	***450	3,000	34,993	46,689
1988	7,979	52,023	37,784	14,239	300	2,750	34,734	48,973
1987	7,638	49,800	33,021	16,779	200	2,500	30,321	47,100
1986	6,688	43,606	30,219	13,387	75	2,000	28,144	41,531
Total*	105,172	685,723	523,366	162,357	106,675	38,050	377,741	540,998

Notes:
Litters: As reported by the National Greyhound Association (NGA), the U.S. registry organization.
Total Born: Derived by multiplying the total number of litters by an average of 6.52 pups per litter (this is the conservative average that industry sources report).
Individuals Registered to Race: As reported by the NGA in The Greyhound Review, the official industry publication. Each owner must pay an additional fee to the NGA to have a greyhound individually registered.
Culled: This column shows the total number of dogs who disappear annually between birth and individual registration by 18 months of age. Very few greyhound puppies or young dogs are ever delivered to greyhound rescue groups.
*To arrive at an estimated sixteen-year total of greyhounds killed, one must also subtract the number of dogs still in the racing system (approximately 40,000), the number of puppies/youngsters currently at farms (approximately 28,500) and the breeding stock required to produce thousands of litters a year (about 500 males and 1,500 females).
**A liberal estimate of figures from those in the adoption community.
***Organized, large scale adoption efforts did not take place until the mid-1990's. During the late 1980's it is estimated that only a few hundred dogs made it into adoptive homes nationwide. For over 50 years all greyhounds were routinely destroyed.

SOURCE: "U.S. Racing Greyhound Breeding Statistics and Analysis of the Annual Numbers of Dogs Killed from 1986–2001," Greyhound Protection League, Penn Valley, CA, 2003

(NGA), the American Greyhound Track Operators Association (AGTOA), and the American Greyhound Council (AGC; a joint effort of the NGA and AGTOA). The NGA represents greyhound owners and is the official registry for racing greyhounds. All greyhounds that race on U.S. tracks must first be registered with the NGA. The AGTOA represents greyhound track operators. The AGC manages the industry's animal welfare programs, including farm inspections and adoptions.

According to information available on the Web site of the AGC in 2003, there are approximately 1,500 greyhound breeding farms in 43 states. These farms and racing kennels have an annual payroll of $37.5 million and account for $68 million each year of community spending. Greyhound tracks generate $190 million in tax revenues and contribute more than $10 million per year to charities and community causes.

THE WELFARE OF RACING GREYHOUNDS. The HSUS is strongly opposed to greyhound racing for the following reasons:

- It is not governed by the federal Animal Welfare Act under the USDA, as are other commercial animal enterprises, such as zoos and circuses.

- The industry severely overbreeds greyhounds in the hopes of producing winners, leading to the destruction of thousands of puppies each year.

- A racing greyhound's career is typically over at the age of four, well below its average lifespan of 12 years, meaning that thousands of adult dogs are also destroyed each year when they are no longer useful.

The AGC says that it has adopted standard guidelines for the care of greyhounds and the maintenance of kennel facilities based on the veterinary textbook *The Care of the Racing Greyhound.* All of the nation's greyhound breeding farms and kennels are subject to unannounced inspections to verify that they are complying with the industry's animal welfare guidelines. Violators can be expelled from the sport.

Statistics on the AGC Web site claim that greyhound tracks contribute about $1 million each year to local greyhound adoption programs and that 18,000 dogs are adopted annually. The organization insists that more than 90 percent of all registered greyhounds are retired to farms for breeding purposes or adopted out as pets.

The National Coalition Against Legalized Gambling claims that there were more than 75 well-documented cases of cruelty and abuse in the greyhound industry during the 1990s involving thousands of dogs that were shot, starved, abandoned, or sold to research laboratories.

Animal welfare groups estimate that 12,000 to 20,000 adult greyhounds are destroyed each year by the racing industry. The Greyhound Protection League claims that 5,901 greyhound puppies were culled (killed) in 2001 alone. (See Table 6.3. Note that some of these numbers are calculated from estimates.) More than half a million greyhound puppies and adult dogs are believed to have been killed by the industry between 1986 and 2001.

In May 2002 a 68-year-old Alabama man was arrested and charged with felony animal cruelty after the remains of 2,000–3,000 greyhounds were found on his property. The man, who worked as a security guard at the Pensacola Greyhound Park in Florida, said that the track sometimes paid him $10 apiece to shoot the dogs and dispose of their carcasses on his farm. He admitted that he had been killing greyhounds upon request for 40 years. Although he claimed the dogs died instantly, autopsy results showed that some dogs were shot in the neck, not the head, and likely suffered before they died. It is a felony in Alabama to torture an animal. In November 2002 three more people were indicted in the case, all of whom were affiliated with Florida dog racing tracks.

In early 2003 the greyhound racing industry was severely hurt by an epidemic that struck many racing dogs in Alabama and Florida. Races across the country had to be cancelled. Although the symptoms were similar to those of kennel cough, a common infectious but generally nonserious disease, some of the infected dogs died. Autopsies indicated that the illness might be a much more serious disease called canine streptococcal toxic shock syndrome (STSS). Animal welfare groups complain that tracks continue to let sick dogs race, risking further exposure and spread of the disease.

Sled Dog Racing

The sport of sled dog racing is small but extremely popular throughout Alaska, Canada, and parts of northern Europe. In North America the sport traces its origins to Native Americans, who for centuries have used hearty dogs bred for cold weather to pull their sleds. Typical draft animals, such as horses and oxen, were unsuitable for this purpose because of their weight and food requirements.

There are a variety of dogs used in sledding, including the Malamute (named for the Malemiut Inupiat tribe), Siberian huskies, Samoyeds, and special crossbreeds. Most sled race dogs are relatively small, weighing only about 50 pounds. They are compact and muscular and grow a thick winter coat. Mushers (sled drivers) say they develop a special bond with their dogs and that the dogs love to race.

Sled dogs were used by famous polar explorers, including Richard Byrd and Robert Peary, to traverse dangerous terrain in harsh weather conditions. The Royal Canadian Mounted Police used sled dogs to patrol northern parts of Canada beginning in the late 1800s.

The most famous sled dog race, the Iditarod, traces its origins to 1908, when a gold rush occurred near the town of Iditarod in central Alaska. Steamboats could bring visitors and supplies to the town only during the short warm season from around June to September. During the remainder of the year the rivers were frozen, and sledding was the only means of travel available.

In 1925 a diphtheria epidemic swept through Alaska. Doctors in Nome reported that they were out of serum and needed more immediately to save the town's hundreds of residents. Teams of sled dogs were organized in villages along the way to relay the serum more than 600 miles from Nenana to Nome in just over five days. The final leg of the journey was accomplished in a ferocious blizzard by a musher named Gunnar Kaasen. The lead dog of his team, named Balto, came to be known as Balto the Wonder Dog.

The event attracted attention worldwide and brought fame and glory to the mushers and dogs involved, particularly Balto. A statue of Balto was erected in Central Park in New York City with an inscription that reads "Dedicated to the indomitable Spirit of the sled dogs that relayed the antitoxin 600 miles over rough ice, treacherous waters; through Arctic blizzards from Nenana to the relief of stricken Nome in the winter of 1925. Endurance. Fidelity. Intelligence."

The fame was short-lived. Balto and the other dogs on the team were sold to a vaudeville promoter within a year of their historic run. In 1927 a businessman from Cleveland, Ohio, saw the dogs in a shabby "dime-a-look" show in Los Angeles. The dogs were sick and obviously mistreated. A massive media campaign conducted by Cleveland newspapers raised $2,000 to buy the dogs and ship them to the Cleveland zoo. The dogs were a popular attraction and were well cared for the remainder of their lives. After his death, Balto was stuffed and mounted and is now an exhibit in the Cleveland Museum of Natural History.

THE IDITAROD. During the 1940s and 1950s, sled dog teams were hired by the U.S. military to help in rescue and retrieval operations whenever planes crashed in the Alaskan wilderness. One musher who participated in these events was Joe Redington. In 1967 he helped organize a sled dog race called the Iditarod Trail Seppala Memorial Race. By 1973 the Iditarod Trail Sled Dog Race was run between Anchorage and Nome, a distance of roughly 1,150 miles. The race became an annual event, growing in popularity every year and bearing the nickname the "Last Great Race on Earth."

The Iditarod is held in early March of each year and includes dozens of teams competing for thousands of dollars in prize money. In general the race is completed in anywhere from 8 to 16 days. The speed record (set in 2002) is 8 days, 22 hours, and 46 minutes. The 2003 race was plagued by unusually warm weather and light snowfall. The winning time exceeded 9 days, with the last finisher taking just over 15 days to complete the race. The total prizes paid out in 2003 were around $600,000.

Mushers are allowed to start the Iditarod with up to 16 dogs. A typical team includes 15 dogs, one of which is the leader. The others are arranged in pairs behind the lead dog. The pair closest to the sled carries the heaviest load among the dogs. No dog substitutions are allowed during the race. If one or more dogs drop out for any reason, they cannot be replaced. The remainder carry the load. The dogs wear booties on their paws to help protect against cuts and abrasions.

The Iditarod includes about 24 checkpoints along the way. Each team is required to take three breaks during the race: one 24-hour break and two 8-hour breaks. Mushers leave dogs that are sick, tired, or injured at one of the checkpoints for transport back to the starting point. According to race officials, each checkpoint has a veterinarian available.

Hazards of the race include the weather conditions, wildlife, and unpredictable terrain. Temperatures can drop to as low as -40 degrees F during the race. However, unusually warm temperatures (up to 50 degrees F) are also a problem as they can contribute to heat stress in the dogs and cause spoilage of dog food stored along the route.

The Iditarod received little media attention outside of Alaska until 1985, when a woman (Libby Riddles) won the race for the first time. Another woman, Susan Butcher, won the Iditarod every year between 1986 and 1990. The resulting publicity greatly boosted the profile of the race but also brought more scrutiny and criticism from animal welfare organizations.

THE WELFARE OF SLED DOGS. In 1991 an Anchorage musher was charged with animal cruelty after 2 badly injured puppies were found along with 12 dead puppies in a crate in his truck. The man admitted to shooting and bludgeoning the puppies, which were from his sled dog breeding stock. He had not checked to make sure that they were all dead and had left them in the truck for at least nine hours. He was sentenced to 160 hours of community service and was suspended from the Iditarod.

A sports reporter for the *Anchorage Daily News* defended the man, saying that he was not a bad person, just "naive, misinformed, misguided, and confused." The reporter acknowledged that there is a "dark side of the sport" in that mushers must get rid of puppies sometimes and homes are difficult to find for them. "They do it because they can't afford the estimated $500 a year it takes to feed and care for dogs which won't be part of their racing teams" (Lew Freedman, "Musher Who Killed Puppies Pays by Losing Sport He Loved Most," October 9, 1991).

The negative publicity from this incident, as well as publicized dog deaths during Iditarods held in the early 1990s, caused many corporate sponsors to drop their participation in the race. In 1995 the HSUS asked the Alaska attorney general to investigate alleged animal abuses in the Iditarod. The attorney general refused the request, noting that the dogs were treated in conformance with accepted veterinary practices during the race.

Iditarod organizers implemented stricter rules, including reducing the number of dogs required to start the race from 20 to 16, meaning fewer dogs were exposed to racing hazards. They also expanded their efforts to educate people about the measures that are taken to protect the dogs. Today the Iditarod receives its sponsorship mostly from Alaska-based companies.

The HSUS opposes the Iditarod Trail Sled Dog Race, arguing that the sled dogs are forced to run "too far and too fast" in brutal weather and racing conditions. Critics complain that the pressure to run the Iditarod faster every year pushes the dogs beyond their limits. They point out that the historic diphtheria run made by Balto and other sled dogs in 1925 was conducted by several relay teams, not one team of dogs.

In addition, the HSUS makes the following allegations:

- The race experiences dog deaths and injuries almost every year.

- At least 118 sled dogs are known to have died during the race since its inception, including 15–19 dogs in the first race alone. Two dogs died in 2001 and one dog died in 2002. Dogs have died from heart and other organ failures due to overexertion; pneumonia; and injuries, including being strangled in towlines (the ropes that stretch from the dogs' harnesses to the sled) and rammed by sleds.

- At least three mushers have been disqualified from races for beating or kicking dogs or forcing dogs to run through dangerously deep slush. Two of the dogs in these cases died.

- Race dogs have suffered heat stress, dehydration, diarrhea, pulled tendons, and cut paws due to their participation in the Iditarod.

- Sled dog breeders kill puppies that are unable or unwilling to become good racers.

The HSUS also complains that the majority of sled dogs are confined to short tethers in large dog yards when they are not racing. Tethering as a means of primary confinement is not permitted by the USDA for its licensed dog breeders and is opposed by the HSUS.

Iditarod mushers and supporters acknowledge that the race is grueling and can be dangerous, but they believe that sufficient rules and safeguards are in place to protect the dogs from injury and abuse. Many people involved in the sport believe that the dangers and wildness of the race enhance its allure.

The Sled Dog Action Coalition (SDAC) is another organization opposed to the Iditarod. Begun in 1999 by a former schoolteacher, the SDAC Web site lists hundreds of quotes from newspaper reporters, mushers, and other sources regarding abuses and mishaps that take place during racing and training. The SDAC calls for specific reforms to be made in race procedures to ensure the safety of the sled dogs. These reforms include:

- Performance of an electrocardiogram, chest X ray, blood workup, and urine test on each dog prior to the race

- Performance of a complete physical exam on each dog by a veterinarian at each race checkpoint

- Certification of all mushers in canine first aid or CPR

- More rest periods during the race

- Establishment of minimum vet-to-dog ratios

The SDAC notes that the Iditarod uses only about 35 veterinarians to oversee as many as 1,000 dogs that participate in the race.

The Iditarod is not the only sled dog race. The International Sled Dog Racing Association (ISDRA) was formed in 1966. The organization has more than 850 members and sanctions up to 75 races each year. These include traditional sled dog races as well as gig races, in which dogs pull wheeled rigs, and ski-joring and bike-joring, in which dogs pull people on skis and bicycles, respectively. There are events for adults and children.

The ISDRA has an animal welfare policy that requires race participants to abide by the following statement: "There shall be no cruel, inhumane or abusive treatment of any dog, through deliberate action or inaction, through knowledge or ignorance, with or without implement, nor shall anyone deny a dog adequate care."

Rodeos

The word rodeo comes from the Spanish word *rodear,* meaning to surround. Originally a rodeo was a roundup of cattle that happened once or twice a year. Open-range grazing was common in western North America during the 1800s, and cowboys were hired to round up the cattle and herd them to market. Following these cattle drives, as they were called, the cowboys would often congregate

and hold informal contests to show off their skills at riding and roping.

In 1897 the mayor of Cheyenne, Wyoming, decided to hold a festival to attract tourists to the town. The first Cheyenne Frontier Days included competitions and exhibitions of typical cowboy skills, such as racing ponies, roping cattle, and riding broncos. (*Bronco* is a Spanish word that means rough and wild. It was used by cowboys to describe an unbroken horse—that is, a wild horse that had not been trained to accept a rider. There were several million wild horses in the Old West at that time.)

The Cheyenne Frontier Days festival was so popular that it became an annual event and was eventually called a rodeo, as were similar events that all originated in western states during that same time period. In 1912 the western Canadian town of Calgary, Alberta, held the first Calgary Stampede. This rodeo grew to be the largest one in the world.

THE RODEO BUSINESS. Rodeos have expanded their traditional fan base and now take place all over North America, even in big cities. They are seen by their fans as wholesome family entertainment that glorifies the rugged and hardworking cowboys of the Old West.

According to the Fund for Animals, as of May 2001 about 5,000 rodeos were conducted each year, most by amateur organizations. The Animal Protection Institute reported in spring 2002 that a dozen professional organizations sponsor about 1,000 rodeos each year. Professional rodeo stars travel from event to event and compete for millions of dollars in prize money. Most big-money rodeos in the United States are sponsored by the Professional Rodeo and Cowboy Association (PRCA). According to information posted on its Web site in 2003, the PRCA sanctions around 700 rodeos each year with prizes in excess of $34 million. Besides professional rodeos, the organization also sponsors amateur rodeo events for children and youth.

The animals used in rodeos include horses, bulls, steers (male cattle that have been castrated prior to reaching sexual maturity), and calves. Typical rodeo events include:

- Bareback bull riding—The rider has one hand tied while the bull is held securely in an enclosure called a chute. When the bull is released from the chute, it tries to buck the rider off. The goal for the rider is to remain on the bucking bull for as long as possible without touching the bull or the equipment with his free hand. Each ride is judged based on the rowdiness of the animal and on the ability of the rider to maintain the proper position and form during the ride. The riders earn extra points for spurring the bull during the ride.

- Saddle bronc riding—The riding action and judging are similar to those described for bull riding. The rider's score is based on the bucking action of the horse, the rider's form and control, and the way in which the rider spurs the horse. The length of his spurring stroke is important.

- Bareback horse riding—Bareback horse riding is similar to bronc riding, except that the rider has no saddle. A leather and rawhide rigging is attached to the horse and the rider holds on to it with only one hand during the ride. Scoring is based on the rowdiness of the horse and the rider's spurring action and ability to maintain the proper form.

- Steer wrestling—A steer wrestler, or bulldogger, begins on horseback. A steer is released from its pen and the bulldogger pursues it while another rider on horseback (the hazer) keeps the steer running in a straight line. When the bulldogger pulls even with the steer, he slips off his horse, grabs the steer by its horns, and twists them to throw the steer to the ground. The clock stops when the bulldogger has all four of the steer's legs pointing in the same direction.

- Calf roping—Calf roping (or tie-down roping) requires a rider on horseback to pursue a running calf. The rider ropes the calf, slips off his horse, and throws the calf to the ground. He uses a thin rope carried in his teeth to tie together three of the calf's legs. The binding must be strong enough to hold the calf for at least six seconds or the run does not count.

- Steer roping—Steer roping is similar to calf roping except much more difficult because of the size and strength of a steer. Also, the steer is roped around the horns rather than around the neck. Steer roping requires a large amount of space and is held only at a few large rodeos.

- Team roping—Team roping is similar to steer roping, except that two riders on horseback participate. The header chases and ropes the steer around its horns and/or neck while the heeler chases and ropes the steer's two hind legs and pulls them out from under the animal, causing it to fall to the ground.

- Barrel racing—Riders on horseback sprint in a cloverleaf pattern around three barrels positioned around an arena. The object is to complete the circuit as quickly as possible without tipping over any barrels. Quarter horses are commonly used in barrel racing.

THE WELFARE OF RODEO ANIMALS. The PRCA defends the treatment of animals used in rodeos it sponsors. The organization has an extensive animal welfare program that governs the care and handling of rodeo animals and requires that a veterinarian be on-site during a rodeo. Injury statistics compiled by these on-site independent veterinarians show an extremely low injury rate at PRCA rodeos. A survey released in 2000 covered the 1999 National Finals Rodeo and 56 other rodeos. Out of 71,743 animal exposures, the survey reported only 38 injuries, an injury rate of 0.05 percent. The 2001 survey covered 67 PRCA rodeos and showed an injury rate of only 0.03 percent.

Many animal welfare organizations are opposed to rodeos. They argue that rodeos are not representative of Old West ranching ways but are businesses that use animals as pieces of athletic equipment. They say that most injured rodeo animals are not humanely euthanized but are sent to slaughterhouses without receiving veterinary attention or painkillers. They also point out that today's rodeo animals are not naturally wild and unbroken as they might have been when rodeos first started in the 1800s but are relatively tame animals that must be physically provoked into displaying wild behavior. This is particularly true for the bucking animals.

According to "Born to Buck?" (Diana Rowe Martinez, *Rodeo and Cowboys,* Suite101.com, http://www.suite101.com/article.cfm/rodeo_and_cowboys/51740), bucking animals, or roughstock, as they are called, are supplied to rodeos by stock contractors. Prior to the 1950s, semi-wild horses that roamed the western United States were used for this purpose. They became scarce as ranchers began breeding gentler dispositions into their stock and eliminating horses that were difficult to control by destroying them or selling them to slaughterhouses.

A Montana stock contractor named Ernest Tooke was one of the first to produce a line of large strong bucking broncs by mating an Arabian stallion with draft horses. Contractors also use selective breeding to obtain bucking bulls for rodeos. The gentler buckers are supplied to youth and amateur-level rodeos, while the "tough and unpredictable" stock are saved for high-paying professional events.

Some regular horses become roughstock if they do not have the disposition to be work or pleasure horses. When not on the road or performing, roughstock are kept in open fields and isolated from human contact as much as possible. People in the rodeo business commonly use the words ornery and rank to describe roughstock behavior. They argue that roughstock buck because it is their nature, not because they are tortured to do so.

Rodeo opponents say that bucking is unnatural behavior provoked in rodeo animals by tormenting them with painful straps and spurs. They also claim that bucking animals are sometimes poked with cattle prods or sharp sticks or rubbed with caustic ointments right before they are released from their chutes in order to incite more frenzied bucking action during the ride.

Bucking horses do wear flank straps that encourage them to kick their legs high in the air, according to the

PRCA. However, the PRCA requires that the flank strap be lined with fleece or neoprene and placed loosely around the horses. On its anti-rodeo Web site, the animal rights group People for the Ethical Treatment of Animals (PETA) says the straps are cinched tightly around the animals' sensitive abdomen and groin areas, causing the animals to buck to try to throw off the painful devices. The PRCA denies that the straps are pulled tight, arguing that a tight strap would actually restrict a horse's movement and not permit it to jump into the air.

Riders in several rodeo events wear and use spurs. The PRCA requires that the spur points be dull and that the wheel-like rowels on the spurs be able to roll along the animal's hide, rather than be locked. The organization contends that this prevents any injury to the animal from spurring. Riders who violate these rules or injure an animal are subject to disqualification. PETA argues that even dull spurs are painful because they are kicked into the animals' sides. They compare being poked by a dull spur to being hit by a hammer.

Besides bucking animals, activists are particularly critical of the calf-roping events. They complain that calves have their tails twisted or raked against a rail to ensure that they will leave the chute at a full run. The PRCA argues that the techniques used in events such as calf and steer roping were used on Old West ranches to catch and immobilize cattle needing medical treatment. In early 2003 the PRCA announced that the term "calf roping" was no longer to be used at PRCA rodeos. The term "tie-down roping" will be used instead.

Dr. Peggy Larson is a veterinarian who once participated in rodeos and has cared for rodeo animals. In a 2002 interview with the Association of Veterinarians for Animal Rights ("An Interview with Peggy Larson," *Directions,* Winter 2002), she described her concerns about rodeo animal welfare.

She considers steer wrestling to be one of the least harmful rodeo events and calf-roping to be one of the worst. She describes calves that have died or had to be euthanized because of broken limbs, backs, and necks caused by the sudden jerk of the rope. The calves also suffer oxygen deprivation while the rope is cinched tightly around their necks during the tie-down. Dr. Larson is concerned that calves are jabbed with electric prods in order to get them to leave their chutes at a full run.

She also describes rodeo horse training methods, including the use of wire attachments on the horse's bit. Dr. Larson says that these wires stab painfully into the horse's gums when the reins are pulled and can even sever the tongue.

Although many activists complain about the use of flank straps on bucking horses, Dr. Larson does not think that these straps are painful to the animals. She is much more concerned about tissue damage caused by repeated spurring, particularly in the horses' shoulder areas. Also, she worries that these blunt injuries do not have time to heal between shows. Although Dr. Larson believes that spurring of horses should be outlawed in rodeos, she states, "I do not believe that rodeo can ever be made humane and still remain popular."

CHARREADAS. Besides traditional American rodeos, there is another type of rodeo growing in popularity. A Mexican rodeo is called a *charreada,* and its cowboys are called *charros.* Although charreadas held in the United States are generally small-time events, with only a few hundred spectators, they are harshly criticized by animal welfare groups. Charreadas include many of the same events as American rodeos but may also include *manganas,* or horse-tripping, and tailing. Horse tripping is a roping event in which charros try to lasso the legs of a running horse and bring it tumbling to the ground. In a tailing event, a charro on a horse grabs the tail of a running cow or steer and tries to jerk the animal to the ground.

Horse welfare groups, including the California Equine Council, have been very critical of horse tripping and describe numerous injuries associated with it. According to the Animal Protection Institute, horse tripping was banned in the states of California, Florida, Texas, New Mexico, Illinois, Maine, and Oklahoma as of spring 2002. Because charreadas are primarily conducted and attended in the United States by Hispanics, some Hispanic groups have complained that prohibiting horse tripping is discriminatory.

Cockfighting

Cockfighting is performed by cocks outfitted with sharp spikes called gaffs on their legs. Two cocks are thrown into a pit together where they fight to the death. Cockfighting was banned by most states during the 1800s. As of November 2002, it was illegal in 48 states. (See Table 6.4.)

According to the HSUS, as of that date, cockfighting was legal in parts of Louisiana and New Mexico. (See Table 6.4.) It was a felony in 27 states and a misdemeanor offense in 21 others. States differ in their treatment of cockfight spectators and those caught in possession of birds for fighting.

Because cockfighting is still legal in some parts of the United States and in Mexico and many Asian countries, there is a commercial breeding industry in America. However, the federal Animal Welfare Act prohibits the interstate transport of birds for cockfighting into states with laws against cockfighting. As of May 2003 the law also prohibits the transport of fighting gamecocks into or out of states where cockfighting is still legal and bans the exporting of fighting gamecocks to foreign countries.

TABLE 6.4

Cockfighting state laws as of November, 2002

State	Outlawed	Type of activity Cockfighting	Possession of birds for fighting	Being a spectator at a cockfight
Alabama	1896	*Misdemeanor*	**Legal**	**Legal**
Alaska	1953	Felony	Felony	*Misdemeanor* [5]
Arizona	1998	Felony	Felony	*Misdemeanor*
Arkansas	1879	*Misdemeanor* [3]	**Legal**	**Legal**
California[6]	1905	*Misdemeanor*	*Misdemeanor* [7]	*Misdemeanor*
Colorado	1913	Felony	Felony [7]	Felony
Connecticut	1862	Felony	Felony	Felony
Delaware	1852	Felony	Felony	*Misdemeanor*
Florida	1986	Felony	**Legal**	*Misdemeanor*
Georgia	1933	*Misdemeanor* [3]	**Legal**	**Legal**
Hawaii	1884	*Misdemeanor*	**Legal**	**Legal**
Idaho	1883	*Misdemeanor*	**Legal**	*Misdemeanor*
Illinois	1921	Felony [2]	Felony [2,7]	*Misdemeanor*
Indiana	1926	Felony	*Misdemeanor* [7]	*Misdemeanor*
Iowa	1868	*Misdemeanor*	**Legal** [7]	*Misdemeanor*
Kansas	1889	*Misdemeanor*	**Legal**	*Misdemeanor*
Kentucky	1893	*Misdemeanor*	**Legal**	*Misdemeanor*
Louisiana	**Legal**	**Legal**	**Legal**	**Legal**
Maine[1]	1903	Felony	Felony	*Misdemeanor*
Maryland	1890	Felony	**Legal**	**Legal**
Massachusetts	1836	Felony	Felony	*Misdemeanor*
Michigan	1915	Felony	Felony [7]	Felony
Minnesota	1871	Felony	Felony	*Misdemeanor*
Mississippi	1880	*Misdemeanor*	**Legal**	**Legal**
Missouri	1998	Felony	**Legal** [7]	*Misdemeanor*
Montana	1895	Felony	Felony	**Legal**
Nebraska	1873	Felony[2]	Felony[2]	Felony[2]
Nevada	1919	Felony[2]	**Legal**	Felony[2]
New Hampshire	1887	*Misdemeanor*	*Misdemeanor*	*Misdemeanor*
New Jersey[1]	1880	Felony	Felony	Felony
New Mexico	**Legal**	**Legal**	**Legal**	**Legal**
New York	1881	Felony	Felony	*Misdemeanor*
North Carolina	1881	Felony[2]	**Legal**	*Misdemeanor*
North Dakota	1891	Felony	Felony	*Misdemeanor*
Ohio	1929	*Misdemeanor*	*Misdemeanor*	*Misdemeanor*
Oklahoma	2002	Felony	Felony	*Misdemeanor*
Oregon	1970	*Misdemeanor*	**Legal**	*Misdemeanor*
Pennsylvania	1869	Felony	Felony	Felony
Rhode Island	1896	Felony	Felony	Felony
South Carolina	1887	*Misdemeanor*	*Misdemeanor*	*Misdemeanor*
South Dakota	1903	*Misdemeanor*	**Legal**	*Misdemeanor*
Tennessee	1881	*Misdemeanor*	*Misdemeanor*	*Misdemeanor*
Texas	1907	Felony	**Legal**	**Legal**
Utah	1888	*Misdemeanor*	**Legal**	*Misdemeanor*
Vermont	1854	Felony	Felony	Felony
Virginia	1887	*Misdemeanor* [4]	**Legal**	*Misdemeanor*
Washington	1901	*Misdemeanor*	*Misdemeanor*	*Misdemeanor*
West Virginia	1923	*Misdemeanor*	**Legal**	*Misdemeanor*
Wisconsin	1889	Felony	Felony	*Misdemeanor*
Wyoming	1895	*Misdemeanor*	*Misdemeanor*	*Misdemeanor*
Totals	**48 Illegal**	27 Felony	20 Felony	9 Felony
	2 Legal	*21 Misdemeanor*	*8 Misdemeanor*	*31 Misdemeanor*
		2 Legal	**22 Legal**	**10 Legal**

[1]These states do not have felony or misdemeanor offenses per se but rather have penalties equivalent to felonies and misdemeanors.
[2]A repeated offense can trigger a felony prosecution.
[3]While not specifically prohibited by state law, cockfighting can be prosecuted under the general anticruelty statute.
[4]While not specifically prohibited by state law, cockfighting can be prosecuted under the general anticruelty statute as well asother statutes addressing cockfighting.
[5]In Alaska a first offense is a violation and a second offense is a misdemeanor.
[6]While cockfighting-related activities are prosecutable as misdemeanor crimes, felony charges may be leveled against persons responsible for the mutilation of birds. (See *The People v. Modesto Ruiz Baniqued et al., Superior Court No. 97F06010.*)
[7]Possession of cockfighting implements is prohibited. In Iowa, only use of cockfighting implements is prohibited.

SOURCE: Adapted from "Cockfighting State Laws," in *The HSUS on Animal Fighting: The Final Round,* The Humane Society of the United States, Washington, DC, November 2002

In January 2003 police in Maui arrested 28 people following a yearlong investigation into connections between cockfighting and organized crime on the island. Police expressed concerns that cockfighting is increasingly linked to mobsters and drug traffickers. In February 2003 Mississippi police arrested 29 people after busting an ongoing cockfight. The police confiscated hypodermic needles that were being used to inject the birds with steroids. Two cocks were found dead. Another 18 had to be euthanized because of injuries or because they displayed excessive aggressiveness toward humans.

According to the *Atlanta Journal and Constitution* (Drew Jubera, "The Fight of Its Life: Cockfighting Is Big Business in Louisiana, But a New Federal Law Threatens the Sport and Angers Legions of Loyal Fans," March 9, 2003), the Louisiana cockfighting industry generates millions of dollars in revenue. The state has more than 70 cockfighting pits that draw spectators from across the country. The larger pits can seat hundreds of people and charge gamecock owners as much as $1,000 to participate in a fight. Winners can earn $50,000 in these matches. Superior gamecocks sell for up to $300 apiece.

A *Journal* reporter interviewed people involved in cockfighting to find out why they participated in the sport. Most said that they admired the natural fighting talents of cocks. Although they admitted that the sport was violent, they did not think that it was cruel to the birds. One breeder insisted that it would be crueler to keep the birds from fighting, because they love fighting so much.

Dogfighting

Dogfighting in America has its roots in the bear- and bullbaitings of the Middle Ages. Legend has it that bulldogs got their name because butchers used them to help control unruly bulls and to participate in bullbaitings. After baiting was outlawed, these same dogs were bred for dogfighting.

Dogfighting is conducted between two dogs placed in a pit or small boarded arena. The fights are usually held in warehouses or abandoned buildings. American pit bull terriers are most commonly bred and specially trained for this purpose because they have powerful jaws. Fights can go on for hours, sometimes to the death. Generally a fight goes on until a dog gives up or an owner concedes defeat.

Fighting dogs are judged on their "gameness." Gameness is determined by a dog's willingness and eagerness to fight and its reluctance to yield or back down during the fight. Selective breeding and grueling, sometimes cruel, training methods are used to enhance gameness.

In December 2000 the Harvard Medical School's *Weekly Addiction Gambling Education Report* published its research findings on the cultural aspects of dogfighting in the southern United States. Researchers inter-

TABLE 6.5

Dogfighting state laws as of November, 2002

State	Type of activity		
	Dogfighting	Possession of dogs for fighting	Being a spectator at a dogfight
Alabama	Felony	Felony	Felony
Alaska	Felony	Felony	*Misdemeanor*
Arizona	Felony	Felony	Felony
Arkansas	Felony	Felony	*Misdemeanor*
California	Felony	Felony	*Misdemeanor*
Colorado	Felony	Felony	Felony
Connecticut	Felony	Felony	Felony
Delaware	Felony	Felony	*Misdemeanor*
Florida	Felony	**Legal**	*Misdemeanor*
Georgia	Felony	**Legal**	Felony
Hawaii	Felony	Felony	**Legal**
Idaho	*Misdemeanor*	**Legal**	*Misdemeanor*
Illinois	Felony	Felony	*Misdemeanor*
Indiana	Felony	*Misdemeanor*	*Misdemeanor*
Iowa	*Misdemeanor*	**Legal**	*Misdemeanor*
Kansas	Felony	Felony	*Misdemeanor*
Kentucky	Felony	Felony	*Misdemeanor*
Louisiana	Felony	Felony	*Misdemeanor*
Maine[1]	Felony	Felony	*Misdemeanor*
Maryland	Felony	**Legal**	*Misdemeanor*
Massachusetts	Felony	Felony	*Misdemeanor*
Michigan	Felony	Felony	Felony
Minnesota	Felony	Felony	*Misdemeanor*
Mississippi	Felony	Felony	Felony
Missouri	Felony	Felony	*Misdemeanor*
Montana	Felony	Felony	Felony
Nebraska	Felony[2]	Felony[2]	*Misdemeanor*
Nevada	Felony	**Legal**	Felony[2]
New Hampshire	Felony	Felony	Felony
New Jersey[1]	Felony	Felony	Felony
New Mexico	Felony	Felony	Felony
New York	Felony	*Misdemeanor*	*Misdemeanor*
North Carolina	Felony	Felony	Felony
North Dakota	Felony	Felony	*Misdemeanor*
Ohio	Felony	Felony	Felony
Oklahoma	Felony	Felony	*Misdemeanor*
Oregon	Felony	Felony	*Misdemeanor*
Pennsylvania	Felony	Felony	Felony
Rhode Island	Felony	Felony	Felony
South Carolina	Felony	Felony	*Misdemeanor*
South Dakota	Felony	Felony	*Misdemeanor*
Tennessee	Felony	Felony	*Misdemeanor*
Texas	Felony	*Misdemeanor*	*Misdemeanor*
Utah	Felony	Felony	*Misdemeanor*
Vermont	Felony	Felony	Felony
Virginia	Felony	**Legal**	*Misdemeanor*
Washington	Felony	*Misdemeanor*	*Misdemeanor*
West Virginia	*Misdemeanor*	**Legal**	*Misdemeanor*
Wisconsin	Felony	Felony	*Misdemeanor*
Wyoming	*Misdemeanor*	*Misdemeanor*	*Misdemeanor*
Totals	46 Felony	37 Felony	17 Felony
	4 Misdemeanor	*5 Misdemeanor*	*32 Misdemeanor*
	0 Legal	**8 Legal**	**1 Legal**

[1]These states do not have felony or misdemeanor offenses per se but rather have penalties equivalent to felonies and misdemeanors.
[2]A repeated offense can trigger a felony prosecution.

SOURCE: Adapted from "Dogfighting State Laws," in *The HSUS on Animal Fighting: The Final Round,* The Humane Society of the United States, Washington, DC, November 2002

viewed 31 men involved in dogfighting in Louisiana and Mississippi. They found that dogfighting was closely associated with the men's need to assert their masculinity. A "game" dog brought the owner status and prestige among other dog owners. Any dog showing cowardice or a willingness to quit reflected poorly on its owner's masculinity and was killed.

Fighting dogs are often trained on treadmills or devices called catmills. A catmill holds a small animal, such as a cat or dog, just out of reach of the training dog while it runs. Police report that these bait animals are often pets stolen from local neighborhoods and are usually killed during the training.

According to the HSUS, dogfighting is illegal in all 50 states. (See Table 6.5.) It is a felony in 46 states, and a misdemeanor in the others. Even being a spectator at a dogfight is a felony in some states. Possession of a dog for fighting is illegal in 42 states.

Animal welfare groups want to strengthen state laws to make possession of a fighting dog a felony in every state. They also ask major newspapers not to accept advertisements selling dogs that use descriptive words like "game dog" or "game bred," as these terms imply that the dog is intended for fighting. The HSUS asks people to notify the organization whenever such ads appear in their local newspapers.

The Ohio Dog Fighting Task Force estimated in 2001 that around 30,000 people and 250,000 dogs were involved in organized dogfighting in the United States. According to a 2002 article in the *Columbus Dispatch*, incidents increased by 300 percent between approximately 1992 and 2002 (Kathy Lynn Gray, "Blood Sport: A Dramatic Rise in Illegal Dogfighting Overwhelms Authorities and Strikes Fear in Some Neighborhoods," May 5, 2002). Law enforcement and animal control officers across the country report huge increases in the number of pit bulls they have confiscated in recent years. One county in Ohio seized nearly 2,000 pit bulls in 2002. More than half of the dogs showed injuries or scars typical of fighting.

In April 2002 police in North Carolina raided an ongoing dogfight near Asheboro. They found a wooden enclosure with bloodstained carpet in which the dogs were fighting. Two men were arrested for dogfighting and cruelty to animals, both felonies. Dozens of live and dead dogs were found at the scene. Three dogs had to be euthanized by authorities because of the extent of their injuries.

In July 2002 a California man received a 7-year prison sentence for running an extensive dogfighting ring out of his home. More than 50 pit bull terriers were confiscated, along with dogfighting equipment. Information obtained during the investigation led police to another 40 fighting dogs around the state.

In January 2003 ABC News reported on the growing concern of police in dealing with organized dogfights. The report described a raid at a Columbus, Ohio, auto body shop in which 40 people were arrested and nearly $25,000 in cash was confiscated, along with some handguns and drugs. The spectators had come from as far away as Alabama to see the fight. Police believe that dogfighting has changed from a small-time rural activity to a well-organized business that advertises over the Internet. They are increasingly concerned about the number of drug dealers and gang members they see involved in dogfighting and the large amounts of money that are bet, often tens of thousands of dollars.

CHAPTER 7
ENTERTAINMENT ANIMALS

Entertainment animals are those that perform or are displayed publicly to thrill, amuse, and delight people. These animals appear in circuses, carnivals, animal shows and exhibits, amusement and wildlife theme parks, aquariums, zoos, museums, fairs, and motion pictures and television programs. Although these venues are diverse, they all have one thing in common—they use animals for human purposes. Many of these purposes are purely recreational. Others combine recreation with educational goals, such as teaching the public about the conservation and preservation of endangered species. In either case, the animals are a source of income for their owners.

Entertainment animals include both wild and domesticated types. Wild exotic animals like elephants, lions, and tigers are the most popular. They are objects of curiosity because people do not encounter them in their daily lives. The word "exotic" means foreign or not native but also suggests an air of mystery and danger that is very alluring to people, who will often pay to see exotic animals lying in cages. Domestic animals, on the other hand, must do something to make money, since most people will not pay to see ordinary dogs and cats lying around. They might, however, pay to see them jump through fiery hoops or walk on their hind legs pushing baby carriages. They will pay even more to see wild animals do such things because that is truly extraordinary.

This, the unnatural basis of the exotic animal business, is what makes it unacceptable to animal rights groups. They believe that wild animals should live in the wild, unaffected by human interference, and not forced to do things that do not come naturally to them. Animal welfarists fear that exotic animals are not housed, trained, and cared for in a humane manner, particularly at circuses, carnivals, and roadside zoos and parks. Animal welfare can be very poor in these facilities because the people in charge lack the knowledge, resources, or will to provide proper care to exotic species. Performing animals must be trained to do what they do, and some trainers use cruel and abusive methods.

Animal rights advocates feel that even nonperforming wild animals live unnatural lives because they are captives. They are either removed from their natural habitats or born into captivity. Some people argue that this is beneficial to the animals and the perpetuation of their species. Animals in the wild face many dangers, including natural predators, starvation, hunters, and poachers. Their habitats in Asia and Africa are shrinking as human developments take up more and more space.

Some exotic animals live longer in captivity than they would in the wild, and some species might die out completely if humans did not capture specimens of them and preserve them. Large zoos and circuses do this kind of work. But they are also in the entertainment business, earning money by displaying captive animals to the public. Does the end justify the means? This is one of the fundamental questions in the debate over animals in entertainment.

HISTORY

The use of animals for entertainment dates back thousands of years. Even so many years ago, societies were most interested in exotic animals. Archaeological evidence shows that lions were kept in cages in Macedonia as far back as 2000 B.C. Egyptian, Chinese, Babylonian, Assyrian, and Roman rulers also collected wild animals, as did the Abbasid princes of Arabia. Ancient collections often included elephants, bears, giraffes, and the big cats. Historians believe that wild animals were kept and shown off by rulers as a symbol of power and wealth.

The Greeks were among the first to collect wild animals to learn about them. Their collections had an educational purpose. By contrast, the Roman Empire focused on the wild nature of the animals. The emperors entertained themselves and the public by holding spectacles in which animals fought to the death with each other and with human gladiators. These events took place in great circular arenas called circuses. One of the most famous was Circus Maximus.

Animal entertainment based on violence, particularly dog- and cockfighting and bull- and bearbaiting, continued in Europe throughout the Middle Ages. Captive wild animals were also popular as items of curiosity. European explorers brought back exotic species from all over the world to put in exhibits called menageries. The French word *ménagerie* means housing for domestic animals. Wild animal menageries used cages or small pits to protect people from the animals and still allow easy viewing.

King Henry I of England (1068–1135) established Britain's royal menagerie in the town of Woodstock. Later this collection was moved to the Tower of London, where it remained for several hundred years. It featured many exotic animals that were captured from the wild or presented as gifts to British royalty by other leaders. At various times, these animals included African elephants, leopards, lions, camels, and even a polar bear and a porcupine. The royal menagerie was the longest continuously running animal exhibit in the world.

Some medieval entrepreneurs took their menageries on the road. They traveled the countryside, collecting money from curious spectators. By the end of the 1700s, these traveling menageries were called circuses. It was also during this century that the first real zoos were established in France, Spain, and Austria. However, historians note that the Aztec civilization of Mexico had large zoos at least two centuries before this. The first British and American zoos opened to the public in the mid-1800s.

Wild-animal performances were perfected in the traveling menageries, circuses, and shows of the 1800s. Famous animal trainers of the period include Henri Martin (1793–1882) of France and the American Isaac Van Amburgh (1801–65). Supposedly, Van Amburgh was the first man to entertain a crowd by putting his head into a lion's mouth in 1833. His act also included a lion and lamb that would lie peacefully side by side. Van Amburgh was greatly admired for his heroic and wondrous feats. In portraits he was depicted in gladiator costume, and in the press he was described as a "conqueror" of wild animals.

Most acts of the time focused on the ferocity of the animals and the braveness of the trainer. Lions were trained to roar and swat at the trainers, who fended them off with whips and chairs. These daring acts thrilled audiences, but the training methods used could be brutal. Trainers had to establish absolute dominance over their animals to prevent them from actually attacking.

Zoos, circuses, and other forms of "wild" animal entertainment were especially popular in England and America during Victorian times (the late 19th century). Historians note that many performing animals suffered terribly from poor care. In his article "Romantic Rhinos and Victorian Vipers: The Zoo as Nineteenth-Century Spectacle," professor Ashton Nichols reports that large mammals in captivity in the mid-1800s lived for an average of only two years and faced an "immeasurable amount of disease, suffering, and death."

Wild animals were not the only animal entertainers of the time. During the 19th century, horses, dogs, and other domesticated animals performed in equestrian acts and variety shows throughout Europe and the United States. Near the end of the century, animal acts were incorporated into a new form of American entertainment—vaudeville. Vaudeville shows consisted of short theatrical acts performed on stage. They usually included jugglers, singers, dancers, magicians, comedians, and performing animals.

The Library of Congress maintains a collection of vaudeville memorabilia on its Web site (http://memory. loc.gov/ammem/vshtml/vshome.html). As of 2003, the collection included playbills and even audio and video recordings of various vaudeville acts. Three of the films depicted popular animal acts: *Laura Comstock's Bag-Punching Dog,* a troupe of performing dogs and cats in *Stealing a Dinner,* and *Jumbo—The Trained Elephant.* The Web site reports that a variety of other animals, including sheep, pigs, bears, donkeys, monkeys, and birds, also performed in vaudeville shows. Vaudeville remained popular until about 1920, when it was overshadowed by radio and motion pictures.

These new entertainment media also featured animal acts. A German shepherd dog named Rin Tin Tin became a popular movie star during the 1920s after he was rescued from a German kennel during World War I (1914–17). He was featured in 26 movies and reportedly received more than 10,000 fan letters a week. Rin Tin Tin died in 1932. The next year, a movie called *Black Beauty* was released, based on a popular book about a horse's life and hardships in 19th century England. A decade later, a dog whose real name was Pal became an entertainment sensation in the 1943 movie *Lassie Come Home.* A Lassie radio show followed in 1947, and a television show in 1954. The original television show aired for 17 years. Numerous other movies and television shows were produced featuring Pal's descendents starring as Lassie.

The movie and television industry became major media outlets for animal entertainment during the latter part of the 20th century. Circuses and other traditional shows featuring live wild animal acts faded in popularity as they competed with new venues, such as theme parks and aquariums with exotic animals. In 1962 the first Sea World marine park opened in San Diego, California. The San Diego Zoo's Wild Animal Park was established in

1969. Busch Gardens of Florida began in the late 1950s as a beer-tasting factory open to the public. Over the following two decades the company added elaborate bird and animal acts and amusement park rides to create a theme park. During the late 1990s and early 2000s Sea World and Walt Disney World both added massive animal theme parks to their existing attractions.

Exotic animal acts have evolved during the 20th century. Shows today are often marketed as a chance for people to get closer to nature and to help protect endangered species. Tourists pay to swim with captive dolphins at beach resorts. Sea World in Orlando, Florida, advertises "amazing animal encounters" for its guests with killer whales, dolphins, sea lions, and stingrays. Las Vegas magicians Siegfried and Roy make a point of highlighting their work to conserve the extremely rare white tigers and white lions that perform in their shows.

U.S. LEGISLATION AND REGULATION

Performing animals in the United States had little legal protection until 1970 when the Animal Welfare Act (AWA) was amended to include animals exhibited to the public. Regulation and enforcement of the act is handled by the U.S. Department of Agriculture (USDA) Animal and Plant Health Inspection Service (APHIS) animal care unit. Animal exhibitors that exhibit animals for compensation and either obtain or dispose of animals in commercial transactions must be licensed. Exhibitors that do not receive compensation and do not buy, sell, or transport animals only need to register.

Licensing is required for:

• Zoos (except those operated by the federal government)

• Exhibits, shows, and acts that feature captive marine mammals (dolphins, porpoises, whales, polar bears, sea otters, seals, walruses, and other mammals with fins or flippers)

• Tourist attractions exhibiting animals, such as road-side zoos

• Carnivals and circuses

• Promotional exhibits in which regulated animals are used to promote or advertise goods and services

• Owners that exhibit animals doing tricks or otherwise performing for a live audience or on tape

Exemptions from the license requirement are granted for pet and horse shows, rodeos, hunting events, exhibits of farm animals at agricultural events, private collectors who do not publicly show or sell animals, enterprises that keep animals in a wild state (such as game preserves and hunting preserves), and exhibits that feature animals not covered by the AWA—mainly birds, reptiles, and fish.

TABLE 7.1

Licensed and registered exhibitors of animals by facilities and number of sites, fiscal year 2001

	Licensed exhibitors		Registered exhibitors	
	Facilities	**Sites**	**Facilities**	**Sites**
Total United States	2,531	3,437	18	20
Alabama	44	58	0	0
Alaska	9	9	0	0
Arizona	31	38	0	0
Arkansas	27	37	0	0
California	250	356	0	0
Colorado	34	39	0	0
Connecticut	41	53	0	0
Delaware	7	10	0	0
District of Columbia	0	0	0	0
Florida	264	431	1	1
Georgia	53	75	2	2
Guam	3	3	0	0
Hawaii	16	18	0	0
Idaho	18	23	0	0
Illinois	136	181	2	2
Indiana	71	90	0	0
Iowa	44	58	0	0
Kansas	27	39	0	0
Kentucky	18	26	1	1
Louisiana	20	26	0	0
Maine	8	17	0	0
Maryland	29	40	0	0
Massachusetts	40	56	0	0
Michigan	98	123	4	4
Minnesota	56	72	2	2
Mississippi	15	20	0	0
Missouri	68	101	0	0
Montana	17	18	0	0
Nebraska	15	18	0	0
Nevada	49	71	0	0
New Hampshire	19	24	0	0
New Jersey	48	58	0	0
New Mexico	13	15	0	0
New York	118	151	0	0
North Carolina	49	60	0	0
North Dakota	16	25	0	0
Ohio	68	103	4	4
Oklahoma	24	34	0	0
Oregon	48	55	0	0
Pennsylvania	112	144	0	0
Puerto Rico	6	6	0	0
Rhode Island	7	8	0	0
South Carolina	22	28	0	0
South Dakota	20	29	0	0
Tennessee	36	44	0	0
Texas	210	290	0	0
Utah	15	18	0	0
Vermont	4	6	0	0
Virgin Islands	0	0	0	0
Virginia	54	68	1	2
Washington	31	40	0	0
West Virginia	9	11	0	0
Wisconsin	93	113	1	2
Wyoming	1	1	0	0

SOURCE: Adapted from "Table 1: Number of Licensees and Registrants by Facility and Number of Sites," in *Animal Welfare Report, Fiscal Year 2001,* (APHIS 41-35-075), United States Department of Agriculture, Animal and Plant Health Inspection Service, Washington, DC, 2002

Under the AWA, licensed exhibitors must provide "adequate care and treatment in the areas of housing, handling, transportation, sanitation, nutrition, water, general husbandry, veterinary care, and protection from extreme weather and temperatures." The exhibitors are required to keep records detailing the veterinary care that the animals

FIGURE 7.1

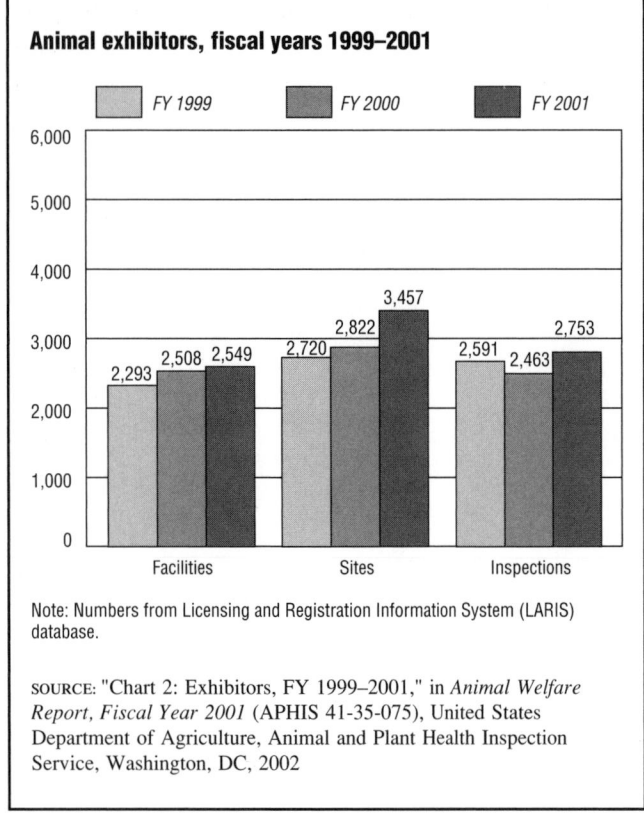

Animal exhibitors, fiscal years 1999–2001

Note: Numbers from Licensing and Registration Information System (LARIS) database.

SOURCE: "Chart 2: Exhibitors, FY 1999–2001," in *Animal Welfare Report, Fiscal Year 2001* (APHIS 41-35-075), United States Department of Agriculture, Animal and Plant Health Inspection Service, Washington, DC, 2002

TABLE 7.2

Localities that ban animal acts as of October 2002

Localities that ban circuses, rodeos, and other animal acts

California	**Massachusetts**
Corona	Braintree
Encinitas	Provincetown
Pasadena	Quincy
Rohnert Park	Revere
	Weymouth
Colorado	
Boulder	**Missouri**
	Richmond
Connecticut	
Stamford	**New York**
	Greenburgh
Florida	
Hollywood	**North Carolina**
Lauderdale Lakes	Orange County
	Washington
Maryland	Port Townsend
Takoma Park	Redmond

Localities outside the United States that ban animal acts

Brazil	**Colombia**
Cotia	Bogotá
Rio de Janeiro	São Leopoldo
Canada	**Costa Rica**
Argyle	Nationwide
Bridgewater	
Burlington	**Finland**
Burnaby	Nationwide
Chilliwack	
Coquitlam	**Greece**
Digby	Thessaloniki
Guelph	Kalamaria
Kamploops	Patra
Kanata	
Kelowna	**India**
Langley	Nationwide
Malahide	
Maple Ridge	**Ireland**
Mont Royal	Nationwide
Nanaimo City	
Nanaimo district	**Israel**
New Westminster	Nationwide
North Cowichan	
North Vancouver City	**Singapore**
Parksville	Nationwide
Port Colbarne	
Saanich	**Sweden**
Salmon Arm	Nationwide
Shelbourne	
St. Laurent	
Surrey	
Vancouver	
Victoria	
Windsor	
Yarmouth	

SOURCE: Adapted from "Localities That Ban Animal Acts," in *Legislation Prohibiting Animal Acts,* In Defense of Animals, Mill Valley, CA, October 2002 [Online] http://www.idausa.org/campaigns/circuses/circusban.html [accessed May 19, 2003]

receive. Table 7.1 shows the list of licensed and registered exhibitors by state during 2001. The state of Florida has the most licensed animal acts (431), followed by California (356), Texas (290), Illinois (181), and New York (151).

Regulations are also designed to ensure public safety. Dangerous animals can be publicly exhibited only under the direct control of an experienced trainer. There are time limits for exhibits, and the animals have to be fed and watered and handled in a humane manner that prevents unnecessary stress or discomfort. Physical abuse and food withholding are not permissible training methods. Traveling exhibits have to submit their performance schedules to APHIS before each tour. Exhibitors that violate standards are subject to warnings and civil actions such as license suspensions or fines.

Criticisms of the AWA and APHIS

The AWA regulations are criticized by animal welfarists as being minimal standards that provide little protection and are poorly enforced. Penalties for violating the AWA are civil, not criminal. In fiscal year 2001 the animal care unit of APHIS employed fewer than 100 inspectors who were responsible for inspecting thousands of facilities all over the country. The USDA reports that it conducted 2,753 inspections in 2001. (See Figure 7.1.)

According to press releases on the USDA Web site in 2003, charges were filed against 11 animal exhibitors during 2002 for violating AWA regulations. No details were

given about the alleged violations. The accused were all small roadside zoos, ranches, farms, and sanctuaries located in Colorado, Iowa, Illinois, Kansas, Ohio, Louisiana, Missouri, Texas, Utah, and Wisconsin.

Animals are often protected by state and local anti-cruelty laws. However, the Humane Society of the United

States (HSUS) complains that some states exempt USDA-licensed animal acts (particularly circuses) from meeting anticruelty laws. Animal rights groups also say that the USDA refuses to allow its inspectors to testify in criminal cruelty cases. Some local governments forbid or tightly regulate animal acts. Table 7.2 lists U.S. and foreign cities that have banned animal acts as of October 2002.

The HSUS advocates one of two legislative approaches at the local level:

- A ban on any mental and physical harassment of wild animals for the purpose of entertainment and a ban on their use in unnatural behaviors (such as jumping through hoops, wrestling with people, etc.)

- A ban on the use of all wild animals for entertainment unless regulations are in place to ensure their safety and that of the public

CIRCUSES

Circuses have used performing animals, mostly horses, elephants, lions, tigers, bears, and monkeys, for centuries. Historians trace the modern circus to the British entrepreneur Philip Astley (1742–1814), an accomplished equestrian and horse trainer. During the late 1700s, he put together an elaborate traveling show that performed in many European countries. Circus entertainment soon spread to the United States. One of the first American circuses was presented in Philadelphia in 1793 by John Bill Ricketts, another British equestrian.

Early circuses were small affairs with a few jugglers and acrobats and usually a horse act. Over time they became associated with elephants. One of the most famous was an African elephant named Old Bet. Old Bet's owner was Hackaliah Bailey, the man who founded the Barnum and Bailey circus. Old Bet was shot and killed in Maine in 1816 by protesters who were angry that she was performing on a Sunday. Another famous show elephant was named Little Bet. She could actually do tricks, including removing the cork from a bottle and sitting on command like a dog. In 1822 Little Bet was shot and killed by a group of boys who wanted to see if her hide could withstand the bullets.

In the late 1880s showman P. T. Barnum bought an elephant named Jumbo from the London Zoo. At the time, Jumbo was the largest captive elephant in the world. Jumbo traveled around North America in a specially equipped railcar. She died in 1885 after being hit by a train. By the end of the 1880s, circuses were very popular in the United States. The five Ringling brothers of Wisconsin started a circus in 1884. They later bought the Barnum and Bailey circus. The Ringling Bros. and Barnum and Bailey Circus performed its first show in 1918.

Circuses have always used oddities, both human and animal, to attract audiences. During the 1950s some circuses allegedly deprived ponies of milk to stunt their growth so they could exhibit them as miniature horses. A small horse named Angel was billed as the world's smallest horse. Angel traveled with circuses, carnivals, and county fairs for several decades. In 1997 she was rescued by the Horse Protection Society of China Grove, North Carolina. A picture on the organization's Web site in 2003 showed her at the time of her rescue with huge patches of hair missing and crippling leg deformities. Angel was nursed back to health and became the group's official mascot until her death in 2002.

In 1984 the Ringling Brothers and Barnum & Bailey circus attracted widespread criticism for exhibiting four surgically altered goats as living unicorns. Horns had been implanted into the goats' skulls to make them look like the mythical creatures. The ASPCA called on the public to boycott the circus in protest. Federal officials examined the animals and ordered the circus to quit advertising them as unicorns. According to animal rights group People for the Ethical Treatment of Animals (PETA), the man who supplied the animals to the circus was a serial killer who tortured and murdered several women before being arrested in 1985.

Animal rights and welfare groups are very critical of circuses that feature animals. They complain that the animals are treated poorly and spend long hours in small cages or chained to the ground. The HSUS makes the following claims against circuses:

- Many circus animals are not owned by the circuses but are leased from exotic animal dealers under seasonal contracts.

- Circuses do not provide proper veterinary care for the animals they own or lease.

- Circus animals spend too much time in transport in trucks and railcars that are not air conditioned or heated.

- Traveling circus animals are often deprived of food and water for long periods.

- Circus training methods include beatings and food deprivation.

The Outdoor Amusement Business Association (OABA) denies allegations that the circus industry condones abuse or mistreatment of its animals. In an October 1, 1999, press briefing, spokeswoman Heidi Herriot made the following points:

- Circus breeding programs produced the first Asian elephant born in captivity in the 1800s.

- The majority of circus elephants in the United States at the time of the briefing were more than 30 years old. By comparison, animals living in the wild often do not even reach maturity because of threats in their natural habitats.

- Studies conducted by the Royal Society for the Prevention of Cruelty to Animals (RSPCA) and Texas A&M University show that circus animals are "more peaceful, livelier, and less stressed than their counterparts in zoos."

- Reports that circus elephants are dying in record numbers due to abuse, illness, and malnutrition are false.

- Circuses "lead the way" in ensuring Asian elephant propagation in the United States.

- Banning elephant performances could advance the extinction of Asian elephants because circuses would have less money to invest in breeding programs.

- Animal rights groups inflate the number of people allegedly injured by circus elephants.

- U.S. government records show that no circus patrons died during the decade preceding the press briefing nor had any contracted diseases from circus elephants.

In addition, the OABA pointed out that the welfare of circus animals is regulated by the USDA, many state fish and wildlife agencies, and many local government agencies. The spokeswoman said, "There are more regulations in place for circus animals than there are for our children."

Major animal welfare and rights groups, such as the HSUS and PETA, advocate animal-free circuses. On its Web site in 2003, the HSUS listed 19 animal-free circus productions that tour the United States. One of the most famous is the Cirque du Soleil (Circus of the Sun), based in Montreal, Canada. In January 2003 the Reuters News Service interviewed Cirque du Soleil's artistic director Pierre Parisien (January 9, 2003 [Online] http://209.157.64.200/focus/f-news/k-red/browse [accessed August 1, 2003]). Parisien explains that the company has no intention of using animals in its shows. Referring to circus animals, he says "we do not agree with the way they are trained and I'm not sure the place of an elephant or a tiger is to stand in a cage half of its life and perform all around the world."

Elephants

Among all circus animals, elephants often receive the most attention from animal rights and welfare groups. History shows that elephant-human encounters can sometimes turn tragic for both sides. In 1826 Chunee the performing elephant was killed in England for displaying menacing behavior. It took more than 150 shots and over an hour to kill the animal, and witnesses reported that the elephant was in agony during the ordeal. The incident was widely reported in the British press and helped to gain sympathy for captive wild animals in the country.

In 1916 Mary the circus elephant was hung from a crane in Erwin, Tennessee, after killing her trainer, Red Eldridge. Eldridge had been on the job only one day. He had no experience with elephants and was a janitor before joining the circus. Witness accounts of the attack differ. Some people said it was completely unwarranted. Others said that Eldridge hit Mary in the mouth with a stick. The hanging was botched several times, and Mary's foot and hip were broken before she was finally killed. According to local historians, an autopsy conducted on the elephant revealed that she had abscessed teeth, a very painful condition that had never been treated.

In 1994 an elephant named Tyke escaped from a Circus International performance in Hawaii after killing her trainer and injuring dozens of others. The frightened elephant ran frantically around the city streets until being killed by police with nearly 100 shots. On its anticircus Web site, PETA lists hundreds of other captive animal attacks that have occurred since 1990. PETA claims that these rampages result from the animals' rebelling against years of abuse and deprivation.

Elephants are particularly difficult to keep in confinement because of their immense size. Welfarists claim that many circus elephants are mistreated, malnourished, and sick with tuberculosis. A common tool for training elephants is called an ankus. An ankus is a long rod with a hook on the end. Critics charge that elephant trainers beat the animals with the rod and poke the hook into tender areas of the elephant's hide behind its ears.

PETA's Web site describes the life of a 51-year-old circus elephant named Lota. She lived at the Milwaukee zoo from 1954 until 1990, when she was acquired by the Hawthorn Corporation, a company that trains exotic animals and leases them to circuses. PETA claims that Hawthorn handlers beat the elephant and that she suffered from malnutrition and tuberculosis. The company has been criticized by animal welfare groups for years for its problems. Hawthorn was also the exhibitor of Tyke, the elephant that escaped from the Hawaii circus in 1994.

According to PETA, Hawthorn was charged in April 2003 with a long list of violations of the AWA, including failing to provide veterinary care to elephants with severe illnesses, using abusive training methods, and allowing unsafe public contact. PETA is asking the USDA to revoke Hawthorn's exhibitor license and confiscate its animals. A well-respected elephant sanctuary in Tennessee has agreed to take Lota if she is confiscated.

In 2002 the animal rights group In Defense of Animals (IDA) sponsored speaking engagements around the country for a former circus animal trainer. The trainer described beatings administered to elephants with bullhooks. He claimed that brutal training methods are routinely used at the Clyde Beatty–Cole Brothers Circus and Ringling Brothers and Barnum & Bailey Circus. IDA also obtained video footage of what it says are abusive training methods being practiced on circus animals.

The Ringling Brothers and Barnum & Bailey Circus defends its elephant training and breeding programs. The circus, which is owned by Feld Entertainment, operates an animal retirement facility and the Center of Elephant Conservation (CEC) in Florida. The CEC was founded in 1995 to conserve, study, and breed Asian elephants. According to company officials, the CEC is a $5 million 200-acre facility dedicated to preserving the species, of which only 35,000 are left in the wild. The CEC is not open to the public.

The CEC says that it is responsible for more than 30 percent of the viable Asian elephant calves born in North America between 1992 and 2002. During that period, 15 elephants were born at the CEC, the last in May 2002. A videotape of the latest calf, named P.T., is provided on the facility's Web site (www.ringling.com/cec/). A company press release noted that the birth "takes us one step farther from extinction of the species." Feld Entertainment says that the corporation works with scientists and conservation groups to protect African elephants. The company claims to have a herd of 70 African elephants, which it says is the "largest and most diverse gene pool outside of Southeast Asia."

Animal rights groups complain that breeding elephants to work in the circus is not really conservation. They believe that wild animals should live undisturbed in their natural environments and that resources should be focused on protecting and expanding natural habitats. They do not generally advocate the use of captivity as a conservation tool.

MOVIES AND TELEVISION

Animals have been performing in movies and television shows since those media were invented. (See Figure 1.4 in Chapter 1, Figure 7.2, and Figure 7.3.) During the filming of the 1939 movie *Jesse James,* a horse was killed when it was forced to jump off a cliff for a scene. Public complaints led to the formation of the film-monitoring unit of the American Humane Association (AHA). The AHA opened an office in Los Angeles in 1940.

In 1980 the AHA was awarded a contract with the Screen Actors Guild (SAG) to monitor the safety and welfare of animals appearing in movies and television shows featuring SAG performers filmed in the United States. The Producer-Screen Actors Guild Codified Basic Agreement of 1998 includes a provision that producers must notify the AHA prior to using animals on a set and provide AHA representatives with access to the set while animals are being filmed. This applies to movies, television shows, commercials, and music videos that include SAG performers.

The AHA reviews scripts and works with animal trainers and production staff to ensure that animals are not harmed during filming. During 2002 the AHA monitored

FIGURE 7.2

A still from the movie *Billy Rose's Jumbo,* featuring Jimmy Durante. *The Kobal Collection. Reproduced by permission.*

more than 850 productions in the United States and six other countries. The AHA's contractual authority does not extend beyond the United States. However, producers sometimes invite the AHA to oversee animal filming at foreign locations. The AHA has no oversight authority on non-SAG productions, such as reality shows and documentaries. The AHA has publicly criticized the television shows *Survivor* and *Fear Factor* for incidents in which animals were killed or injured by the shows' contestants.

The AHA guidelines are laid out in the document *American Humane Association Guidelines for the Safe Use of Animals in Filmed Media*. The guidelines cover what filmmakers and crew should do prior and during production to ensure animal safety. These guidelines cover the treatment of animals present during production, whether they are performing, off-camera, or even visiting the set. The basic guidelines are listed on the AHA Web site.

In addition, there are general guidelines that deal with working conditions, feeding, watering, performance of stunts, safety, costumes, makeup, special effects, housing, transportation, and veterinary care. There are also species-specific guidelines for dogs, cats, birds, fish, insects and

FIGURE 7.3

Cast members Tommy Norden, Brian Kelly, and Luke Halpin with dolphin star Bebe, who played Flipper on the 1960s television show of the same name. *AP/Wide World Photos/NBC. Reproduced by permission.*

arachnids, horses and livestock, exotic animals, apes and monkeys, reptiles, and wildlife.

The AHA rates movies based on their adherence to these guidelines. Ratings for hundreds of recently released movies are provided on the AHA Web site (http://www.ahafilm.info).

The ratings given are "Acceptable," "Believed Acceptable," "Questionable," "Unknown," and "Unacceptable." An acceptable rating means that the AHA supervised animal treatment during filming and found it to be humane. Only films that receive an acceptable rating are permitted to show the AHA's endorsement line: "No animals were harmed during the filming of this motion picture." This message appears on screen during the closing credits. In 2003 the AHA Web site listed more than 1,000 movies that have received this rating.

The questionable rating means that AHA monitors witnessed some questionable practices during filming but that no animals were harmed. Fewer than 40 movies have received this rating. An unacceptable rating means that animals suffered "deliberate cruelty" during filming. As of 2003, 54 movies were listed under the unacceptable category.

If the AHA does not actually supervise animal treatment during filming, it may assign ratings of believed acceptable or unknown. A rating of believed acceptable indicates that the AHA does not believe that any animals were mistreated during filming based on interviews with cast members, review of scripts, and screenings of the film. If AHA is unable to obtain or verify any of this information, it issues an unknown rating. In 2003 several hundred movies were listed with a believed acceptable rating and 60 movies with an unknown rating.

The AHA Web site also describes in detail how particular animal scenes were filmed in dozens of movies. Usage of deceptive camera angles, body doubles, fake blood, computer graphics, and other tricks is described.

In 2001 the *Los Angeles Times* printed an article that was critical of the AHA's role in overseeing animal filming (Ralph Frammolino and James Bates, "Questions Raised About Group That Watches Out for Animals in Movies," February 9, 2001). The article claims that the AHA provides too little oversight and is reluctant to criticize the major movie studios, which fund its work. The AHA's budget comes from a fund that is overseen by producers and the SAG. The article notes that this fund included $1.5 million in 2001, and disputes claims by the AHA that its observers oversee filming of approximately 850 productions each year. The authors claim that a review of internal AHA documents shows that "the number of films monitored is considerably fewer." The AHA employed only nine full-time observers and 25 part-time observers during 2001.

The article also lists particular productions from the late 1990s in which animals were injured or killed during filming, yet which still received an endorsement line or acceptable rating from the AHA. These include the movies *The 13th Warrior* and *Simpatico* and an episode of the television show *Dr. Quinn, Medicine Woman.* The article claims that AHA employees complained about these productions and were frustrated by the lack of response from the organization. According to the authors of the article, at least one AHA employee has accused the AHA of "caving in to the studios on major investigations."

The AHA issued a press release in response to the *Los Angeles Times* article in which it defended its actions. It blamed the specific incidents listed in the article on "tragic accidents" and unauthorized use by movie studios of the AHA endorsement line ("American Humane Association Statement Regarding AHA Film and Television Unit," February 9, 2001).

ZOOS

The word "zoo" is short for zoological garden. The term, taken from the Greek word *zoion,* meaning animal, first came into English use in the mid-1800s. The London Zoological Society established a garden around 1828 to display its collection of wild animals. At first the garden was private, accessible only to members who paid a subscription fee. The society wanted to distinguish itself from the common animal exhibits of the time. However, the need for funds drove the society to open the garden to the public in 1846. The new zoo was hugely popular, receiving more than 100,000 visitors during its first year. The royal menagerie at the Tower of London was closed around this time and its animals presented to the zoo.

In 1874 the first American zoo opened to the public in Philadelphia. It featured animals from around the world, as well as elaborate gardens, architecture, and art. Early zoos kept wild animals in cages, but during the mid-1800s, a German exhibitor named Carl Hagenbeck, Jr., advocated the use of natural settings for zoo animals. In 1907 he opened a zoo in which the animals were exhibited on "artificial islands" that resembled their natural habitats. He felt that this approach was better for the animals and for the spectators. Hagenbeck was ahead of his time. Although few other zookeepers adopted his ideas at the time, they were one of the hallmarks of a top zoo by the end of the 20th century.

Accredited Zoos

In 1924 the American Association of Zoological Parks and Aquariums was founded. Today it is called the American Zoo and Aquarium Association (AZA). It is a nonprofit organization that works to advance conservation, education, science, and recreation at zoos and aquariums. The AZA's stated goal is "to work cooperatively to save and protect the wonders of the living natural world." Zoos and aquariums that meet AZA's professional standards can be accredited by the organization. In 2000 there were more than 200 AZA-accredited zoos and aquariums, located mostly in North America. They housed more than 750,000 animals.

In 2000 the AZA noted that each year accredited zoos and aquariums:

- Receive 134 million visitors (more than attend major league football, basketball, and baseball games combined)
- Receive more than $96 million in financial support and millions of volunteer work-hours from patrons
- Dedicate $52 million to educational programs
- Educate more than 12 million people, including more than 9 million students and nearly 85,000 teachers
- Participate in around 2,000 conservation projects all over the world
- Publish thousands of publications on animal issues
- Employ more than 45,000 workers

The AZA also works to ensure the long-term breeding and conservation of a variety of species. As of 2003 more than 160 species of mammals, birds, reptiles, amphibians, fish, and invertebrates were protected under its Species Survival Plan.

The zoos accredited by the AZA in the United States are generally well respected by the public and even by many animal welfarists. For example, the HSUS acknowledges that large zoos educate the public about wildlife and help to conserve, preserve, and restore endangered species. However, this does not spare accredited zoos from some criticisms.

In February 1999 the *San Jose Mercury News* published a series of articles by Linda Goldstein titled "Zoo Animals to Go." The series makes these allegations about major U.S. zoos:

- Zoo overbreeding has led to thousands of surplus exotic animals in this country.

- Zoos purposely overbreed some animals to produce babies that are popular with the public and bring in crowds.

- Older and less popular animals are quietly discarded and often end up at rundown roadside zoos and exotic animal auctions.

- Unwanted but healthy animals were euthanized at the Detroit zoo during the 1990s.

- A handful of dealers preferred by the major zoos have become wealthy from the sales of unwanted exotics given or sold to them by the zoos.

- Some surplus zoo animals wind up on the black market, where they are killed for their valuable hides or parts.

In August 2002 a reporter with *U.S. News and World Report* reported on the animal disposal practices of some major U.S. zoos (Michael Satchell, "Cruel and Usual," August 5, 2002). The reporter tracked down a dozen primates, birds, and other exotic animals that had left the prestigious Rosamond Gifford Zoo in Syracuse, New York, for a menagerie in Texas. He found the animals living in filthy cages alongside an interstate highway amidst trash and weeds. The menagerie had gone out of business.

The executive director of the Rosamond Gifford Zoo, which is accredited by the AZA, said that she had relied on references and information supplied by the Texas facility to make her decision. However, the reporter pointed out that if the director had checked with the USDA she would have found that unfavorable inspection reports had been issued for the menagerie.

As posted on its Web site in 2003, the AZA's code of ethics requires accredited institutions to acquire animals from and dispose of animals to other AZA institutions or to non-AZA members with "the expertise, records management capabilities, financial stability, and facilities required to properly care for and maintain the animals." The *U.S. News and World Report* article claims that this procedure is often violated by AZA zoos that "loan" or "donate" unwanted animals to unaccredited roadside zoos and animal parks. These facilities are frequently substandard and provide poor care. The article quotes a HSUS spokesperson as saying that the practice is "the dirty little secret" of the respectable zoos.

Satchell based his accusations on a review of database records from the International Species Information System (ISIS), as well as interviews with government, zoo, and animal rights personnel. ISIS is used by major zoos to track animal transfers. The article concludes that large zoos in New York, California, Hawaii, Tennessee, Georgia, Colorado, Arizona, Alabama, Missouri, and Washington, D.C., have transferred unwanted animals to substandard facilities and to dealers with alleged links to the exotic animal trade.

Elephants are perennially popular zoo attractions. (See Figure 7.4.) However, some major zoos have also been criticized for importing wild elephants from Africa and Asia to replenish the diminishing captive population in the United States. According to a May 2003 press release from the animal organization Born Free, the U.S. captive herd will die out within a few decades. Although the organization admits that wild elephants face many man-made dangers in the wild, it does not believe that captivity in zoos is the answer. Instead Born Free advocates a focus on conservation and protection efforts for wild elephants in their natural habitats. Zoo proponents argue that keeping elephants in captivity raises public awareness about their plight and will help their cause in the long run.

In May 2003 the San Diego Wild Animal Park came under intense criticism from animal welfare groups when it decided to transfer all of its African elephants to other facilities and import seven young elephants from the African country of Swaziland. Three groups—Born Free, In Defense of Animals, and Elephant Alliance—filed a formal complaint with the U.S. Fish and Wildlife Service (USFWS) to try to stop the process.

The groups criticized the park for subjecting the existing herd of older elephants to the trauma of moving. One of the elephants, a male named Chico, had been at the park for 25 years. The groups also argued that the young elephants would be better off at one of the multiacre elephant preserves that has offered to take them, rather than at the one-acre facility at the San Diego Wild Animal Park.

The Wild Animal Park argues that the elephants that they want to import would be subject to culling (killing) due to overcrowding and drought in their Swaziland habitat. When the USFWS reinstated the park's permit to import after investigating the animal rights groups' complaint, the Save Wild Elephants Coalition (made up of a number of animal rights groups) filed a federal lawsuit requesting a preliminary injunction against the importation. However, according to an August 9, 2003, story posted on the Web site of the *San Diego Union-Tribune* (James Steinberg, "Judge Denies Move to Block Importation"), on August 8 U.S. District Court Judge John D. Bates declined to issue such an injunction. This should allow the San Diego park to import its 7 elephants, while

FIGURE 7.4

Zoo patrons watch an elephant in Providence, Rhode Island. *Jim McElhom*

as part of the same shipment, the Lowry Park Zoo in Tampa, Florida, will import 4 elephants.

Unaccredited Zoos

Approximately 90 percent of the zoos in this country are not accredited by the AZA. There are thousands of these small "roadside zoos," petting zoos, animal parks, and similar exhibits that display animals to the public. The HSUS says that these small zoos often barely meet minimal federal standards for animal care. Most of these facilities include exotic animals, such as lions and tigers. Many are run by entrepreneurs with little experience in the proper care of exotic animals and with limited financial resources. Some call themselves animal preserves and achieve tax-exempt status so that they can solicit donations for their "conservation" work.

In May 2002 the USDA announced charges against the Corpus Christi Zoo in Corpus Christi, Texas, for violations of the AWA regarding veterinary care, handling, and housing. The small zoo is not affiliated with the city but is operated by the non-profit Corpus Christi Zoological Association. In December 2002 a local newspaper report-ed that the association had closed the zoo and intended to turn it into a refuge for exotic cats. The zoo housed only a few dozen animals, including two lions, four tigers, and some llamas, sheep, pot-bellied pigs, wolf-dog hybrids, birds, and reptiles. Local officials had complained that the zoo was giving the city "a black eye" because of bad publicity (Sara Lee Fernandez, "Zoo Closes Gates to Public Except by Appointment," *Corpus Christi Caller-Times,* December 3, 2002).

In August 2002 *U.S. News and World Report* described another animal park under investigation by the USDA. The Noah's Land Wildlife Park in Texas became a nonprofit animal preserve in 2000 after struggling financially for years. At the time it included only four tigers that were housed in horse trailers. Despite a lack of financial resources, the facility allowed the tigers to breed, which produced 26 cubs in two years. In addition, the preserve keeps a few bears, primates, deer, and antelope. The article describes the animals as living in "grim squalor" in cinderblock cages. Although the park director admits to having fund-raising difficulties, she has allegedly refused offers from accredited sanctuaries to take the animals.

Since the USDA refuses to comment on open investigations, no more recent information on either of the cases noted above was available as of July 2003. However, animal welfare groups say such stories are not unusual. They complain that poorly run facilities often receive bad inspection reports for years but are still not closed down. The Gentry Wild Wilderness Safari in Gentry, Arkansas, is an excellent example. The park's checkered past was described by a local newspaper in June 2002 (Robin Mero, "Wilmoth Settles," *The Morning News*, Springdale, Arkansas, June 28, 2002).

According to the article, the owner of the 200-acre drive-through park has been ticketed and fined numerous times for animal violations since 1988. In 1995 he paid an $8,000 civil penalty in an out-of-court settlement as a result of charges based on violations from 1992 to 1994. USDA inspections conducted in 1999–2000 resulted in a host of new charges that the facility violated AWA requirements for proper veterinary care, recordkeeping, housekeeping, and housing of its animals. This resulted in a $10,000 civil penalty that was also settled out of court. Half of the penalty is a fine. The other half must be spent upgrading the facility and training employees.

ANIMAL THEME PARKS

Animal theme parks are large tourist attractions that combine elements of zoos (or aquariums) and amusement parks to entertain the public. According to the National Amusement Park Historical Association, theme parks have their origins in the pleasure gardens of Medieval Europe. These gardens featured live entertainment, games, and other forms of recreation. Although their popularity faded in Europe, pleasure gardens evolved into amusement parks in the United States and were widely popular by the end of the 1800s.

The first oceanarium (a very large saltwater aquarium) in the United States is thought to be Marine Studios of Florida. Later named Marineland, the oceanarium opened in June 1938 and received 20,000 visitors its first day. Its popularity led to the opening of a similar facility, Marineland of the Pacific, in southern California in 1954. These oceanariums were more like amusement parks than traditional educational aquariums. They relied on performing dolphins, pilot whales, seals, and sea lions to entertain crowds.

In 1963 came the release of the popular movie *Flipper,* about a dolphin who befriends a young boy. It became a hit television show a year later in 1964. Public demand for performing dolphins and other sea creatures skyrocketed. In 1964 a young man named George Millay developed a marine life park called Sea World in San Diego, California, and in 1965 Sea World acquired Shamu, a female orca (killer whale) captured from the wild.

Shamu was one of many orcas captured during the early 1960s for use in the entertainment industry. According to a 1997 PBS *Frontline* story ("A Whale of a Business"), the first captive orca had been collected for Marineland of the Pacific in 1961. The animal lived for only one day. She repeatedly smashed herself against the walls of her tank until she died. A table available on the PBS Web site in 2003 listed 133 known orcas captured between 1961 and 1997, along with their lifespans in captivity. Many lived only for a few months, while the average lifespan for an orca in the wild is 30–50 years. PBS estimated that 102 of the 133 Orcas had died.

The original Shamu survived for six years. In the intervening years, Sea World has continued to acquire orcas and call at least one of them by the stage name Shamu for performance purposes. Eventually the company trademarked the name.

During the 1970s and 1980s, Sea World marine parks opened in Ohio, Florida, and Texas. In 1989 they were purchased by the Anheuser-Busch company, which already operated Busch Gardens, a popular park in Florida featuring bird acts, animal shows, and amusement park rides. In 2000 the company opened another theme park, also in Florida, named Discovery Cove, where visitors can experience wildlife up-close and swim with dolphins and stingrays. The stingers are cut off of the stingrays to make them harmless to people. An aviary includes hundreds of exotic birds that people can hand feed. According to company officials, the Sea World marine parks, Busch Gardens, and Discovery Cove were home to more than 60,000 animals as of 2003. The company noted on their Web site in the same year that "These animals serve as ambassadors for their species by helping to entertain, educate and inspire millions of people."

Many animal welfare and rights groups are critical of the Anheuser-Busch theme parks and Disney's Animal Kingdom, an attraction opened at Disneyworld of Florida in 1998. On its Web site, PETA has referred to these parks as "deadly destinations" and has noted that hundreds of animals that have died at these facilities due to improper care. PETA argues that living conditions are not healthy for the animals in captivity and disputes claims by the companies that own animal parks further conservation efforts. In 2003 PETA's Web site said that "Disney bulldozed tens of thousands of acres of wildlife habitat in the central Florida flatlands, killing native gopher tortoises and other animals" to build its Animal Kingdom, a park for imported wild animals.

The HSUS has focused its efforts on eliminating dolphin petting pools at animal theme parks. These are areas of shallow water around which visitors can gather and touch and feed dolphins. In spring 2003 the HSUS released a report titled *Biting the Hand That Feeds: The*

Case Against Dolphin Petting Pools. The report notes that animal theme parks are increasingly offering such opportunities for the public to experience physical contact with wild animals and marine life via feeding, petting, and swimming programs. In 1998 the federal government developed regulations for some swim-with-the-dolphin programs. These regulations included provisions regarding dolphin access to refuge areas, maximum interaction time, staff training, and safety measures. The HSUS says the regulations were suspended in 1999 due to pressure from the theme park industry, and in any event, the regulations did not cover petting pools and swimming programs held in shallow wading pools.

The HSUS report also provides a number of arguments against holding cetaceans (dolphins, whales, porpoises, etc.) in captivity to entertain humans and particularly against using them in petting pools. HSUS field investigations conducted between 1996 and 2003 revealed that visitors to petting pools are not properly supervised by theme park staff and expose themselves and the animals to various health and safety hazards, including:

• Dropping foreign objects, such as sunglasses, keys, coins, souvenirs, etc., into the pools

• Not washing their hands before or after feeding the animals

• Feeding the animals human snack foods

• Feeding the animals fish that have been dropped on the ground or even stepped on

• Holding babies and small children out over the water to get a better look at the animals

• Touching the animals' eyes and blowholes

• Poking at the animals with maps and other objects to get their attention

Besides these problems, the HSUS notes that many of the dolphins in petting pools appear obese and show signs of injury from aggressive competition over food. Encouraging the public to feed captive dolphins also sets a dangerous precedent, the HSUS feels. The government actively discourages people from feeding wild dolphins under the Marine Mammal Protection Act. Finally, the HSUS disputes the claim by the theme park industry that petting pools are educational, noting that "hand-feeding dead fish to obese dolphins in a cramped, overcrowded and featureless tank of chemically treated water provides visitors with scant insight into normal dolphin behavior in the natural environment."

CHAPTER 8
SERVICE ANIMALS

Service animals are those that work for humans doing particular tasks. These tasks may be as mundane as pulling plows or as sophisticated as finding underwater mines. Throughout history, animals have helped humans hunt wildlife, herd livestock, guard people and property, and wage warfare. Currently, animals are also trained for more humanitarian causes, such as rescuing the lost and providing aid and comfort to people with certain physical and psychological needs.

Whatever the task may be, the common factor is that service animals help humans with their needs and desires. Many people see this as a clever use of resources. Others see it as a form of slavery. Many animal rights activists believe that animals should not be used for any purpose by humans. However, they rarely speak out against uses that the public views as benevolent, but they are extremely critical of military uses of animals because the animals are exposed to great danger. This is also true for animals doing some police and rescue jobs.

Welfarists are also concerned that working animals should be trained and treated with care. Animal groups recommend that only positive reinforcement be used when service animals are trained. They also point out that service animals should be carefully screened to ensure that they are a good match with their potential human partners. Finally, they remind people that the needs of service and assistance animals must be considered along with the needs of the people being served.

HISTORY

The first service animals were probably dogs domesticated from wolves around 13,000 B.C. Humans learned to use the natural instincts and skills of the dogs to help them chase down and capture prey. As other animals were domesticated over the next 10,000 years, they too became useful for doing tasks.

All ancient cultures put animals to work. At first, the primary focus was feeding people. Societies dependent on hunting used dogs to help them and also enlisted more exotic species, such as mongooses and birds of prey. Agricultural societies had different needs. They used cats to protect the grain supplies and dogs to protect and herd livestock. Herding is actually a controlled form of hunting. Wolf packs sometimes hunt by sending a few of the fastest members out to circle prey and chase it back toward the remainder of the group. This instinct to chase and contain prey is associated with herding breeds of dogs, such as collies, sheepdogs, and cattle dogs. Some herding dogs even bite at the heels of livestock to move them along.

Oxen, donkeys, camels, horses, mules, and other beasts of burden pulled plows in the fields, carried loads on their backs, and pulled carts to market. Even small farm animals were put to work. Sheep and pigs were led across fields at planting time to step on seeds and push them into the ground. Sheep were also used to trample on grain to thresh it after it was harvested.

As civilizations grew, they developed public services and engaged in commerce and warfare with each other. This required animals that could travel well. Horses became very important as a means of transportation and in delivering mail. Many historians credit King Darius the Great (550–486 B.C.) of Persia with establishing the first elaborate postal system to use horses. The Roman Empire's postal system used horses for "express" mail and oxen for less urgent deliveries. Some ancient societies also used carrier pigeons to deliver important messages.

The military use of animals has a very long history. Many horses, camels, and even elephants were ridden into battle by soldiers and died along with them. Armies used beasts of burden to haul their ammunition and supplies. Some smaller animals also had military uses. For example, carrier pigeons and dogs made effective battlefield messengers.

FIGURE 8.1

A Pony Express rider and his horse, circa 1861. *National Archives and Records Administration*

Valuable Traits Encouraged

The role of service animals in hunting, agriculture, transportation, and warfare changed little over thousands of years. Breeding was manipulated to produce strains that served particular purposes. This was especially true for horses and dogs.

HORSES. According to anthropologist Sandra Olsen, as cited on the Web site of the Carnegie Museum of Natural History in 2003, "The horse has had a bigger impact on societies through the ages than any other animal."

Archaeologists believe that prehistoric horses were small, only about 12 hands (four feet) tall. Probably they were too small to even be ridden by humans. Horses were hunted and later farmed for meat. Over time the largest, strongest, and fastest were mated with each other to provide desired characteristics. Around 4000 B.C. ancient humans decided to put horses to work. Archaeological excavations in the Ukraine dating to this time period have uncovered horse teeth showing signs of wear, likely from a bit or other control device held in the mouth. These devices were improved and expanded over the years to provide greater versatility. Horses graduated from pulling carts and chariots to carrying riders.

Horses became invaluable to humans. The development of Western civilization would not have been possible without their services. They carried riders, pulled carriages and stagecoaches, and did all manner of jobs. American colonists and pioneers relied heavily on horses to settle new frontiers and to deliver news and mail. Horses reached their heyday in the Old West of the 19th century. The Pony Express is a famous example. This mail delivery system operated from April 1860 to November 1861 between St. Joseph, Missouri, and San Francisco, California, a distance of more than 1,900 miles. (See Figure 8.1.)

DOGS. Dogs were highly valued by many ancient societies, including the Greeks and Romans. After the fall of the Roman Empire, dogs in Europe mostly lost their status as working animals. Many were left to fend for themselves and became half wild. They roamed in packs, terrorizing villages and stealing livestock for food. Millions of dogs (and cats) were killed by superstitious people who feared that they were agents of evil. Dogs were accused of being werewolves, and cats were accused of witchery. Both were massacred during times of plague.

Dogs were still valued in hunting and herding, particularly by noblemen, aristocrats, and other landowners. Some dogs performed other roles. For example, during the 18th century, Dalmatians were used as carriage dogs. They could run alongside and underneath a carriage for miles and guide horses through busy streets. They also kept other small animals out from under the horses' feet and protected riders from thieves and highwaymen.

European colonists brought dogs with them to America and found the Native Americans already using them for hunting, sentry duty, and pulling sleds in the frozen north, and as pack animals. Eventually the colonists used trained dogs to attack Native Americans in battle.

Changing Roles

In the United States, service animals continued in their traditional roles until the late 1800s. Then the urbanization and innovations of the Industrial Revolution slowly eliminated the need for many of them. Motorized vehicles took over nearly all of the work formerly done by horses and beasts of burden in transportation, warfare, and agriculture. Over the next century, many people turned to electronics instead of dogs to guard their property and to chemicals instead of cats to kill rodents. Some vital tasks previously performed by working animals have become activities of sport and recreation—for example, hunting and herding with dogs and using horses to pull carriages.

However, the use of animals (particularly dogs) in military and public service continues to grow. In addition, animals serve as aides and comfort givers to people with specific physical and mental needs.

HUNTING

Early Times

Hunting was the first task in which animals were put into service to humans. Prehistoric hunters took advantage of the natural instincts and skills of carnivorous (meat-eating) animals, like dogs, which had been domesticated from wolves. The hunters trained the dogs to accompany them on hunts and turn over any captured prey. Prehistoric cave paintings show humans and dogs cooperating to pursue and capture large prey.

The ancient Egyptians used a variety of animals to help them hunt, including dogs, mongooses, and birds of prey. A drawing in a Cairo museum shows a man hunting waterfowl along the Nile River with his mongoose. Mongooses were considered sacred and called "Pharaoh's cats."

Falconry

Falconry is thought to date back to around 2000 B.C. in China. It is a form of hunting conducted with the use of trained birds of prey, such as falcons, hawks, owls, or eagles. These birds are also called raptors. Falconry was particularly important in the Middle East and is discussed at length in the Koran, the holy book of Islam. It became popular among European nobility during the Crusades and was fashionable until the invention of firearms.

Falconry is still practiced today as a sport in the United States. (See Figure 8.2.) There are very strict licensing requirements, because the sport uses wild birds that are protected species. Animals commonly hunted using falconry are rabbits, squirrels, pigeons, quail, and waterfowl.

Dogs

Dogs have been historically used in hunting. In the United States, dogs are used to hunt upland game birds and waterfowl, such as pheasant, quail, partridge, ducks, and pigeons. Dogs are also used to hunt squirrels, bears, raccoons, mountain lions, foxes, and other prey. The primary dog breeds used in hunting are beagles, spaniels, griffons, retrievers, setters, pointers, and hounds. Dogs that hunt mostly by scent are called scenthounds, and dogs that hunt mostly by sight are called sighthounds. Hunting dogs perform a variety of tasks, including tracking prey, pointing prey out to the hunter, and retrieving downed prey after it is shot.

CONTROVERSIES OVER HUNTING DOG USE. Hunting with dogs has become a controversial issue in some areas where it is common. In April 2003 the *Atlanta Journal and Constitution* reported on increasing conflicts in south Georgia between hunters using dogs and landowners (Stacy Shelton, "Hunters Howling," April 13, 2003). Dog running, as it is called, is a long-standing tradition in rural areas of the state. Landowners accuse hunters of letting their dogs trespass onto private property during deer-hunting season (mid-October to mid-January). Hunters say that property owners are being unreasonable and have killed at least one hunting dog. The landowners claim that hunters have threatened them and told them that they should fence their property if they do not want hunting dogs on it.

FIGURE 8.2

A falconer holds a peregrine falcon wearing a hood and jesses. *Photograph by Robert J. Huffman. Field Mark Publications. Reproduced by permission.*

This has become a major issue in recent years as rural areas of the state undergo residential development. The hunters are fighting attempts by the state legislature to outlaw dog running. The Georgia Dog Hunting Association supports legislation that would require hunters to purchase special permits and display their permit numbers on their vehicles and their hunting dogs. In this way, trespassers could be easily identified and reported to authorities. Some companies that own huge tracts of land in south Georgia, such as the International Paper Company, have decided not to allow dog hunting on their property anymore.

One form of hunting conducted with the help of dogs and horses is fox hunting. This has been practiced in the United Kingdom for hundreds of years. Hunters on horseback pursue foxes across the countryside using packs of hounds. Animal welfare groups have been trying to get it outlawed since the 1940s because they consider it cruel to the foxes. In 1999 Prime Minister Tony Blair pledged to outlaw fox hunting. In February 2002 Scotland passed a bill outlawing mounted hunting with dogs. A few organized fox hunts are held in the United States, mainly in southern and eastern states.

GUARD DUTY

Animals have been used historically to guard people and property from various threats. Prehistoric humans were the first to figure out that dogs could warn them of the approach of wild animals. The ancient Greeks and Romans used dogs to guard their towns and military fortresses.

Guard duty encompasses several tasks by animals. One task is to alert humans to danger. Another task is to provide physical protection from danger. Many animals can provide alerts, but not protection. For example, canaries were once used in mines to warn miners that dangerous gases were present. Because canaries are sensitive to very small dosages of these gases, their deaths gave the miners time to leave dangerous areas before they too were overcome. This was not a trained or voluntary response by the canaries. By contrast, dogs can alert people to an approaching predator and defend them against it.

Today dogs are still the most popular type of guarding animals. Besides their traditional guard duties, dogs are increasingly used to warn humans about impending natural phenomena, such as earthquakes. For years, researchers have been studying claims that dogs can somehow sense when an earthquake is about to happen. The speculation is that dogs may hear rumbling noises or sense vibrations occurring deep within the earth that precede actual ground movement.

Guarding Livestock

Historically the best guards for livestock (cows, sheep, goats, etc.) have been dogs. Guard dogs protect livestock from common predators, such as coyotes, mountain lions, bears, and wild dogs. This is one job that dogs continue to do on a regular basis.

Livestock guard dogs do not herd the animals and have been bred not to chase or harm them. The most common breeds used in the United States are great Pyrenees, komondors, akbash, kangal, kuvasz, Anatolian shepherds, and maremma. These are large dogs when fully grown, weighing at least 75 pounds. The dogs live with the herds and are generally calm and peaceful unless a predator is detected. Then the dogs will chase the predator away.

Llamas and donkeys are also used as guard animals by some sheep producers in the western United States. According to statistics from Colorado State University, 9 percent of sheep producers in the state used guard llamas during 1999. Another 3 percent used guard donkeys. Llamas and donkeys are both naturally protective of sheep and aggressive toward coyotes and wild dogs. However, they are afraid of mountain lions and bears. Their main advantages are that they live longer and are less prone to accidents than guard dogs. In the Alps, donkeys are also used to guard sheep.

Guarding Territory and People

Dogs are also the most popular animal used for guarding territory and people. This job requires large breeds that are strong, protective, and very territorial. The breeds most often used for this work are Doberman pinschers, rottweilers, komondors, German shepherds, and chows.

Guard dogs are not the same as watchdogs. Watchdogs bark when a stranger approaches them or their territory. Even small dogs, like chihuahuas, make good watchdogs. Guard dogs are intended to scare away and even attack intruders. Many guard dogs are employed by security companies. They work with handlers and human guards to patrol sites or protect individuals. Other guard dogs work without human accompaniment. They are placed on commercial and industrial properties, such as junkyards, at night.

Animal welfarists are highly critical of the use of unaccompanied guard dogs at commercial and industrial sites. They claim that these working dogs are given a minimum amount of food, water, and veterinary care, are kept in isolation in very dangerous environments, and are treated cruelly to instill aggressive behavior.

Friends of Animals is a nonprofit animal welfare group headquartered in Darien, Connecticut. The Winter 2002/2003 issue of the group's newsletter, *ActionLine*, describes the hardships endured by some New Jersey guard dogs (Megan Metzelaar, "Guard Dog Update"). According to the article, many guard dogs are leased from security companies. They are rotated around to different properties so that the dogs will not become accustomed to and possibly friendly with people in that area. The constant uncertainty makes the dogs feel vulnerable and insecure, which makes them even more aggressive. Critics say that the constant movement also makes it difficult for concerned people to monitor the condition of the dogs and report abuse and neglect to authorities.

MANUAL LABOR

The dictionary definition of "manual labor" is work that requires physical skill and energy. One of the first great civilizations to put animals to work was the ancient Egyptians. They used a variety of animals for transportation and as beasts of burden or pack animals, mainly donkeys, oxen, camels, horses, and hinnies. (A hinny has a horse for a father and a donkey for a mother.) These animals were also used to pull plows in the fields and to thresh grain in mills. During the Middle Ages, humans developed effective animal control devices, such as stirrups, collars, and shoes, that allowed animals to work even harder.

In the United States, mechanized equipment has replaced most of the work done by beasts of burden. Draft horses and mules are still used by a few farmers, particularly

FIGURE 8.3

A Sri Lankan farmer uses oxen to plow a rice paddy. © *Tim Page/CORBIS. Reproduced by permission.*

those in communities with traditional farming ways, such as the Amish. Nearly all developing countries rely heavily on draft animals for agricultural work. (See Figure 8.3.) According to the Food and Agriculture Office (FAO) of the United Nations, horses, mules, cattle, buffaloes, donkeys, and camels are widely used to help farmers plow, plant, and weed crops and in transportation, hauling, logging, and land excavation. The FAO reports that even developing countries such as India, Mexico, and Brazil still rely on animal power to do many tasks.

In the United States, some tasks historically performed by animals have become activities of leisure. For example, entrepreneurs in many large cities offer old-fashioned carriage rides to tourists. (See Figure 8.4.) Animal welfarists are very critical of these ventures. They complain that carriage horses are forced to work under hazardous conditions on city streets crowded with traffic and often do not receive proper housing and care.

On its Web site in 2003, the horse protection group Equine Advocates listed tragedies involving carriage horses that occurred between 1994 and 2000. Several horses have been hit by cars and at least one was electrocuted. The group says that horse-drawn carriage rides have been banned in several major cities for welfare reasons.

In her 1997 book *The Horse: The Most Abused Domestic Animal,* animal welfarist Greta Bunting lists a host of problems associated with commercial carriage horses:

- The horses work long hours exposed to bad weather, dangerous traffic, and exhaust fumes.

- The horses are not fed and watered as often as they should be by their operators in order to cut down on "messes" on the streets.

- The horses experience many leg and hoof problems from walking repeatedly on asphalt and concrete surfaces.

- Some of the horses do not receive proper veterinary care.

- Retired carriage horses are often sent to the slaughterhouse.

ODD JOBS

Over the years, creative humans have found some unusual jobs for animals to do. Europeans have long used dogs and pigs to seek out truffles. Truffles are small fungi that grow underground. They are highly prized in gourmet

FIGURE 8.4

A Belgian horse carriage offers recreational rides to city dwellers and tourists. *Photograph by Cory Langley. Reproduced by permission.*

cooking and are rare and expensive, selling for up to $500 per pound in 2003. Edible truffles are found primarily in the forests of France and Italy and in the American Northwest.

Truffle-hunting dogs and pigs are able to sniff out truffles and dig them up. Sows are particularly useful for this task because truffles emit a fragrance that is similar to a hog's sexual hormone. Although sows require less training than dogs to find truffles, they are also more prone to eat the fungi when they find them. Well-trained truffle-hunting dogs sell for as much as $20,000. They are much more mobile than sows and can travel better over rough terrain.

The incredible ability of dogs to sniff out particular odors has been put to use in other fields as well. During the past decade dogs have been put to work in the mold and pest control industries. These detector dogs sniff out colonies of destructive termites and mold spores in and under homes. Companies claim that the dogs are able to squeeze into tight crawlspaces and smell through walls—tasks that human inspectors cannot do.

One facility that trains termite and mold-detecting dogs is the Florida Canine Academy (FCA). According to owner Bill Whitstine, dogs are better than sensing devices at pinpointing hidden problem areas in a house. This saves the homeowner money because demolition of walls and floors is not needed. Also, people can spot-treat infested areas rather than blanket-treat the entire structure.

The primary breeds used for this type of work are beagles, rat terriers, Labrador retrievers, Jack Russells, and border collies. Dogs trained at FCA receive nearly 1,000 hours of training in obedience, odor identification, building searches, socialization, and riding in vehicles.

LAW ENFORCEMENT

Law enforcement agencies around the world use animals (mostly dogs and horses) to help them perform security work. Dogs are, by far, the most common animals used.

Dogs

Many dogs are used by U.S. law enforcement agencies at the local and national levels to perform important tasks. These agencies include police and sheriff departments, arson investigators, the Federal Bureau of Investigation (FBI), the U.S. Department of Customs, the U.S. Department of Agriculture (USDA), the U.S. Department of Corrections, and the Drug Enforcement Agency (DEA).

The dogs are specially trained to work with officers during searches and arrests and to sniff out illegal substances. Dogs have incredibly sensitive noses. Their sense of smell is several thousand times better than that of humans. Dogs can smell tiny quantities of substances and can distinguish particular scents with amazing accuracy. This natural ability has proven to be an extremely useful tool in law enforcement applications.

Many of the dogs used in law enforcement are rescued from dog pounds and animal shelters or donated by owners. The dogs undergo extensive training along with their potential handlers. Most popular are hunting breed mixes, such as German shepherds, golden retrievers, and Labrador retrievers. Beagles are preferred for many sniffing jobs.

The use of dogs by local police dates back to 19th-century Europe. British policemen on patrol often took their pet dogs with them as they walked the streets. Many police stations had mascot dogs just for this purpose. The successful use of dogs by military units during World War I brought added attention to the use of dogs in police work. During the 1930s British police set up official programs for the training and use of police dogs.

In 1907 the New York City police department (NYPD) incorporated police dogs into its work. However, the value of dogs for this work was not immediately recognized in the United States. They were used by only a dozen police forces through the early 1950s. Police dogs were sometimes used during the civil rights protests of the 1960s. (See Figure 8.5.)

The United States Police Canine Association Inc. was founded in 1971. The organization works to establish minimum standards for the training of police dogs in searching buildings and other areas for suspects and evidence, tracking criminals and lost people, pursuing and apprehending fleeing criminals, and protecting their human handlers.

Police dog work is very dangerous for the dogs. Many have died on duty. In 2000 a charity called Pennies to Protect Police Dogs, Inc., was started by a 12-year-old Florida girl. As of June 2003, the organization had raised more than $200,000 and contributed 239 custom-fit bulletproof vests to police dogs employed at 83 agencies in 14 states.

Many fire departments use dogs as part of their arson investigation teams. Arson dogs are specially trained to sniff for the presence of accelerants, such as gasoline, at sites where arson is suspected. Because of their incredible sense of smell, arson dogs can detect tiny amounts of accelerants lingering on surfaces inside buildings and vehicles or on people's clothes. The dogs indicate a find either by sitting or attempting to gain eye contact with their handlers. Because arsonists often hang around the scene of the crime, arson dogs are discreetly led through

FIGURE 8.5

A policeman and police dog confront a man at a civil rights protest in Birmingham, Alabama. *AP/Wide World Photos. Reproduced by permission.*

crowds gathered to watch fires to sniff for the presence of accelerants on people's clothing or belongings. Any suspicious finds are subjected to detailed laboratory testing.

The USDA uses dogs at international airports and border crossings to sniff people's luggage for banned plant and animal products. People sometimes try to sneak in items that could pose a disease threat to America's crops and animals. As of June 2001, the USDA was using more than 60 dog teams composed primarily of beagles, known as the "Beagle Brigade." The dogs attend the USDA National Detector Dog Training Center in Orlando, Florida. According to USDA officials, the dogs can correctly sniff out banned items 90 percent of the time after two years of experience. The Beagle Brigade intercepts approximately 75,000 banned products each year. The dogs work for 5 to 10 years and must be well-behaved around crowds.

U.S. Customs has been using sniffer dogs since the 1970s to seek out illegal drugs being smuggled into the country. As of July 2002, more than 500 narcotics dogs worked at airports, seaports, and border crossings around the country. The dogs have discovered millions of pounds of marijuana, cocaine, heroin, and other drugs hidden in vehicles and cargo entering the United States. During 2001 they led customs agents to more than 1 million

FIGURE 8.6

An officer and a narcotics sniffer dog inspect lockers at a New York high school. *AP/Wide World Photos. Reproduced by permission.*

TABLE 8.1

Some mounted police programs, as of July 1, 2003

Florence, AL	Dover, NH
Gadsden, AL	Hampton, NH
Scottsdale, AZ	Camden County Park Police, NJ
Los Angeles County, CA	Morris County Park Police, NJ
Monterey County, CA	Union County, NJ
Oxnard, CA	New Mexico Mounted Patrol
Placer County, CA	Albuquerque, NM
San Bernardino, CA	Las Vegas, NV
Santa Monica, CA	Chautauqua County, NY
San Jose, CA	New York City, NY
South Lake Tahoe, CA	Niagara County, NY
Ventura County, CA	Rochester, NY
Bridgeport, CT	Rockland County, NY
New Haven, CT	Stillwater, OK
Denver, CO	Tulsa, OK
Douglas County, CO	Fayette County, OH
New Castle County, DE	Franklin County, OH
Daytona, FL	Oxford, OH
Ft. Lauderdale, FL	Toledo, OH
Gainesville, FL	Portland, OR
Lake County, FL	Providence, RI
Marion County, FL	Charleston, SC
Orlando, FL	Hendersonville, TN
Pembroke Pines, FL	Memphis, TN
Polk County, FL	Nashville, TN
Chicago, IL	State Park Police, TN
Waterloo, IA	Baytown, TX
Indiana University, IN	Fort Worth, TX
Indianapolis, IN	Grayson County, TX
Porter County, IN	Harris County, TX
Wichita, KS	Texas City, TX
Covington, KY	Ogden, UT
Lexington, KY	Portsmouth, VA
Ouachita Parish, LA	Virginia Beach, VA
Boston, MA	Clark County, WA
U. of Massachusetts, MA	University of Wisconsin, WI
Portland, ME	Huntington, WV
St. Paul, MN	US Border Patrol, San Diego Sector
St. Louis County Parks, MO	

SOURCE: "USA Mounted Sites," in *MountedPolice.com,* 2003 [Online] http://www.mountedpolice.com/links.html [accessed June 16, 2003]

pounds of marijuana and 26,000 pounds of cocaine, resulting in the arrest of nearly 8,000 people. More than $20 million in cash was also confiscated. The dogs undergo a 13-week training program at the Canine Enforcement Training Center in Front Royal, Virginia. The Customs Service says that dogs that do not graduate and those that retire from service are either adopted by their handlers or placed in good homes. Drug sniffer dogs are also sometimes used in schools. (See Figure 8.6.)

Horses

Horses have been used in law enforcement work for centuries. They were the fastest and surest form of transportation for officers for many years. Even after cars became common, many law enforcement agencies continued to use mounted patrols. (See Table 8.1 for a list of some such programs in the United States and Figure 8.7 for a photo of mounted police in action in the 1940s.)

Mounted units are popular in both rural and metropolitan areas. According to information on the Web site of the United Mounted Peace Officers of Texas in 2003, Texas authorities use about 100 horses for patrols around the state. They are particularly useful in backcountry areas on dirt roads and rugged terrain. Several large U.S. police departments use mounted patrols for crowd control and to provide greater visibility of officers on the streets.

In 1871 the NYPD established a mounted unit to help officers control reckless carriage drivers and riders. It was responsible for 429 arrests during its first year alone. By the turn of the century, the program used nearly 400 horses and was responsible for crowd control during strikes, rallies, parades, and other public demonstrations. As of April 2002 the NYPD was using approximately 100 horses. All of them were geldings (castrated males) that were housed at six stables located throughout the city. The horses are donated by owners or purchased specifically for use in the program.

Mounted units are not without controversy. There have been injuries to horses, police, and members of the public. Because mounted units often perform crowd control during protests and demonstrations, the horses and the riders are exposed to people who may be angry and confrontational. There are reports of police horses being pelted with marbles and even garbage. Protesters claim that police often charge their horses into crowds, knocking over and injuring people.

Walking for many hours on city streets under stressful conditions is not easy on the horses. A few instances are

FIGURE 8.7

Mounted police handle labor unrest in Philadelphia in 1946. *The Library of Congress*

reported each year of police horses throwing off or kicking their riders. A 2002 article by a Columbia University journalism graduate student quotes a mounted officer as saying, "when the animals are exhausted, they tend to lash out at officers and grooms" (Emily Fancher, "Caring for the Horses at the NYPD Mounted Unit is a Full-Time Job," Columbia News Service, April 30, 2002 [Online] http://www.jrn.columbia.edu/studentwork/cns/2002-04-30/353.asp [accessed July 28, 2003]).

SEARCH, RESCUE, AND RECOVERY

Search and rescue (SAR) and body recovery work are performed by a variety of public service agencies in conjunction with private organizations. Animals that assist in SAR work are generally considered very valuable and noble by modern societies. These animals, primarily dogs, use natural and learned behaviors to help find missing humans, rescue people in danger, and recover bodies after disasters strike.

Many of the talents that were bred into dogs to assist in hunting, fishing, and herding have proved very useful in SAR tasks. For example, dogs originally bred to track down animals during hunting are now used to track down missing people. These dogs help find escaped criminals, kidnap victims, children that have wandered away, lost hikers, and many other people in need. Historians believe that bloodhounds were first used for "mantrailing" during the 16th century.

Newfoundland dogs were originally valued by Canadian fishermen because they showed a natural ability to retrieve items and people that fell overboard. Today they patrol European beaches along with human lifeguards. Saint Bernards were bred from sturdy cow-herding dogs in Switzerland. Monks living in the snow-covered mountains used the dogs to find lost travelers and people buried in avalanches. German shepherds were bred to be intelligent, diligent, and hardworking sheepherders. These traits are useful in a variety of SAR operations. In fact, some SAR agencies accept only German shepherds into their training programs.

According to the National Association for Search and Rescue (NASAR), there are hundreds of SAR dog units

FIGURE 8.8

A golden retriever guide dog helps a visually impaired woman across the street. *Photograph by Peter Skinner/Science Source/Photo Researchers, Inc. Reproduced by permission.*

across the country. The breeds most often used for this work are German shepherds, Dobermans, rottweilers, golden retrievers, giant schnauzers, and Labrador retrievers.

One of the most remarkable displays of SAR dogs occurred in 2001 after the September 11 terrorist attacks on the United States. More than 350 dogs scoured the rubble of the World Trade Center (WTC) in New York City, along with their human trainers, looking for survivors and corpses. Dog units participated from all over the United States and from foreign countries. The work was very difficult. SAR dogs suffered from paw cuts and burns, dehydration, burning eyes, and psychological stress. Some handlers reported that their dogs became depressed after not finding any live victims and could not eat or sleep normally.

The dogs, like all of the rescue workers, were exposed to fumes and fibers in the wreckage that might be damaging to their health. In March 2002 veterinary researchers at the University of Pennsylvania announced a three-year project to study and track any health problems in SAR dogs used at the WTC site. The researchers fear that these dogs may show a higher rate of cancer due to their exposure to potentially carcinogenic chemicals and other unknown toxins.

MEDICAL SERVICE

Animals that provide for the physical and mental well-being of humans are perhaps the most admired of all working animals. They guide, aid, assist, and comfort people with all kinds of physical and mental disabilities, impairments, and problems.

Aiding the Physically Impaired

Many people troubled with physical impairments rely on trained dogs to improve their quality of life. Assistance Dogs International, Inc. (ADII) is a coalition of nonprofit organizations that train and place assistance dogs. According to ADII, assistance animals fall into three broad categories:

- Guide animals for the blind and visually impaired

- Hearing animals for the deaf and hearing impaired

- Assistance animals for those with other physical disabilities

Under the Americans with Disabilities Act (ADA), service animals must be allowed access to all facilities and transportation vehicles that are open to the public. This means that service animals and their partners must be permitted to enter stores, subways, and other businesses. A service animal is defined as any animal "individually trained to work or perform tasks for an individual with a disability."

Many organizations that train service animals recommend that the animals wear colorful vests that identify them as service animals. These vests may display in large letters "Service Animal" or "Working Animal" and "Do Not Pet." Several companies sell such vests, as well as identifying patches and bandanas, for guide animals.

HELP FOR THE BLIND OR VISUALLY IMPAIRED. The most common type of medical service animal is the guide dog for the blind. (See Figure 8.8.) As of 1993 (the most recent data available), approximately 7,000 guide animals for the blind were in use in America, according to the American Foundation for the Blind.

The first modern training program for the use of dogs to assist the blind dates to 1819. Johann Klein founded a training institute in Vienna, Austria. Although Klein wrote about his work, it received little notice for another century. Following World War I (1914–18), German doctors established the first known training school for guide dogs. They were intended to assist soldiers blinded during the war. During the 1920s, a wealthy American woman named Dorothy Eustis wrote a magazine article, "The Seeing Eye," about the German school for the *Saturday Evening Post*. Eustis was a dog trainer at the time, working in Switzerland.

A blind American man named Morris Frank heard about the guide dogs and asked Eustis to train one for him. In exchange he promised to start a training school in the United States. Frank and his trained dog Buddy, a German shepherd, became the first guide dog team in the United States. Frank's school, the Seeing Eye, was founded in Morristown, New Jersey, in 1929 and was still in operation in 2003.

The school breeds its own German shepherds, Labrador retrievers, and golden retrievers. Puppies are raised by volunteer foster families until they are 18 months old. At that time, the dogs return to the school to attend a four-month training program conducted by certified trainers. Then the dogs are matched up with blind owners, and both undergo a 27-day training regimen.

The dogs learn to follow directional commands from their owners, such as "forward," "left," and "right." The dogs are taught to disobey a command if doing so would lead the blind person into danger. Blind people with guide dogs complain that well-meaning sighted people sometimes interfere with their activities by distracting and petting the dogs or pulling on their harnesses. According to the Seeing Eye, guide dogs for the blind typically work for seven to eight years and are then adopted as pets by their owners or others.

Another famous training program is called Guide Dogs for the Blind. It was founded in California in 1942 with the primary purpose of training guide dogs for veterans blinded during World War II (1939–45). As of 2003, the organization had large campuses in California and Oregon. One of its graduates became famous following the terrorist attacks of September 11, 2001—a guide dog named Roselle led a blind man named Michael Hingson down 78 floors to safety after the World Trade Center (WTC) was hit.

Guide Dog Users, Inc. (GDUI) is an affiliate of the American Council of the Blind. GDUI estimated in December 2001 that it costs up to $60,000 to properly train a guide dog team. The organization reports increasing problems with attacks on guide dogs by aggressive dogs while walking on city streets. It wants state laws enacted that will protect blind people and their guide dogs from any harassment or obstruction. In December 2001 GDUI published a booklet titled *A State Legislator's Handbook on Guide Dog Protection*. The booklet describes recent attacks on guide dogs and their devastating physical, emotional, and financial consequences.

Dogs are not the only animals that guide the blind. In 1999 a retired horse trainer, Janet Burleson, established the Guide Horse Foundation in Kittrell, North Carolina, to train miniature horses to do this work. Miniature (or pygmy) horses stand about two feet tall and are known for their calm and intelligent nature. Burleson started the foundation after successfully teaching her own miniature horse to guide a blind woman around a busy shopping mall.

Guide horses have several advantages over guide dogs. First, they live much longer—an average of 30–40 years, more than twice the average life span of a dog. This longevity appeals to many blind people who want to keep the same guide animal for many years. Guide horses are also more suitable for people who are allergic to dogs or afraid of them. The training of guide horses is reportedly much less expensive than that of guide dogs.

HELP FOR THE DEAF OR HEARING IMPAIRED. Hearing dogs are specially trained to alert their deaf or hard-of-hearing owners to particular noises, such as a doorbell, knock at the door, oven timer, crying baby, alarm clock, or smoke alarm. When the dogs hear these noises they make physical contact with their owners and lead them to the source of the noise. Hearing dogs are usually small- to medium-sized mixed breeds. The nonprofit group Dogs for the Deaf, Inc., of Central Point, Oregon, estimated on its Web site in 2003 that it spends approximately $12,000 to train, care for, and place each of its hearing dogs.

HELP FOR OTHER PHYSICAL CONDITIONS. Service dogs do a variety of tasks for people with debilitating conditions, such as paralysis, lameness, epilepsy, or Parkinson's disease. The dogs are trained to pick up dropped items, fetch objects (such as a phone), pull wheelchairs, open and close doors, turn light switches on and off, and perform other tasks as needed. They can even assist people who are unsteady on their feet by providing a means of support and balance. Some service dogs are trained to summon help if their partner needs it. The most common types of service dogs are Labrador retrievers and golden retrievers.

The organization Independence Dogs, Inc., in Chadd's Ford, Pennsylvania, is working with a Pennsylvania hospital to provide service dogs to patients with Parkinson's disease. The dogs are specially trained to nudge walking patients who suddenly freeze because they forget they are moving. The dogs also act as a safety crutch in case a patient stumbles and begins to fall.

Some service dogs are trained specifically to assist children with disabilities. Loving Paws Assistance Dogs is a nonprofit organization based in Santa Rosa, California. The group trains service dogs for children with spinal cord injuries, muscular dystrophy, spina bifida, cerebral palsy, and other disabling conditions. According to estimates on the organization's Web site in 2003, training of a service dog can cost between $15,000 and $20,000.

Other animals beside dogs also work as service animals. The organization Helping Hands in Boston, Massachusetts, trains capuchin monkeys to assist quadriplegic people with their daily activities. Capuchin monkeys are more commonly known as "organ grinder" monkeys. They are small clever animals with limber hands and friendly dispositions. They assist paralyzed people by fetching items, retrieving things that are dropped, and turning lights on and off. Like all service animals, the monkeys also provide much-needed companionship to their human partners.

NOT ALL CASES ARE SUCCESSFUL. Although the vast majority of service animals are greatly appreciated for their work, there have been cases of abuse. In February 2002 a blind man in Pennsylvania was charged with brutally killing his guide dog, Inky. The man allegedly went into a rage while intoxicated and kicked the dog to death. He was sentenced to up to 23 months in prison and ordered to pay $1,000 to a guide dog association. Animal welfarists use the case to point out that service animals and their human partners must be carefully screened and monitored to ensure that a good match is made and that the animals will be cared for properly.

One controversial issue associated with guide dogs is the use of breeding programs to produce them. Many organizations and training schools rescue dogs from pounds and animal shelters. This provides good homes for dogs that might otherwise be euthanized. Animal welfarists are critical of schools that breed their own dogs because there are already so many unwanted dogs in the country. However, some schools complain that the supply of suitable pound and shelter dogs is not sufficient to meet their needs. Paws with a Cause is an organization based in Wayland, Mississippi, that trains service animals. The group announced in the early 2000s that it planned to concentrate on using specially bred dogs rather than shelter dogs for its training program. On its Web site in 2003, the organization presented statistics showing that few shelter dogs meet its criteria for age, temperament, and medical condition. The failure rate for shelter dogs is also higher (87.5 percent) than it is for specially bred dogs (25 percent). Paws with a Cause defends its decision by reminding people that its primary goal is helping people, not rescuing dogs. The group says that it works hard to find alternative jobs and homes for the dogs that fail its program.

Mental and Physical Therapy

Another medical service that animals provide is therapeutic rather than utilitarian. Therapy animals provide emotional support or assist in rehabilitation activities. For example, therapy animals can comfort people undergoing psychological counseling. Many organizations working with abused children use therapy dogs in their programs. Petting and hugging the dogs relaxes the children and allows them to open up to counselors. Similar programs are used to calm children suffering from autism.

Therapy animals also visit hospitals, orphanages, and nursing homes to cheer people who may be lonely or depressed. Dogs are the most common therapy animals. Only gentle and social dogs with very good dispositions are used in this work. The human participants are screened beforehand to ensure that they like animals and find them comforting.

Therapy animals also participate in physical rehabilitation programs, such as hippotherapy, or horse-assisted therapy. The word *hippotherapy* is derived from the Greek word *hippos,* meaning horse. At the Fran Joswick Therapeutic Riding Center in San Juan Capistrano, California, people disabled by strokes or injuries ride horses as part of their rehabilitation. Doctors have believed for some time that horseback riding is beneficial to people who must relearn to walk. As a horse strolls, a rider's hips are gently swiveled back and forth. This causes the rider's legs to swing back and forth in a motion that mimics walking. At the same time, the rider works to keep the upper body centered and facing forward. Riding a horse works nearly every muscle in the human body. Over time, the movement rebuilds the muscle strength, coordination, and balance required for walking. Hippotherapy is highly effective for children and adults suffering from a variety of muscular and neurological problems.

Because therapy animals are not individually trained to assist specific individuals, they are not considered service animals under the ADA. Therefore they are not guaranteed the public access rights under U.S. law that service animals are.

Medical Detection

The idea of using animals in medical detection received credibility following the publication of a 1989 article in the *Lancet,* a distinguished British medical journal. The article, "Sniffer Dogs in the Melanoma Clinic," described a patient who had sought medical help about a worrisome mole on her leg. The woman reported that her dog constantly sniffed at the mole and seemed very interested in it. Doctors discovered that the mole was cancerous and removed it. Similar stories have been reported by other dermatologists. Doctors speculate that dogs may be able to smell some unique scent emitted by cancerous skin cells.

In June 2002 researchers at the Cambridge University Veterinary School in England announced their intent to test dogs at screening human urine samples for a scent unique to prostate cancer cells. The researchers believe that a chemical with a distinctive smell may be present in the urine of prostate cancer sufferers. If dogs could be trained to alert doctors to samples with that smell, it might be a useful screening tool. The researchers call the idea "dognoseis." If it is found that cancerous cells do emit unique scents, the information could be used to construct electronic "noses" for use in diagnosing cancer. As of July 2003 the project was still seeking funding.

Dogs and some other animals may also be able to sense when a person is about to have a seizure. Some seizure-prone people have service dogs to assist them. The dogs are trained to lie by the person's side during a seizure and help them get up afterwards. However, many

FIGURE 8.9

A relief of a Greek horse-drawn chariot. © *Ganni Dagli Orti/Corbis*

of these people claim that their dogs act strangely right before a seizure occurs. Doctors are not certain if dogs can really sense seizures before they occur. However, other stories in the media report on people who claim to have seizure-sensitive dogs and even cats and birds.

MILITARY SERVICE

Of all the service and assistance animals in use, animals used by the military are the most controversial. To animal welfarists and animal rights activists, the use of animals by the military can be extremely disturbing. These animals are often put into tremendous danger, and many of them die during their service. On the other hand, members of the military say that service animals have saved many human lives in battle. They argue that animal deaths in war are regrettable, but permissible, if human lives are saved. Animal rights activists and welfarists argue that animals involved in warfare do not know what they are fighting for or against and have very poor chances of surviving.

Although some animal work is classified, it is known that the U.S. military has used horses, pigeons, dogs, chickens, dolphins, beluga whales, sea lions, and other marine mammals during combat. Besides horses, many of these animals are still used in modern warfare.

History

Humans have used animals in military roles for at least 3,500 years. Sometime before 1500 B.C., the Mesopotamians used horses to pull their chariots during battle. Figure 8.9 shows an ancient Greek horse-drawn chariot.

Elephants were used in warfare as early as 1100 B.C. They are mostly associated with Alexander the Great (356–323 B.C.) and Hannibal Barca (247–183 B.C.). Hannibal's journey with elephants across the Alps to fight the Romans is famous. However, historians say that the vast majority of his elephants died during the trip. The Roman Empire incorporated elephants into its military after capturing them from defeated armies. Elephants were mostly prized for striking fear into the enemy. Sometimes their heads or ears were painted in bright colors to make them look more frightening. Although they played a key role in some battles, they were also a liability. When panicked, they often ran amok among their own troops.

Roman armies assembled entire formations of attack dogs for battle. Dogs were also used in military campaigns by Attila the Hun (406–453).

Cavalry units in which warriors fought while riding horses date back to around 800–700 B.C. The ancient Scythians are generally credited with mastering war on horseback. Scythia comprised parts of Europe and Asia north of the Black Sea. The Scythians were expert archers and kept large herds of horses. They were among the first to castrate their male horses.

Cavalry units were not widely used in European warfare because heavily armored knights had difficulty maneuvering their lances and swords while on horseback. This changed during the Middle Ages when the stirrup was introduced. In the 1500s European soldiers began using heavy artillery and cannons that were pulled by teams of horses. War dogs were used for guard and messenger duty.

During the Revolutionary War, General George Washington (1732–99) created cavalry units called Continental Dragoons that fought with distinction in several battles. These units were expensive to maintain and were disbanded after the war ended. During the 1800s, however, dragoon regiments were reinstated to fight against Native Americans and the Mexican army on the western frontier. This was the origin of the U.S. Cavalry.

Later in the 19th century, cavalry units were used extensively by both sides during the Civil War (1861–65). Approximately 18,000 horses were involved in an 1863 battle at Brandy Station, Virginia. This is considered the largest cavalry battle ever in the Western Hemisphere. The National Museum of Civil War Medicine in Frederick, Maryland, estimates that 1 million horses in military service died during the Civil War. By the beginning of the 20th century, more than 400,000 troops (and horses) were in the U.S. Cavalry.

The mounted cavalry proved ineffective during World War I. Horses could not penetrate barbed-wire fences and were mowed down by machine guns. According to the PBS Web site, most of the 6 million horses that served the U.S. military in World War I were killed ("Horses and Waging War," in *Wild Horses, An American Romance* [Online] http://www.pbs.org/wildhorses/wildintro.html [accessed July 28, 2003]). The deaths of millions of other horses in military service to other countries severely depleted the world's horse population. World War I was the last war in which horses played a major role. By 1942 all U.S. Cavalry units were disbanded or mechanized.

Coincidentally enough, this is the same year that dogs were first officially inducted into the U.S. Army. Prior to that time, dogs had seen extensive service in European armies, particularly in France, Italy, Germany, and Belgium. In fact, the Germans established the first official school for military dogs in 1884. They used an estimated 30,000 dogs during World War I as sentries, sled dogs, pack animals, and messengers, and to perform other tasks. One of those dogs was a German shepherd puppy captured by an American soldier. The dog wound up in Hollywood, California, and starred in more than 100 movies as Rin Tin Tin. The French military also used about 20,000 dogs in

World War I. At that time dogs were widely used throughout Europe for both military and police work.

The U.S. military used dogs in some military campaigns during the 19th century, particularly in the Seminole Wars, the Civil War, and the Spanish-American War of 1898. Dogs that sometimes accompanied American troops in World War I were officially considered mascots or pets by the U.S. military, but in 1942 dog training began in earnest. A group called Dogs for Defense asked Americans to donate dogs to the army. Dogs were trained for guard and police duty, to pull sleds, to carry packs and messages, to help reconnaissance patrols find hidden enemy soldiers, and to help the medical corps find and rescue wounded soldiers.

Following World War II, the surviving dogs were returned to their owners. This was not the case in later wars. Military officials were afraid of a trained military dog attacking someone in civilian life. It became common practice to euthanize unusable and retired war dogs or leave them behind on the battlefield. Animal welfarists and soldiers complained about this policy, particularly after the Vietnam War.

Military historians estimate that war dogs saved thousands of American soldiers from death or injury during the Vietnam War. Approximately 4,000 service dogs guarded troops, alerted them to booby traps, and pulled the wounded to safety. On its Web site, the U.S. War Dog Association lists the names of nearly 300 dogs that were killed in action during the war. Most service dogs that survived the war were left behind in Vietnam when American troops pulled out. The fate of these dogs is unknown. Many veterans, including the Vietnam Dog Handlers Association, are lobbying for a national memorial to be built in Washington, D.C., to honor the service of war dogs. According to a November 26, 2000, article in *Stars and Stripes,* 30,000 dogs have served in the U.S. military since World War II (Scott Schonauer, "New Law Allows Adoption of Military Dogs").

In November 2000 President Bill Clinton signed a new law into effect that allows retired military dogs to be adopted rather than euthanized. New owners have to agree not to hold the government responsible for any injuries or damages caused by former military dogs. Because of their extensive training, the dogs are expected to be useful in law enforcement and rescue work.

In recent decades, animals that have died in battle have been recognized as war heroes. The Dickin is an award presented by the PDSA, a British organization that provides veterinary care for animals in low-income neighborhoods. Since World War II, the PDSA has awarded Dickin medals to 32 pigeons, 18 dogs, 3 horses, and 1 cat for their performance in battle. Most of the animals performed acts that saved the lives of many soldiers.

Current Uses

According to the Department of Defense, as of fall 2001, the military used around 1,400 dogs that were working as sentries, detecting land mines and bombs, and performing search, rescue, and recovery tasks. In April 2003 the HSUS donated $9,000 to buy 30 cooling vests for K-9 dogs in battle with the U.S. Marines in Iraq. The vests wrap around the dogs' midsections and have pockets for inserts that remain cool for hours. The HSUS was worried that the dogs would suffer from hot desert temperatures (as high as 120 degrees F) during the summer months. The dogs perform various tasks, including guard duty, bomb detection, scouting, and even helping apprehend enemy soldiers.

Other military animals used by the United States during the 2003 invasion of Iraq include dozens of pigeons and chickens. Both were deployed as early-warning alerts in the event of a chemical or biological attack. However, their use is not considered a success. Nearly every chicken died after only days in the desert due to heat, stress, illness, or injury. Some may have been killed and eaten by hungry U.S. troops. The chickens were replaced with nearly 200 pigeons, but these birds too died in large numbers.

More successful was the use of some specially trained dolphins. U.S. forces used two bottle-nosed Atlantic dolphins named Makai and Tacoma to seek out underwater mines along the Iraqi coast. The dolphins were trained to find the mines without detonating them and alert handlers to their presence.

Frontline reported on the U.S. Navy's historical use of dolphins and other marine mammals in "A Whale of a Business" (PBS, Boston, Massachusetts, 1998). The navy began its Marine Mammal Program in 1960. Marine mammals were trained to perform tasks such as filming objects underwater, retrieving and delivering equipment, and guarding vessels against enemy divers. They were used during the Vietnam War and later in the Persian Gulf during the 1980s.

Dolphins are trained to detect enemy divers and attach restraining devices to them so they can be apprehended by human handlers. These devices include a line with a buoy that floats to the surface. Sea lions are trained to actually pursue any fleeing divers who go ashore. Mine-hunting dolphins identify and mark mines so that they can be decommissioned or later exploded safely.

The use of animals in the 2003 invasion of Iraq was criticized by animal rights and welfare groups, including PETA, the HSUS, and United Poultry Concerns. In an April 1, 2003, letter to Secretary of Defense Donald Rumsfeld, a PETA spokeswoman and wildlife biologist complained that "these animals never enlisted, they know nothing of Iraq or Saddam Hussein, and they probably won't survive." Other activists have accused the military of wasting animals needlessly when sophisticated equipment could be used instead.

CHAPTER 9
PETS

Pets are animals that humans keep for pleasure rather than utility. Their value is mostly emotional. They help to fulfill human desires for companionship, affection, entertainment, and ownership.

The American Pet Products Manufacturers Association (APPMA) was founded in 1958 and is the nation's leading pet industry trade group. More than 650 companies were members of the association as of 2003. Every two years, the APPMA releases data on pet ownership. According to the *2001/2002 National Pet Owner's Survey,* more than 350 million animals are kept as pets in the United States. Cats, dogs, ornamental fish, and tropical birds are the most popular. Other common pets include horses, rabbits, livestock, pigeons and poultry, guinea pigs, turtles, snakes, ferrets, gerbils, lizards, and miscellaneous reptiles and rodents. More than one-third of American households had a dog or a cat. Nearly half owned more than one type of pet. The breakdown by pet is shown in Figure 9.1.

The American Veterinary Medical Association (AVMA) performed a pet census in 1991, 1996, and 2001. (See Figure 9.2 and Figure 9.3.) The latest survey was detailed in the *2001 U.S. Pet Ownership & Demographics Sourcebook.* The survey found that the pet cat population was 68.9 million, up from 57 million in 1991. There were 61.6 million pet dogs, up from 52.5 million in 1991. Pet horse, rabbit, turtle, lizard, reptile, and ferret populations have also increased since 1991.

Pets have a unique status. Legally, they are considered personal property. This offers them some protection under the law, as damaging someone else's property is a crime. From a psychological standpoint, most pets enjoy a higher value. Many people say they consider pets to be members of the family, almost like children. The APPMA notes that U.S. pet owners spent $28 billion in 2000 on pet supplies, equipment, and services. The status of pet species differs in different societies—for example, most

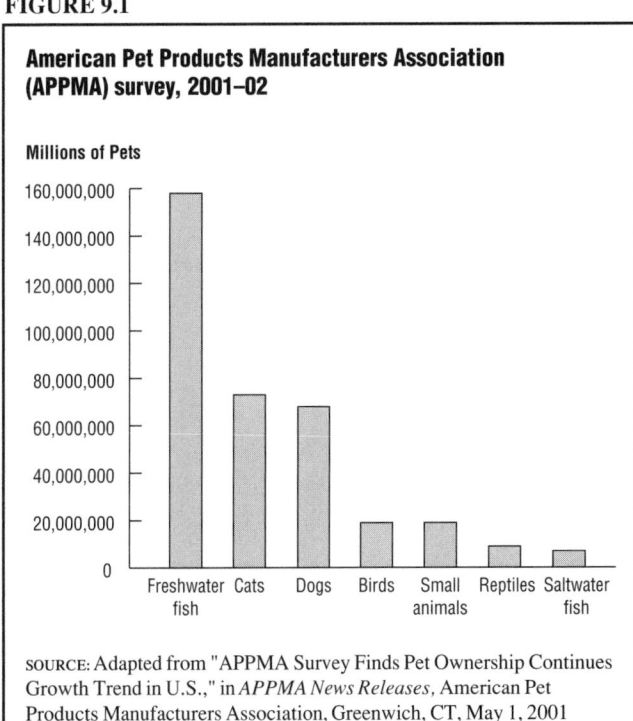

FIGURE 9.1

American Pet Products Manufacturers Association (APPMA) survey, 2001–02

Millions of Pets

SOURCE: Adapted from "APPMA Survey Finds Pet Ownership Continues Growth Trend in U.S.," in *APPMA News Releases,* American Pet Products Manufacturers Association, Greenwich, CT, May 1, 2001 [Online] http://www.appma.org/press/news_releases/2001/nr_05-01-01.asp [accessed July 11, 2003]

Americans would not consider eating a dog, cat, or horse, but this taboo does not exist in some other cultures.

It surprises many pet owners to learn that some animal rights groups are opposed to the idea of keeping pets. For example, the group Animal Freedom is based in Holland. On its Web site in 2003, one writer pointed out how different a dog's life is as a pet compared to life in the wild:

- Wild dogs can attain various social rankings within their packs, while pet dogs are limited to the lowest social rank.

- Wild dogs can move about freely, while pet dogs have their movements restricted.

FIGURE 9.2

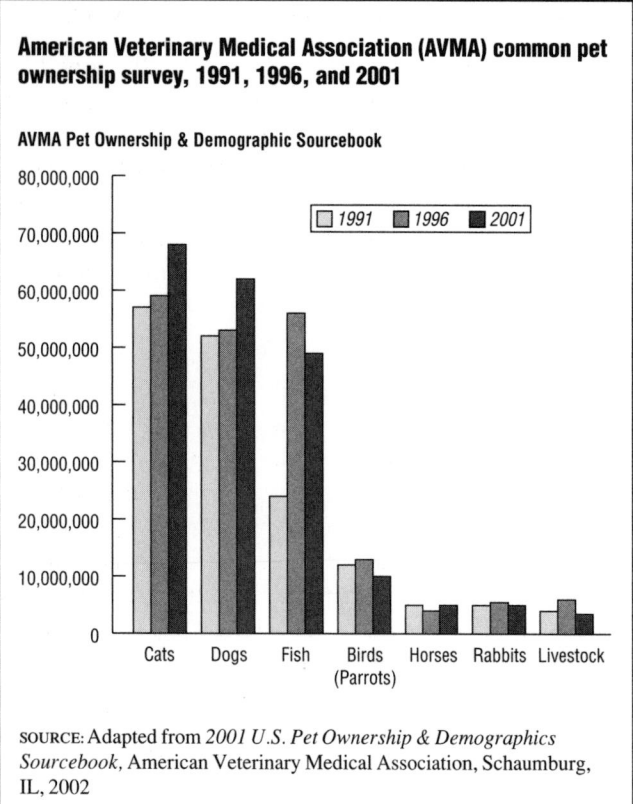

American Veterinary Medical Association (AVMA) common pet ownership survey, 1991, 1996, and 2001

AVMA Pet Ownership & Demographic Sourcebook

SOURCE: Adapted from *2001 U.S. Pet Ownership & Demographics Sourcebook,* American Veterinary Medical Association, Schaumburg, IL, 2002

FIGURE 9.3

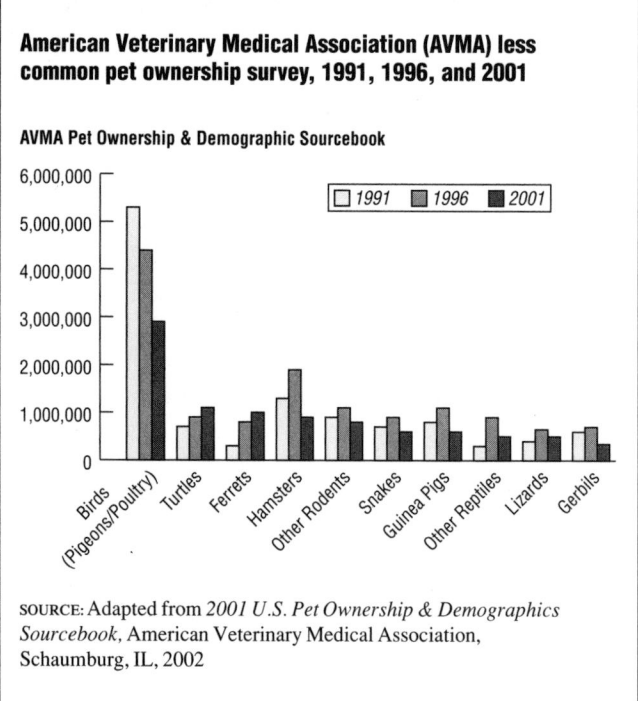

American Veterinary Medical Association (AVMA) less common pet ownership survey, 1991, 1996, and 2001

AVMA Pet Ownership & Demographic Sourcebook

SOURCE: Adapted from *2001 U.S. Pet Ownership & Demographics Sourcebook,* American Veterinary Medical Association, Schaumburg, IL, 2002

• Wild dogs can socialize among themselves, while pet dogs are often kept isolated from other members of their species.

• Wild dogs express their sexuality freely, while the sexuality and reproduction of pet dogs are controlled by people.

• Wild dogs eat as they choose, while pet dogs eat what and when people want to feed them.

This writer concluded that "although there are plenty of people who want nothing but the best for their dogs, this doesn't change the fact that in the end people impose their wills on dogs."

Pet ownership is a thorny issue in the animal rights debate. Some activists are outspoken that any use of any animal for any human purpose is wrong. However, when it comes to pets, many consider this stance too radical. A great number of those who work to improve animal welfare are pet owners. Most animal rights groups and animal welfarists focus their attention on particular pet problems, such as neglect, abuse, and overpopulation. They are particularly critical of breeders and pet stores that sell pets to the public. The keeping of wild animals as pets is condemned by most or all major organizations working for animal rights and welfare.

Some groups say that people keep pets for the wrong reasons. They argue that some people get pets to compen-

sate for their inability to engage in healthy social contact with other people. Pets may be a crutch or a time-filler to these people. Others rely on pets to build their egos or make them feel good about themselves in some way. The ability to control another living being can be a powerful motivator. Some people see pets as disposable items to be kept as long as they are useful or fun, and discarded when they are not. Many people think that taking care of a pet is educational for children because it teaches them responsibility and respect for other living creatures. Some people believe that keeping a pet has a spiritual basis, and that it brings them closer to nature.

The common thread in all of these reasons is that they focus on the needs and wants of the pet owner rather than the pet. Some people feel this is only fair, as it is the pet owner who provides food, shelter, and care. Shouldn't people be able to keep animals as pets as long they take care of them? There is a movement by some humane organizations to refer to pets as "companion animals" and to owners as "guardians." These terms demonstrate the desire of these groups to elevate pets from property status to wards or dependents.

HISTORY

Historians are not sure when humans first started keeping animals as pets. Keeping an animal for pleasure rather than for food or work was possible only for people who were well off and so had the resources to feed extra mouths. Dogs most likely were the first pets, because they were domesticated so long ago. The ancient Romans are known to have kept pets, particularly dogs and birds. Cats and horses were also popular with Romans and may have been considered pets, but they were also working animals. The origins of ornamental goldfish date back to the 7th century in China, where Buddhist monks first raised them in ponds. By the 14th century the Chinese were keeping goldfish indoors in bowls as pets.

During the Middle Ages many pet cats were put to death with their owners on suspicion of witchcraft. It was during this period that dog breeding became popular in Europe. Although many dogs were bred for herding, guarding, and hunting traits, some breeds were tailored to pet owners who desired certain coat characteristics, sizes, and behaviors. Pet ownership was mostly limited to the upper classes of society—royalty, aristocrats, and landowners.

The first American colonists brought a few pets with them to the New World. However life was hard in the colonies, and resources were scarce. Few people had extra food to give to an animal unless it was being fattened up for slaughter or earning its keep by working. Some dogs and cats may have been called pets, but they also performed useful tasks such as guard duty and killing rats. The modern age of pet keeping began in the mid-1800s when a thriving middle class of society emerged. This was the first time that many people had the time and money to keep animals solely for companionship and pleasure.

According to historian Kasey Grier of the University of South Carolina, tropical birds, such as parrots, were highly valued in American society before recorded music became available. They were the first animal companions for which goods were specifically marketed, including bird food, medicines, cages, and other accessories. The Pet Food Institute reports that the first commercially prepared dog food was introduced in England around 1860. The first goldfish were bred in the United States in 1878. Dogs, tropical birds, and ornamental fish were the house pets of choice well into the 20th century. The keeping of horses for personal enjoyment rather than for work also grew. In 1947 kitty litter was introduced to U.S. consumers, making it much easier to keep cats indoors. They too became prized as pets.

Some unusual pets have interesting histories. Guinea pigs (or cavies) are rodents that originated in South America. It is believed that during the 1500s Spanish explorers introduced them to Europe, where they became popular house pets. Queen Elizabeth I (1533–1603) of Britain is said to have kept a guinea pig as a pet.

The first recorded instances of people keeping rats for pets are traced to 19th-century London. Professional rat catchers earned a living by ridding the city of rodents. A rat catcher named Jack Black was among the first to take in and breed rats with unusual colorings and fur for collectors. Another man named Jimmy Shaw ran a rat pit, or a sporting house in which dogs competed to see who could kill the most rats. Legend has it that Shaw kept and bred rats with unique colorings and sold them as pets.

Gerbils are rodents that were originally found in Mongolia during the 1800s by French missionaries. The animals were used in laboratory research beginning in the 1950s and became popular as pets during the 1970s. Hamsters are rodents native to Syria and other Middle East countries. They were brought to the United States in the 1930s as laboratory research animals and eventually became popular as pets.

The ferret craze began in the 1970s. Ferrets are descendents of European polecats and members of the weasel family. There is some disagreement among scientists and politicians about whether ferrets are completely domesticated or not. They have been banned as pets in California, Hawaii, and some municipalities (including New York City). In California ferrets are classified as "detrimental animals" and are believed to pose a threat to native wildlife. In New York City, ferrets are considered a threat to public health and safety.

SHELTERS, POUNDS, AND EUTHANASIA

Despite the popularity of pets, millions of them wind up in public and private shelters each year. The vast majority are dogs or cats. They are turned in by owners who no longer want them or are picked up as strays. Some are lost pets that can be reunited with their owners, but many are homeless animals with no place to go. According to information on the Web site of the Humane Society of the United States (HSUS) in 2003, there are 4,000–6,000 shelters operating in the United States that receive 6–8 million dogs and cats each year. Approximately half of these animals are euthanized (killed). The remainder are adopted or reclaimed by owners.

History

According to the Humane Society of the United States (HSUS), the first public "pounds" were constructed during the 1700s to impound stray livestock. As American society changed from rural to urban, these facilities switched their focus to stray dogs and became dog pounds. Rabies was a serious public health threat well into the 20th century, with thousands of cases reported each year. The vast majority of cases were contracted by people from domestic dogs, so animal control departments operated dog pounds as part of public health and safety programs. Their mission was to protect people rather than to ensure the welfare of the dogs.

Following World War II (1939–45), rabies vaccinations for dogs became mandatory in the United States. This program, combined with effective stray dog control, dramatically reduced the occurrence of rabies in dogs. The New York State Health Department recorded up to

200 rabid dogs in the state each year between 1925 and 1944, but by 1959 that number had dropped to 20–50 each year, and by 1989 dog rabies had been virtually eliminated in the state. Similar results were obtained across the country. Pounds continued to pick up stray dogs (and cats, by this time) but did so more to control aggressive and nuisance animals and "clean the streets" than as rabies protection. Pounds also became centralized facilities for people to get rid of unwanted pets.

Dog pounds came to be called animal shelters. They held stray animals for a few days (if there was room) to see if their owners would reclaimed them. If not, unwanted strays and pets were sold to research laboratories or given to anyone who wanted them. Unclaimed and unplaced animals were killed using whatever means were available. Public animal shelters received little funding from local governments, and humane treatment and euthanasia were not a priority in most jurisdictions.

This began to change as the animal welfare movement gained momentum during the 1960s and 1970s. Shelters came under increasing pressure to focus on welfare issues in addition to public health and nuisance concerns. Some municipal governments began contracting their shelter operations to nonprofit animal welfare organizations, like local humane societies and rescue groups. These organizations held fund-raisers and were able to secure private donations to help shelters operate. However, most shelters continued to euthanize large numbers of animals as the homeless animal population surged out of control.

Euthanasia

The word "euthanasia" comes from a Greek term meaning "good death." During the 1800s, it was first used to describe mercy killing conducted with the approval of the law. Today, euthanasia of animals is conducted on a massive scale. The Web site of the HSUS in 2003 estimated that 3 to 4 million shelter animals are euthanized each year. Although the public assumes these animals are killed by lethal injection, this is not always true.

The AVMA maintains a list of approved euthanasia methods for various types of animals. According to the AVMA, "Euthanasia techniques should result in rapid loss of consciousness followed by cardiac or respiratory arrest and the ultimate loss of brain function. In addition, the technique should minimize distress and anxiety experienced by the animal prior to loss of consciousness." However, the AVMA admits that "the absence of pain and distress cannot always be achieved."

Acceptable euthanasia methods for dogs and cats include intravenous injection of barbiturates (such as sodium pentobarbital or secobarbital) or potassium chloride/anesthetic or gassing the animals with inhalant anesthetics (such as ether), carbon dioxide, or carbon monoxide gas. In addition, gassing with nitrogen or argon is considered acceptable with some reservations on dogs and cats, as are the use of electrocution and penetrating captive bolts (bolts shot at point-blank range from a gun into the animal's skull, which if shot at the proper location destroy enough brain tissue to kill the animal instantly) on dogs only. Each of the methods, along with its advantages and disadvantages, is described in the "2000 Report of the AVMA Panel on Euthanasia" published in the *Journal of the American Veterinary Medical Association* on March 1, 2001.

The report notes that injection of barbiturates intravenously (within a vein) is the preferred method of euthanasia for horses, dogs, cats, and other small animals. Advantages include rapid and smooth action, minimal physical distress to the animal if the procedure is performed correctly, and relatively low cost compared to other options. The main disadvantages are that each animal must be personally restrained for the procedure, and personnel must be properly trained in giving injections. Also, barbiturates are federally controlled substances that can be purchased only using a Drug Enforcement Administration registration and order form. Their use is controlled by state law, and there are specific record-keeping requirements that must be met.

As of 2003, the HSUS recommended injection of sodium pentobarbital as the preferred euthanasia method for companion animals. Intravenous injection is the recommended route of delivery, but intraperitoneal (within the peritoneal cavity in the abdomen) injection is considered acceptable for cats, kittens, and puppies in which intravenous injections cannot be administered easily. Intracardiac injection (within the heart) is considered acceptable only if the animal is already unconscious. Intrahepatic injection (within the liver) is not considered acceptable, because of lack of scientific study on the procedure. The HSUS recommends that euthanasia of each animal be carried out by two people—one to hold the animal and one to administer the injection. Both the AVMA and the HSUS stress that shelter personnel performing euthanasia must be well trained.

Lethal injection is a hands-on procedure in which animals and personnel come into close physical contact. When shelters first began practicing humane euthanasia, it was thought that a hands-off approach would be easier for the workers performing euthanasia. Gas chambers were common because the euthanizer could perform the procedure from outside the chamber by opening a valve or flipping a switch.

Many shelters still use gassing to euthanize unwanted animals. Although the use of poisonous gases is considered acceptable by the AVMA, the organization notes that "any gas that is inhaled must reach a certain concentration in the alveoli before it can be effective; therefore, euthanasia with any of these agents takes some time." Animal welfarists roundly condemn gassing as a means of euthanasia. In 1998 the state of California passed a law prohibiting the use of carbon monoxide chambers for euthanizing shelter animals.

In August 2003 the news organization CNN reported a story about a dog surviving a gas chamber at the animal shelter run by the city of St. Louis, Missouri ("Miracle Dog Survives Gas Chamber," August 7, 2003, http://www.cnn.com/2003/US/Midwest/08/07/offbeat.dog .survivor.ap/index.html [accessed August 12, 2003]). An animal control officer says that when she opened the door after the gassing, the dog was standing there, wagging his tail. She asked a local rescue group (Stray Rescue of St. Louis) to take the dog, saying she did not have the heart to gas him again. The head of the rescue group called the dog's survival "a miracle or divine intervention." The dog was given the name Quentin (after the infamous San Quentin prison in California) and put up for adoption.

Animal shelter workers have an incredibly stressful and emotionally demanding job. Many get into the line of work because they care about animals. Most humane organizations believe that the solution to the euthanization problem lies in aggressive sterilization campaigns, better education of pet owners, and successful adoption programs.

No-Kill Shelters

Despite the disturbing nature of the issue, some animal welfare groups note that euthanasia rates have been dropping. The number of euthanized cats and dogs has dropped considerably in this country, from about 13.5 million deaths per year in 1973 to 3–5 million deaths in 2002, while over the same period the total number of cats and dogs has nearly doubled. (See Table 9.1.)

Some animal welfarists and members of the public criticize shelters for using euthanasia at all. They believe that every animal that enters a shelter has a right to life. Critics say that this viewpoint is unrealistic. They point out that some animals are too aggressive, injured, or sick to be adopted. There is no practical alternative but to euthanize them. Also, some pet owners rely on shelters rather than private veterinarians to euthanize their sick and elderly pets.

During the 1990s the concept of "no-kill" shelters became very popular. The name implies that no animals are ever euthanized in these shelters—an idea that appeals to many people. In reality, most no-kill shelters still euthanize animals that are unadoptable. Some traditional shelters (or open-admission shelters, as they are called) do not like the use of the term no-kill. They feel it can be very misleading and accuse some organizations of using the phrase just to gain financial support and political favor. Welfare organizations argue among themselves about the exact definition of no-kill and which animals are adoptable.

TABLE 9.1

Shelter euthanasia of owned animals, 1973, 1982, 1992, and 2000

Year	Total owned dogs and cats	Euthanized	Approximate % of owned animals euthanized
1973	65 million	13.5 million	21.0
1982	92 million	8–10 million	10.0
1992	110 million	5–6 million	5.5
2000	120 million	4–6 million	4.5

SOURCE: Deborah J. Salem and Andrew N. Rowan, "Table 1: Shelter Euthanasia of Owned Animals," in The State of the Animals 2001, The Humane Society of the United States, Washington, DC, 2001

The truth is that all shelters (public and private) operate with limited space, personnel, and financial budgets. They must make life-and-death decisions about the animals that enter. These decisions are based on moral, political, social, and financial considerations. Professor Taimie Bryant teaches courses about animal law and nonprofit organizations at the UCLA law school. In a 1998 article, she argued that traditional shelters are reluctant to give up the use of euthanasia, seeing it as a necessary evil and an issue that pits themselves, performers of a public service, against a public that refuses to spay and neuter its pets ("California Legislation for Companion Animals: Hayden Law" [Online] http://www.maddiesfund.org/nokill/nokill _legis_hayden.html [accessed August 1, 2003]). Shelters, on the other hand, feel euthanasia is the most compassionate option, though not at all a desirable one. In the January-February 1996 issue of its Animal Sheltering magazine, for example, the HSUS noted, "Euthanasia of shelter animals to make room for others is a tragic necessity that prevents animal suffering."

While the HSUS wishes euthanasia were not necessary, it also recognizes some of the practical drawbacks of the no-kill idea. In the January-February 2002 issue of Animal Sheltering was a series of articles titled "What Would It Take?" by Nancy Lawson and Carrie Allen. The articles describe how the no-kill idea became an advertising and fund-raising slogan for some animal organizations that use it to set themselves apart from traditional shelters.

Popularization of the no-kill idea is generally credited to Richard Avanzino, president of the San Francisco Society for the Prevention of Cruelty to Animals (SPCA) from 1976 to 1999. During this time period, the city achieved the lowest euthanasia rate of any urban city in the nation. The San Francisco SPCA started adoption, spay/neuter, and animal management programs that became models for every other welfare organization. In 1992 Avanzino spoke at an HSUS workshop in Las Vegas on the no-kill movement. He advocated no-kill as a concept and a mission for welfarists, not as a weapon to use against traditional shelters in fund-raising campaigns.

The articles also recount the difficulties that some organizations encountered when they tried to become no-kill shelters. In 1995 the Humane Society of Gallatin Valley in Bozeman, Montana, decided to institute a no-euthanasia policy. However, as the only shelter in the city it also decided to continue accepting any animal that was relinquished. The shelter soon became overwhelmed, and animal welfare suffered. The director reports that "animals who came in adoptable quickly became unadoptable in a crowded environment that wore on their temperaments and made them sick."

The same problem led some organizations to limit their shelter admissions. Critics say that such shelters do not really serve their communities by accepting only the "cute and cuddly" and turning away difficult-to-adopt animals. This practice is seen as self-serving. It allows these shelters to practice a true no-kill policy but burdens neighboring shelters with the animals they turn away. However, the opposite policy can be just as troublesome. In the articles, various people describe well-meaning shelter groups that refused to euthanize any animals, even typically unadoptable animals like aggressive dogs. These animals took up cage space and resources that could have been devoted to animals with a reasonable chance of being adopted. Deciding which course of action is a better one is difficult.

The no-kill label is a powerful public relations tool. Many people prefer to donate money to an organization or shelter that advertises itself as no-kill. However, no-kill does not necessarily mean no euthanasia. It also does not guarantee that the animals are being properly cared for and kept in clean, uncrowded, disease-free conditions. Critics say that some people who want to warehouse or hoard animals adopt the label in order to raise funds.

Some organizations and shelters that follow the no-kill philosophy downplay use of the label to describe themselves. For example, the Best Friends Animal Sanctuary was founded in 1984 and is the largest animal sanctuary in the country. Funded by private donations and located on 23,000 acres near Kenab, Utah, the sanctuary housed roughly 1,800 animals of all kinds as of 2003. Approximately 80 percent are dogs and cats. The remainder includes horses, burros, birds, rabbits, goats, livestock, and other animals. Best Friends takes in animals from all over the country. Some come from shelters where they were considered unadoptable and were going to be euthanized. They may be old, crippled, or sick with chronic illnesses, or may have been traumatized by abuse or neglect. In exchange for taking these animals, the sanctuary asks many of the shelters to take back adoptable animals from Best Friends.

According to information available on the Best Friends Web site in 2003, approximately 75 percent of the animals that come into the sanctuary are readily adoptable or become so following rehabilitation. Others are kept permanently at the sanctuary. Best Friends founder Michael Mountain is a solid supporter of the no-kill policy. The sanctuary defines no-kill as follows: "No-kill means that animals are not destroyed except in cases of terminal and painful illness, when compassion demands euthanasia because there is no reasonable alternative." As of 2003, Best Friends did not display a no-kill label on its Web site. Instead, it used the slogan "No More Homeless Pets."

Another major organization that supports the no-kill idea is called Maddie's Fund. It was founded by Dave and Cheryl Duffield and named after their beloved miniature schnauzer Maddie, who died of cancer in 1997. According to information available on its Web site in 2003, Maddie's Fund is a $240 million foundation with the goal of making the United States a "no-kill nation where all healthy (adoptable) and treatable (underage, sick, injured and poorly behaved) shelter dogs and cats find loving new homes." On its Web site, the organization describes its principles and funding opportunities. Maddie's Fund advocates a community approach in which animal control agencies, shelters, humane organizations, and private-practice veterinarians work together to achieve no-kill status. The fund provides grants to community coalitions, veterinary medical associations, and colleges of veterinary medicine for programs that advance the no-kill goal.

Several programs had been completed by Maddie's Fund as of July 2003:

• A $12 million feral cat–altering program operated by the California Veterinary Medical Association from July 1999 to May 2002 performed free spay/neuters on approximately 168,000 feral cats.

• A $2.2 million spay/neuter program operated by the California Veterinary Medical Association from July 2001 to May 2002 performed low-cost surgeries on 35,000 dogs and cats belonging to low-income caregivers in California.

• A $343,500 spay/neuter program operated by the Utah Veterinary Medical Association assisted 5,000 dogs and cats of low-income Utah residents and feral cats in the state.

A number of other programs funded by Maddie's Fund are ongoing around the country.

Several major cities are already operating or working toward no-kill status. In 1994 the San Francisco SPCA formed an adoption pact with city animal control officials to become the first U.S. city with a no-kill policy. Shelters in Miami, Florida; Richmond, Virginia; and Austin, Texas, have followed suit. In December 2002 officials in New York City announced plans to convert all of the city's shelters to no-kill by the year 2008. The effort is being spearheaded by the Mayor's Alliance. Experts believe that the program has an excellent chance of success because the Mayor's Alliance is a neutral party rather than a particular animal group with its own agenda. Animal welfare organizations in the city do not have a history of working well together on common goals. The program will increase public awareness about adoptions and spay/neuter programs at the shelters. A new agreement was reached on how the city's animal control operations will coordinate with rescue groups and shelters to reach the no-kill goal.

Spaying and Neutering

Overpopulation of dogs and cats is a tremendous problem. It is aggravated by the fact that these animals reproduce at very high rates. A fertile cat can have three litters of four to six kittens each every year. Over a seven-year period, this cat and her offspring can produce 420,000 kittens. A fertile dog can have two litters each year, each including 6–10 puppies. Over a six-year period, this results in 67,000 more puppies. According to data available in 2003 on the Web site of SpayUSA, a nonprofit organization founded in 1992 to reduce pet overpopulation, approximately 70,000 puppies and kittens are born every day in America. This means that 25 million more dogs and cats require homes each year.

Experts generally agree that massive and sustained birth-control methods must be implemented on dog and cat populations to bring the problem under control. Surgical sterilization of female animals is called spaying, and involves removal of the ovaries, fallopian tubes, and uterus. Male animals are neutered or castrated by having their testicles removed. Pet owners commonly refer to these sterilization procedures as "fixing" or "altering" an animal. Increasingly, animal groups use the term *neuter* to refer to sterilization of either males or females.

Veterinarians have been promoting spaying and neutering of pets for several decades. According to the AVMA, sterilization has many medical, behavioral, and social benefits, including:

- Female pets do not go into heat (have fertile cycles) during which scents are emitted that attract male animals. Dogs in heat also discharge blood droplets. Sterilization eliminates bloodstains on floors and carpets and the problems associated with male animals that gather and often fight over females in heat.

- Sterilization usually stops male cats (toms) from marking their territory by spraying strong-smelling urine.

- Sterilization makes pets more attentive to their owners and more likely to stay at home than wander.

- Sterilized females cannot develop uterine infections and are less likely to develop mammary cancer.

- Sterilized males usually become less aggressive.

- Sterilization causes most pets to be more affectionate and gentle with their human companions.

- Sterilization helps reduce the number of stray and unwanted animals in the community. This is advantageous for public health and safety reasons and reduces the enormous cost to taxpayers and private agencies of capturing, impounding, and destroying millions of unwanted animals each year.

Some pet owners are resistant to spaying and neutering their pets. Their reasons can include one or more of the following:

- Surgery costs too much or is too painful for the pet.

- Having a litter can be good for the pet and educational for the children.

- Fixed animals get fat and lazy.

- Backyard breeding is a fun hobby that brings in extra money.

- Male animals do not need to be fixed because they do not have litters.

- Neutering male dogs robs them of their masculinity and makes them less protective as guard dogs.

- Sterilization is unnatural.

Many states and municipalities actively encourage spaying and neutering of pets as a means to reduce overpopulation. Those with licensing programs usually charge pet owners a lower registration fee if their pets are sterilized. In 2003 the fees for unfixed pets were typically $10–$25 higher than for fixed pets. A number of states also sell special license plates that benefit spay/neuter programs.

Increasingly, animal shelters spay and neuter dogs and cats prior to adoption or require new owners to do so within a certain time period. In 1998 a law was passed in California that requires pre-adoption sterilization of dogs and cats. The San Francisco SPCA was one of the first humane groups in the United States to offer low-cost and early spay/neuter surgery.

Low-cost clinics are often run by humane organizations. They operate under nonprofit status, which allows them to save on overhead and tax costs. They offer discounted rates either to the general public or to those people who have adopted an animal from their shelter. The rates can be as much as 50 percent less than those charged by veterinarians in private practice. Such clinics are not without controversy. Some veterinarians complain that the clinics have an unfair advantage because of their nonprofit status. A few states have passed laws that prohibit veterinarians associated with nonprofit groups from operating low-cost spay/neuter clinics. Advocates of the clinics insist that they provide a much-needed service and help to reduce animal overpopulation.

In the past, veterinarians recommended sterilization for dogs and cats around six months of age. During the mid-1990s, many humane organizations began advocating early spay/neuter (ESN) programs. Most clinics practicing ESN will perform the surgery on kittens and puppies at least eight weeks old. Shelters flooded with kittens and puppies have heartily embraced the practice because it allows them to sterilize young animals before they are adopted. Some veterinarians are worried about the long-term effects of ESN surgery on the animals' young bones and express concern that it could cause abnormalities in skeletal growth. However, as of 2003, no definitive scientific studies had proven this. Veterinarians report that puppies and kittens that undergo ESN recover from the surgery much quicker than their older counterparts.

In April 2003 the FDA approved use of the drug Neutersol (zinc gluconate neutralized by arginine) for chemical sterilization of 3- to 10-month-old puppies. The drug is injected into the testicles and works by stopping the production of sperm. It does not eliminate the hormone testosterone, as traditional neutering does. This may be a drawback, as testosterone is considered a major factor in behavior problems seen in unaltered dogs. According to the manufacturer, Neutersol is 99.6 percent effective, and the injection does not require that the puppy be put under general anesthesia. The FDA recommends that puppies be sedated prior to the injection to eliminate movement and to help with any pain. Neutersol is expected to be used mostly at animal shelters that wish to sterilize dogs prior to adoption but do not have ready access to a surgical clinic.

Owner Turn-ins

Many of the animals turned into shelters are pets that people have tired of or either do not want to or cannot take care of anymore. The National Council on Pet Population Study and Policy (NCPPSP) was formed in 1993. It is a national group of humane organizations, breeder groups, and veterinary associations with the goal of lowering the number of surplus pets in the country.

NCPPSP researchers performed a survey in 1997 at 12 shelters around the country to find out why dog and cat owners were turning in their pets. The top 10 reasons that owners gave are shown in Table 9.2. Many owners gave multiple reasons for giving up their pets. In general, the study found that the owners had unrealistic expectations for their pets and lacked the knowledge or will to work out problems that arose.

Moving was the number one reason given by owners relinquishing their dogs to the shelters. (See Table 9.2.) However, the researchers found upon interviewing these owners that there were deeper issues involved, mainly behavior problems. In other words, owners that were moving decided to give up their dogs rather than take them along, because the dogs were unruly. The survey

TABLE 9.2

The top ten reasons for pet relinquishment

Dogs	Cats
1. Moving	1. Too many in house
2. Landlord issues	2. Allergies
3. Cost of pet maintenance	3. Moving
4. No time for pet	4. Cost of pet maintenance
5. Inadequate facilities	5. Landlord issues
6. Too many pets in home	6. No homes for littermates
7. Pet illness(es)	7. House soiling
8. Personal problems	8. Personal problems
9. Biting	9. Pet illness(es)
10. No homes for littermates	10. Inadequate facilities

Note: The listings here represent responses given as reasons for relinquishment. Up to five reasons could be given for each animal as owners often cite multiple issues.

Animals relinquished for euthanasia due to illness or age, and animals turned in as strays were excluded from this list as these reasons do not necessarily represent breaking of the human-animal bond. Eight of the top ten reasons for both species are shared.

SOURCE: "The Top Ten Reasons We Give Up Our Pets," in *Exploring the Surplus Cat and Dog Problem,* National Council on Pet Population Study and Policy, New London, MN, 1997

indicated that if the dogs were better behaved, they might have been kept and taken along to the new residence. Similar findings have been reported by humane organizations investigating dog turn-ins at other shelters.

Many organizations believe that shelters need to place greater emphasis on behavior problems. Some shelters now offer training classes to new dog owners or have volunteers work with shelter dogs on basic obedience lessons. It is hoped that this will reduce the number of shelter-adopted dogs that are later relinquished. Breeders and veterinarians are being urged to encourage new dog owners to enroll in obedience classes or seek help from professional trainers. All people involved in reducing pet overpopulation agree that pet owners need to be better educated about the responsibilities and issues involved in raising pets.

Pound Seizure

Following World War II, the use of animals in laboratory testing and experimentation increased greatly. Researchers turned to pounds and shelters for a quick and cheap supply of unwanted animals. Many states passed laws that required publicly operated shelters to turn over animals to institutions that requested them, a practice called pound seizure. Animal welfarists were disturbed by this development and blamed the National Society for Medical Research (now the National Association for Biomedical Research) for pushing pound seizure legislation. Many welfare organizations contracted with their local municipalities to privatize shelter operations so that their shelter would not be subject to the laws.

In 1990 the federal Animal Welfare Act (AWA) was amended to set a minimum holding period of five days for shelter animals before release to research institutions.

This is designed to provide a window of opportunity for owners to find their missing pets or for the animals to be adopted by new owners. The AWA also includes record-keeping requirements for dealers who sell shelter animals to research institutions.

Animal rights activists and welfarists widely condemn pound seizure. According to the Web site of the American Anti-Vivisection Society (AAVS) in 2003, three states—Utah, Oklahoma, and Minnesota—still required publicly funded shelters to provide dogs and/or cats for research purposes. Most states legally allow pound seizure or do not address the issue. In some states the decision is left up to local government authorities. A few states require owners giving up animals to indicate whether or not they give permission for release to research institutions. On its Web site, the AAVS includes a state-by-state listing of laws regarding pound seizure.

According to information on the Web site of the organization In Defense of Animals (IDA) in 2003, 13 states had outlawed pound seizure: Connecticut, Delaware, Hawaii, Maine, Maryland, Massachusetts, New Hampshire, New Jersey, New York, Pennsylvania, Rhode Island, Vermont, and West Virginia. IDA claims that some cash-strapped shelters engage in pound seizure illegally to raise funds. There are also accusations that shelters hide some animals from public view during the required five-day holding period and then sell them to dealers or research facilities. IDA suggests that pound seizure puts all pets in a community at greater risk of being stolen.

The Michigan Society for Medical Research (MSMR) says that Massachusetts alone prohibits the use of pound-seizure animals in medical research, and that the other 12 states listed above specifically prohibit the use of pound-seizure animals obtained from in-state shelters. In other words, these 12 states do permit the use of pound-seizure animals obtained from out-of-state shelters only. This means that 49 states allow pound seizure in some form.

Those who support pound seizure argue that animals that are going to be euthanized by shelters anyway should be used in research. They feel the benefits to humankind outweigh animal welfare concerns. Welfarists fear that pets turned over to laboratories will suffer from poor care and die slow, painful deaths as the subjects of medical experiments. They believe that euthanasia at the shelter is preferable to this alternative.

The Physician's Committee for Responsible Medicine (PCRM) is a nonprofit organization concerned with medical issues. The group advocates alternatives to animal experimentation for educational and research purposes. According to PCRM, research institutions prefer test animals that are relatively calm, well socialized, and easy to handle. However, these types of animals are also the most likely to be adopted from shelters. Therefore, PCRM

disputes the claim that pound seizure is justified because the animals involved would be euthanized anyway.

PUPPY MILLS AND PUREBREDS

Many animal welfare groups blame dog overpopulation in part on puppy mills. They define puppy mills as breeder facilities that supply puppies to the wholesale market. Wholesale breeders are considered Class A animal dealers by the U.S. Department of Agriculture (USDA). These breeders usually sell their puppies to brokers, which are considered Class B animal dealers by the USDA. Many brokers are also breeders. The brokers sell the puppies to pet stores, who in turn sell them to the public.

In 1990 the HSUS launched a boycott of pet stores selling puppies from the seven states responsible for breeding the most puppies in the United States: Arkansas, Iowa, Kansas, Missouri, Nebraska, Oklahoma, and Pennsylvania. The organization claimed that many puppy breeding facilities in these states did not provide adequate veterinary care, food, shelter, and socialization for their puppies. According to the HSUS, thousands of puppy mills still exist in the United States as of 2003.

Animal welfare groups generally believe that Missouri has more puppy breeding facilities than any other state. A 2001 article in the *Pinnacle Newspaper* says that Missouri breeders exported 12,000 puppies in that year (Kate Woods, "Dying for Love" [Online] http://www.pinnaclenews.com/oldsite/archvs01_p/pupmill419cont/p61401.html [accessed August 12, 2003]). IDA says that Missouri's 1,100 puppy breeding facilities did $2 billion in business in 2001.

In response to negative publicity about puppy mills, several states have passed so-called "lemon laws" to protect consumers buying puppies at pet stores. Such laws typically enable consumers to be reimbursed by pet stores that sell them puppies that turn out to be in poor health. The HSUS says that 17 states had puppy lemon laws or regulations as of August 2001 and hopes that such laws motivate pet stores to pressure breeders to improve the conditions in which puppies are raised.

Puppy mills exist because of the demand for purebred dogs, or those which have been bred from members of a recognized breed over many generations. This ensures that certain appearance and behavior traits are maintained within a breed. Breeding of this type has been practiced for centuries. During the Middle Ages, it was popularized by European monks who earned money by breeding dogs with particular traits for aristocrats and members of royalty. It resulted in breeds that were notable for a specific task, such as hunting wildfowl, or had desirable features in their size, shape, fur, ears, and so forth.

Maintaining desirable qualities in a bloodline requires careful choice of mating partners. For example, an excellent hunting dog mated with a poor hunting dog will likely produce offspring that are not good hunters, and so the desirable qualities would be lost. Mating together two excellent hunting dogs will greatly increase the likelihood that the offspring are also great hunters. This makes them much more valuable. Purebred dogs can sell for hundreds of dollars. Purebred enthusiasts are passionate about protecting certain qualities within a breed, and reputable breeders work to ensure that breed characteristics are maintained and that purebred puppies are placed in good homes.

The American Kennel Club (AKC) was formed in 1884. It is the largest not-for-profit organization in the United States that registers purebred dogs. The second-largest registry is maintained by the United Kennel Club (UKC), which was founded in 1898. These are the two most respected purebred registries in the country. They supply registration papers for purebred dogs, based on information supplied by breeders who are members of their respective clubs. These papers provide a written record of a particular dog's ancestry.

Neither the AKC or the UKC guarantees the quality of a purebred dog. They simply track ancestry records based on the information they are given by breeders. It is an honor system. Unscrupulous breeders can provide false information and register dogs that are not really purebreds, but mixes (or mutts). Such breeders can also breed dogs with known genetic disorders. Dog enthusiasts encourage consumers to buy only from reputable local breeders and to ask to see the sire (father) and dam (mother) of the puppy they are interested in purchasing. A personal visit ensures the consumer that the breeder is operating a clean and well-kept business.

All major animal welfare organizations are opposed to commercial puppy breeding because of the severe pet overpopulation problem. They do not believe that puppies should be commercially bred because millions of unwanted puppies and dogs are euthanized at shelters. The HSUS estimated on its Web site in 2003 that approximately 25 percent of the dogs that wind up in shelters are purebred. Purebred dogs can generally be identified by their coloring, fur, and characteristic appearance.

Kim Townsend operates a Web site (http://www. nopuppymills.com) that describes her reasons for opposing puppy mills. She also offers information to people who are thinking about purchasing or have purchased a puppy from a pet store. Consumers who purchase pet store puppies can determine where the puppies came from by researching the supplier (breeder) and distributor (broker) numbers that should appear on the paperwork supplied by the store. These 7-digit alphanumeric codes are USDA registration numbers (for example, 43-A-0123 or 43-B-4444).

Consumers are urged to contact the USDA and ask for copies of federal inspection reports conducted on the breeder and broker of any puppy they purchase. Backyard breeders and hobby breeders do not have to register with the USDA. Townsend claims to maintain a database of information on thousands of private breeders and brokers that people can research.

The AKC does not support random large-scale breeding of dogs for commercial purposes. The organization conducts inspections of breeders who use the AKC registry and breeders, retail pet shops, and brokers who conduct 25 or more registration transactions per year or breed seven or more litters of puppies per year. The AKC has also begun random DNA testing to ensure that breeders are supplying accurate information about the purebred dogs they are registering.

FERAL CATS

Feral cats are cats that have reverted to a semi-wild state because of lack of human contact and socialization. They avoid humans and often live in colonies. They may be born into this condition or adjust to it after being stray, lost, or abandoned for a long time. Feral cats are often confused with strays, but there is a difference. Stray cats generally appear scruffy and unclean because they do not groom themselves. They are used to human care and suffer from stress and hunger without it. Feral cats are adjusted to a wild manner of living. If a natural food source is prevalent, they survive fairly well in the wild.

The problem is that they also reproduce well. Many animal welfare groups advocate a trap-neuter-return (TNR) management plan for feral colonies. In these programs, feral cats are humanely trapped, vaccinated, sterilized, and returned to their colonies. In most cases, volunteers feed the colonies and conduct TNR activities. Kittens and any particularly tame adult cats go into adoption programs. In general, it is very difficult to turn a truly feral cat into a pet. Where it is possible, it requires a great deal of time and effort. Most welfarists believe that their time is better spent sterilizing the cats than trying to tame them.

Alley Cat Allies was founded in 1990 in Washington, D.C., to provide information on feral and stray cats. Many animal control departments try to control feral cat colonies by capturing and euthanizing the cats. According to Alley Cat Allies, the TNR approach is much more effective and less costly.

PET ABUSE AND NEGLECT

According to the HSUS, thousands of animal abuse and neglect cases are reported to authorities each year. Tracking these cases is difficult because there is no national database or tracking system. The HSUS compiles statistics on high-profile abuse cases based on media reports. Their most recent report is titled *The Humane Society of the United States (HSUS) First Strike Campaign 2002*

TABLE 9.3

Breakdown of animal abuse victims, 2002

Animal Type	Percentage of cruelty cases
Companion animals	76%
Farm animals	15%
Wildlife	5%
Exotic animals	2%
Multiple types	2%

SOURCE: "The following is a percentage breakdown of animal abuse victims for 2002," in *The Humane Society of the United States (HSUS) First Strike Campaign 2002 Report of Animal Cruelty Cases,* The Humane Society of the United States, Washington, DC, 2002

TABLE 9.4

Common offenses perpetrated on animals, 2002

Common Offenses	Percent of violent cases	Percent of cases involving males	Percent of cases involving females
Shooting	20%	97%	3%
Beating	16%	95%	5%
Torturing	11%	90%	10%
Mutilation	11%	92%	8%
Throwing	8%	94%	6%
Burning	6%	100%	0
Animal fighting	8%	89%	11%
Kicking	3%	100%	0
Suffocating	2%	78%	22%
Poisoning	3%	94%	6%
Stabbing	5%	95%	5%
Hanging	3%	83%	17%
Dragging	2%	100%	0
Animal sexual abuse	1%	89%	11%
Drowning	2%	85%	15%

SOURCE: "The following table is a breakdown of common offenses perpetrated on animals," in *The Humane Society of the United States (HSUS) First Strike Campaign 2002 Report of Animal Cruelty Cases,* The Humane Society of the United States, Washington, DC, 2002

Report of Animal Cruelty Cases. The report covers calendar year 2002 and presents data related to 1,400 cases. Just over half (59 percent) involved intentional cruelty, while 41 percent involved extreme animal neglect.

The HSUS defines abuse (or cruelty) as purposefully depriving an animal of food, water, shelter, socialization, or veterinary care or maliciously torturing, maiming, mutilating, or killing an animal. These are considered intentional acts that give the abuser pleasure. Neglect is not considered to be intentional, but results in an animal not receiving proper shelter, food, water, attention, grooming, or veterinary care.

Companion animals were the victims in 76 percent of the cruelty cases examined by the HSUS. (See Table 9.3.) More than half of the animals involved in these cases either died from the abuse or had to be euthanized.

As shown in Table 9.4, shooting, beating, torturing, and mutilation were the most common violent offenses committed against animals. Overall, males were responsible for 92 percent of the cruelty cases. Adults (aged 20 and up) accounted for three-fourths of the cruelty cases, while teenagers accounted for 22 percent. Cases involving dogs outnumbered those involving cats by a margin of three to one. The HSUS believes that dog cases are more likely to be reported to authorities.

The HSUS statistics show that approximately 12 percent of the intentional animal cruelty cases also involved some form of concurrent family violence—for example, child abuse. Authorities have long known about the link between animal abuse and family violence. The American Humane Association (AHA) was founded in 1877 as a collection of organizations working against child and animal abuse. It now operates the National Resource Center on the Link Between Violence to People & Animals. The AHA works to strengthen animal abuse laws and to advocate early intervention in cases where children abuse animals to prevent the violence from escalating. According to the AHA, a large majority of families being treated for child abuse incidents also report instances of animal abuse.

Another form of animal abuse is called pet hoarding. This occurs when people collect large numbers of pets and do not provide proper care for them. The animals are often kept inside the home and allowed to urinate and defecate there. Hoarders are oblivious to the negative effects of their actions on their pets and even on themselves. They see themselves as animal rescuers. Most will not admit that the severe overcrowding is unsanitary and unhealthy for the animals. The AMVA estimated in 2002 that there are 700 cases of pet hoarding annually in the United States.

Dr. Gary Patronek is the founder of the Hoarding of Animals Research Consortium. The group studies the hoarding problem and works to increase awareness among mental-health and social-service workers. In 1999 Patronek examined 54 cases of animal hoarding from around the country. Each hoarder kept an average of 39 animals, mostly cats, dogs, farm animals, and birds. Patronek found that most hoarders were unmarried females living alone. Nearly half were at least 60 years old. In a majority of the cases, animal feces and urine were in the person's living quarters. The hoarders' beds had been soiled by feces and urine in more than 25 percent of the cases. Although sick or dead animals were involved in the vast majority of the cases, most of the hoarders refused to acknowledge that there was a problem with the animals. Patronek believes that hoarding is a pathological problem. Some psychiatric experts suspect that it is a psychological disorder similar to obsessive-compulsive behavior.

In January 2003 authorities discovered the worst case of animal hoarding in U.S. history. An elderly couple living in rural Malheur County, Oregon, was found to have more than 550 dogs in and around their home. The dogs were scattered around the property, with some living inside the home, some in pens, and some in abandoned cars. Many of the dogs were sick and malnourished. More than 100 had to be euthanized. The remainder were distributed among various shelters and rescue groups in the area. The couple was charged with criminal neglect, animal neglect, and criminal mischief. Authorities discovered that they had been charged with similar offenses in 1996 related to the keeping of 200 dogs at their prior residence.

In 2001 Illinois became the first state to pass legislation dealing specifically with animal hoarding as a crime separate from animal cruelty or neglect. The Illinois law is considered by some animal activists to be model legislation for other states because it recognizes that hoarding may be a mental-health problem and recommends psychiatric treatment for offenders.

EXOTIC PETS

The word "exotic" means foreign or not native. However, when the word is used to describe pets, it refers to wild animals that are not normally considered pets. These include lions, tigers, wolves, bears, primates, certain rodents and reptiles, and many other species. Exotic pets appeal to people because they are different. The animals may not provide devotion, companionship, or affection, many being essentially wild, but they are novel, "cool," and fascinating.

Many people feel they have the right to keep any animal as long as they provide proper care for it. Critics say that exotic animals belong in their natural habitats and not in cages, where they can suffer from abuse, neglect, and boredom. Welfarists believe that even well-treated exotic pets should not be kept in captivity because it violates their wild nature.

One of the most popular exotic pets in 2003 was the sugar glider. Sugar gliders are small members of the possum family that live in the treetops in tropical regions like Australia and Tasmania. They have loose skin flaps between their wrists and ankles that allow them to leap and glide through the air for up to 300 feet. Sugar gliders are cute, furry little creatures that are heavily marketed in the United States as pocket pets. People purchase sugar gliders from pet stores and breeders and keep them in cages that are typically about three feet high and two to three feet wide and deep. Owners hang tiny baskets and perches from the tops of the cages so they can watch the animals jump between them. The vast majority of the animals are raised by breeders, not imported from the wild.

Some people think it is wrong to keep wild animals, even those born in captivity, in captivity. Exotic breeders argue that an animal born and raised in a cage does not miss the wild because the animal has never experienced it. Crit-ics do not agree with this argument. They believe that captive-born wild animals retain the natural urges and instincts of their species. Under this reasoning, a sugar glider that was born and raised in a cage would be frustrated because it would still have the urge to glide long distances above the treetops, even though it had never done so.

Exotic pets are offered for sale in pet stores, on the Internet, at auctions, and in trade publications, such as *Animal Finder's Guide*. The National Alternative Pet Association (NAPA) operates a Web site that in 2003 listed more than 250 breeders, dealers, and shops that specialize in exotic pets. The site also provides information and Internet links for a variety of clubs and organizations for exotic pet owners. NAPA complains that people with exotic pets suffer from discrimination and have difficulties finding food, supplies, veterinarians, shelters, and rescue groups for their animals. Zoos are often unwilling to provide needed information and will not take unwanted exotic pets.

Exotic pets are banned in some jurisdictions. On its Web site in 2003, NAPA complained that "even though many exotic pet species have been bred in captivity for a long time now, the laws still treat them like second class pets in some areas." The organization believes that a few bad incidents involving exotic pets have been blown out of proportion, and that exotic-pet owners are unfairly blamed for declining populations of endangered species. On the contrary, NAPA insists that captive breeding is the only chance for some species. NAPA claims that many public shelters and wildlife rescue groups give preference to zoos and will euthanize exotic animals instead of allowing private individuals to take them.

Most or all major animal rights and welfare groups oppose the keeping of exotic pets, expressing concern about degradation of natural populations and the care that captive animals receive. Wildlife collectors are blamed for harming sensitive habitats and killing nontarget animals. Animal rights activists and welfarists tend to be opposed to the removal of wild animals from their natural habitats for any purpose. Besides the obvious dangers to the animals, removal can have devastating consequences on the natural habitats of the animals left behind.

For example, People for the Ethical Treatment of Animals (PETA) reports that trappers in Argentina cut down thousands of tropical trees to capture baby macaws for collectors. This has destroyed vital habitat for the remaining animals. Tropical fish in the Philippines are sometimes caught by spraying low doses of cyanide into the water. The chemical temporarily stuns the fish, but it is very poisonous to the fragile coral reefs in which they live. Baby orangutans are often caught by shooting their mothers because the babies cling to their dead mothers' bodies instead of running away. Animal groups publicize these concerns to note that exotic animals are not only an animal welfare issue but also an environmental and conservation issue.

The exotic pet trade is a multibillion-dollar industry. It has both legal and illegal elements. According to PETA's Web site in 2003, birds are smuggled into the United States more than any other exotic animals. The birds are force-fed before the trip and have their beaks taped shut. Their wings are also clipped. PETA says that up to 80 percent of tropical birds in each shipment die during transit. Welfare groups claim that on average, more than half of all wild animals captured for the pet trade die before they reach their final destination.

Exotic animals that do survive long enough to be pets can suffer from poor nutrition and care at the hands of inexperienced and uninformed owners. The animals may be subjected to painful procedures like wing clipping, defanging, and declawing. Welfarists believe that only accredited zoos and sanctuaries should care for wild animals kept in captivity. This ensures the proper care for the animals and protects the public safety.

Pat Hocter is the publisher of the *Animal Finder's Guide*. He says he had raised hundreds of exotic cats (lions, tigers, ligers, cougars, leopards, jaguars, bobcats, and servals) as well as many breeds of monkeys and baboons, fancy livestock, wolves, coyotes, reptiles, and fish. In a quote on his Web site in 2003, he noted that "the last hope before extinction for many animal species is captive breeding."

In 2002 a group of animal welfare organizations joined with the Oakland Zoo to form the Captive Wild Animal Protection Coalition (CWAPC). The CWAPC plans to compile a database of information on wild animals kept as pets in the United States and work to outlaw the practice. An undated fact sheet available on the CWAPC Web site in 2003 suggests that there are approximately 173 million tropical birds, 8.8 million reptiles, 10,000–20,000 big cats, 5,000–7,000 tigers, and 3,000 primates being kept as pets in the United States. The CWAPC also estimates that 90 percent of all exotic pets die within the first two years of captivity, and considers exotic pet ownership to be both inhumane to the animals and dangerous to people. The CWAPC hopes to significantly reduce the availability and population of dangerous exotic pets by the end of 2006 through its public education programs.

Reptiles and Amphibians, or Herps

The branch of zoology that deals with reptiles and amphibians is called herpetology; therefore, many people refer to these animals as "herps." Popular herp pets include snakes, turtles, frogs, and lizards. Demand for herps increased greatly in the United States during the 1990s due in part to the popularity of the *Jurassic Park*

movies and *The Crocodile Hunter* television show. According to the APPMA, the number of herp pets increased from 2 million in 1991 to 9 million in 2001.

Pet stores and breeders market herps to the public as pets that need much less care, space, and attention than traditional pets such as dogs and cats. Also, herps are considered good for people with allergies because they have no fur. Finally, herp enthusiasts praise ownership as a conservation measure because it helps to preserve species that may be endangered in their natural environment. They argue that familiarizing the public with traditionally feared or disliked species, such as snakes, would engender more public respect for such animals and encourage more people to conserve wild populations.

Herpetologists at the Smithsonian Institution (SI) in Washington, D.C., have a different view. The SI staff of the National Museum of Natural History (NMNH), Division of Amphibians and Reptiles, noted on the NMNH Web site in 2003 that they "discourage anyone from keeping an amphibian or a reptile as a pet." The primary reason is lack of proper care. The SI staff note that herps are often transported and kept in unhealthy and overcrowded conditions. SI is particularly critical of pet stores, saying that it is not uncommon to see malnourished, sick, and even dead herps in the cages. The Web site also points out that herps are not low-maintenance pets, as claimed by pet stores and breeders. Although herps do require less attention than pet dogs and cats, they still have very particular diet, space, and social needs that must be met to keep them healthy. Many owners are not aware of these needs or are unable or unwilling to meet them.

Zoos have their own complaints about herp pets. Zookeepers say that they receive numerous phone calls from owners who need advice on how to care for a herp or want to donate it a zoo. There is a common misconception among people who buy baby herps (particularly alligators and pythons) that they can always give them to zoos if the animals get too big to handle. Accredited zoos concentrate on endangered species with known genetic histories. They will not accept pet herps for this reason. Many herp owners release their pets into the wild when the animals get too big or become too much trouble. These animals face many dangers in an unknown environment. They compete with native herps for food and resources and can spread new diseases among them.

Tigers

In June 2003 Dr. Eric Miller, director of the St. Louis Zoological Park, testified before a U.S. House of Representatives committee that there are between 5,000 and 10,000 pet tigers in the United States and that this number exceeds the number of wild tigers living throughout Asia. Wild tigers are considered an endangered species, and private ownership of them is prohibited by the Endangered

Species Act. However, ownership of a captive-born endangered animal is legal in many states.

Accredited zoos have been collecting wild tigers for decades. Many of these tigers were bred in captivity to produce very popular zoo babies to bring in crowds. This resulted in an oversupply of adult tigers, many of which wound up in private hands. Pet owners, breeders, circuses, and roadside zoos have interbred different varieties of these animals, resulting in a large population of generic (not purebred) tigers.

Accredited zoos work to preserve endangered tiger species through selective breeding programs. Only pure-bred tigers with traceable ancestries are used. Generic tigers, or mutts, as they are called, have no value to these programs. According to the environmental journal *The Ecologist,* biologists do not believe that mutt tigers could even survive in the wild. Sloppy breeding to produce pop-ular pet characteristics has diluted traits that subspecies would need in particular environments. For example, jun-gle tigers have been interbred with Siberian tigers. The resulting offspring are not equipped to live in the extremes of the tropical jungle or in frigid Siberia. Also, tiger cubs born in captivity are often separated from their mothers after only a few days or weeks. In the wild, cubs would stay with the mother for up to two years and learn neces-sary survival skills. Captive-born cubs are often declawed and defanged to make them easier to handle. Welfarists complain that pet tigers are often kept chained or confined in small enclosures and may be beaten into submission.

PET STORES

According to the financial company NASDAQ, the pet industry was a $29 billion business in 2001. Animal rights groups and many welfare organizations are critical of pet stores that sell animals, particularly those that sell puppies (due to concerns about puppy mills) and exotic animals. The two largest companies in the pet supply industry are PETsMART and PETCO Animal Supplies. Together they accounted for nearly 15 percent of the entire market in 2001.

PETsMART was founded in 1987 and had $2.5 bil-lion in sales in 2001 at more than 500 stores around the country. The company has never sold dogs and cats. Instead, it allows local animal shelters and rescue groups to set up adoption centers in its stores to adopt these ani-mals directly to the public. As of March 2003 PETs-MART reported that this program had resulted in the adoption of 1.4 million dogs and cats. The company does sell small animals (such as gerbils and hamsters), reptiles, and birds. This has drawn criticism from animal rights groups such as PETA. On its Web site, PETA complains that these animals are purchased by PETsMART from commercial breeders and often suffer during their captivi-ty from stress, injuries, and illnesses.

PETA is much more critical of PETCO Animal Sup-plies, a company founded in 1965. NASDAQ reports that PETCO had $1.3 billion in sales in 2001 at more than 600 stores. PETCO does not sell dogs and cats. After receiving complaints from customers about animal care at various PETCO stores, PETA launched a public relations campaign against the company in 1994, nicknaming it "PETNO" and setting up a Web site that lists the alleged complaints. The most serious allegations involve the refusal of store man-agers to pay for veterinary treatment for sick birds or to humanely euthanize those that are critically ill. PETA says that there were numerous incidents in PETCO stores in which very sick birds were placed in store freezers to die.

In 2003 PETA's Web site claimed that PETCO has a very poor record of providing proper veterinary care, hous-ing, food, and other services for the animals that it sells. PETCO denies these allegations and insists that it cares for its animals properly. A quote on the PETCO Web site in 2003 stated "We are deeply distressed if any animal in our stores suffers, and when we know of a concern, we imme-diately investigate the incident and take prompt and appro-priate action." The company also points out that it donated more than $12 million to animal welfare organizations between 1999 and 2003 and has allowed animal shelters and rescue groups to hold adoptions in its stores. As of 2003, PETCO is one of the corporate sponsors of the Web site www.petfinder.org, which lists thousands of pets up for adoption by shelters and rescue groups across the country.

Pet stores selling animals are criticized by animal rights groups and some animal welfare organizations for contributing to pet overpopulation, particularly of exotic birds. In July 2003 an article in the *Los Angeles Times* reported on the growing problem of unwanted pet birds in the United States (Mira Tweti, "Plenty to Squawk About," July 20, 2003). The reporter provides scientific estimates that there are approximately 27,000 exotic parrots living wild across the country that were previously pet birds. The article blames major pet store chains, such as PETsMART and PETCO, for heavily marketing parrots to customers.

The reporter is most critical of the common pet store practice of selling unweaned birds. Most exotic birds require several months to be weaned, but commercial bird breeders sometimes ship unweaned baby birds to pet stores, where they can be hand-fed by syringe by store employees. According to Tweti, this practice stems from the common misperception that baby birds must be sepa-rated from their parents at an early age and hand-fed by humans in order to be tame and affectionate pets. Instead, Tweti suggests, birds sold as hand-reared in pet stores are actually "emotionally deprived" due to the stress of being separated from their parents at such an early age. As of July 2003, PETA and many bird rescue groups were advo-cating passage of a bill by the California legislature to outlaw the sale of unweaned birds in pet stores.

TABLE 9.5

Practicing veterinarians as of September 2002

	Total as of September 2002 No.	Number of Veterinarians*			2001 Earnings Mean Individual Income Before Taxes** $
		Percent of Total %	Percent Male %	Percent Female %	
Private Clinical Practice					
Large animal exclusive	1,827	4.0	83.3	16.7	84,526
Large animal predominant	2,925	6.4	85.1	14.9	73,080
Mixed Animal	3,839	8.4	67.0	33.0	73,602
Small animal predominant	4,967	10.9	65.9	34.1	78,952
Small animal exclusive	28,575	62.6	52.8	47.2	84,447
Equine	2,101	4.6	65.1	34.9	108,405
Other	1,431	3.1	55.4	44.6	105,753
Total Private Practice	**45,665**	**14.3**	**67.8**	**32.2**	**83,979**
Public & Corporate Employment					
College or University	4,032	45.1	57.1	42.9	83,059
Federal government	1,233	13.8	65.5	34.5	80,479
State or local government	339	3.8	35.1	64.9	69,549
Uniformed services	472	5.3	65.7	34.3	74,971
Industrial	1,523	17.0	69.5	30.5	137,175
Other	1,335	14.9	30.6	69.4	84,576
Total Public & Corporate	**8,934**	**100.0**	**53.9**	**46.1**	**92,229**
Employment Unknown	6,878				
Grand Total	**61,477**				

*Includes active AVMA member (Regular, Recent Graduates, and Educational) and Non-members (Excludes non-members born prior to 1932 and non-members who received their veterinary degree prior to 1958)
**Excludes an estimated 12% return to owners' equity in practice real estate.

SOURCE: "U.S. Veterinarians," in *Veterinary Market Statistics,* American Veterinary Medical Association, Schaumburg, IL, September 2002 [Online] http://www.avma.org/membshp/marketstats/usvets.asp [accessed July 11, 2003]

HEALTH AND SAFETY ISSUES

Veterinary Care

Increasing pet ownership has resulted in greater demand for veterinary care. The AVMA represents the interests of more than 60,000 veterinarians. A breakdown of these veterinarians by field of practice, gender, and earnings is presented in Table 9.5. Nearly half work exclusively with small animals in private practice. There are 27 colleges of veterinary medicine in the United States that had a combined enrollment of 9,746 students during the 2001–02 school year.

According to the AVMA's *2001 U.S. Pet Ownership & Demographics Sourcebook,* dog owners were far more likely to visit the vet than cat owners. Only 25 percent of cat owners visited the vet at least once per year, compared to 83 percent of dog owners. Nearly half of dogs and cats were more than six years old. This percentage is way up from the 1987 census, indicating that pets are living longer lives. The AVMA credits better living conditions, health care, and nutrition as reasons for pets' growing life spans. Also, statistics indicate that more people are adopting older pets than ever before. The survey indicates that pet owners spent $19 billion in 2001 on veterinary services, up from $11.1 billion in 1996.

Many devoted pet owners are willing to spend thousands of dollars on specialized medical services for their pets. Organ transplants, chemotherapy, and other expensive procedures are becoming more commonplace for pets. According to the AVMA, the number of animal cardiologists in the United States increased by 75 percent between 1996 and 2002.

The APPMA 2001/2002 National Pet Owner's Survey found that approximately 1 percent of dogs and 1 percent of cats were covered by veterinary health insurance.

Risks to People

ZOONOSES. The largest health risks to people from pets are zoonoses and animal bites. Zoonoses are diseases that can be passed from animals to humans, and they occur in domesticated and wild animals. However, zoonoses in livestock, cats, and dogs are well known, heavily researched, and largely controlled through vaccination programs. Diseases passed to humans from reptiles, rodents, rabbits, and primates are a different matter. They are more difficult to control.

In May 2003 an outbreak of monkeypox in the Midwest captured widespread media attention. Monkeypox is a disease that is related to smallpox but not nearly as lethal. Scientists believe that several people caught monkeypox from pet prairie dogs, which in turn had caught the disease from infected Gambian rats. The import of all African rats was subsequently banned by the U.S. Department of Health and Human Services. Health experts fear that other zoonoses not previously seen in the United States will emerge unless the trade in wild and exotic pets is curtailed.

SALMONELLOSIS. The Centers for Disease Control and Prevention (CDC) estimates that 70,000 people get salmonellosis each year from contact with reptiles. Salmonellosis, an infection caused by the bacteria *Salmonella,* can cause diarrhea, fever, and abdominal cramps in patients for several days. It does not generally require hospitalization. According to the Los Angeles County Department of Health Services, iguana lizards and turtles are the major sources of salmonella infection in children.

TIGER ATTACKS. The Captive Wild Animal Protection Coalition reports that captive tigers killed 2 children and 6 adults and seriously injured 60 others between 1990 and 2000 in the United States.

DOG BITES. According to the AVMA, approximately 4.7 million Americans are bitten by dogs each year. More than half of the victims are children. Up to 800,000 people seek medical attention for dog bites annually and approximately 12 die from their wounds. According to an estimate on the American Society for the Prevention of Cruelty to Animals (ASPCA) Web site in 2003, intact (unneutered) male dogs account for nearly three-fourths of reported dog bite incidents.

IMPORTANT NAMES AND ADDRESSES

American Anti-Vivisection Society
801 Old York Road, #204
Jenkintown, PA 19046
(215) 887-0816
(800) SAY-AAVS
E-mail: aavs@aavs.org
URL: http://www.aavs.org

American Humane Association
63 Inverness Drive East
Englewood, CO 80112
FAX: (303) 792-5333
(866) 242-1877
URL: http://www.americanhumane.org

American Meat Institute
1700 North Moore Street
Suite 1600
Arlington, VA 22209
(703) 841-2400
FAX: (703) 527-0938
E-mail: webmaster@meatami.com
URL: http://www.meatami.com/

American Pet Products Manufacturers Association, Inc.
255 Glenville Road
Greenwich, CT 06831
(203) 532-0000
FAX: (203) 532-0551
E-mail: info@appma.org
URL: http://www.appma.org

American Rescue Dog Association
P.O. Box 151
Chester, NY 10918
(845) 469-4173
E-mail: jlittle@vsrda.org
URL: http://www.ardainc.org

American Society for the Prevention of Cruelty to Animals (ASPCA)
424 E. 92nd Street
New York, NY 10128
(212) 876-7700

E-mail: membership@aspca.org
URL: http://www.aspca.org/site/PageServer

American Veal Association
1500 Fulling Mill Road
Middletown, PA 17057
(717) 985-9125
FAX: (717) 985-9127
E-mail: info@vealfarm.com.
URL: http://www.vealfarm.com

American Veterinary Medical Association
1931 North Meacham Road
Suite 100
Schaumburg, IL 60173
(847) 925-8070
FAX: (847) 925-1329
E-mail: avmainfo@avma.org
URL: www.avma.org

American Zoo and Aquarium Association
8403 Colesville Road
Suite 710
Silver Spring, MD 20910-3314
(301) 562-0777
FAX: (301) 562-0888
URL: http://www.aza.org/

Animal and Plant Health Inspection Service (APHIS)
U.S. Department of Agriculture (USDA)
4700 River Road, Unit 84
Riverdale, MD 20737
(301) 734-4981
E-mail: APHIS.Web@aphis.usda.gov
URL: http://www.aphis.usda.gov/

Animal Concerns
EnvironLink Network
P.O. Box 8102
Pittsburgh, PA 15217
E-mail: support@animalconcerns.org
URL: http://www.animalconcerns.org/

Animal Legal Defense Fund
127 Fourth Street
Petaluma, CA 94952-3005
(707) 769-7771
FAX: (707) 769-0785
E-mail: info@aldf.org
URL: http://www.aldf.org/

Animal News Center
153 East 57th Street
Suite 6E
New York, NY 10022
(212) 319-0428
FAX: (646) 497-1205
E-mail: president@anc.org
URL: http://www.anc.org/

Animal Protection Institute
1122 S Street
Sacramento, CA 95814
(916) 447-3085
FAX: (916) 447-3070
E-mail: info@api4animals.org
URL: http://www.api4animals.org

Animal Welfare Institute
P.O. Box 3650
Washington, DC 20027
(703) 836-4300
FAX: (703) 836-0400
URL: www.awionline.org

Animals Voice
1354 East Avenue #R-252
Chico, CA 95926
FAX: (530) 343-2498
(800) 82-VOICE
E-mail: info@animalsvoice.com
URL: http://www.animalsvoice.com

Association of Veterinarians for Animal Rights
P.O. Box 208
Davis, CA 95617
(530) 759-8106

FAX: (530) 759-8116
E-mail: info@avar.org
URL: http://AVAR.org

Best Friends Animal Sanctuary
5001 Angel Canyon Road
Kanab, UT 84741-5001
(435) 644-2001
FAX: (435) 644-2078
E-mail: info@bestfriends.org
URL: http://www.bestfriends.org/

Canadian Sealers Association
P.O. Box 8005
St. Johns, Newfoundland, Canada A1B 3M7
(709) 722-1721
FAX: (709) 738-1661
E-mail: sealers@canada.com
URL: http://www.sealers.nf.ca/

Compassion Over Killing
P.O. Box 9773
Washington, DC 20016
(301) 891-2458
E-mail: INFO@COK.NET
URL: http://www.cok.net

Defenders of Wildlife
1130 17th Street, NW
Washington, DC 20030
(202) 682-9400
E-mail: info@defenders.org
URL: http://www.defenders.org/

Delta Society
580 Naches Avenue SW
Suite 101
Renton, WA 98055-2297
(425) 226-7357
FAX: (425) 235-1076
E-mail: info@deltasociety.org
URL: http://www.deltasociety.org/

Farm Animal Reform Movement (FARM)
P.O. Box 30654
Bethesda, MD 20824
(888) ASK-FARM
E-mail: farm@farmusa.org
URL: http://www.farmusa.org/

Farm Sanctuary
P.O. Box 150
Watkins Glen, NY 14891
(607) 583-2225
FAX: (607) 583-2041
E-mail: activist@farmsanctuary.org
URL: http://www.farmsanctuary.org/

Friends of Animals
777 Post Road
Darien, CT 06820
(203) 656-1522
E-mail: Info@friendsofanimals.org
URL: http://www.friendsofanimals.org/

GREY2K USA Education Fund
P.O. Box 440142
Somerville, MA 02144
(617) 666-3526
FAX: (617) 666-3568
(866) 2GREY2K
E-mail: Info@GREY2KUSAEDU.org
URL: http://www.grey2kusaedu.org

Greyhound Protection League
P.O. Box 669
Penn Valley, CA 95946
(800) 446-8637
URL: http://www.greyhounds.org/

Guide Dog Users, Inc.
14311 Astrodome Drive
Silver Spring, MD 20906
(301) 598-5771
FAX: (301) 871-7591
(888) 858-1008
E-mail: webmaster@gdui.org
URL: http://www.gdui.org/

Guide Horse Foundation
P.O. Box 511
Kittrell, NC 27544
(252) 433-4755
E-mail: e-mail: info@guidehorse.com
URL: http://www.guidehorse.org

Humane Farming Association
P.O. Box 3577
San Rafael, CA 94912
(415) 771-CALF
FAX: (415) 485-0106
E-mail: hfa@hfa.org
URL: http://www.hfa.org/

Humane Society of the United States (HSUS)
2100 L Street, NW
Washington, DC 20037
(202) 452-1100
URL: www.hsus.org

In Defense of Animals
131 Camino Alto, Suite E
Mill Valley, CA 94941
(415) 388-9641
FAX: (415) 388-0388
E-mail: ida@idausa.org
URL: http://www.idausa.org/index.shtml

International Association of Assistance Dog Partners
38691 Filly Drive
Sterling Heights, MI 48310
(586) 826-3938
URL: http://www.iaadp.org/

International Fund for Animal Welfare
411 Main Street
P.O. Box 193
Yarmouth Port, MA 02675
(508) 744-2000

FAX: (508) 744-2009
(800) 932-4329
E-mail: info@ifaw.org
URL: http://www.ifaw.org/

International Institute for Animal Law
30 North LaSalle Street, Suite 2900
Chicago, IL 60602
(312) 917-8850
FAX: (312) 263-5013
E-mail: IIAL@AnimalLawIntl.org
URL: http://www.animallawintl.org

International Professional Rodeo Association
P.O. Box 83377
Oklahoma City, OK 73148
(405) 235-6540
FAX: (405) 235-6577
E-mail: membership@iprarodeo.com
URL: http://www.iprarodeo.com

International Sled Dog Racing Association
22702 Rebel Road
Merrifield, MN 56465
(218) 765-4297
FAX: (218) 765-3246
E-mail: dsteele@brainerd.net
URL: http://www.isdra.org

Jane Goodall Institute
8700 Georgia Avenue, Suite 500
Silver Spring, MD 20910-3605
(301) 565-0086
FAX: (301) 565-3188
E-mail: info@janegoodall.org
URL: http://www.janegoodall.org

Johns Hopkins Center for Alternatives to Animal Testing (CAAT)
111 Market Place, Suite 840
Baltimore, MD 21202
(410) 223-1693
E-mail: caat@jhsph.edu
URL: http://caat.jhsph.edu/

Last Chance for Animals
8033 Sunset Boulevard #835
Los Angeles, CA 90046
(310) 271-6096
FAX: (310) 271-1890
E-mail: info@lcanimal.org
URL: http://www.lcanimal.org/

Maddie's Fund
2223 Santa Clara Avenue, Suite B
Alameda, CA 94501
(510) 337-8989
FAX: (510) 337-8988
E-mail: info@maddiesfund.org
URL: www.maddiesfund.org

Michigan Society for Medical Research
P.O. Box 3237
Ann Arbor, MI 48106
(734) 763-8029

FAX: (734) 930-1568
E-mail: MISMR@umich.edu
URL: http://www.mismr.org/

National Animal Interest Alliance
P.O. Box 66579
Portland, OR 97290
(503) 761-1139
FAX: (503) 761-1289
E-mail: President@NAIAonline.org
URL: http://www.naiaonline.org/

National Association for Biomedical Research
818 Connecticut Avenue NW
Suite 200
Washington, DC 20006
(202) 857-0540
FAX: (202) 659-1902
E-mail: info@nabr.org
URL: http://www.nabr.org/

National Association for Search and Rescue
4500 Southgate Place
Suite 100
Chantilly, VA 20151
(703) 222-6277
FAX: (703) 222-6283
E-mail: info@nasar.org
URL: http://www.nasar.org

National Chicken Council
1015 15th Street, NW, Suite 930
Washington, DC 20005-2622
(202) 296-2622
FAX: (202) 293-4005
E-mail: ncc@chickenusa.org
URL: http://www.nationalchickencouncil.
com

National Council on Pet Population Study & Policy
P.O. Box 341
New London, MN 56273
E-mail: nationalcouncil@petpopulation.org
URL: http://www.petpopulation.org

National Greyhound Association
P.O. Box 543
Abilene, KS 67410
(785) 263-4660
E-mail: nga@ngagreyhounds.com
URL: http://www.ngagreyhounds.com/

National Institute for Animal Agriculture (NIAA)
1910 Lyda Avenue
Bowling Green, KY 42104
(270) 782-9798
FAX: (270) 782-0188
E-mail: NIAA@animalagriculture.org
URL: http://www.animalagriculture.org/

National Pork Producers Council
7733 Douglas Avenue

Urbandale, IA 50322
(515) 278-8012
FAX: (515) 278-8011
E-mail: flynnk@nppc.org
URL: http://www.nppc.org

National Trappers Association
P.O. Box 632018
Nacogdoches, TX 75963
E-mail: NTAheadquarters@nationaltrap-pers.com
URL: http://www.nationaltrappers.com/

National Wildlife Federation
11100 Wildlife Center Drive
Reston, VA 20190-5362
(800) 822-9919
URL: http://www.nwf.org

New England Anti-Vivisection Society
333 Washington Street
Suite 850
Boston, MA 02108
(617) 523-6020
FAX: (617) 523-7925
E-mail: info@neavs.org
URL: http://www.neavs.org

North American Riding for the Handicapped Association (NARHA)
P.O. Box 33150
Denver, CO 80233
FAX: (303) 252-4610
(800) 369-7433
E-mail: narha@narha.org
URL: http://www.narha.org

Outdoor Amusement Business Association, Inc.
1035 S. Semoran Boulevard, Suite 1045A
Winter Park, FL 32792
(407) 681-9444
FAX: (407) 681-9445
(800) 517-OABA
E-mail: oaba@aol.com
URL: http://www.oaba.org/

PAWS with a Cause
4646 S. Division
Wayland, MI 49348
(800) 253-PAWS
E-mail: paws@ionline.com
URL: http://www.ismi.net/paws

People for the Ethical Treatment of Animals (PETA)
501 Front Street.
Norfolk, VA 23510
(757) 622-7382
FAX: (757) 628-0786
E-mail: info@peta.org
URL: http://www.peta.org/

Performing Animal Welfare Society
P.O. Box 849
Galt, CA 95632

(209) 745-2606
FAX: (209) 745-1809
E-mail: info@pawsweb.org
URL: http://www.pawsweb.org/site/home-page.htm

Pet-Abuse.com
P.O. Box 2995
Del Mar, CA 92014-5995
FAX: (775) 659-5430
(866) 240-1179
E-mail: info@pet-abuse.com
URL: http://www.pet-abuse.com

Professional Rodeo Cowboys Association
101 ProRodeo Drive
Colorado Springs, CO 80919
(719) 593-8840
URL: http://www.prorodeo.com/

Psychologists for the Ethical Treatment of Animals
P.O. Box 1297
Washington Grove, MD 20880
(301) 963-4751
E-mail: info@psyeta.org
URL: http://www.psyeta.org/

Scientists Center for Animal Welfare
7833 Walker Drive, Suite 410
Greenbelt, MD 20770
(301) 345-3500
FAX: (301) 345-3503
E-mail: info@scaw.com
URL: http://www.scaw.com/

Showing Animals Respect and Kindness (SHARK)
P.O. Box 28
Geneva, IL 60134
(630) 557-0176
FAX: (630) 557-0178
E-mail: info@sharkonline.org
URL: http://www.sharkonline.org/

Sled Dog Action Coalition
P.O. Box 562061
Miami, FL 33256
E-mail: SledDogAC@aol.com
URL: http://www.helpsleddogs.org

Society for Animal Protective Legislation
P.O. Box 3719
Washington, DC 20027
(703) 836-4300
FAX: (703) 836-0400
E-mail: sapl@saplonline.org
URL: http://www.saplonline.org/

Therapy Dogs International, Inc.
88 Bartley Road
Flanders, NJ 07836
(973) 252-9800
FAX: (973) 252-7171
E-mail: E-mail: tdi@gti.net
URL: http://www.tdi-dog.org

TRAFFIC
1250 24th Street, NW
Washington, DC 20037
(202) 293-4800
FAX: (202) 775-8287
E-mail: tna@wwfus.org
URL: http://www.traffic.org

United Gamefowl Breeders Association
73345 Bowen Road
Albany, OH 45710
(740) 596-4807
FAX: (740) 596-4352
E-mail: ugba@ohiohills.com
URL: http://winnerscircle.hypermart.net/ugba/

United Poultry Concerns, Inc.
P.O. Box 150
Machipongo, VA 23405
(757) 678-7875
FAX: (757) 678-5070

E-mail: info@upc-online.org
URL: www.upc-online.org

U.S. National Agricultural Library
U.S. Department of Agriculture
10301 Baltimore Avenue
Beltsville, MD 20705-2351
(301) 504-6212
FAX: (301) 504-7125
E-mail: awic@nal.usda.gov
URL: http://www.nal.usda.gov/awic/

United States Police Canine Association
P.O. Box 80
Springboro, OH 45066
(800) 531-1614
E-mail: uspcadir@aol.com
URL: http://www.uspcak9.com

U.S. Poultry & Egg Association
1530 Cooledge Road
Tucker, GA 30084

(770) 493-9401
FAX: (770) 493-9257
E-mail: ssmall@poultryegg.org
URL: http://www.poultryegg.org/

U.S. Sportsmen's Alliance
801 Kingsmill Parkway
Columbus, OH 43229
(614) 888-4868
FAX: (614) 888-0326
E-mail: info@USSPORTSMEN.org
URL: http://www.wlfa.org/

Wildlife Society
5410 Grosvenor Lane, Suite 200
Bethesda, MD 20814-2144
(301) 897-9770
FAX: (301) 530-2471
E-mail: TWS@Wildlife.org.
URL: http://www.wildlife.org/

RESOURCES

Several resources useful to this book were published by agencies of the U.S. Department of Agriculture (USDA), including the Economic Research Service, National Agricultural Statistics Service, Animal and Plant Health Inspection Service (APHIS), and Food Safety and Inspection Service. Other federal agencies providing information were the U.S. Fish and Wildlife Service (USFWS), U.S. Department of Customs, Centers for Disease Control and Prevention (CDC), National Science Board, National Institutes of Health (NIH), Food and Drug Administration (FDA), U.S. Forest Service (FS), National Park Service (NPS), Bureau of Land Management (BLM), National Marine Fisheries Service, and U.S. Department of Labor.

The General Accounting Office (GAO) is the investigative arm of the U.S. Congress. One GAO publication used for this book was *Wildlife Services Program: Information on Activities to Manage Wildlife Damage* (GAO-02-138).

State agencies and educational institutions providing information included Alberta Farm Animal Care (Canada), California Horse Racing Board, Cambridge University Veterinary School, Colorado State University, Massachusetts Institute of Technology McCormick Library of Special Collections, Oregon State University, Smithsonian Institution, the State University of New Jersey Rutgers Cooperative Extension, Tufts University School of Veterinary Medicine, University of Arizona, University of Nebraska–Lincoln, University of Saskatchewan College of Agriculture, University of South Carolina, and the Virginia Cooperative Extension. The University of New Mexico School of Law, Center for Wildlife Law, and Michigan State University Animal Legal and Historical Center were invaluable resources for legal documents.

Information on animal industries and businesses was obtained from associations including the American Greyhound Council, Inc. (AGC), American Meat Institute (AMI), American Pet Products Manufacturers Association (APPMA), American Veal Association (AVA), American Zoo and Aquarium Association (AZA), Food Marketing Institute, International Sled Dog Racing Association, International Whaling Commission (IWC), National Council of Chain Restaurants, National Pork Producers Council, National Renderers Association, National Turkey Federation, Outdoor Amusement Business Association (OABA), Pet Industry Joint Advisory Council, the Jockey Club, U.S. Fur Commission, and U.S. Trotting Association.

The Web sites of the Ringling Brothers and Barnum and Bailey Circus, Hanneford Family Circus, Florida Canine Academy, and Paws with a Cause were very informative. The Web site of Dr. Temple Grandin (www.grandin.com) was particularly useful as a resource on animal husbandry and slaughtering in the modern agriculture industry.

Organizations involved in animal issues that provided helpful statistics and information include the American Veterinary Medical Association (AVMA), Assistance Dogs International, Inc., Foundation for Biomedical Research, Michigan Society for Medical Research (MSMR), Minnesota Foundation for Responsible Animal Care, MountedPolice.com, National Alternative Pet Association (NAPA), National Association for Search and Rescue, Physician's Committee for Responsible Medicine (PCRM), RDS, U.S. Sportsmen's Alliance, United States Police Canine Association, Inc., and United States War Dog Association. The following resources describe environmental issues that also affect animals: *The Ecologist* magazine, Monterey Bay Aquarium, Sierra Club, and Union of Concerned Scientists.

Historical articles and exhibits that proved useful were provided by the Web sites of the Agropolis Museum (France), Brooklyn College at City University of New York, Cairo Museum, Carnegie Museum of Natural History,

Chicago Historical Society, Cleveland Museum of Art, Cleveland Museum of Natural History, Dickinson College, Kashmiri Overseas Association, Liverpool John Moores University, Minnesota State University, San Jose State University, the Art Institute of Chicago, the Institute of Human Origins, United States Armor Association, University College (Canada), University of Michigan, University of New Castle, the Museum of Antiquities (UK), and the University of Notre Dame Jacques Maritain Center.

A wealth of information was obtained from groups devoted to the causes of animal protection, welfare, and rights. These include Alley Cat Allies, American Humane Association (AHA), Animal Legal Defense Fund (ALDF), Animal News Center, Inc., Animal Protection Institute (API), Animal Rescue Foundation, Association of Veterinarians for Animal Rights, Best Friends Animal Sanctuary, Blue Horse Charities, Defenders of Wildlife, Doris Day Animal League, Farm Sanctuary, Friends of Animals, Fund for Animals, Greyhound Protection League (GPL), Humane Society of the United States (HSUS), In Defense of Animals (IDA), Maddie's Fund, National Anti-Vivisection Society (NAVS), National Council on Pet Population Study and Policy, New England Anti-Vivisection Society (NEAVS), NoPuppyMills.com, People for the Ethical Treatment of Animals (PETA), Petabuse.com, Psychologists for the Ethical Treatment of Animals, Sled Dog Action Coalition, Society for the Protection of Animal Rights Egypt, and United Poultry Concerns (UPC).

Animal rights activists and opponents have written some important books that were valuable resources for this work. They include *Animal Liberation* by Peter Singer (HarperCollins Publishers, New York, NY, 1975, 1990, 2002), *Animals, Property, and the Law* by Gary L. Francione (Temple University Press, Philadelphia, PA, 1995), *Rattling the Cage, Toward Legal Rights for Animals* by Steven M. Wise (Perseus Books, Cambridge, MA, 2000), and *The Animal Rights Debate* by Carl Cohen and Tom Regan (Rowman & Littlefield Publishers, Lanham, MD, 2001).

The following news organizations and outlets were useful for providing timely stories related to animals: ABCNews.com, *Anchorage Daily News,* Animal Planet, Associated Press, *Atlanta Journal & Constitution,* BBC News, Columbia News Service, the *Los Angeles Times,* National Geographic News, Nature Publishing Group, the *New York Times,* Reuters News Service, *San Jose Mercury News, The Morning News* (Springdale, AR), Time.com, *U.S. News and World Report,* and the *Washington Post*. The PBS *Frontline* documentaries "Modern Meat" and "The Story of Navy Dolphins" were very helpful. The Gallup Organization supplied polling results on animal issues.

INDEX

retired racing horse adoption, 106
roots of, 102
Thoroughbred races, 1990-2002, 104
(f6.1)
welfare of racing horses, 104–106
Horses
in circuses, 121
domestication of, 3f, 4
guides for the blind, 141
horse meat, popularity of, 71
horse sports, 102, 102t
hunter-gatherers and, 1
hunting with, 133–134
Islam and, 7
law enforcement with, 138–139
manual labor by, 134–135
military service, 143–144, 143f
mounted police handle labor unrest in
Philadelphia, 1946, 139f
mounted police programs, 138t
Native Americans and, 11
pet ownership history, 149
Pony Express rider and his horse, circa
1861, 132f
Premarin controversy, 71–72
rodeos and, 110, 111–112
Romans and, 8
service animals, history of, 131, 132
therapy with, 142
Wild Horses Act, 14
"Horses and Waging War" (PBS Web site),
144
How Can We Price Early-Weaned Pigs?
(Meyer and Lazarus), 70
HREA (Health Research Extension Act),
90–91
HSUS. *See* Humane Society of the United
States
Human-animal interaction, history of, 1–18
Age of Enlightenment, 10–11
America, 11–12
ancient cultures/religions, 4–8, 5t, 6f
animal protection milestones, 15t–17t
blood sports, 11
British law, 13
England, 12–13
human domestication of animals, 2–4, 3f
Keiko, *18*
medieval period, 9–10
prehistoric times, 1–2, 2f
twentieth century, 14–18
U.S. law, 13–14
Human injuries/fatalities
hunting-related, 45
tiger attacks/dogbites, 162
from wildlife bites or attacks, 34, 34t
Human rights, 19
Humane endpoints, 98
Humane Farming Association, 53
Humane Law Enforcement (HLE), 17
Humane Methods of Slaughter Act of 1958
does not apply to chickens, 68
does not apply to ritual slaughter, 65
passage of, 14
requirements of, 53
Humane Society of Gallatin Valley
(Bozeman, Montana), 152

Humane Society of the United States
(HSUS)
animal abuse/neglect and, 156–157
animal acts and, 120–121
animal cruelty charges against game
warden, 41
animal-free circus advocate, 122
animal theme parks and, 128–129
bearbaiting and, 47
claims against circuses, 121
cooling vests donated by, 145
dogfighting and, 115
founding of, 14
fur farming and, 77
gavage and, 69
greyhound racing opposition of, 107
increased membership in, 21
Iowa's hog farms and, 57
no-kill shelters and, 151
opposition to canned hunting, 45–46
Pain and Distress Initiative, 98
plan to kill cormorants and, 40
purebred dogs and, 156
rescue/rehabilitation facilities and, 50
shelters and, 149
sled dog racing opposition of, 109–110
stance of, 24
wildlife control with hunting and, 46
*The Humane Society of the United States
(HSUS) First Strike Campaign 2002
Report of Animal Cruelty Cases* (HSUS),
156–157
Humans
dissection of, 80, 81, 82 (f5.5)
endangered species interests *vs.*, 43
guard dogs for, 134
health issues, farm animals and, 75–76
pets and health risks to humans, 161–162
service animals for, 131
vivisection of, 80
Hume, David, 12
Humpback whale, 30f
Humphrey, Hubert, 14
Hunter-gatherers, 1
"Hunters Howling" (Shelton), 133
Hunting
conservationists and, 31–32
hunters/days of hunting, by type of game,
45t
official hunting seasons in colonies, 31
public opinion on banning, 28, 28 (f2.4)
recreational hunting, 44–46
service animals for, 131, 132–134
valuable wildlife, 29
wildlife control method, 46–47
Hunting fees, 47
Hunting rights, 31
Huntingdon Life Sciences (HLS), 86
Husbandry, 4
Huss, Rebecca J., 26
Hywel the Good, 10

I

IACUC (Institutional animal care and use
committee), 89

ICCVAM (Interagency Coordinating
Committee for the Validation of
Alternative Methods), 97
IDA. *See* In Defense of Animals
Iditarod Trail Sled Dog Race, 108–109, 110
IFCS (International Federation of
Cynological Sports), 103
Illinois, 26, 158
In Defense of Animals (IDA)
circus and, 122
The Coulston Foundation research
facility and, 87, 88
hunting as wildlife control method and,
46
lawsuit against USDA, 86
pound seizure information from, 155
San Diego Wild Animal Park and, 126
In-ocean farms, 72
In vitro tests, 97
Independence Dogs, Inc., 141
India, 5–6
Indus, 5
Industrial Revolution, 132
Injuries
human, hunting-related, 45
rodeo-related, 111
tiger attacks/dogbites, 162
wildlife bites or attacks, 34, 34t
Inky (guide dog), 142
Institute of Behavioral Research (Silver
Springs, MA), 86
Institutional animal care and use committee
(IACUC), 89
Interagency Coordinating Committee for the
Validation of Alternative Methods
(ICCVAM), 97
*Interests and Rights: The Case Against
Animals* (Frey), 20
International endangered species protection,
43–44
International Federation of Cynological
Sports (IFCS), 103
International Hunter Education Association,
45
International Sled Dog Racing Association
(ISDRA), 110
International Species Information System
(ISIS), 126
International trade, 48–49
International Whaling Commission (IWC),
49
*An Introduction to the Principles of Morals
and Legislation* (Bentham), 12–13, 24
Iowa, 57, 70
Iraq invasion of 2003, 145
Irradiation, 76
ISDRA (International Sled Dog Racing
Association), 110
ISIS (International Species Information
System), 126
Islam, 7
IWC (International Whaling Commission),
49

J

Jainism, 6
Japan, 49

Huntingdon Life Sciences case and, 86
investigation of unaccredited zoos,
127–128
National Detector Dog Training Center,
137
regulation of entertainment animals, 119
research animals registered with USDA,
fiscal year 2001, 93, 93 (f5.12)
research facilities and, 89, 90
Swine 2000 Report of, 70
USFWS works with, 33
U.S. Fish and Wildlife Service (USFWS)
bird control and, 40
Endangered Species Act administered by,
41
hunting as wildlife control method and,
46–47
mission statement of, 27
San Diego Wild Animal Park complaint
and, 126
work of/wildlife laws enforced by, 32–33
U.S. Fish Commission, 32
U.S. General Accounting Office (GAO), 34,
34t
U.S. News and World Report
animal park investigation article in, 127
sealing industry report in, 48
zoo article in, 126
U.S. Sportsmen's Alliance (USSA), 46–47
U.S. War Dog Association, 144
USDA. *See* U.S. Department of Agriculture
USDA Forest Services (USFS), 43
USFWS. *See* U.S. Fish and Wildlife Service
USSA (U.S. Sportsmen's Alliance), 46–47
Utah Veterinary Medical Association, 152
Utilitarianism, 24

V

Value, of wildlife, 29
Van Amburgh, Isaac, 118
Vanderbilt University, 98
Variant Creutzfeldt-Jakob disease (vCJD),
75–76
Vaudeville, 118
VCJD (variant Creutzfeldt-Jakob disease),
75–76
Veal, 60–61
Vegans, 26, 73
Vegetarianism
animal rights application and, 26
increase of, 73
R.G. Frey on, 21–22
Vehicles, collisions with animals, 40
Vesalius, Andreas
portrait of, 82 (f5.6)
"Some Observations on the Dissection of
Living Animals", 11
work of/vivisection by, 81
Veterinarians
care of pets, 161
pet store care, 160
practicing veterinarians as of September
2002, 161t
requirement under Animal Welfare Act,
89
rodeos and, 111, 112
sled dog racing and, 110

spaying/neutering and, 153–154
Veterinary medical schools, 95–96, 95t
Victoria, Queen of England, 13
Victorian Street Society, 81
Vietnam Dog Handlers Association, 144
Vietnam War, 144, 145
Virginia, 31
Visually impaired, guide dog for, 140–141,
140f
Vivisection
in Age of Enlightenment, 11
antivivisection movement, 80
argument against, 12
defined, 79
history of, 80–82
in U.S., 13
Voltaire, FranÁois-Marie Arouet de
animal vivisection and, 12
discovery of animals' feeling organs, 81
portrait of, 84 (f5.9)

W

Wales, 10
Wallace, Robin, 43
Walt Disney's Animal Kingdom, 128
War dogs, 143, 144, 145
Ward Egg Ranch (CA), 68
Warrick, Joby, 62–63
Washington, 43
Washington, George, 103, 144
Washington Post, 62–64
Washington State Bar Association, 27
Waste, factory farming, 57
Watchdogs, 134
Weapons, hunting, 44
*Weekly Addiction Gambling Education
Report* (Harvard Medical School), 114
Weier, John, 43
Welfare-friendly farming
certified organic sales, 2002, 74f
changes towards, 73–75
percent of sites that gave antibiotics/feed
additives to grower/finisher pigs by
primary reason/route of administration,
75t
Welfare state, defined, 23
Welfarism, 23–24
Welfarists. *See* Animal welfarists
Wendy's Corporation, 74, 75
West Indian manatees, 42–43
Western University of Health Sciences
College of Veterinary Medicine, 96
"A Whale of a Business," PBS *Frontline*
story, 128, 145
Whales
humpback, 30f
Minke, 49
Shamu (orca), 128
Whaling, 49
"What Would It Take?" (Lawson and Allen),
151
Whitstine, Bill, 136
Wild animals
categorized by ownership, 27
as entertainment animals, 117–119
Wild Bird Conservation Act, 33
Wild-caught animals, 96

Wild Horses Act, 14
Wild Horses, An American Romance (PBS
Web site), 144
Wild Idea Buffalo Company, 41
Wildlife, 29–50
animal rabies cases, 34f
canned hunts, sample prices for, 46t
CITES list of party countries, 44t
estimates of annual human
injuries/fatalities from, 34t
federal laws impacting wildlife, 33t
Gifford Pinchot, 32 (f3.3)
government agencies that control, 32–34
government wildlife regulation, goals of,
34–38, 40–44
gray wolf, 42f
gray wolf populations, 42t
history of, 30–32
humpback whale, 30f
hunters/days of hunting, by type of game,
45t
John Muir, 32 (f3.2)
killing wildlife, 44–50
questions in debate over, 29–30
rescue/rehabilitation of, 50
resources damaged by injurious wildlife,
related emerging concerns, by state,
35t–39t
summary of listed species,
endangered/threatened, 41t
threat/value categorization, 29
Wildlife commodities
big cats, 48
seals, 48
types of, 47–48
Wildlife control, 46–47
Wildlife damage
animal rabies cases, 1955-2001, 34f
annual human injuries/fatalities from
wildlife bites or attacks, 34t
to health/safety, 34–38, 40
to property/pleasure, 40–41
resources damaged by injurious wildlife,
related emerging concerns, by state,
35t–39t
Wildlife recreationists, 47
Wildlife refuges
hunting at, 46–47
USFWS and, 32–33
*Wildlife Services Program: Information on
Activities to Manage Wildlife Damage*
(GAO report), 34, 34t
*Wildlife Services: The Facts About Wildlife
Damage Management* (APHIS), 40
Wildlife Services (WS), 33–34, 40
"Wilmoth Settles" (Mero), 128
Wilson-Sanders, Susan, 82, 83
Wise, Mike, 106
Witchcraft Act of 1563, 10
Witches, 9
Wolves
endangered/threatened, 42
gray wolf, 42f
gray wolf populations, 42t
herding/hunting by, 131
wolf bounty acts, 31
Women, 28